JESUS AND ISRAEL

JESUS AND ISRAEL

JULES ISAAC

EDITED, AND WITH A FOREWORD, BY

CLAIRE HUCHET BISHOP

TRANSLATED BY

SALLY GRAN

HOLT, RINEHART AND WINSTON

NEW YORK   CHICAGO   SAN FRANCISCO

Grateful acknowledgment is made to the following pub-
lishers who have generously granted permission to reprint
from their publications: The Division of Christian Education, National Council of Churches, for quotations from
the *Revised Standard Version of the Bible*, 1946, 1952.
The RSV has been followed except when other English
renditions come nearer the French text through which
the author develops a specific point.

Excerpts from *Évangile selon saint Marc; Évangile selon
saint Luc; Évangile selon saint Matthieu; Évangile selon
saint Jean; L'Évangile de Jesus Christ.* J. Gabalda et Cie,
Editeurs. Paris

The blindstamp on the jacket reproduces a medal by
Jules Isaac's younger son, who engraved the original
following a drawing he made with his father's permission
in 1960. The medal was struck at the Paris Mint.

Library of Congress Catalog Card Number: 69-10236
FIRST EDITION
Published in France under the title *Jésus et Israël*,
© 1959 by Fasquelle Éditeurs, Paris.
DESIGNER: VINCENT TORRE
SBN: 03-072550-X
Printed in the United States of America

CONTENTS

List of Abbreviations   ix
Foreword by Claire Huchet Bishop   xi
Preface to the 1959 Edition   xxi
Preface to the 1948 Edition   xxiii

INTRODUCTION

Preliminary Observations on the Old Testament

PROPOSITION 1. The Christian religion is the daughter of the Jewish religion. The New Testament of the Christians is built upon the foundation of the Old Testament of the Jews. If only for this reason, Judaism is deserving of respect.   3

PART I

Jesus, the Christ, a Jew "According to the Flesh"

PROPOSITION 2. Jesus, the Jesus of the Gospels, only Son and Incarnation of God for the Christians, in his human lifetime was a Jew, a humble Jewish artisan. This is a fact of which no Christian has a right to be unaware.   11

PROPOSITION 3. Insofar as we can know of them through the Gospels, Jesus' family was Jewish: Mary, his mother, was Jewish, and so were all their friends and relatives. To be at once an anti-Semite and a Christian is to try to marry reverence with abuse.   15

PROPOSITION 4. On each New Year's Day the Church commemorates the circumcision of the Infant Jesus. It was not without hesitation and controversy that early Christianity abandoned this rite sanctioned by the Old Testament.   19

PROPOSITION 5. The name *Jesus Christ* is basically Semitic, even though its form is Greek: *Jesus* is a Hellenization of a Jewish name; *Christ* is the Greek equivalent of the Jewish word *Messiah*.   22

PROPOSITION 6. The New Testament was written in Greek. In the course of the centuries, the Catholic Church has quoted it in Latin, a Latin which is the result of translation. But Jesus, like all the Palestinian Jews he was addressing, spoke Aramaic, a Semitic language closely related to Hebrew.   27

PART II

The Gospel in the Synagogue

PROPOSITION 7. It is commonly maintained that at the time of the coming of Christ, the Jewish religion had degenerated into mere legalism without a soul. History does not support this verdict. In spite of Jewish legalism and its excesses, everything at this period attests to the depth and intensity of the religious life of Israel. 33

PROPOSITION 8. The teaching of Jesus took place in the traditional Jewish setting. According to a very liberal Jewish custom, "the carpenter's son" was permitted to speak and teach in the synagogues, and even in the Temple at Jerusalem. 43

PROPOSITION 9. Jesus was born and lived "under the [Jewish] law." Did he intend or announce its abrogation? Many writers hold that he did, but their statements exaggerate, distort, or contradict the most important passages in the Gospels. 49

PROPOSITION 10. Nothing would be more futile than to try to separate from Judaism the Gospel that Jesus preached in the synagogues and in the Temple. The truth is that the Gospel and its entire tradition are deeply rooted in Jewish tradition and in the attempts at renovation and purification which had been manifested for almost two centuries in Palestine. 74

PART III

Jesus and His People

PROPOSITION 11. Christian writers deliberately omit the fact that at the time of Christ the Dispersion of the Jews had been a *fait accompli* for several centuries. The majority of the Jewish people no longer lived in Palestine. 89

PROPOSITION 12. Therefore, no one has any right to say that the Jewish people "as a whole" rejected Jesus. It is entirely probable that the Jewish people "as a whole" were not even aware of his existence. 94

PROPOSITION 13. But with rare exceptions, wherever Jesus went the Jewish people took him to their hearts, as the Gospels testify. Did they, at a given moment, suddenly turn against him? This is a notion which has yet to be proved. 101

PROPOSITION 14. In any case, no one has the right to declare that the Jewish people rejected Christ or the Messiah, that they rejected the Son of God, until it is proved that Jesus revealed himself as such to the Jewish people "as a whole" and was rejected by them as such. But the Gospels give us good reason to doubt that this ever happened. 132

PROPOSITION 15. Christ is said to have pronounced a sentence of condemnation and alienation on the Jewish people. But why, in contradiction of his own Gospel of love and forgiveness, should he have condemned his own people, the only people to whom he chose to speak—his own people, among whom he found not only bitter enemies but fervent disciples and adoring followers? We have every reason to believe that the real object of his condemnation is the real subject of guilt, a certain pharisaism to be found in all times and in all peoples, in every religion and in every church. 177

PART IV

The Crime of Deicide

PROPOSITION 16. For eighteen hundred years it has been generally taught throughout the Christian world that the Jewish people, in full responsibility for the Crucifixion, committed the inexpiable crime of deicide. No accusation could be more pernicious—and in fact none has caused more innocent blood to be shed. 233

PROPOSITION 17. Now, in the Gospels, Jesus was careful to name in advance the parties responsible for the Passion: elders, chief priests, scribes—a common species no more limited to the Jews than to any other people. 264

PROPOSITION 18. Joan of Arc was also sentenced by a tribunal of chief priests and scribes—who were not Jewish—but only after a long trial, of which we have the complete and authentic text. This is not true of the trial of Jesus, which was hurried through, whether in three hours or in three days, and is known only by hearsay. No official transcript, no contemporary testimony on the event has come down to us. 285

PROPOSITION 19. To establish the responsibility of the Jewish people in the Roman trial—the Roman death sentence—the Roman penalty, we must ascribe to certain passages in the Gospels a historical validity which is particularly dubious; we must overlook their discrepancies, their improbabilities, and give them an interpretation which is no less biased and arbitrary for being traditional. 311

PROPOSITION 20. To crown its injustices, a certain so-called Christian devotion, only too happy to fall in with a centuries-old prejudice which is complicated by ignorance or misunderstanding of the Gospel, has never wearied of using the grievous theme of the Crucifixion against the Jewish people as a whole. 365

CONCLUSION

PROPOSITION 21 and Last. Whatever the sins of the people of Israel may be, they are innocent, totally innocent of the crimes of which Christian tradition accuses them: they did not reject Jesus, they did not crucify him. And Jesus did not reject Israel, did

not curse it: just as "the gifts . . . of God are irrevocable" (Rom.
11:29), the evangelical Law of love allows no exception. May
Christians come to realize this at last—may they realize and redress their crying injustices. At this moment, when a curse seems
to weigh upon the whole human race, it is the urgent duty to which
they are called by the memory of Auschwitz.   385

Appendix and Practical Conclusion.   The Rectification Necessary in
   Christian Teaching: Eighteen Points   401

LIST OF ABBREVIATIONS

ABS (American Bible Society): *Good News for Modern Man: The New Testament in Today's English,* tr. Dr. Robert G. Bratcher, New York, American Bible Society, 1966.

BT (Babylonian Talmud): *The Babylonian Talmud,* ed. by and tr. under Rabbi Dr. Isidore Epstein, 35 vols., London, Soncino, 1935–1952.

CCD (Confraternity of the Christian Doctrine): *New American Catholic Edition: The Holy Bible,* Douay-Confraternity tr., New York, Benziger, 1961.

JB (Jerusalem Bible): *The Jerusalem Bible,* tr. Joseph Leo Alston *et al.,* Garden City, N. Y., Doubleday, 1966.

KJ (King James): *The Holy Bible,* Revised Version tr., New York, Nelson, 1901.

MR (Midrash Rabbah): *Midrash Rabbah,* ed. by and tr. under Rabbi Dr. Harry Freedman and Maurice Simon, 10 vols., London, Soncino, 1939 (3rd prtg., 1961).

RK (Ronald Knox): *The New Testament of Our Lord and Saviour Jesus Christ,* tr. Msgr. Ronald Knox, New York, Sheed & Ward, 1954.

RSV (Revised Standard Version): *The Holy Bible,* Revised Standard Version tr., New York, World Publishing, Meridian, 1962.

FOREWORD

To state that this book was written over twenty years ago is to run the risk of having the prospective reader set it aside unread. Yet it is brought out today in the United States precisely because the time seems ripe for a wide reading public's interest. Vatican Council II has awakened many Christians to the necessity of revising their attitude regarding the Jews. However, it is doubtful whether the conciliar Statement on the Jews [1] would have taken shape at all had not Jules Isaac, eighteen years prior to the Council's voting, compelled European Christians to come face to face with the responsibility of the centuries-old Christian teaching in the development of a mentality which made the Holocaust of six million Jews possible.

The impact of *Jésus et Israël* stemmed from a number of causes. It was the work of an outstanding French historian, a man whose activities, all during his life, had focused on the field of general history and not on that of the Jewish question, though he was himself Jewish. Author of a seven-volume world history which has been used for several generations now throughout secondary schools and universities, Professor Isaac had also held the high government post of Inspector General of Education for France. A commander of the French Legion of Honor, decorated with the Croix de Guerre, 1914–1918, for bravery, he was well known for his scholarly achievements and his intellectual integrity. The Nazi Occupation of France in 1940 and the subsequent persecution of the Jews impelled Jules Isaac to delve as a historian into the origin and the widespread development of anti-Semitism within nations which had been Christianized for nearly two thousand years. He brought out the result of his study and research in *Jésus et Israël:* the fault lay mainly with Christian tradition and teaching as exemplified in commentaries on the Gospels.

Professor Isaac's demonstration was carried out with an inflexible drive which left no loopholes. And from the point of view of sheer literature, the book was a masterpiece: the rigor of the reasoning came through a brilliance of style where each sentence in itself was a gem in its indisputable clarity and noble forcefulness. Magisterial tone, which one might have expected with such a subject, was absent; the

---

[1] Regarding the Statement, see p. 319, n. 16.

thoughts rebounded in deadly accuracy but with an elegance of inter-play as in an expert tennis game. The consummate skill of the writer, the exigency of the historian served an ardent conviction rooted deep in personal tragedy—while engaged in writing this book, the author had lost his wife and daughter in a German concentration camp. Yet bitterness and hatred were not to be found in his writing, only active compassion and fervor for truth. Moreover, this work was the first of its kind to make a concrete appeal: it called for some specific steps, which were summed up in the Eighteen Points at the end of the book, in order to purify Christian teaching regarding the Jews.

Jésus et Israël rocked European Christians' complacence, particu-larly in France and in Rome. What followed—the Ten Points of See-lisberg issued from Jules Isaac's Eighteen Points,[2] his founding of the Jewish-Christian fellowship L'Amitié judéo-chrétienne, the revising of French catechisms and textbooks, Professor Isaac's private audience with John XXIII on June 13, 1960—have been recorded in the intro-ductions of two of his previously published writings, *Has Anti-Semit-ism Roots in Christianity?* and *The Teaching of Contempt.*[3]

Prior to his death, Jules Isaac did me the honor of entrusting me with the responsibility for the American editions of his works, partic-ularly of *Jésus et Israël.* I can but hope not to have failed his trust. He left it to me to make the desirable cuts for the American edition. Indeed, the 600-page book posed certain problems, one of them being the fact that a number of quotations from French works have become obsolete in the course of twenty years. These have been deleted. Great care, though, has been taken to leave the author's tight demon-stration intact. Nothing has been added to the text save occasionally an indispensable connective word. The only other departures from the 1959, or second, edition of *Jésus et Israël* are that the notes printed at the back of the French book, and containing Professor Isaac's revisions of the first edition, have been incorporated into the body of the present work. Also incorporated are the handwritten corrections made by the author himself in his own French copy, which is in the editor's hands.

In the footnotes, it has been deemed necessary to introduce a num-

---

[2] See the Appendix and Practical Conclusion at the end of the present work for both the Eighteen Points and the Ten Points of Seelisberg.

[3] Jules Isaac, *Has Anti-Semitism Roots in Christianity?*, tr. Dorothy and James Parkes, New York, National Conference of Christians and Jews, 1961; and Jules Isaac, *The Teaching of Contempt: Christian Roots of Anti-Semitism*, tr. Helen Weaver, New York, Holt, Rinehart and Winston, 1964.

ber of typical up-to-date writings, mostly American ones, to emphasize the timeliness of the work and its world-wide relevance. In some
cases, the quoted text may have been revised or withdrawn lately. Yet
its publication date is recent enough for its influence to remain potent
among people living today. In this gathering of additional commentaries, the American Jewish Committee, the Institute of Judaeo-Chris-
tian Studies, and the National Council of Christians and Jews have
been especially helpful.

The American Jewish Committee has also contributed in other very
significant ways to this English edition. The editor is particularly
grateful to Rabbi Marc H. Tanenbaum, National Director of the Interreligious Affairs Department of the AJC, for his active interest and
his sustaining encouragement over the years while this translation
was in progress.

The blindstamp in the cover of the book reproduces a medal by
Jules Isaac's younger son, who engraved the original following a
drawing he had made in 1960 for this purpose with his father's agreement.

The translation has required, besides sure professional competence,
a subtle sensitivity to the telling rhythm of Jules Isaac's prose, a firm
grasp of his dialectic, a capacity to re-create a work of rare intensity
and broad sweep, and a thorough familiarity with the Jewish-Christian question. I trust the reader will feel as I do that Sally Gran has
fully succeeded in this challenging undertaking.[4]

Bible quotations, which Professor Isaac usually provided in full, are
given textually in the present edition where necessary for the understanding of the argument. Otherwise the reference citation alone is
retained. The Revised Standard Version has been used except when
other English renditions come nearer the French text through which
the author develops a specific point. Only in such cases is the particular source indicated. The notation "RSV" does not appear unless
needed to clarify attribution, as when several quotations from more
than one source occur seriatim. The same method has been followed
for New Testament passages which Jules Isaac, who was a distinguished Hellenist, obviously translated directly from the Greek text.[5]

Extensive bibliographical research has been undertaken in order to

[4] For the short texts which introduce the Propositions, we have relied largely
on Helen Weaver's translation in *The Teaching of Contempt*, so as to retain the
published English versions as far as possible.—Tr.

[5] These sources are documented in the List of Abbreviations, p. ix.

present fuller information in the source references. We are especially grateful to Marguerite Dumont, Sister Marie-Bénédicte, N.D.S., Sister Rose Thering, Harry J. Alderman, Father Edward Flannery, Anthony Gran, Daniel Isaac, Professor Fadley Lovsky, and Rabbi A. James Rudin, who have helped us in this work. We are likewise indebted to Joseph Cunneen for locating published English translations of some writings to which Professor Isaac refers.

The fact that the author wrote *Jésus et Israël* while fleeing the Nazis from place to place accounts for incomplete reference data. A scrupulous scholar, Jules Isaac himself deplored these discrepancies. As he wrote:

Back to normal life (almost), when all the reference libraries had reopened, I was tempted, terribly tempted, to take my book apart and redo it. But no, I couldn't do that. What was essential was not to extend bibliographical, exegetical, theological research, which at that point in my life would have easily filled the few years I still had to live.[6]

No, for Professor Isaac the heart of his work lay elsewhere:

What was essential was not erudition, was not expertise, was even more not courtesy, good manners, academic "moderation." What was essential was the Essential, the Text, Scripture, the Word. And, toward the Text, the freshness and directness of the human gaze, a certain openness of soul, a certain emptying, absolute sincerity, and the truth of the battle engaged.[7]

And he goes on to explain why, with such an outlook, taking the research of the historic method school into consideration was out of the question. "With my purpose to focus not on learned studies but on traditional opinion, current opinion in Christendom, what need had I to press farther and run to enroll in the ranks of the *formgeschichtliche Schule* . . . ? I put the commentaries . . . side by side with the texts, exposing the abyss that separated them." [8]

Such indeed was Jules Isaac's original purpose:

To discover whether, as current opinion in Christianity would have it, as a hardy opinion teaches, Jesus had rejected Israel—the Jewish people as a whole; pronounced its downfall, reproved it, and even cursed it; and conversely, whether it was true that Israel had failed to recognize Jesus, refused to see the Messiah and the Son of God in him, rejected him, scoffed

---

[6] Jules Isaac, *Genèse de l'antisémitisme* (Genesis of Anti-Semitism), Paris, Calmann-Lévy, 1956, p. 15.

[7] *Ibid.*, p. 15.

[8] *Ibid.*, pp. 344–345.

at him, crucified him; whether it deserved for nigh on two thousand years the defamatory stigma of "deicide people." . . .[9]

"A hardy opinion," the one most widespread through a two-millennium tradition: Jules Isaac's work dealt with this generally accepted Christian outlook on the Jews since the small minority in Christendom who repudiated it had no influence on the masses. Yet, at first sight today, one may be inclined to find Professor Isaac's concern out of date and the chapters on the "deicide people" superfluous, reflecting a state of affairs prior to Vatican II's Statement on the Jews. Such was my own feeling as a Catholic following the 1964 draft of the Statement. But in the final version, the 1965 text, the word *deicide* was deleted. The attempt at fairness elsewhere in the Statement and the subsequent explanations of the Secretariat for Promoting Christian Unity, which was responsible for the document, could not compensate for this shameful and tragic omission. As Father René Laurentin put it, "The Council text wanted to avoid the problem of deicide precisely because it is a burning issue." [10] It is indeed. Wrote Bishop Stephen A. Leven, of San Antonio, "The word 'deicide' was invented by Christians and has been hurled at the Jews for centuries to justify persecutions and pogroms. It seems fitting that this Sacred Council should specifically reject it." [11]

But the Sacred Council did not. Its failure to do so is bound to have future repercussions. Unfortunately, as Father Laurentin reflects, ". . . history teaches us to be pessimistic. . . . [Supposing] that new persecutions and even genocide erupt, then the Council and the Church will be accused of letting this emotional root of antisemitism, the notion of deicide, grow undisturbed in obscurity." [12] Then will the responsibility lie on the shoulders of the Council Fathers who opposed the previous text, in which *deicide* was named and condemned. Yet these "men of the Church . . . are sincere and worthy of esteem. This proves, quite simply, the effort that is still required to root out the themes which are incompatible with the spirit of the promulgated

---

[9] *Ibid.*, p. 14.

[10] Fathers René Laurentin and Joseph Neuner, S.J., *The Declaration on the Relation of the Church to Non-Christian Religions of Vatican II*, "Vatican II Documents" series, Glen Rock, N. J., Paulist Press, 1966, p. 65.

[11] Bishop Stephen A. Leven, of San Antonio, Tex., letter to the Council Fathers dated October 11, 1965 (mimeo.); in the editor's possession.

[12] Father René Laurentin, "Vote No. 6 on the Deletion of 'Deicide' from the Schema on Non-Christian Religions," Rome, n.d. (fall, 1965), monograph (mimeo.), p. 7; in the editor's possession.

Declaration." [13] Anyone in full agreement with this commentary will understand the lasting value of Jules Isaac's chapters on deicide.

Thus, *Jesus and Israel* remains a future-oriented work. And this also for another reason—that today a number of Christians find it irksome and a waste of energy to delve into anti-Semitic Christian teaching. They advocate going ahead, starting fresh with a clean slate, in a happy new Jewish-Christian fellowship where the past is forgotten. Some even resent this uncovering of Christian turpitude. They seem blatantly unaware that it cannot be so easy for the persecuted to wipe out the awesome memory of the past. To forgive? Yes; the Jews have done it ceaselessly for centuries. But to forget is another matter, all the more so because it is obvious that Christian anti-Jewish prejudice still persists, either actively or under subtle disguise. The apathy of Christian institutions at the time of the Six-Day War in 1967 was not wholly unconnected with the effects of a centuries-old, prejudicial religious tradition which has left a persistent imprint on the Christian subconscious.

If we are sincere about our effort to eradicate this tradition, we have to face the extent and the depth to which we have been conditioned, generation after generation, by false Christian teaching. Then and then only can we hope our Jewish-Christian fellowship will stand on solid foundations. This embarrassing and painful but indispensable trial of purification Jules Isaac makes possible for us. Whoever wishes to be enlightened on the question of Jewish-Christian relations and on the possibility of a candid and authentic dialogue will find *Jesus and Israel* the one basic and invaluable study. Through Professor Isaac's work, as the distinguished writer and deputy mayor of Jerusalem, André Chouraqui, puts it,

The world and the Church will finally be able to see not only the light of Israel's gaze but its true face. Jules Isaac was one of those who have lifted the veil and made this encounter possible, and it is this that constitutes his incomparable greatness; for the encounter of the Church and the Synagogue not only concerns the Jews but indubitably, in our time and our days, bears on the true salvation of men.[14]

However, it would be erroneous to conclude that Professor Isaac made the Christian tradition alone and wholly responsible for anti-

[13] Laurentin and Neuner, *op. cit.,* p. 102.

[14] André Chouraqui, lecture delivered at Marseille, December 16, 1963, and Aix-en-Provence, December 17, 1963; in *Dans l'Amitié de Jules Isaac,* whole issue of *Cahiers de l'Association des Amis de Jules Isaac* (Aix-en-Provence), no. 1, 1968, p. 49.

Semitism. He was fully aware of pre-Christian anti-Semitism—to which he devoted many pages in *Genèse de l'antisémitisme*—as well as of the neopagan Nazi strain. As he states clearly,

To stress the primordial importance of Christian anti-Semitism is not at all to assert that it has been or is unique of its kind. .... What seems to me to be historically demonstrable, because historic investigation has demonstrated it to me personally, is that Christian anti-Semitism far outweighs the two other types [economic and social] in its continuity, its methodicalness, its poisonousness, its breadth, its depth. . . . Spread abroad for hundreds and hundreds of years by thousands upon thousands of voices, Christian anti-Semitism is the powerful, millennial tree, with many and strong roots, onto which all the other varieties of anti-Semitism—even the most antagonistic by nature, even anti-Christian—have come to be grafted in the Christian world.[15]

Neither was Jules Isaac blind to the fact that many an individual Christian has, by his own attitude and deeds, repudiated this noxious Christian tradition. As he continually emphasized, how could he forget that he himself was saved through the heroism of a few Christians? But as a historian, he was compelled to look at the picture as a whole, over the centuries.

Not forgetting the true Christians, nor was he oblivious to Jewish wrongs:

Even less will I pretend that in the old and bitter controversy between Israel and Christianity, the responsibility, the wrongs, the faults and failures are all on one side, the Christian side. . . . In addressing Christians primarily, am I not justified in thinking that the Christian aspect of the problem, the Christian wrongs, Christian responsibility alone should count for them? Or would I be mistaken, then? Is the Sermon on the Mount not law for every Christian? [16]

This is the question addressed now through this book to the English-speaking Christian reader by Jules Isaac, him who was indeed, in his own words, *pro veritate pugnator.*

Claire Huchet Bishop

New York, March 1, 1970

<hr/>

[15] Isaac, *Genèse de l'antisémitisme*, pp. 19, 17–18.
[16] *Ibid.*, p. 21.

PREFACE TO THE 1959 EDITION

The present edition is a very tardy revision.

Given the origins of this book, and the conditions in which it was conceived and written, it did not readily lend itself to rewriting. It had to retain its original character. Nonetheless, certain points of progress in historical knowledge also had to be taken into account, particularly the major contribution of the Dead Sea Scrolls discovered during the last decade.

The original text has been retained, and corrections and observations added where called for.

May this impassioned book, born of the most intense tribulation, still reach readers' minds and hearts.

It is a meditation not made in a day, and has value for all our days; and its sole aim is to purify.

Jules Isaac

PREFACE TO THE 1948 EDITION

> *There is no doubt that the Christians carry a heavy sin regarding the people of Israel.*
>
> NIKOLAI BERDYAEV [1]

> *It is Christianity that has laid the way to Israel's sufferings, to the proscriptions against it today. . . . How guilty we feel in the face of such anguish!*
>
> AUGUSTE LEMAÎTRE [2]

Begun in 1943, in the course of a life already threatened and uprooted, soon to be ravaged and hunted;

finished in 1946, in solitude and seclusion,

this book has a history that explains it and perhaps justifies whatever elements of torment, peculiarity, from some standpoints deformity it contains.

It was born of persecution. Midway in the writing, a tragedy crossed it. How did the book survive? Who could say? It was a miracle, which raises the imperative of a sacred duty—commemoration.

It is not and could not be essentially a textbook, for a discipline like exegesis—the interpretation of Scripture—demands the preparation and consecration of an entire lifetime.

It is the cry of an outraged conscience, of a lacerated heart. It is addressed to men's consciences and hearts. I sorrow over those who will refuse to hear it.

[1] Nicolas Berdiaeff [*sic*], "Le Christianisme et le danger du communisme matérialiste" [Christianity and the Danger of Materialist Communism], *Le Christianisme social*, no. 2–3, April, 1939. [See, in English, as Nicolas Berdyaev, *Christianity and Anti-Semitism*, tr. Alan A. Spears and Victor Kanter, New York, Philosophical Library, 1954. Where we have found a published English translation for a source, we will cite it, but only at the first occurrence of Professor Isaac's own source. We will of course credit it every place where we take our English version from it. —Tr.]

[2] Auguste Lemaître, quoted in David Lasserre, "L'Antisémitisme de l'Église chrétienne" [The Anti-Semitism of the Christian Church], *Cahiers protestants*, no. 1, January–February, 1939.

Yet if it is not a textbook in essence, it is so in its framework, its methods of investigation and discussion, and, I believe I can say, its strict probity. I am the first to regret that it cites writers of negligible —and sometimes beggarly—learning more often than qualified exegetes, whether a Julius Wellhausen or an Albert Schweitzer or a Rudolf Bultmann; but this serves my chosen purpose, which is to focus not on scholarly research but on traditional opinion, current opinion in Christianity, and thus to confront the Christian world with its responsibilities, which are heavy.

Should I apologize for citing Alfred Loisy here rather than Bultmann or Martin Dibelius? For it is fashionable to refer to German writers rather than French. But Loisy, unjustly forgotten today, had considerable renown among my generation. And in Levroux, the little town in the old province of Berry where I was hidden in the spring of 1944 when I wrote Part III of this book, in which exegesis is given the most extensive treatment, it would have been very hard for me to get hold of the writings of Bultmann or Dibelius. I was only too happy to have at my disposal, thanks to the great kindness of my friend Gustave Monod, the four large commentaries by Father Marie-Joseph Lagrange; they were the solid foundation on which I was able to build this work.

Even in the blackest hours, I found the most valued help on my path. I express my infinite gratitude to all those who aided and sustained me.

The reader may wonder to what religion the author belongs. This is easy for him to answer: none. But his whole book witnesses to the fervor that inspires and guides him, fervor for Israel, fervor for Jesus, son of Israel.

Jules Isaac

INTRODUCTION

◇◇

Preliminary

Observations on

the Old Testament

If you do boast, remember it is not you that support the root, but the root that supports you.

ROM. 11:18

PROPOSITION 1

THE CHRISTIAN RELIGION IS THE DAUGHTER OF THE JEWISH
RELIGION. THE NEW TESTAMENT OF THE CHRISTIANS
IS BUILT UPON THE FOUNDATION OF THE OLD TESTA-
MENT OF THE JEWS. IF ONLY FOR THIS REASON,
JUDAISM IS DESERVING OF RESPECT.

Every Christian is aware—or should be aware—that the Holy Scriptures, which he is taught to revere, consist of two distinct books: first
the Old Testament, the established title, whose exact meaning is the
"Old Covenant"; and subsequently (for it is a sequel) the New Testament, or "New Covenant."

But is every Christian aware that the Old Testament, which he
knows either in the Latin translation of Saint Jerome called the Vulgate or in translations into his native tongue, was originally a Semitic
writing, set down in two closely related languages, both Semitic—the
greater part in Hebrew, and some fragments in Aramaic? [1]

Is every Christian aware that the Old Testament, Semitic in substance no less than in form, is the Hebraic Bible, the collection of Israel's holy books, "the Law and the Prophets" of the Jews? Or, to
define it religiously in its essence, God's progressive revelation to a
people elected, expressly chosen by Him—God—for that revelation,
the people elected by God being those called sometimes the Hebrews,
sometimes Israel, sometimes the Judeans or Jews? [2] It is written in
Genesis: [3]

[1] In the Catholic Bible, the Old Testament also includes a certain number of
writings known only through texts in Greek, but in the main translated from Hebrew: the Books of Machabees, the Book of Tobias, Ecclesiasticus, and others.
[2] [It should be noted that throughout the book, whenever Professor Isaac
speaks of "Israel," he is always referring to the Jewish people and never to the
modern State.—Ed.]
[3] [See the Foreword, p. ix, and the List of Abbreviations, p. vii, regarding sources
for quotations from Scripture.—Ed.]

3

[God said to Abraham:] And I will establish my covenant between me and you and your descendants after you throughout their generations for an everlasting covenant, to be God to you and to your descendants after you.

Gen. 17:7

❉   ❉   ❉

Christians are obliged to recognize the election of the people of Israel because their religious doctrine demands it, but they most often do so grudgingly, and try as hard as they can to forget it.

Nikolai Berdyaev [4]

Christians, that election affronts you; it collides with the centuries-old prejudice rooted in your minds and hearts:

But [says Saint Paul the Jew] who are you, a man, to answer back to God?

Rom. 9:20

Might I dare add: see rather whether it is not your prejudice that affronts God. It is quite true that Israel has no right to take pride in the miraculous election; that exalting and terrifying grace imposed on it—Israel, the "Servant"—only duties, too often rejected. It is quite true that the "stiffnecked" people, the people with an "uncircumcised heart" (Lev. 26:41), strayed from the right path thousands on thousands of times; let him among the Christian peoples who has never sinned against God cast the first stone! But each of these thousands on thousands of times—and this is the miracle, this is the grace—there has been a "remnant," a handful of faithful Jews to reply to God's call:

Do you not know what the scripture says of Elijah, how he pleads with God against Israel? "Lord, they have killed thy prophets,[5] they have demolished thy altars, and I alone am left, and they seek my life." But what is God's reply to him? "I have kept for myself seven thousand men who have not bowed the knee to Baal."

Rom. 11:2—5

God was outraged, God punished; but having punished, God pardoned, and that is without exception, says Saint Paul:

For God has consigned all men to disobedience, that he may have mercy upon all.

Rom. 11:32

[4] Nicholas Berdiaeff, "Le Christianisme et le danger du communisme matérialiste," Le Christianisme social, no. 2–3, April, 1939.

[5] [With regard to style points like the capitalization of the terms Prophets, Law, and Scripture, the usage of each source has been followed throughout this book; hence the inconsistencies of treatment.—Tr.]

Long before Saint Paul, God said through the mouth of the Prophet:

> But Sion said, "The Lord has forsaken me; my Lord has
>   forgotten me."
> Can a mother forget her infant, be without tenderness for
>   the child of her womb?
> Even should she forget, I will never forget you.
>
> Is. 49:14–15 [CCD]

> In overflowing wrath for a moment
>   I hid my face from you,
> but with everlasting love I will have compassion
>   on you, says the Lord, your Redeemer.
>
> Is. 54:8 [RSV]

Now, if the Jews, or at least those among the Jews who still obey the Law of Moses, have refused to this day to agree with Christians that the Old Testament, in a sort of spiritual thrust, or rise, or ascent, leads to the New Testament as the summit that crowns it,

could any Christian refuse to agree that the Jewish Old Testament is the foundation, the unshakable bedrock on which the New Testament and consequently the Christian faith are grounded?

To deny this is a type of monstrous heresy which the Church has always fought and victoriously rejected.

"What would remain of our Christian faith," writes Father Henri de Lubac, "if monotheism, the Decalogue, universality, and belief in eternity were torn from it? Is God less our God because a blasphemer chooses to call Him Jehovah?" [6]

Might I here again dare add: and without the Jews' invincible obstinacy, without the separatism (of divine order, according to Scripture: "[I] have separated you from the [other] peoples, that you should be mine" [Lev. 20:26]) that the Judeans, deported and dispersed, practiced systematically after the fall of the Kingdom of Judah in order to safeguard the integrity of their faith and preserve it from all taint, a separatism that earned them the insults and calumnies of a pagan "anti-Semitism" that our Christian anti-Semites are well pleased to discover in pre-Christian history: yes, without all this, I ask, how could Christianity have come into being?

[6] In Father Henri de Lubac, S.J., *et al.*, *Israël et la foi chrétienne* [Israel and the Christian Faith], "Manifeste contre le Nazisme" series, Fribourg, Switz., Éd. de la Librairie de l'Université, 1942, p. 11. [In a letter to the editor dated July 2, 1968, Father de Lubac writes, regarding the "blasphemer," that "It is obviously question here of a Nazi orator. . . ."—Ed.]

Clearly, the Christian belief in the mission, in the divinity of the Son presupposes the anterior fundamental Jewish belief in the divinity of the Father, the One God of Abraham, Isaac, and Jacob, the All-Powerful, the Eternal, Who revealed Himself to Moses in the burning bush under the name of Yahweh (Ex. 3:14–15).[7]

What did Jesus answer the scribe who asked him which commandment is the first of all?

The first is, "Hear, O Israel: The Lord our God, the Lord is one; and you shall love the Lord your God with all your heart, and with all your soul, and with all your mind, and with all your strength." The second is this, "You shall love your neighbor as yourself." There is no other commandment greater than these.

Mk. 12:29–31

Thus do the principal formulas of the Jewish Law, the Jewish faith, the Jewish ethic (Deut. 6:4–5 and Lev. 19:18) recur in the Gospel according to Saint Mark, 12:29–31, and in Jesus' very mouth.

✿   ✿   ✿

Reference to the Old Testament, reference for the purpose of example or justification, reference and deference: such is the position of the New Testament relative to the Elder; such is thus the only fair Christian position. Some theologians think it meritorious to deny that Israel had any worth or genius in itself, or to elevate the New Testament by depreciating the Old. What pettiness before God, the "head of Christ" (1 Cor. 11:3), Whose true presence permeates the Old Testament. Better inspired is the adversary who forces himself to be fair: "In the Jewish 'Old Testament,' the book of divine justice, there are men, things, and sayings on such an immense scale, that Greek and Indian literature has nothing to compare with it. . . . the taste for the Old Testament is a touchstone with respect to [what is] 'great' and 'small.' . . ."[8] Better inspired is that superior theologian who does not fear to proclaim:

The faith of Abraham is already our faith. In its fundamental precepts, the law of Moses is still our law. The great men of Israel are truly our fathers. . . . The majesty of the God of Israel bows us down with her before the

[7] [On the subject of the word *Yahweh*, see CCD, p. 54, n. 3.14; JB, p. 81, n. h; and RSV, p. v.—Tr.]

[8] Friedrich Nietzsche, *Par delà le Bien et le Mal*, tr. H. Albert, Paris, Mercure de France, n.d., sec. 52, p. 97. [Quotation taken from *idem, Beyond Good and Evil*, tr. Helen Zimmern, New York, Modern Library, n.d. (1917), sec. 52, pp. 59–60.—Tr.]

thrice-holy Face. . . . Jeremiah plows out a new dimension in our hearts. Job exhorts us to a manly patience. The Psalms nourish our prayer daily. Daniel and the Machabees teach us faithfulness. And everywhere, from end to end, God's Faithfulness is revealed: "The counsel of the Lord stands for ever, the thoughts of his heart to all generations" (Ps. 33:11).[9]

Far from there being a discontinuity in the Scriptures, there is such a bond, wrought by such a hand, that no human hand could dissolve it, no sword could sunder it. Christian liturgy provides incontrovertible evidence of this by the place it gives the Old Testament—which is tantamount to saying the Jewish genius (enlightened by God), primarily in the two forms in which it is incomparable, and incomparably inspired: Prophecy and Psalm, messages from God and hymns to God.

✿　　✿　　✿

There is more to say than that, from the Christian point of view, the Old Testament is the prelude (albeit grandiose), the prologue, the first and necessary stage in humanity's journey toward God; that it is a preview, a prediction, an annunciation, an advance toward the light. Also to be seen in it, and Christian theology does want to see in it, is a mysterious prefiguring of the New Testament, as a harmony pre-established by the grace of God: a choice theme for doctoral virtuosity, a marvelous exercise with infinite (and sometimes abusive) variations; but equally, and far better, an exalting theme with ample harmonics that Charles Péguy has beautifully orchestrated in his *Mystery of the Holy Innocents:*

> [Overture:]
> *A man had twelve sons.* As the forty-six books of the Old
> Testament proceed before the four Gospels and the
> Acts and the Epistles and the Apocalypse.
> Which closes the procession. . . .
> And as Israel proceeds before Christianity.
> And as the battalion of the just proceeds before the battalion of saints.
> And Adam before Jesus Christ.
> Who is the second Adam.

[9] Lubac, *op. cit.,* p. 38. [Ps. 33:11 in RSV, but 32:11 in CCD, for Pss. 9A and 9B in CCD are numbered 9 and 10 in RSV and other Protestant Bibles, as well as in the ecumenically sponsored JB. Hence all Psalm numbers above 9 will differ by one unit between these sets of sources. We recall this to the readers in case the place citation for a Psalm quotation does not accord with their Bibles.—Ed.]

Thus before any history and before any resemblance to
the New Testament
Proceeds a history of the Old Testament which is its par-
allel and which is its likeness.
A man had two sons. A man had twelve sons.
And thus before every Christian sister
Walks a Jewish sister who is her elder sister and who an-
nounces her coming and who goes before.
And who has spread her tent in the desert. And the well
of Rebecca
Had been dug before the well of the Samaritan
woman. . . .
[Finale:]
. . . the old testament is that arch which rises in a rib,
In a single ridge and the new testament
Is the same arch which falls,
Which descends in a single sweep.
And the rising rib begins from the earth and it is a carnal
rib.
But that sweep which falls comes from the spirit
And it is a spiritual sweep.
And the rib and the ridge that rises issues from time and
it is a temporal rib.
But the sweep that falls comes from eternity and it is
An eternal sweep.
And the key of that mystical arch.
The key itself
Carnal, spiritual,
Temporal, eternal,
Is Jesus,
Man,
God.[10]

[10] Charles Péguy, *Le Mystère des saints Innocents*, in *Cahiers de la Quinzaine*,
13th ser., no. 12, March, 1912, pp. 121–122, 179. [See, in English, in *idem*, *The
Mystery of the Holy Innocents and Other Poems*, tr. Pansy Pakenham, New York,
Harper, 1956.—Tr.]

PART I

❖❖❖

Jesus, the Christ, a Jew
"According to the Flesh"

He was a Jew, a simple Jew. . . .
CHARLES PÉGUY °

Jesus Christ, whom we adore as God, but also truly man, was born in Judea and preached his doctrine there. It was from there that his disciples, all Jews, spread throughout the world. The more scholars study that religious movement, the more they recognize its Jewish point of departure, which for us in no way nullifies its divine originality.
FATHER MARIE-JOSEPH LAGRANGE †

° Charles Péguy, *Le Mystère de la charité de Jeanne d'Arc*, in *Cahiers de la Quinzaine*, 11th ser., no. 6, December, 1909, p. 82. [See, in English, as *idem*, *The Mystery of the Charity of Joan of Arc*, tr. Julian Green, New York, Pantheon, 1950, p. 65.—Tr.]

† Father Marie-Joseph Lagrange, O.P., *Le Judaïsme avant Jésus-Christ* [Judaism Before Jesus Christ], Paris, Gabalda, 1932, p. ix.

PROPOSITION 2

JESUS, THE JESUS OF THE GOSPELS, ONLY SON AND INCARNA-
TION OF GOD FOR THE CHRISTIANS, IN HIS HUMAN LIFE-
TIME WAS A JEW, A HUMBLE JEWISH ARTISAN. THIS IS
A FACT OF WHICH NO CHRISTIAN HAS A RIGHT TO BE
UNAWARE.

Everything we know about Jesus shows that he was Jewish.

Not only Jewish by belief, by religion.

Jewish by birth.

There is no evidence more official or solid, historically speaking, than that of the Apostle Paul, his contemporary (Paul was some ten years younger). Writing of his Jewish compatriots, the Apostle expressed himself thus:

. . . my brethren, my kinsmen by race. They are Israelites, and to them belong the sonship, the glory, the covenants, the giving of the law, the worship, and the promises; to them belong the patriarchs, *and of their race, according to the flesh, is the Christ.*[1]

Rom. 9:3–5

In the same vein, it is written in the Epistle to the Hebrews, which appears in the New Testament following Saint Paul's Epistles, though we cannot attribute it to him:

For it is evident that our Lord was *descended from Judah.* . . .

Heb. 7:14

And in the Revelation to Saint John:

Weep not; lo, *the Lion of the tribe of Judah,* the Root of David, has conquered. . . .

Rev. 5:5

A craftsman, a humble Jewish artisan—so does Jesus appear in the Gospel accounts. According to the first two Gospels, attributed to

[1] [Italics added by the author in this and the two following quotations.—Ed.]

Saints Matthew and Mark, he was known as a carpenter, the son of a
carpenter, more exactly a woodworker, simultaneously a carpenter,
joiner, and wheelwright, living and working with his kith in Nazareth, a small town of Galilee, in northern Palestine.

. . . he began to teach in the synagogue; and many who heard him were
astonished, saying, "Where did this man get all this? What is the wisdom
given to him? What mighty works are wrought by his hands! Is not this the
carpenter, the son of Mary and brother [2] of James and Joses and Judas and
Simon, and are not his sisters here with us?"

Mk.[3] 6:2–3

. . . he taught them in their synagogue, so that they were astonished, and
said, "Where did this man get this wisdom and these mighty works? Is not
this the carpenter's son? Is not his mother called Mary? And are not his
brothers James and Joseph and Simon and Judas? And are not all his sisters
with us? Where then did this man get all this?"

Mt. 13:54–56

If we can believe a tradition taken up by Justin Martyr in the second century, Jesus made ploughs and yokes for oxen.

It was a noteworthy cultural characteristic of the Jewish society of
that time that even the humblest manual labor was not adjudged incompatible with even the noblest spiritual activity. Severe toward
idlers, Jewish wisdom taught, "A man who lives from the labour [of
his hands] is greater than the one who fears heaven" but is supported
by others (Berakoth 8a [and n. 4, BT], and "Artisans may not [need
not] rise before scholars whilst engaged in their work" (Ḳiddushin
33a [BT]). Scholars sometimes were found to be "artisans . . . engaged in their work." A rabbi or master of religious studies might be
a shoemaker; another might be a blacksmith. Saint Paul had learned
and practiced the trade of "tentmaker" (Acts 18:3). Sixteen centuries
later, when the illustrious Jewish philosopher Baruch Spinoza worked

---

[2] In the Catholic interpretation, the words "brother" and "sisters" must be understood here in the sense of "cousins." On this point, see Father Marie-Joseph
Lagrange's commentary in his *Évangile selon saint Marc* [Gospel According to
Saint Mark], Paris, Gabalda, 1910 [repub. 1942], pp. 79–93, or the briefer article "Frères de Jésus" [Jesus' Brothers] in the appendix of Canon A. Crampon's
translation of the Bible, *La Sainte Bible*, rev. ed., Tournai, Desclée, 1939, pp.
340–342. [It should be noted that Canon Crampon is Roman Catholic; the title
canon, not generally employed in the American Catholic Church, continues to be
used in the French.—Tr.]

[3] We quote first from Mark, the second evangelist, because his priority seems
today to be well established and because he must be considered as one of the
primary sources for the first and third Gospels, those of Saints Matthew and
Luke.

at polishing lenses in the Hague, he was only following a very old and very solid national tradition.

It appears furthermore that Jesus was not a craftsman incidentally. He was a craftsman pure and simple. A Jew in the most modest of conditions, a Jew of the people, knowing well the people among whom he lived and loving them, this people, his people, with a marvelous heart that never withdrew from them.

❖   ❖   ❖

Here my path crosses through a singular band of deniers, of Germanic robots set up to prove that common opinion is wrong: Jesus was not a Jew.

Each to his task: you cannot send university professors to kill Jewish old people, women, and children at Auschwitz or Treblinka; to them was reserved the honor of Aryanizing knowledge, some treating physics, others religious history.

These Germans unfortunately had English and French masters, in the first ranks of whom was Houston Stewart Chamberlain, author of *The Foundations of the Nineteenth Century*,[4] one of the Nazi gospels. But in France, among responsible thinkers, I find only one— Reverend Henri Monnier—who let himself go on that slippery bank to the point of writing: "Jesus was not, properly speaking, Jewish; he was Galilean, which is not the same thing." [5] The entire school is in fact grounded on and pivots around this fragile base: Jesus was Galilean; now, Galilee had a very mixed population; hence it is highly probable that Jesus had more Aryan than Jewish blood in his veins. (Note that in Jesus' time, according to the conclusions of historic inquiry,[6] Jews formed the predominant element of the Galilean population, as was evidenced by the strength of the nationalist current in that country; but this matters little to those whose minds are made up.)

It is not surprising that this school reached full flower in Germany, Hitler's Germany. In 1921, a German historian of the caliber of Ed-

---

[4] [Published originally in German as *Die Grundlagen des Neunzehnten Jahrhunderts* in 1899; translated and published in English in 1911.—Tr.]

[5] Henri Monnier, *La Mission historique de Jésus* [Jesus' Historic Mission], Paris, Fischbacher, 1906, p. xxviii.

[6] Emil Schürer, *Geschichte des jüdischen Volkes im Zeitaltes Jesu-Christi* [History of the Jewish People in the Time of Jesus Christ], 3 vols., 4th ed., Leipzig, Hinrichs, 1907, II, 16, n. 35.

uard Meyer could still smile at this "naïvety" and adjudge the discussion superfluous.[7] In 1941, no German historian would have ventured to smile when Dr. Walter Grundmann, professor at the University of Jena, claimed to find even in Jesus' genealogy, as set down by Saint Matthew, proof that Jesus was not Jewish on his mother's side.[8]

In reality, Eduard Meyer's is the only proper attitude toward these racist inventions, which have no reliable foundation and which all the facts and texts deny, as we have already seen and will see in the following pages of this work.

✿ ✿ ✿

Whether other Christians deny or fastidiously conceal Jesus' Jewishness, for all that it is fundamental; whether it makes them feel ashamed, or embarrassed, Péguy the Catholic—here again, I call on him whose faithful companion I was from 1897 on—stresses and marvels at it:

And you Jews, people of Jews, people of the Jews, my God my God, what had this people done to you then, for you to have preferred it to all peoples. . . . What have they done then, *what has it done then to be your elect?* For you to have showered it, thus, with that grace. . . . For you to have made it famous with such radiance, an eternal radiance. . . . You chose, you sifted, you picked among them, from generation to generation you picked among them the long lineage, the high, the mounting lineage of the prophets; and like a summit the last of all; the last of the prophets, the first of the saints; Jesus, who was Jewish, a Jew among you, the race who received the greatest grace; . . . mystery of grace; elect race. . . . He was a Jew, a simple Jew, a Jew like you, a Jew among you. You knew him the way one says of a man: I knew him in the old days. . . . Brothers of his race and of the same lineage. He shed unique tears over you. He wept over that multitude of you. You saw the color of his eyes; you heard the sound of his words. Of the same lineage eternally.[9]

[7] Eduard Meyer, *Ursprung und Anfänge des Christentums* [Origin and Beginnings of Christianity], 3 vols., Stuttgart, Cotta, 1921–1923, II, 425, n. 1.

[8] Walter Grundmann, *Jesus der Galiläer und das Judentum* [Jesus the Galilean and Judaism], Leipzig, 1940, pp. 196–198.

[9] Charles Péguy, *Le Mystère de la charité de Jeanne d'Arc*, in *Cahiers de la Quinzaine*, 11th ser., no. 6, December, 1909, pp. 80–82.

PROPOSITION 3

INSOFAR AS WE CAN KNOW OF THEM THROUGH THE GOSPELS, JESUS' FAMILY WAS JEWISH: MARY, HIS MOTHER, WAS JEWISH, AND SO WERE ALL THEIR FRIENDS AND RELATIVES. TO BE AT ONCE AN ANTI-SEMITE AND A CHRISTIAN IS TO TRY TO MARRY REVERENCE WITH ABUSE.

Let us name in the lead:

> The one who is infinitely queen
> Because she is the humblest of creatures.
> Because she was a poor woman, a pitiful woman, a poor
> Jewess of Judea.[1]

Mary, mother of Jesus.

She was called Mariam or Miriam. Mary is the English transcription of this Semitic name, which was sometimes lengthened to Mariane or, more often, abridged to Maria.

All the other family names were Semitic, given by the evangelists Mark and Matthew in the texts previously cited:

Joseph, whose Galilean pronunciation could be Yosef;

James,

Simon,

Jude,

all English names derived from Hebrew by way of Greek and Latin transcriptions.

The names of friends or family were Semitic, as we know them through the third evangelist, Luke, the only one, moreover, who was not of Jewish origin:

Zechariah, priest of the ministerial division of Abijah; his wife

---

[1] Charles Péguy, Le Porche du mystère de la deuxième vertu [The Porch of the Mystery of the Second Virtue], in Cahiers de la Quinzaine, 13th ser., no. 4, October, 1911, pp. 82–83.

Elizabeth—Elisheba—a relative of Mary's and one "of the daughters of Aaron" (Lk. 1:5);

their son John—Yoḥanan—who would be the Baptist;

in Jerusalem, the devout Simeon (Lk. 2:25);

the prophetess Anna, "the daughter of Phanuel, of the tribe of Asher" (Lk. 2:36).

✿   ✿   ✿

Without needing to comment here on the historic validity of the "childhood accounts" in Luke's Gospel, accounts that are infinitely dear to Christian piety,

we are entitled to say that these passages, taken in themselves, constitute a document of the greatest value, not only literary but religious: nowhere is the link between the New Testament and the Old more visible (or stronger), such a link that one wonders whether Saint Luke, himself Gentile by birth and writing for Gentiles, might not have used some specifically Semitic source.

At the very least, the writer of the third Gospel took inspiration from the purest Hebraic tradition. That it influenced him is surely not a negligible fact.

I require no other proof than the *Magnificat*, the admirable hymn with which Mary replies to Elizabeth's greeting; practically not one word, one verse of it but did not come directly from the Psalms, the Prophets, and the song of Hannah, the mother of Samuel:

> My heart exults in the Lord. . . .
>
> 1 Sam. 2:1
>
> The bows of the mighty are broken, . . .
>   but those who were hungry have ceased to hunger. . . .
>   [The Lord] brings low, he also exalts.
> He raises up the poor from the dust;
>   he lifts the needy from the ash heap. . . .
>
> 1 Sam. 2:4–8
>
> Thou [Lord] wilt show faithfulness to Jacob
>   and steadfast love to Abraham,
> as thou hast sworn to our fathers
>   from the days of old.
>
> Mic. 7:20

And Mary, the mother of Jesus, sings:

My soul magnifies the Lord, and my spirit rejoices in God my Savior; Because he has regarded the lowliness of his handmaid. . . . He has put down the mighty from their thrones, and has exalted the lowly. He has filled the hungry with good things, and the rich he has sent away empty. He has given help to Israel, his servant, mindful of his mercy—Even as he spoke to our fathers—to Abraham and to his posterity forever.

Lk. 1:46–48, 52–55 [CCD]

How can we not be struck by the sound these words make, and especially the last two lines, so specifically Israelite! What solemnity in the recollection of the Old Testament, and this at the beginning of the Gospel—the Gospel of the Gentiles—and from Mary's own mouth: "forever."

The strength of these words is a little troublesome to the honest commentator Father Lagrange. They must "not be too closely linked," he says, "with to *spermati*" (race).[2] "Too closely"—a gracious formula. Somewhat linked, nonetheless; for what else could they be "linked with"? With the reign of God, of Whom Israel is the instrument, proposes the Reverend Father—who does not, moreover, argue the point "too closely."

❋   ❋   ❋

The same evangelist, Saint Luke—a Greek physician, according to tradition—makes a point of telling us that Jesus' family observed the basic prescriptions of Mosaic Law; and this they doubtless did as ordinary people would, not as would doctors of the Law—that is, without any rigorism:

And when the time came for their purification according to the law of Moses, they [Joseph and Mary] brought him [the child Jesus] up to Jerusalem to present him to the Lord (as it is written in the law of the Lord, "Every male that opens the womb shall be called holy to the Lord") and to offer a sacrifice according to what is said in the law of the Lord, "a pair of turtledoves, or two young pigeons."

Lk. 2:22–24

[2] Father Marie-Joseph Lagrange, O.P., commentary on the *Évangile selon saint Luc* [Gospel According to Saint Luke], Paris, Gabalda, 1921 [repub. 1941], p. 51. [Father Lagrange (1855–1936), to whom Professor Isaac refers frequently, was a scholar and the founder of the famous Jerusalem School for Biblical Studies (1890) and of the *Revue biblique* (1892, later titled the *Revue biblique internationale*). Author of numerous erudite works, his four volumes of commentaries on the Gospel texts are particularly well known in the field of exegesis.—Ed.]

The first of these prescriptions is drawn from Exodus 13:2, the second from Leviticus 12:6–8. The offering prescribed by the Law was a lamb, young pigeons, or turtledoves: "And if she [the mother of the newborn] cannot afford a lamb, then she shall take two turtledoves or two young pigeons." The evangelist thus lets us see that Mary and Joseph were poor people who "[could] not afford a lamb."

We also read in Saint Luke that Jesus' "parents," "according to [the] custom" of pious Jews, "went to Jerusalem every year at the feast of the Passover" (Lk. 2:41–42). Thus does Christian piety in its first fervor seem to hold out a hand to Jewish piety.

❀   ❀   ❀

By way of commentary, may I be allowed to insert two parallel quotations here, one from Jacques Maritain and the other from Léon Bloy. The first reads:

It is no small thing for a Christian to hate or despise or want to debase the race from which his God and the immaculate Mother of his God have sprung. This is why the bitter zeal of anti-Semitism always turns against Christianity itself in the end.[3]

The second says:

Suppose that people around you spoke constantly of your father and mother with the greatest contempt and treated them to nothing but offensive insults and sarcasm. How would you feel? Well, this is exactly what happens to Our Lord Jesus Christ. People forget, or rather they do not want to know, that our God made man is a Jew, the Jew par excellence by nature, the Lion of Judah; that his Mother is a Jewish woman, the flower of the Jewish race; that all his ancestors were Jews; that the Apostles were Jews, as were all the Prophets; finally, that the whole of our Sacred Liturgy is drawn from Jewish books. How then to express the enormity of the outrage and blasphemy [4] that consist in vilifying the Jewish race? . . .

Anti-Semitism . . . is the most dreadful blow Our Lord has received in his Passion, which continues still; it is the bloodiest and the most unpardonable because he takes it *on his Mother's Face* and from the hand of Christians. . . .[5]

[3] Jacques Maritain, "L'impossible antisémitisme" [Impossible Anti-Semitism], in Paul Claudel *et al., Les Juifs* [The Jews], "Présences" series, Paris, Plon, 1937, p. 71.
[4] "Outrage and blasphemy": Léon Bloy had practiced them lavishly, condemning that practice some twenty years later with full knowledge of its meaning. In the interim, he had made some precious friendships with Jews.
[5] Léon Bloy, letter dated January 2, 1910, to an unknown woman, in his book *Le Vieux de la Montagne* [The Old Man of the Mountain], Paris, Mercure de France, 1907, p. 303. [See, in English, in Albert Béguin, *Leon Bloy: A Study in Impatience,* tr. Edith M. Riley, London, Sheed & Ward, 1947, pp. 135–136. —Tr.]

PROPOSITION 4

ON EACH NEW YEAR'S DAY THE CHURCH COMMEMORATES
THE CIRCUMCISION OF THE INFANT JESUS. IT WAS NOT
WITHOUT HESITATION AND CONTROVERSY THAT EARLY
CHRISTIANITY ABANDONED THIS RITE SANCTIONED BY
THE OLD TESTAMENT.

The Jewish Infant Jesus was "born under the law" (Gal. 4:4). In keeping with the Law (Lev. 12:3), he was circumcised, like all Jewish boy children, eight days after his birth (Lk. 2:21).

Christmas, the Feast of the Nativity, falling on December 25 on our calendar, New Year's Day comes eight days later. That is why January 1 on all the calendars carries this word: *Circumcision*.[1]

New Year's Day is the commemorative Feast of the Circumcision of the Infant Jesus: a Christian feast in commemoration of a Jewish rite.

❀   ❀   ❀

According to the Old Testament—or at least according to Genesis, which does not conform with Exodus on this point[2]—circumcision was a divine commandment. God had instituted it Himself as a sign of His covenant with Abraham and Abraham's descendants:

And God said to Abraham, "As for you, you shall keep my covenant, you and your descendants after you throughout their generations. . . . You shall be circumcised in the flesh of your foreskins, and it shall be a sign of the covenant between me and you. . . . So shall my covenant be in your flesh

---

[1] [Beginning January 1, 1970, the Church replaced the commemoration of Jesus' circumcision with that of the Motherhood of Mary. However, the official reading of Scriptures for that day still includes Luke 2:21, which tells of the infant Jesus' circumcision.—Ed.]

[2] The passage in Exodus regarding circumcision (4:24–26) is one of the most obscure and difficult to interpret. Circumcision is not included among the com-

an everlasting covenant. Any uncircumcised male who is not circumcised in the flesh of his foreskin shall be cut off from his people; he has broken my covenant."

Gen. 17:9, 11, 13–14

Here is the explanation, in the first place, of the importance that pious Jews attached and continue to attach to the observation of this rite of the flesh. Among the numerous pagans who were attracted to the Jewish religion in those days and gravitated toward Jewish communities (already dispersed throughout the whole of the ancient world ³), only those who, whatever their age, agreed to undergo the rite of circumcision became members of the community, under the name *proselytes.* In all likelihood, these were only a small minority; the others, the great majority of the sympathizers, remained outside the community, and were called *God-fearers.* From this it is not unreasonable to deduce that circumcision was the most serious obstacle to the diffusion and expansion of Judaism.

Here is the explanation, in the second place, of the gravity of the controversy that arose in the first Christian communities—formed of Jews—among those who demanded that the strict observance of the Law, beginning with circumcision, be imposed on all converts, Gentiles as well as Jews:

But some men came down from Judea and were teaching the brethren, "Unless you are circumcised according to the custom of Moses, you cannot be saved." And when Paul and Barnabas had no small dissension and debate with them, Paul and Barnabas and some of the others were appointed to go up to Jerusalem to the apostles and the elders about this question.

Acts 15:1–2

The meeting of the Apostles and the Elders, called the Council of Jerusalem, discussed the issue lengthily, and ultimately pronounced in favor of Paul and Barnabas (Acts 15:6–29). Circumcision was therefore not obligatory for Christians from the Gentile world—a decision of capital importance, by virtue of which Christianity, freed of this obstacle, took wing in the pagan world, leaving far behind it a willingly harnessed Judaism.

mandments of the Decalogue. According to Exodus 31:12–17, it is the observation of the Sabbath rest that must be considered as the sign of the covenant concluded between God and Israel through the intermediary of Moses.

³ On the Diaspora, or Dispersion, see Jules Isaac, *La Dispersion d'Israël* [The Dispersion of Israel], Algiers, C.C.J.J., 1954.

❈   ❈   ❈

Already in antiquity, the Jewish custom of circumcision excited Greek and Roman anti-Semites to mockery. Christian anti-Semitism was quick to take up this coarse mockery in its own account,[4] as if it did not know

that the Infant Jesus was circumcised;

that the question of circumcision occasioned a discussion of the greatest gravity among the Apostles and the first Christians, themselves circumcised;

that Saint Paul declared: "For I tell you that Christ became a servant to the circumcised . . ." (Rom. 15:8),

and that, giving himself the title of Apostle to the pagans or Gentiles, he recognized Saint Peter as the Apostle "to the circumcised" (Gal. 2:7);

and finally, that there are circumcised Christians: the Abyssinians.

This religious (but also medical) surgery, moreover, is not a specifically Jewish custom. Spread through Egypt from the time of the Old Kingdom, principally among priests (Israel perhaps adopted it from Egypt); in Arabia prior to the time of Muhammad; and then in the whole Muslim world and all the way to Oceania, it is still practiced today by an important segment of the world population, approximately a seventh of the human race.

[4] It is a fact that the Fathers of the Church were the first to give the example. Saint Ephraim, in the fourth century, called the Jews "circumcised dogs" (see Jean Juster, *Les Juifs dans l'Empire romain* [The Jews in the Roman Empire], Paris, Guethner, 1914, I, 264).

PROPOSITION 5

THE NAME *Jesus Christ* IS BASICALLY SEMITIC, EVEN
THOUGH ITS FORM IS GREEK: *Jesus* IS A HELLENIZA-
TION OF A JEWISH NAME; *Christ* IS THE GREEK EQUIV-
ALENT OF THE JEWISH WORD *Messiah.*

The name *Jesus* is the Greek transcription *Iesous* of the Hebrew name *Jeshua* (*Yeshua*) or *Jehoshua*, which is also transcribed *Joshua*, and which means "Yah[weh] is salvation."

The evangelists Matthew and Luke emphasize in their narratives the importance they attached to such a name with such a meaning:

. . . an angel of the Lord appeared to him [Joseph] in a dream, saying, ". . . she [Mary] will bear a son, and you shall call his name Jesus, for he will save his people from their sins."

Mt. 1:20–21

[The angel Gabriel said to Mary,] "And behold, you will conceive in your womb and bear a son, and you shall call his name Jesus.

He will be great, and will be called the Son of the Most High; and the Lord God will give to him the throne of his father David. . . ."

Lk. 1:31–32

And at the end of eight days, when he was circumcised, he was called Jesus, the name given by the angel before he was conceived in the womb.

Lk. 2:21

Actually, *Jesus* was a rather widespread name among the Jews. One of the books of the Old Testament, the Wisdom of Sirach, or Ecclesiasticus,[1] which dates from the second century before Christ, had as its author "Jesus, son of Eleazar, son of Sirach," of Jerusalem.[2] In

---

[1] As we said earlier (p. 3, n. 1), Ecclesiasticus appears in the Catholic Bible but not in the Protestant.

[2] [See the Introduction to the Book of Sirach (Ecclesiasticus) in CCD, p. 662. The different spellings "Eleazar" here and "Eliezer" in the next sentence accord with the two places in the source.—Tr.]

the genealogy given by the evangelist Saint Luke, we find a "Jesus, the son of Eliezer" (Lk. 3:29 [CCD; RSV has "Joshua"]). In the list of Jewish high priests who succeeded each other at Jerusalem from the advent of Herod the Great in 37 B.C. to the capture of the city by Titus and the destruction of the Temple in A.D. 70, we count no fewer than four Jesuses.[3]

The name *Jesus* thus had nothing—in itself—that could attract the attention of his Jewish fellow citizens, nothing singular, nothing exceptional. It was a Jewish name, pure and simple.

       ✣   ✣   ✣

"Jesus Christ" exactly equals "Jesus the Messiah." The Greek word *christos* is the equivalent of the Semitic word *mashiah* or *meshiha*, messiah, which means "anointed," "he who has been anointed," "by Yahweh" being understood.

Calling Jesus "the Christ" is thus equivalent to calling him "the Messiah" (of Israel), "the Anointed" (by Yahweh).[4] In other words, it relates to the Jewish religion, to the traditional Jewish belief in the coming of a Savior, a messenger from God, as we find it expressed in the fourth Gospel, attributed to Saint John:

[Jesus said to the Samaritan woman at Jacob's well,] "You [Samaritans] worship what you do not know; we [Jews] worship what we know, for salvation is from the Jews. . . ." The woman said to him, "I know that Messiah is coming (he who is called Christ); when he comes, he will show us all things." Jesus said to her, "I who speak to you am he."

Jn. 4:22, 25–26

       ✣   ✣   ✣

Messianic hopes took on very different forms in Israel. In the most generally accepted and popular Jewish tradition, the Messiah was to be a descendant of the glorious king of Israel, David. And in Christian tradition, Jesus was indeed a descendant of King David, despite the modest circumstances of his family. Saint Paul asserts this at the beginning of the Epistle to the Romans, and repeats it in the Second

---

[3] Emil Schürer, *Geschichte des jüdischen Volkes im Zeitaltes Jesu-Christi*, 3 vols., 4th ed., Leipzig, Hinrichs, 1907, II, 269–273.

[4] See Proposition 14, below, concerning the problem of Jesus' messiahship.

Epistle to Timothy, 2:8 (although the Pauline authenticity of this Epistle is in doubt).

Revelation 5:5 and 22:16 contain similar declarations, but the fourth Gospel, also attributed to Saint John, seems to dismiss or be unaware of the Davidic ancestry.

Saint Luke, drawing up the Acts of the Apostles, puts these words in the mouths of the Apostles Peter and Paul:

[Peter:] Being therefore a prophet, and knowing that God had sworn with an oath to him [David] that he would set one of his descendants upon his throne. . . . This Jesus God raised up. . . .

                                                                    Acts 2:30, 32

[Paul:] Of this man's [David's] posterity God has brought to Israel a Savior, Jesus, as he promised.

                                                                    Acts 13:23

But words set down some thirty or forty years after they were spoken cannot be guaranteed as literally exact.

The first page of the New Testament contains a "genealogy of Jesus Christ, the son of David, the son of Abraham" (Mt. 1:1–17). The third Gospel, according to Saint Luke, likewise gives a genealogy of Jesus, which is carried back to "Adam, the son of God" (Lk. 3:38). But for accuracy's sake, we should observe that both trace the transmission of Davidic blood to Jesus through Joseph, who for Christians is only Jesus' "adoptive" father, and also that the two genealogies do not conform with each other absolutely.[5] (Nor do the accounts of the two evangelists agree on the circumstances of Jesus' birth: though both have him born in Judea, at Bethlehem, the "city of David," Matthew 2:1 shows Jesus' family settled in Bethlehem, while according to Luke 2:4–7, they were at first established in Galilee at Nazareth, and went to Bethlehem because a census had been ordered by imperial Roman edict.)

Numerous times in the first Gospel Jesus is addressed with the messianic title "Son of David" (Mt. 9:27; 15:22; 20:30–31; 21:9, 15), and on one occasion—the same—in the Gospels of Saint Mark (10:48) and Saint Luke (18:38), but not once in the fourth Gospel, according

---

[5] On the difficulties raised by the concordance as well as the divergence between these genealogies, see the Catholic interpretation given in Canon A. Crampon's article "Généalogie de Jésus-Christ" [Genealogy of Jesus Christ] in the appendix to the first edition of his Bible (*La Sainte Bible*, Paris, Desclée, Lefebvre, 1905, p. 343), or in Father Marie-Joseph Lagrange's commentary in *L'Évangile de Jésus-Christ* (Paris, Gabalda, 1928 [8th ed., 1953], pp. 29–30). [See the latter, in English, as *idem, The Gospel of Jesus Christ*, tr. by members of the English Dominican Province, 2 vols., Westminster, Md., 1938.—Tr.]

to Saint John. And again for accuracy's sake, we should observe that in none of the Gospel narratives does Jesus proclaim himself Son of David. On the contrary, in an account common to the first three Gospels, called the Synoptics,[6] if Jesus alludes to the Davidic descent of the Messiah, his purpose does not seem to be to confirm it or attribute it to himself:

And as Jesus taught in the temple, he said, "How can the scribes say that the Christ is the son of David? David himself, inspired by the Holy Spirit, declared,

> 'The Lord said to my Lord,
> Sit at my right hand,
> till I put thy enemies under thy feet.' [7]

David himself calls him Lord; so how [do people think] is he his son?"

Mk. 12:35–37; the same account, aside from some variations
in form, in Mt. 22:41–45 and Lk. 20:41–44

Were Jesus' objection and the interrogation that follows only a problem posed to perplex the scribes (doctors of the Law), as some theologians would have it? Since Jesus furnished no answer to it, the theologians are themselves perplexed in the bargain.

Should we share their perplexity? Yet is it the answer, affirmative or negative, that is important? Or isn't it rather the lesson Jesus gave scholars of all times, a lesson that seems clear and can be formulated thus:

There is no common measure between the Messiah and human greatness. Lineage has no bearing. . . .

Which in no way detracts from Jesus' humanity—his Jewish humanity—but which makes all controversy about genealogies superfluous, makes the genealogies themselves superfluous. How many times does the incomprehension of the Master's disciples, those both nearest and dearest to him, come through in the Gospels? Here it is the incomprehension of the evangelists, and along with them the genealogists, that comes through and surprises us; more surprising still if we refer to the key text given in Mark 3:31–35, and without much change in Matthew 12:46–50 and Luke 8:19–21:

[While Jesus was teaching,] . . . his mother and his brothers came; and standing outside they sent to him and called him. And a crowd was sitting about him; and they said to him, "Your mother and your brothers are out-

[6] *Synoptics:* "which can be seen at one view"; that is, presenting a measure of parallelism. The expression has had currency since the eighteenth century.
[7] Ps. 110:1.

side, asking for you." And he replied, "Who are my mother and my brothers?" And looking around on those who sat about him, he said, "Here are
my mother and my brother! Whoever does the will of God is my brother,
and sister, and mother."

Mk. 3:31–35

PROPOSITION 6

THE NEW TESTAMENT WAS WRITTEN IN GREEK. IN THE COURSE OF THE CENTURIES THE CATHOLIC CHURCH HAS QUOTED IT IN LATIN, A LATIN WHICH IS THE RESULT OF TRANSLATION. BUT JESUS, LIKE ALL THE PALESTINIAN JEWS HE WAS ADDRESSING, SPOKE ARAMAIC, A SEMITIC LANGUAGE CLOSELY RELATED TO HEBREW.

Owing to time-honored tradition, sacred writings appear in the Catholic world as Latin writings. Those dearest to Christian piety carry Latin titles, following their opening words: the *Ave Maria*, the *Magnificat*, the *Benedictus*, the *Nunc dimittis*, the *Pater noster*. Such an illustrious writer as the great Catholic poet Paul Claudel has actually discussed the meaning that must be given certain Latin words in the Gospel text, as if the original text were in Latin.[1]

But the Latin of the Church, the Latin of the missal, is only a translation. The oldest text of the whole New Testament is a Greek text: Gospels and Epistles, Acts of the Apostles and Revelation have come down to us only in Greek. Except for Jesus' words, it is not certain whether they ever had another form.

What language did Jesus use, then? Not Latin, not Greek, not even Hebrew, but Aramaic, as did all Palestinian Jews of that time. That Jesus may have known or understood Greek is not impossible; the Greek language was spread throughout Palestine as in all the Levant, especially in the cities (but Jesus was from the country). Opinions are very divided on this point, and no text allows us to decide among them.

There remains one thing sure, and one only: Jesus' tongue was Aramaic.

[1] See Paul Claudel, *Un Poète regarde la Croix*, Paris, Gallimard, 1938, p. 18, n. 1. [See, in English, as *idem, A Poet Before the Cross*, tr. Wallace Fowlie, Chicago, Regnery, 1958, p. 14, n. 10.—Tr.
[Since Vatican II, the use of the vernacular has been adopted. However, Latin is retained on special occasions.—Ed.]

27

And Aramaic was a Semitic language very closely related to Hebrew.

Several centuries before Jesus Christ, in the sixth and fifth centuries, it had spread from northern Syria into all of western Asia, where it appeared as a kind of international tongue in commercial and other relations among the very diversified people of that region. By the first century, Aramaic had also become the ordinary language of the Jews of Palestine: when the Torah—the Law—was read in Palestinian synagogues, each verse read in Hebrew was translated at once into Aramaic.

✿   ✿   ✿

Thus, the Latin of the Catholic missal and the French, English, or German of the Protestant Bibles are translations from the Greek. But when it gives us Jesus' teachings, the Greek text of the Gospels is itself only a translation, from Aramaic into Greek.

When, according to a tradition mentioned around the mid-second century by Bishop Papias, the Jew Levi, a former revenue agent who had become the Apostle Matthew, collected and "arranged" the *logia*, or sentences of Jesus, this collection was in a Semitic language, in Aramaic most probably, "and everyone translated them as best he could." [2]

The original collection of "The Sayings of Jesus" has not come down to us, so that unfortunately it is impossible to compare the Greek text given in the Gospels with the Aramaic. But the Semitic original repeatedly surfaces from under the Greek text, and the exegete must persistently try to catch it. Jesus' speech follows the rhythms of Hebraic teaching.[3] The Greek of the Gospels is so impregnated with Semitisms that an expert has been able to write: "The Gospels constitute a Jewish book in their terms, their modes of ex-

[2] Papias' testimony, the most important in this connection, appears in Eusebius of Caesarea, Church History, 3:39:16. [While Professor Isaac worked with each classical writing in either its original language or a French translation, or both, we will generally cite it only in English, so as to reduce the length of the footnote. The divisions of such works (into books, sections, and the like) have of course long been standardized.—Ed.]

The text in Eusebius says "in a Hebraic language," but qualified scholars think that "Hebraic" here is the same as "Aramaic" (Father Marie-Joseph Lagrange, O.P., ed. and tr., Évangile selon saint Matthieu [Gospel According to Saint Matthew], Paris, Gabalda, 1922 [repub. 1941], pp. xviii–xix).

[3] On this question, the reader is referred to the scholarly works of Father Marcel Jousse, notably "Le Formalisme araméen des récits évangéliques" [The Aramaic Form of the Gospel Accounts], Ethnographie, December 15, 1945.

pression, . . . in their maxims, proverbs, and parables, in their descriptions of customs and usages; it is the most stirring book that the Jewish genius, though it repudiates it, has ever produced." [4]

❡   ❡   ❡

The oldest of the Greek Gospels, which is the second Gospel—Saint Mark's—conserved and included in its Greek text a number of Jesus' words as they must have been spoken, in Aramaic. Too rare but all the more precious exceptions, thanks to which it is granted us to hear the Word itself, in its pure state, without the interposition of the screen of a Greek translation or a translation of a translation.

[The miracle of the daughter of Jairus:] Taking her by the hand he said to her, "Talitha cumi"; which means, "Little girl, I say to you, arise."

Mk. 5:41

[The miracle of the deaf-mute:] . . . and looking up to heaven, he sighed, and said to him, "Ephphatha," that is, "Be opened." And his ears were opened, his tongue was released. . . .

Mk. 7:34–35

[Prayer at Gethsemane:] And going a little farther, he fell on the ground and prayed. . . . And he said, "Abba, Father, all things are possible to thee; remove this cup from me. . . ."

Mk. 14:35–36

[Jesus on the cross:] And at the ninth hour Jesus cried with a loud voice, "Eloi, Eloi, lama sabachthani?" which means, "My God, my God, why hast thou forsaken me?" [5]

Mk. 15:34

The evangelist Matthew has likewise given this cry of pain, in the following form:

And about the ninth hour Jesus cried with a loud voice, "Eli, Eli, lama sabachthani?" that is, "My God, my God, why hast thou forsaken me?"

Mt. 27:46

Mark's text is more correct Aramaic; the text of the first Gospel, half Hebrew and half Aramaic, is more likely, since the bystanders say: "This man is calling Elijah" (Mt. 27:47).

Saint Matthew and Saint Luke retained another Aramaic word in this sentence spoken by Jesus: "You cannot serve God and mammon [money]" (Mt. 6:24; Lk. 16:13).

[4] Paul Vulliaud, La Clé traditionnelle des Évangiles [The Key to the Gospels from Tradition], Paris, Thiébaud, 1936, pp. 88–89.
[5] Ps. 22:1.

PART II

◇◇◇

The Gospel
in the Synagogue

[Jesus said:] . . . I have always taught in synagogues and in the temple. . . .

JN. 18:20

PROPOSITION 7

IT IS COMMONLY MAINTAINED THAT AT THE TIME OF THE COMING OF CHRIST, THE JEWISH RELIGION HAD DEGEN-ERATED INTO MERE LEGALISM WITHOUT A SOUL. HISTORY DOES NOT SUPPORT THIS VERDICT. IN SPITE OF JEWISH LEGALISM AND ITS EXCESSES, EVERYTHING AT THIS PERIOD ATTESTS TO THE DEPTH AND INTENSITY OF THE RELIGIOUS LIFE OF ISRAEL.

How could there have emerged from a world which was falling to ruins—a world of ossified belief in the letter, of a narrow-minded caste-spirit and materialistic piety, a world of scepticism, doubt, and libertinism—a human nature so incomparably pure, so God-united and holy and gracious, so inwardly detached and free and genuine as his? [1]

This model quotation is from a German Catholic theologian of merit, Karl Adam, who was simply following in the tracks of a long line of Catholic and Protestant writers

from Calvin: "Things had so degenerated among that people, everything was full of such great abuse, the priests had so dimmed the pure light of doctrine through unconcern or malice that there was hardly any respect any more for the Law";[2]

to Bossuet, declaring that in the time of Jesus Christ, the Jewish religion "was turning into superstition";[3]

[1] Karl Adam, *Jésus le Christ* [Jesus the Christ], tr. E. Ricard, Paris, Casterman, 1934 [5th ed., 1943]. [Quotation taken from *idem, The Son of God.*, tr. Philip Hereford, New York, Sheed & Ward, 1934, p. 183.—Tr.]

[2] Jehan Calvin, *Sur la Concordance ou Harmonie composée de trois évangélistes, asçavoir S. Matthieu, S. Marc et S. Luc* [On the Concordance or Harmony Composed of Three Evangelists, To Wit Saint Matthew, Saint Mark, and Saint Luke], vol. I of *Commentaires de M. Jehan Calvin sur le Nouveau Testament* [Commentaries by Mr. John Calvin on the New Testament], Paris, Meyrueis, 1854, p. 155.

[3] Jacques-Bénigne Bossuet, *Discours sur l'Histoire universelle* [Discourse on Universal History (1681)], vol. V of *Oeuvres de Bossuet* [Works of Bossuet], Paris, Méquignon Junior et Leroux, 1846, pt. II, Chap. XIX, p. 393. [See, in English as *idem, An Universal History from the Beginning of the World, to the Empire of Charlemagne*, tr. Ephilstone, New York, Moore, 1821.—Tr.]

to Jean-Jacques Rousseau in *Émile* (which might well have served as a model for Karl Adam): "But where among his own did Jesus learn that pure and lofty ethic which he alone taught and exemplified? From the core of the most violent fanaticism sounded the highest wisdom; and the simplicity of the most heroic virtues brought honor to the vilest of all peoples . . .";[4]

and closer to us, voices more obscure, more mediocre, but no less heeded:

from Edmond Stapfer, the respected Protestant historian and theologian, peremptory in his description: "Among the Jews, aside from rare and moving exceptions, the same was true of prayer as of almsgiving, fasting, everything else: it was only a mechanical act and a meritorious repetition"; and: "For the true Jew, rite was all. The unique requirement was to put himself right with God by fulfilling the rite, whatever his interior disposition. . . . The very essence of Judaism was practice and the fulfilled act";[5]

to that other Protestant theologian, Gunther Dehn, the German professor chosen (in 1936) to inaugurate a series of French evangelical writings: "For centuries, Israel was as if abandoned by God; the living God of the fathers had become a remote God, inaccessible. Schools, teachers, the exercise of justice, religious zeal—all that was past. . . ." [6]

[4] Jean-Jacques Rousseau, "Profession de foi du Vicaire Savoyard" [Profession of Faith of the Savoyard Vicar], *Émile*, Paris, Hachette, 1937, bk. IV, p. 187. [See, among many English editions, in *idem, Émile*, tr. Barbara Foxley (1911), New York, Dutton, 1955.—Tr.]

[5] Edmond Stapfer, *La Palestine au temps de Jésus-Christ* [Palestine in the Time of Jesus Christ], Paris, Fischbacher, 1898, p. 372; *idem, Jésus-Christ pendant son ministère* [Jesus Christ During His Ministry], vol. II of *Jésus-Christ, sa personne, son autorité, son oeuvre* [Jesus Christ: His Person, His Powers, His Works], Paris, Fischbacher, 1897, pp. 98, 217. [Edmond Stapfer, 1844–1908, Dean of the Faculté de Théologie (Protestant Theological Seminary) in Paris, was an outstanding New Testament exegete. His works, reprinted over and over again, have had a considerable influence both in France and in Switzerland.—Ed.]

[6] Gunther Dehn, *Le Fils de Dieu, commentaire à l'Évangile de Marc* [The Son of God: Commentary on the Gospel of Mark], Paris, Je Sers, 1936 [repub. Geneva, Labor et Fides, 1957], p. 32. [And following those voices are still others, contemporary with us. Perhaps most distressing are the damaging distortions which religious instruction materials continue to broadcast. For example: "Jesus was rejected by the representatives of a withered religion" (Delcuve); "[Mary] was like a beautiful flower on an old, rotted tree" (De Lorimier); "For He [Jesus] challenged their [the Jews'] hypocrisy, their form of religion that was void of concern for human values, and their observances of minute commands while violating the great principles and demands of justice, mercy and human dignity"; ". . . our Lord's claim was offensive to them so much so that they sought to kill Him" (*Bible School Journal*). The first two quotations have Catholic sources: G. Delcuve, *Jésus-Christ, notre Sauveur* (Jesus Christ, Our Savior), 3rd ed., "Témoins du Christ"

There are others, to be sure. There are the scholarly studies *Judaism in the First Centuries of the Christian Era*, by George Foot Moore (1927–1930) *Judaism Before Jesus Christ*, by Father Marie-Joseph Lagrange (1932); *Palestinian Judaism in the Time of Jesus Christ*, by Father Joseph Bonsirven (1935),[7] which are better and more solidly informed, and hence fairer in their judgments. But these great works do not form the general opinion.

That is why even today, "aside from rare and moving exceptions," Christians of all persuasions do not hesitate to pass a harsh verdict against first-century Judaism—and why their judgment must be brought face to face with historic reality here, insofar as impartial investigation can lay that reality bare.

                                    ✿   ✿   ✿

There is one, at least one, historically incontestable fact: at the beginning of the first century (of the Christian era), the whole Jewish people and the Jewish people alone professed the strictest monotheism. In this regard, the hard battle fought by the Prophets had been won. The whole of Israel's credo was contained in the opening words of the *Shema*ᶜ, the prayer devout Jews recited morning and evening:

> *Shema*ᶜ *Yisra'el*: Hear, O Israel:
> The Lord our God, the Lord is one.
> Deuteronomy Rabbah 2:31, on Deut. 6:4 [MR]

Wouldn't the absolute adherence to this article of faith, the strictness of this monotheism, be "the very essence of Judaism" in the final

series, V, Tournai, Casterman, Éd. de Lumen Vitae, 1960, p. 121; and J. de Lorimier, *Histoire de notre salut* (Story of Our Salvation), teacher's manual, Ottawa, Fides, 1962, p. 113, both quoted in Canon François Houtart and Jean Giblet, eds., *Les Juifs dans la catéchèse: Étude des manuels de catéchèse de langue française* (The Jews in Catechesis: Study of Catechesis Manuals in the French Language), Louvain, Centre de Recherches socio-religieuses and Centre de Recherches catéchétiques, 1969, pp. 264, 194. The second set of sentences, from *Bible School Journal* (Methodist), January–March, 1968, pp. 211, 77, was kindly communicated to me by Dr. Gerald Strober, Consultant on Religious Curricula to the American Jewish Committee, New York, who quotes them in the manuscript of a book currently in preparation (Xerox), p. 54.—Éd.]

[7] George Foot Moore, *Judaism in the First Centuries of the Christian Era*, 3 vols., Cambridge, Mass., Harvard University Press, 1927–1930; Father Marie-Joseph Lagrange, O.P., *Le Judaïsme avant Jésus-Christ*, Paris, Gabalda, 1932; Father Joseph Bonsirven, S.J., *Le Judaïsme palestinien au temps de Jésus-Christ, sa théologie*, 2 vols., Paris, Beauchesne, 1935. [An abridged version, published in French in 1950, was translated as *Palestinian Judaism in the Time of Jesus Christ*, New York, Holt, Rinehart and Winston, 1964; and New York, McGraw-Hill Book Company, 1965 (paperback).—Tr.]

analysis? And from this, in turn, would come its unyielding refusal to accept the dogma of the Trinity. "There," writes Nikolai Berdyaev, "lies the abyss that separates the Christian conscience from the Israelite conscience." [8] I think so too. But an abyss to regard with respect. It will not be filled by pouring cartloads of insult and calumny into it.

Pagan idolatry inspired a holy and uncontrollable horror in the Jews. The pagans, astonished at an intransigence they could not understand, replied with contempt or jeering mockery. The lack of understanding between the pagans and the Jews was total. Tacitus recounts that in 63 B.C., when Pompey the Great entered the Temple at Jerusalem as a conqueror, he scandalized the Jews by wanting to proceed into the Holy of Holies to discover the mysterious god of this people at last; great was his disillusionment to find that the sanctuary contained no divine image: "*vacuam sedem et inania arcana,*" "empty place and groundless mysteries" (*Histories,* 5:9). From this it was only a short step, quickly taken, to concluding that the Jews were derisive of others, that they were an impious, atheistic, godless people. All kinds of absurd calumnies thus found acceptance in the pagan world. They were subsequently applied to Christians. Following which, Christians turned up to collect them and apply them again to Jews.

But what Christian would venture to imitate the pagans?—as if he did not know the first commandments of the Decalogue:

I am the Lord your God, who brought you out of the land of Egypt, out of the house of bondage.

You shall have no other gods before me.

You shall not make for yourself a graven image, or any likeness of anything that is in heaven above, or that is in the earth beneath, or that is in the water under the earth; you shall not bow down to them. . . .

Ex. 20:2–5; see Deut. 5:6–9

These commandments, the most solemn in Scripture, the Jews obeyed faithfully, strictly, fiercely, many to the point of sacrificing their very lives.

On the great gate of the Temple, Herod had a gold eagle placed, and the people struck it down; Pilate provoked a revolt by having his troops enter Jerusalem carrying [sacred] images of the emperors; to avoid a similar up-

[8] Nicolas Berdiaeff, "Le Christianisme et le danger du communisme matérialiste," *Le Christianisme social,* no. 2–3, April, 1939.

rising, Vitellius, going from Antioch to Petra, ceded to the demands of the Jews and made a long detour rather than march through Palestine. When Caligula wanted to have his statue placed in the Temple at Jerusalem, popular feeling was such that Petronius, the governor of Syria, retreated. . . .[9]

The great-grandsons of those who had answered the call of the Machabees in the second century B.C. and had fought a battle to the death—ultimately victorious despite the disproportion of the forces —against the encroachments of Greek paganism were prepared, if necessary, to sustain the same struggle, even more disproportionate, against the encroachments of Roman paganism. The most uncompromising, the Zealots, advocated rebellion and practiced terrorism: they were crucified, they were burned alive—nothing stopped them. Call their unconquerable and sometimes provocative zeal fanaticism, "fanatic nationalism": very well. But is this really evidence of "ossified belief" and "materialistic piety"? Don't forget, Christians, that these people were dedicated to the cause of God. One of them, Simon the Zealot,[10] was one of the twelve Apostles of Christ. In *The State in the New Testament*,[11] the first part of which is devoted to Jesus' life and trial, Oscar Cullmann expresses the opinion that one cannot understand the history of Jesus unless the anti-Roman movement of the Zealots is accorded prime importance; he thinks that there must have been other Zealots or former Zealots besides Simon among the Twelve, perhaps Judas.

❂   ❂   ❂

In the realm of religion, as in any other—more than in any other —we must beware of hasty generalizations, of global accusations. The Jews contemporary with Jesus, his compatriots, did not make up a

---

[9] Father Jules Lebreton, S.J., *Histoire des origines du dogme de la Trinité* [History of the Origins of the Dogma of the Trinity], 2 vols., Paris, Beauchesne, 1928, I, 104. [See, in English, as *idem, History of the Dogma of the Trinity from Its Origins to the Council of Nicaea*, tr. A. Thorold, London, Burns, Oates & Washbourne, 1939.—Tr.]

[10] So named according to the most widely accepted tradition and translation. Yet Father Lagrange thinks that the word *Zealot* should be replaced with the word *Zealous*, understood in the most general meaning of a burning zeal for God (Father Marie-Joseph Lagrange, O.P., *L'Évangile de Jésus-Christ*, Paris, Gabalda, 1928, p. 138).

[11] Oscar Cullmann, *Dieu et César* [God and Caesar], Neuchâtel, Delachaux et Niestlé, 1956. [See, in English, as *idem, The State in the New Testament*, tr., New York, Scribner, 1966.—Tr.]

homogeneous mass, exactly alike in their beliefs, doctrines, and religious practices. Distinctions have to be drawn.

An "ossified belief in the letter," a "narrow-minded caste-spirit and materialistic piety" could indeed be found in Israel, primarily in Jewish high society, which held the power (under Roman control), the honor, and the wealth. But oh, stringent Christian judges, are these specifically Jewish traits? Power, honor, wealth, have they withered only Jewish hearts, debased only Jewish souls? The high priesthood of Jerusalem—in charge of the Temple, the sole sanctuary of the Jewish cult; the head of the Sanhedrin, the Great Council and High Court of Judea—formed a proud and contemptuous class, harsh toward those under its jurisdiction, set against anyone who seemed to threaten the status quo, from which it profited. But what valid reason is there to identify the whole Jewish people, and even the whole priesthood, with that selfish and exclusive oligarchy? It is not implausible to believe that Jewish priests still included in their number men of heart and duty, like Zechariah in the Gospels; men worthy of those who, in the siege of the year 63—before Christ—had celebrated the liturgical service in the Temple under Roman attack until the last day, and who had finally been massacred before the altar, before God.

Among persuasions, the leading class was Sadducean. The Sadducees, whom an already long tradition set in opposition to the Pharisees, constituted the political party confronting the religious party, opportunists antagonistic to any excess or fanaticism, conservative, old-fashioned believers wedded to the letter of the Law and hostile to any innovation, in the temporal domain as in the spiritual. But what was their influence on the religious life in Israel of the time? Almost nil. Entrenched in the high priesthood, Sadduceeism shared its unpopularity and its disrepute. We can take the word of Monsignor Louis Duchesne, whose *Ancient History of the Church,* while dating back to 1905, is yet reliable, owing to its unusual honesty:

The luxury, the depravity, the religious indifference that the leaders of the priesthood displayed, their servility before the Roman authorities, their contempt for the messianic hopes and the doctrine of resurrection had deprived them of the affection of the people.[12]

[12] Msgr. Louis Duchesne, *Histoire ancienne de l'Église,* 3 vols., 5th ed., Paris, Fontemoing, 1911, I, 12. [See, in English, as *idem, Early History of the Christian Church from Its Foundations to the End of the Fifth Century,* 3 vols., New York, Longmans, Green, 1922–1925.—Tr.]

The religious influence was held by the scribes and the Pharisees,[13] who are moreover burdened with (Christian) posterity's harshest judgment. The Pharisees, we have said, were the religious party, and we know the meaning the word *pharisaical* has taken on since: exaggerated, hypocritical, ostentatious devotion, false sanctity, rigid pietism, more attentive to the letter than to the spirit, more concerned with external observances than with inner fervor. But to what degree does this disparaging definition apply to the historic Pharisees? Exactly as much as the definition of the word *jesuitical* to the Jesuits.[14]

Of course Israel did not lack for hypocrites, for affected, sententious, and pretentious puritans; they are denounced and excoriated in the Jewish Talmuds as they are in the Gospels; but what "organized piety can ever wholly escape . . . hypocrites"?[15] Tartuffe belongs to all religions, all times, all countries. It is very true that Pharisee rigorism had its faults: an excess of scruples and subtlety in interpreting the Law led to the hollowest casuistry (thirty-nine kinds of activity forbidden on the Sabbath); an obsessive fear of any impure contact tended to separate "the saints" not only from the foreigner, the accursed pagan, but from the rest of the Jewish people, the ignorant mass of the *ammei ha-aretz* or common people, the plebeians; the plethora of external observances, of abstinences, fasts, ablutions, purifications, left hardly any place for the exercise of true piety, which is not a ritual technique but a spiritual life, an effusion of the heart. The influence of the Pharisee rabbis was therefore not without danger for Judaism; and it is not surprising that it elicited sharp reactions on Jesus' part. But once this is said, the facts, the writings, good sense, everything indicates that historic Phariseeism does not admit of a definition synonymous with either hypocrisy or formalism, as so many Christian writers still maintain—and as if the true faith required such a masking of historic truth. "A greater misreading of history," writes

[13] The two terms are not exactly equivalent. *Scribe* denotes a profession, that of "doctor of the Law"; *Pharisee* denotes membership in a group or association of pious men whose object was the knowledge and practice of the Law, written or oral.

[14] [In order to recall this distinction throughout the book, we will use the unconventional form *Phariseeism* in references to the historic Pharisees, reserving the accepted spellings of *pharisaism* and its derivatives for the timeless species called, pejoratively, "pharisees."—Ed.]

[15] Max L. Margolis and Alexander Marx, *Histoire du peuple juif*, tr., Paris, Payot, 1930, p. 150. [Quotation taken from *idem*, *A History of the Jewish People* (1927), New York, Harper & Row, Harper Torchbooks, 1965, pp. 158, 157.—Tr.]

R. Travers Herford, the best historian of Phariseeism, "it is scarcely possible to imagine." [16]

We cannot doubt that there were men of conviction, of high moral worth, of sincere and pure devotion, faithful to the teaching of the Prophets, among the most influential of the Pharisees. Jewish history and the Talmuds bear this out, as do the Gospels. When Jesus was a child, six thousand Pharisees courageously refused to give the oath of loyalty to the pagan emperor that Herod wanted to impose on them. In that time or shortly before, the teacher Hillel summed up the Law in these most evangelical terms: "What is hateful to you, do not [do] to your neighbour; that is the whole Torah, while the rest is the commentary thereof . . ." (Shabbath 31a [BT]). And again he said, ". . . judge not thy fellow-man until thou hast reached his place"; and again: "In a place where there are no men, strive . . . to be a man" (Aboth 2:4, 5 [BT]). Phariseeism had its faults, but it also had its merits (from which Christianity would profit largely): it enriched the Jewish religion, continuing in its evolution, in its spiritual progress, with new beliefs—in the resurrection of the dead, in a judgment beyond the grave; trust in God, hope in His justice, messianic expectation were thereby strengthened; without eliminating the sacrificial Temple rites, prayer and the reading of the Law in the Synagogues moved to the forefront of religious life and in a certain way spiritualized it; finally, the new expansion of Judaism won it numerous adepts —proselytes or God-fearers—in the pagan world. When Christianity applies itself to casting aspersions on Pharisee Judaism, it is forgetting everything it owes it; and it is being not only unjust but ungrateful. [17]

✿ ✿ ✿

But powerful as the body of Pharisees was in Israel, it was not the only one. An astonishing diversity of sects is suspected, if not known, to have existed. Would it be this diversity that reveals what the emi-

[16] R. Travers Herford, *Les Pharisiens*, tr. Gabrielle Moyse, Paris, Payot, 1928. [Quotation taken from *idem*, *The Pharisees* (1924), Boston, Beacon Press, 1962, p. 238—Tr.]

[17] [Though marked progress has been made toward a more accurate presentation of the Pharisees, yet a number of Christian publications still favor the derogatory approach. Witness this commentary in a 1968 encyclopedia of the Bible: "In addition, if we understand 'Israel' to be [the] religious, pharisaic Judaism of the time of Jesus, it was certainly condemned by God forever. . . . The unfaithful Judaism of the time of Jesus, as well as before his coming, remains forever

nent scribe Karl Adam, of Tübingen, has called "a world which was falling to ruins"? A less biased mind would see it perhaps as the sign of an intense religious life, perhaps also as the effect of multiple influences from without—Persian, Babylonian, Hellenic, some would say Pythagorean.

Among all the Jewish sects of that time, the best known, though it has remained mysterious in many ways, is the Essenian. If we accept the conclusions of the most qualified experts, most of the manuscripts discovered in grottoes near the Dead Sea relate to the Essenian sect. This most important discovery has given rise to innumerable articles and controversies. Elsewhere,[18] I have attempted to outline some fundamental characteristics of pre-Christian Judaism in the light of the Dead Sea Scrolls; they only corroborate my thesis, which Millar Burrows confirms: "One of the most significant aspects of pre-Christian Judaism which finds expression in them is its devotional spirit." [19]

In Jesus' time, Essenism was about a century and a half old. Other and perhaps more recent sects existed, such as the gathering of the "Sons of the New Covenant," revealed in a document published in 1910. It is now recognized that this writing, called the Damascus Document, belongs to the same collection and relates to the same sect as the Dead Sea Scrolls. Pious hermits could also be found in Palestine, living as ascetics, with one or more disciples in their company; the historian Josephus declares that he spent three years of his youth with one of these holy men, called Banos. So strong still were the creative urge and the fervor of that "degenerate" Judaism that it seemed to be generating doctrines, salvific formulations, continuously. Who was that Yoḥanan, John the Baptist, who called the Jews to repen-

condemned" ("Reprobación," article in A. Diez-Macho and S. Bartina, eds., *Enciclopedia de la Biblia*, Barcelona, Garriga, 1965, VI, 158; quoted in G. Rossetto, review, *Sidic* [Rome], vol. II, no. 1, 1969, p. 16). The same disparagement is expressed in these quotations from recent American catechetical materials: "Jesus and the Pharisees were in open conflict. The Pharisees represented the one primary evil against which Jesus preached. He represents the one faith they could not tolerate, and they conspired to kill Him" (*The Gate* [Lutheran Church-Missouri Synod], October–December, 1967, p. 33); and: ". . . it becomes clear that for Jesus the whole Pharisaic tradition is a sham" (*To Save All People* [United Church of Christ], 1967, p. 148; both quoted in Strober, *op. cit.*, p. 39).—Ed.]

[18] See Jules Isaac, "L'Histoire contre les mythes, vues sur le judaïsme préchrétien à la lumière des manuscrits de la Mer Morte" [History Versus Myths: Views on Pre-Christian Judaism in the Light of the Dead Sea Scrolls], *Cahiers de l'Alliance israélite universelle*, March–April, 1956.

[19] Millar Burrows, *Les Manuscrits de la Mer Morte*, tr., Paris, Laffont, 1957. [Quotation taken from *idem*, *The Dead Sea Scrolls*, New York, Viking, 1956, p. 327.—Tr.]

tance and baptized them in the waters of the Jordan as a sign of purification? Was he the founder of a new sect, or a new prophet, or, as some believed,[20] Elijah returned to the earth as a precursor of the messianic era? John baptized not far from the place where the Essenian community lived. There are close analogies between his teaching and that found in the Dead Sea Scrolls.

And in the fifteenth year of the reign of the Roman Emperor Tiberius (Lk. 3:1), probably in the year 28, Yohanan saw coming to him, to be baptized in his turn in the waters of the Jordan, one "who is mightier than I" (Lk. 3:16), Yeshua—Jesus of Nazareth.

[20] See Mal. 3:23; Ecclus. 48:10–12. Neither Malachi nor the Son of Sirach speaks explicitly of the Messiah, but they say that Elijah [CCD: Elias] is to announce "the day of the Lord," the day of Yahweh.

PROPOSITION 8

THE TEACHING OF JESUS TOOK PLACE IN THE TRADITIONAL
JEWISH SETTING. ACCORDING TO A VERY LIBERAL JEW-
ISH CUSTOM, "THE CARPENTER'S SON" WAS PERMITTED
TO SPEAK AND TEACH IN THE SYNAGOGUES, AND EVEN
IN THE TEMPLE AT JERUSALEM.

There is a Christian practice of contrasting the Church and the Synagogue; the latter is shown with blindfolded eyes, to signify its blindness.[1] But how many people, reading Scripture, know exactly what a
synagogue was in the time of Jesus Christ? (Many don't even know
what a synagogue is in our own times.)

The synagogue was not a temple; it was not a sanctuary, properly
speaking. There was only one sanctuary in Israel, one temple consecrated to God, the Temple of Jerusalem:[2] there and there alone,
priests celebrated the cult of Yahweh with daily sacrifices; there and
there alone, on the principal religious feasts—Passover, the Feast of
Tabernacles, the Dedication—were magnificent ceremonies staged in
the midst of a great gathering of the population, drawn not only from
Palestine but from all parts of the world where Jewish communities
existed.

---

[1] [On the south porch of the Cathedral of Strasbourg, for example, stands a
statue representing the Synagogue or Old Convenant, and the eyes are blindfolded. Using the same image, a modern commentary alleges: "Placed by God on
the road which led to Christ, it [Judaism] is now a misguided religion, a 'stumbling block'; for it refuses today to recognize Him Whom it announced. . . . The
Synagogue with veiled eyes remains the often painful witness of its own blindness" (A. Durand and H. Holstein, Jésus-Christ, maître de pensée [Jesus Christ,
Master of Thought], rev. ed., "Fils de Lumière" series, Paris, De Gigord, 1960,
pp. 117–118; quoted in Canon François Houtart and Jean Giblet, eds., Les Juifs
dans la catéchèse de langue française, Louvain, Centre de Recherches socio-
religieuses and Centre de Recherches catéchétiques, 1969, pp. 165, 184).—Ed.]

[2] No importance can be attached to the cases—exceptional ones—of the Judeo-
Egyptian temples on Elephantine Island and at Leontopolis, which were founded
by Jewish military colonies and whose orthodoxy was doubtful.

43

But if the Temple of Jerusalem was the single sanctuary of the Jewish cult and the rallying point for all Israel, the primary center of Jewish religious life was the synagogue.

The Greek word *synagoge*, which means "meeting" (as "assembly" is the meaning of the Greek work *ekklesia*, from which the word for "church" in the Romance languages comes—*église, iglesia*, etc.), is the translation of Hebraic or Aramaic words meaning "meeting house" or "house of prayer." Such was the synagogue: a building where devotional meetings took place, where Jews assembled to pray.

Where and when did the custom of these devotional meetings arise? We cannot say for sure, but probably in Chaldea during the Exile in the sixth century B.C. In Jesus' time, every Jewish village in Palestine and every organized Jewish community outside Palestine had its synagogue.

What did they do there? They prayed, sang the Psalms, and—mainly on the Sabbath, but also on the second and fifth days of the week—read and commentated on the sacred texts, the Law and the Prophets. The importance accorded to the study of the Law assured the pre-eminence of the Pharisee rabbis. But any Jew could participate in elucidating the verses for the day; any transient Jew was allowed to take the floor, invited to give news of his community.

In considering such an institution objectively—an institution so new, so democratic, one might even say so "lay," so devoid of any ritualism—observe, Christians, that the religious customs of that sullied Judaism were not without their virtue; the proof of this is that they served as models for the primitive Church. "The synagogue . . . ," writes the Protestant historian Albert Réville, "is the mother of the Christian Church and also of the Muslim mosque." [3] And in Adolphe Lods's words, the synagogue represented "the first attempt to carry out worship in the spirit." [4]

Who cares? The proper thing to do is to follow a centuries-old tradition and declare, along with generations of writers, "For the true Jew, ritual was everything."

For the blind mother, a thankless daughter.[5]

[3] Albert Réville, *Jésus de Nazareth* [Jesus of Nazareth], 2 vols., Paris, Fischbacher, 1906, I, 95.

[4] Adolphe Lods, *La Religion d'Israël* [The Religion of Israel], Paris, Hachette, 1939, p. 224.

[5] [A French proverb, meaning that where a mother is blind to her daughter's shortcomings, the latter eventually turns against her. Here Professor Isaac is playing on the word *blind* because of the Christian tradition, which he has mentioned above, of representing the synagogue blindfolded.—Ed.]

✿   ✿   ✿

. . . and forgetful.

Like all devout Jews, Jesus went to the synagogue regularly on the Sabbath (Lk. 4:16). He went to pray, to sing, to hear the reading and elucidation of the Law and the Prophets. It was there that he was formed, there that he was taught by the rabbis, before teaching there himself. For it was in the synagogue that the Gospel was preached for the first time, in some modest Galilean synagogue, perhaps at Capernaum, on the banks of the Sea of Galilee.

As soon as he began his evangelical ministry, most likely in Galilee, Jesus availed himself of the liberal Jewish custom that allowed him to take the floor in the synagogue to read and commentate on the Law or the Prophets. The four Gospels tell us this:

And they went into Capernaum; and immediately on the sabbath he [Jesus] entered the synagogue and taught.

Mk. 1:21

And he [Jesus] went about all Galilee, teaching in their synagogues and preaching the gospel of the kingdom. . . .

Mt. 4:23

This he [Jesus] said in the synagogue, as he taught at Capernaum.

Jn. 6:59

Luke gives us more than a brief indication; he has us enter the synagogue at Nazareth with Jesus; we see him, we hear him:

And he came to Nazareth, where he had been brought up; and he went to the synagogue, as his custom was, on the sabbath day. And he stood up to read. . . .

Lk. 4:16

✿   ✿   ✿

And the four Gospels tell us also that having begun to teach in the synagogue, Jesus continued:

And he went throughout all Galilee, preaching in their synagogues and casting out demons. . . . And many were gathered together, so that there was no longer room for them, not even about the door. . . .

Mk. 1:39; 2:2

And Jesus went about all the cities and villages [of Galilee], teaching in their synagogues and coming to his own country he taught them in their synagogue. . . .

Mt. 9:35; 13:54

And he [Jesus] was preaching in the synagogues of Judea.[6] . . . Now he was teaching in one of the synagogues on the sabbath. [In Luke's account, this took place at the time Jesus was "journeying toward Jerusalem."]

Lk. 4:44; 13:10, 22

Even more explicit, more categoric, is John's witness:

Jesus answered him [the high priest], "I have spoken openly to the world; I have always taught in synagogues and in the temple, where all Jews come together. . . ."

Jn. 18:20

It is true that the fourth Gospel seems to contradict itself here, since earlier (9:22; 12:42) the evangelist speaks of a decision made by "the Jews"[7]—the Jewish leaders—to exclude from the synagogue anyone who recognized Jesus as the Messiah, meaning *a fortiori* Jesus in person. But should we grant the historicity of a decision that no other witness, no other evangelist confirms, and that on the contrary belies everything we know from Scripture itself, from the Acts of the Apostles, of "the providential role of the synagogue in the work of evangelizing"?[8] After Jesus and like him, it was in the synagogues that the Apostles Peter and Paul preached. Quite clearly, Alfred Loisy is right, rather than Father Lagrange: "Such an excommunication . . . certainly did not exist in the early days of Christian preaching, much less in Jesus' time."[9]

A Jewish custom, preaching in the synagogue. Another Jewish custom: preaching in the open air, as the Gospels describe it to us.

"There is a crowd all around where there is preaching," it is said in the Mishnah.[10] The rabbis preached everywhere, on the village square and in the countryside as well as in the synagogue.

Jesus did as they did.

❉   ❉   ❉

[6] Some manuscripts read "Galilee" instead of "Judea." But the reading "Judea" seems the better, and should be understood here in the sense of "Jewish country."

[7] On this use of the term "the Jews," see pp. 113–114.

[8] Father Jules Lebreton, S.J., *La Vie et l'enseignement de Jésus-Christ*, 2 vols., Paris, Beauchesne, 1931 [19th ed., 1951], I, 119. [See, in English, as idem, *The Life and Teaching of Jesus Christ Our Lord*, tr. Francis Day, 2 vols., London, Burns, Oates & Washbourne, 1935.—Tr.]

[9] Alfred Loisy, *Le quatrième Évangile* [The Fourth Gospel], Paris, by the au., 1903 [repub. Paris, Nourry, 1921], p. 314; cf. Father Marie-Joseph Lagrange, O.P., ed. and tr., *Évangile selon saint Jean* [Gospel According to Saint John], Paris, Gabalda, 1924 [repub. 1947], p. 266.

[10] *Mishnah:* collection of traditional prescriptions that complete the Law; the Mishnah is the old oral tradition, set down in writing in the second century A.D.

In Jerusalem, Jesus taught in the Temple. There were numbers of synagogues in the Holy City, but anyone preaching in the Temple was sure to reach a larger audience.

The Temple of Jerusalem was a vast and sumptuous structure. Rebuilt [11] by Herod the Great beginning in the year 19 B.C., it was not completely finished and was still being worked on in the years 28–30, apparently during Jesus' public life.

Whether Jesus came to Jerusalem only at the end of his ministry, on the eve of Passover and the Passion, as the Synoptic Gospels say; or whether he had stayed there several times on the occasion of various religious feasts, as the fourth Gospel says, there is one fact at least on which the four evangelists agree: his presence, and his teaching, in the Temple. We see him there, a Jew among the Jews, now in the porticoes of the great court, now in the inner court, walking, gazing about, discussing, confounding his opponents—Sadducees or Pharisees:

[Mark:]   And he [Jesus] entered Jerusalem, and went into the temple; and when he had looked round at everything . . . he went out to Bethany with the twelve [11:11].

And they came again to Jerusalem. And as he [Jesus] was walking in the temple, the chief priests and the scribes and the elders came to him . . . [11:27].

And as Jesus taught in the temple, he said . . . [12:35].

And he sat down opposite the treasury [of offerings], and watched the multitude putting money into the treasury [12:41].

[Jesus said to those who came to arrest him,] "Day after day I was with you in the temple teaching, and you did not seize me . . ." [14:49].

[The same details are found in Mt. 21:23; 26:55; Lk. 19:47; 20:1; 21:1, 37; 22:53.]

[John:]   About the middle of the feast [of Tabernacles] Jesus went up into the temple and taught [7:14].

So Jesus proclaimed, as he taught in the temple . . . [7:28].

[11] The first Temple had been built by Solomon on the site chosen by David; it was therefore constructed in the tenth century B.C. Its foundations still exist. Destroyed by the Chaldeans in 586 B.C., the Temple was rebuilt after the return from Exile, under Persian rule, around 520–515 B.C. But in the course of the wars in the second and first centuries B.C., this second Temple had been not only desecrated but badly damaged, which was the reason for the large-scale reconstruction and beautification undertaken by Herod.

Early in the morning he [Jesus] came again to the temple; all
the people came to him, and he sat down and taught them
[8:2].[12]

These words he [Jesus] spoke in the treasury, as he taught in
the temple . . . [8:20].

It was the feast of the Dedication at Jerusalem; it was winter,
and Jesus was walking in the temple, in the portico of Solomon [10:22–23].

[Jesus said,] ". . . I have always taught in synagogues and in
the temple, where all Jews come together . . ." [18:20].

Thus, from the first to the last day, Jesus constantly exercised his
ministry in the religious and cultic setting of the people to whom he
belonged, the Jewish people.

[12] [RSV, p. 95, n. r; Lk. 7:53–8:11 are not included in the body of the RSV
text.—Tr.]

PROPOSITION 9

JESUS WAS BORN AND LIVED "UNDER THE [JEWISH] LAW."
DID HE INTEND OR ANNOUNCE ITS ABROGATION? MANY
WRITERS HOLD THAT HE DID, BUT THEIR STATEMENTS
EXAGGERATE, DISTORT, OR CONTRADICT THE MOST IM-
PORTANT PASSAGES IN THE GOSPELS.

Perhaps Ernest Renan is the writer who has gone the farthest along
the road to perilous statements concerning Jesus' attitude toward the
Law. He shows (or imagines) Jesus repulsed by

. . . all these old Jewish institutions. . . .
An idea . . . that henceforth seemed rooted in his mind was that there
was no possible pact with the old Jewish cult. The abolition of the sacrifices
that had caused him such disgust, the suppression of an impious and
haughty priesthood, and in general the abrogation of the Law appeared to
be of absolute necessity to him. From this moment on, his chosen role was
no longer as a Jewish reformer but as a destroyer of Judaism. . . .
In other words, Jesus was no longer Jewish. . . .
The Law would be abolished, and he would be the one to abolish it.[1]

There is a curious echo of this on the Protestant side, specifically
from Edmond Stapfer, who follows Renan step by step, word for
word:

Up till now, [Jesus] had been a Jewish reformer; henceforth he would be the
destroyer of Judaism. . . . He was convinced that he would abolish the Law
of Moses. . . . Mosaism was dead, it had only to disappear.[2]

More critical and subtler, Maurice Goguel's thought lies in the
same direction. "The idea of abrogating the religion of Israel" was "a

---

[1] Ernest Renan, Vie de Jésus, 4th ed., Paris, Michel-Lévy, 1863 [repub. 1956],
pp. 215, 221, 223, 236. [See, among many English editions, as idem, The Life of
Jesus, tr. (1863), New York, Modern Library, 1927.—Tr.]
[2] Edmond Stapfer, Jésus-Christ pendant son ministère, vol. II of Jésus-Christ,
sa personne, son autorité, son oeuvre, Paris, Fischbacher, 1897, pp. 203, 255.

seed" in Jesus' mind from the outset.[3] "Jesus' ministry in Jerusalem ended in a break with Judaism. . . . It was the accomplishment of the Law . . . which led Jesus to discover that the role of the Law and the prophets . . . had been outlived, and that a new era had opened in the history of religion."[4] Yet the conclusion retreats slightly: "If [Jesus] thought that the dispensation of Judaism should be abrogated, it was not the religion of the Jews but the Jews themselves he condemned" for being slaves to the letter of the Law. "Jesus broke away from empirical Judaism out of fidelity to ideal Judaism, and he did not have the feeling that he was founding a new religion."[5]

So far we have been dealing with scholarly Protestant opinions. We find Catholic opinion in these statements of Father Albert Vincent, professor at the Faculté Catholique of Strasbourg, who is elsewhere a fair-minded historian: "There was . . . an abrogation of everything that constituted the specificity of Judaism and gave it an essentially transitory character. This is what Christianity teaches: Jesus Christ abrogated the Law."[6]

There it is, quite plain: "Jesus Christ abrogated the Law. This is what Christianity teaches."

But Christ himself, what did he teach?

Let us continue to reread the Gospels, let us allow the texts—that is, Jesus himself—to speak, insofar as the evangelists have been faithful transcribers. It would seem that at least two of the four would willingly have undertaken to de-Judaize Christ, had they been able.

❖   ❖   ❖

Point one: the Temple, the "Jerusalemite cult."

Our earlier observations—Jesus' presence in the synagogues and the Temple from the beginning to the end of his ministry, the insistence with which Jesus referred to this—are already conclusive facts.

Pierre Lestringant notes: "Nowhere else [but in Mt. 23:23] does Jesus direct his disciples to observe the Jerusalemite cult and the ritu-

---

[3] Maurice Goguel, La Vie de Jésus-Christ, Paris, Payot, 1932, p. 294. While it is this edition which will be cited in subsequent notes, the quotations themselves are still to be found in the final stage of this work: Jésus, Paris, Payot, 1950. [See the earlier edition, in English, as idem, The Life of Jesus, tr. O. Wyon, New York, Macmillan, 1933.—Tr.]

[4] Ibid., pp. 408, 540.

[5] Ibid., p. 570.

[6] Father Albert Vincent, Le Judaïsme [Judaism], Paris, Bloud et Gay, 1932, p. 74.

als of private life. On the contrary, everything leads us to believe that in general he deliberately abstained from them himself." [7] Let us pass over "the rituals of private life" for a moment. If "Jerusalemite cult" means principally sacrificial rites, isn't it most surprising that "nowhere," at no moment, did Jesus make any explicit pronouncement against those bloody rites which some Jewish sects, notably the Essenes, did not hesitate to reject? Where did he exhibit that disgust Renan speaks of?

For the simple passing references to the words of the Prophet Hosea, "I desire mercy, and not sacrifice" (Mt. 9:13; 12:7), cannot be construed as a condemnation. The Gospel according to Saint Mark does not conceal the fact that on this point Pharisee piety agreed with Jesus: "You are right, Teacher," said the scribe who was questioning Jesus in the Temple; "you have truly said that . . . to love him [God] with all the heart, . . . and to love one's neighbor as oneself, is much more than all whole burnt offerings and sacrifices" (Mk. 12:32–33).

And how do we reconcile this supposed rejection of the "Jerusalemite cult," of the "old Jewish cult," with that violent act of purification, the expulsion of the vendors from the Temple (more precisely, from the large outside court to which they had succeeded in gaining entry)? Isn't that purifying anger a manifest sign of the veneration which Jesus never ceased to profess for the Jewish Sanctuary, for the "House of God"? Isn't it justified in the Gospel according to Saint John, 2:17, with these words from the Jewish Psalmist?—

For zeal for thy house has consumed me. . . .

Ps. 69:9

Let us reread two accounts, Mark's and John's (Matthew's and Luke's do no more than reproduce Mark's text closely):

And he [Jesus] entered the temple and began to drive out those who sold and those who bought in the temple, and he overturned the tables of the money-changers and the seats of those who sold pigeons; and he would not allow any one to carry anything through the temple. And he taught, and said to them, "Is it not written, 'My house shall be called a house of prayer for all the nations' ? [8] But you have made it a den of robbers." [9]

Mk. 11:15–17

[7] Pierre Lestringant, *Essai sur l'unité de la Révélation biblique* [Essay on the Unity of Biblical Revelation], Paris, Je Sers, 1942, p. 45.
[8] Is. 56:7.
[9] Jer. 7:11.

The Passover . . . was at hand, and Jesus went up to Jerusalem. In the
temple he found those who were selling oxen and sheep and pigeons, and
the money-changers at their business. And making a whip of cords, he
drove them all, with the sheep and oxen, out of the temple; and he poured
out the coins of the money-changers and overturned their tables. And he
told those who sold the pigeons, "Take these things away; you shall not
make my Father's house a house of trade."

Jn. 2:13–16

If the priestly authorities reacted to Jesus' act as to an affront, devout Jews could only approve of it; and nothing says that they did
not approve of it. We read in the Talmud:

A man should not enter the Temple mount either with his staff in his hand
or his shoe on his foot, or with his money tied up in his cloth, or with his
money bag slung over his shoulder, and he should not make it a short cut.

Berakoth 62b [BT]

People are quick to counter this all-consuming zeal regarding the
House of God, which Jesus confirmed so publicly, with particular
Gospel passages which they endow with a questionable meaning.
They say:

1. Jesus prophesied the downfall of the Temple:

Do you see these great buildings? There will not be left here one stone
upon another, that will not be thrown down.

Mk. 13:2; almost identical passage in Mt. 24:2; Lk. 21:6

But the great Prophets Isaiah and Jeremiah were also prophets of
woe or punishment; should they also be counted as "destroyers of Judaism"?

2. Jesus is said to have declared that he would destroy the Temple
and rebuild it in three days:

I will destroy this temple that is made with hands, and in three days I will
build another, not made with hands.

Mk. 14:58

But the evangelist adds, these were "false witness[es]" who reported
these words, and "Yet not even so did their testimony agree" (Mk.
14:57, 59).

According to Matthew, the "false witnesses" came forward to state:

This fellow said, "I am able to destroy the temple of God, and to build it in
three days."

Mt. 26:61

And finally, according to John, Jesus is supposed to have said:

Destroy this temple, and in three days I will raise it up.

Jn. 2:19

But this evangelist comments, ". . . he spoke of the temple of his body" (Jn. 2:21)—that is, he prophesied his death and Resurrection.

That a saying of this sort was attributed to Jesus is again evidenced by the taunts hurled at the Crucified: "Aha! You would destroy the temple and build it in three days . . ." (Mk. 15:29; Mt. 27:40). Goguel concludes from this that the utterance about the Temple is "fully authoritative," that "it expresses the conviction Jesus had reached at the end of his ministry that nothing more could be hoped for from Israel." [10] But can such an absolute opinion be based on such a weak foundation, on a simple conjecture that goes beyond the texts, themselves uncertain and divergent?

3. During a discussion with the Pharisees, Jesus unhesitatingly said of himself:

. . . something greater than the temple is here.

Mt. 12:6

But utterance is found again in Matthew and also in Luke in another and far more likely form:

. . . something greater than Jonah is here. . . . something greater than Solomon. . . .

Mt. 12:41–42; see Lk. 11:31–32

Moreover, a comparison of greatness is not a negation, as the narrative attests later on; for it is the same evangelist, Matthew, who ascribes the following words to Jesus:

Woe to you, blind guides, who say, "If any one swears by the temple, it is nothing; but if any one swears by the gold of the temple, he is bound by his oath." You blind fools! For which is greater, the gold or the temple that has made the gold sacred?

Mt. 23:16–17

4. There remain the words to the Samaritan woman, the only words which bring into question not only the existence but the religious mission of the Temple:

Woman, believe me, the hour is coming when neither on this mountain [Gerizim, the site of the Temple of the Samaritans] nor in Jerusalem will you worship the Father. . . . But the hour is coming, and now is, when the true worshipers will worship the Father in spirit and truth. . . .

Jn. 4:21, 23

[10] Goguel, op. cit., pp. 491, 493.

But this admirable passage soars above and beyond historic reality, as do so many others of the fourth Gospel. It is impossible to discern how much is Jesus and how much the evangelist in these dazzling transmutations. This one goes far, to the point of rejecting all materiality of cult, all need of a sanctuary for "the true worshipers." What has become then of the respect Jesus professed for "my Father's house" ? A sentiment some seventy years old, dead and buried for the evangelist, but which everything leads us to believe was very much alive in Jesus.

✿   ✿   ✿

"One would seek in vain in the Gospel for a religious practice recommended by Jesus." [11] A bold statement that may be inverted: one would seek in vain in the Gospel for a religious practice discouraged by Jesus.

That Jesus stressed above all the worship of "the Father in spirit and truth,"

that he ranked the ritual commandments of the Law well below the commandments of love, of charity, of morality, of justice,

that he dismissed with a sovereign gesture the minute requirements of an exaggerated legalism,

agreed; who could challenge the evidence?

But there is other evidence that respect for the texts—and for Jesus' teachings—requires us to recognize: in his eyes, *one attitude does not exclude the other.*

As we have seen, Jesus refrained from condemning sacrificial rites themselves. He did not condemn one of the ritual commandments. And not only did he not speak against the rites, but on occasion he recommended their practice and himself set the example for it:

[Jesus said to the leper he had cured:] . . . go, show yourself to the priest, and offer for your cleansing what Moses commanded. . . .

Mk. 1:44

So if you are offering your gift at the altar, and there remember that your brother has something against you, leave your gift there before the altar and go; first be reconciled to your brother, and then come and offer your gift.

Mt. 5:23–24

[11] Renan, *op. cit.,* p. 225.

The scribes and the Pharisees sit on Moses' seat; so practice and observe whatever they tell you, but not what they do; for they preach, but do not practice.

Mt. 23:2–3

And here, in words even more significant and explicit:

Woe to you, scribes and Pharisees, hypocrites! for you tithe mint and dill and cummin, and have neglected the weightier matters of the law, justice and mercy and faith; these you ought to have done, without neglecting the others.

Mt. 23:23

True, three of the four quotations come from Matthew, whose Gospel is in certain ways the most Judaizing. Does it have less authority for Catholic and Protestant orthodoxy for that reason? Not that I know of. Exegesis is free to make the necessary qualifications, if it can.

Whether one accepts it or not, it is a fact attested to by the Gospels, more particularly by the Synoptics, that to his final hour Jesus did not stop practicing the basic rites of Judaism.

We have seen him participate, "as his custom was" (Lk. 4:16), in the Sabbath services at the synagogue.

We have seen him go to the Temple of Jerusalem to celebrate the great religious feasts: Tabernacles (Jn. 7:14), Dedication (Jn. 10:22), Passover (numerous references in the four Gospels).

We cannot doubt that he recited the daily prayer called the Shema꜄; his answer to the scribe who questioned him in the Temple is positive proof:

And one of the scribes . . . asked him, "Which commandment is the first of all?" Jesus answered, "The first is, 'Hear, O Israel [Shema꜄ Yisra'el]: The Lord our God, the Lord is one. . . .' "

Mk. 12:28–29

We see him wearing on his garment the four woolen tassels—tzitzit in Hebrew, kraspeda in Greek—prescribed by the Law (see Num. 15:38–39; Deut. 22:12). Jesus' tzitzit are mentioned in the three Synoptic Gospels:

And behold, a woman who had suffered from a hemorrhage for twelve years came up behind him and touched the fringe of his garment. . . .

Mt. 9:20; Lk. 8:43–44

. . . and besought him that they might touch even the fringe of his garment; and as many as touched it were made well.

Mk. 6:56; Mt. 14:36

We see him again, before eating, say the accustomed Jewish bene-
diction at the moment of breaking bread:

And taking the five loaves and the two fish he looked up to heaven, and
blessed, and broke the loaves. . . .

Mk. 6:41; Mt. 14:19; Lk. 9:16; Jn. 6:11; the same in
Mk. 8:6; Mt. 15:36; and in Mk. 14:22; Mt. 26:26; Lk. 22:19

And what Christian can fail to know that on the very eve of the
day appointed for the Passion, Jesus, according to the Synoptics, took
care to have the ritual meal for the Jewish Passover prepared for himself and his disciples?

And on the first day of Unleavened Bread, when they sacrificed the passover lamb, his [Jesus'] disciples said to him, "Where will you have us go
and prepare for you to eat the passover?"

Mk. 14:12; the same in Lk. 22:7–9; Mt. 26:17

The ritual meal ended, Jesus and his disciples did not leave until
they had sung "a hymn," one of the Hallel series of Psalms,[12] according to rite:

And when they had sung a hymn, they went out to the Mount of Olives.

Mk. 14:26; Mt. 26:30

Such were the acts, a few hours before the Cross, of this "destroyer
of Judaism" who "was no longer Jewish," whose "ministry in Jerusalem ended in a break with Judaism," who "deliberately abstained
from" observing "the Jerusalemite cult and the rituals of private life."

⁙   ⁙   ⁙

Some will oppose my arguments here with, among others, the case
of the Sabbath—of Jesus' "violations" of the Sabbath. This is indeed a
test case most worthy of serious examination.

In the religious life of Israel, there was no rite more sacred—or
more scoffed at or imitated by pagans[13]—than the weekly Sabbath
rest, whose observation is included among the Ten Commandments
God gave Moses on Sinai:

---

[12] [Scholars think that in Jesus' time only one or two Psalms were sung, possibly 113 and 114.—Ed.]

[13] Juvenal, Satires, 14:105–106. According to Saint Augustine, Seneca attacked
the Jewish custom of weekly rest, which he said was accepted everywhere and
caused people to lose "a seventh of their life."

Remember the sabbath day, to keep it holy. Six days you shall labor, and do all your work; but the seventh day is a sabbath to the Lord your God; in it you shall not do any work, you, or your son, or your daughter, your manservant, or your maidservant, or your cattle, or the sojourner who is within your gates. . . .

Ex. 20:8–10

And the commandment was reiterated in solemn terms:

You shall keep the sabbath, because it is holy for you. . . . It is a sign for ever between me [the Lord] and the people of Israel. . . .

Ex. 31:14, 17

Such was the principle, respected throughout Israel, and no one would have dared rise up against it:

Blessed is the man who does this,
    and the son of man who holds it fast,
who keeps the sabbath, not profaning it. . . .

Is. 56:2

As for the practice, the subtle mind of the doctors of the Law had so contrived as to particularize it down to the least detail. There were thirty-nine kinds of work forbidden on the Sabbath, and discussions on what was or was not licit were pursued out of sight (and out of breath). Day by day the casuistry over the Sabbath bloomed with new prescriptions, disconcerting in their minutiae and sometimes their puerility. The most intransigent in this respect were the Pharisees of the school of Shammai (hostile to the followers of Hillel).

Professor Gunther Dehn, quoted earlier, states that "The old commandment . . . had become a monstrous mass of incomprehensible constraints, thanks to the art of the scribes." [14] Yet, after a close study, Father Joseph Bonsirven, a qualified expert, granted that "The principle seems to have been applied intelligently and liberally on the whole, aside from certain excesses, always inevitable in these matters." [15]

Let us return now to the Gospels, and, in proper order, consider the words and deeds.

[14] Gunther Dehn, *Le Fils de Dieu, commentaire à l'Évangile de Marc*, Paris, Je Sers, 1936, p. 60.
[15] Father Joseph Bonsirven, S.J., *Le Judaïsme palestinien au temps de Jésus-Christ, sa théologie*, 2 vols., Paris, Beauchesne, 1935, II, 177.

First deed, first indictment against Jesus: crossing a field on a Sabbath day, and doubtless being hungry, the disciples took some ears of grain to eat, and Jesus let them do it:

One sabbath he was going through the grainfields; and as they made their way his disciples began to pluck ears of grain. And the Pharisees said to him, "Look, why are they doing what is not lawful on the sabbath?" And he said to them, "Have you never read what David did, when he was in need and was hungry, he and those who were with him: how he entered the house of God, when Abiathar was high priest, and ate the bread of the Presence, which is not lawful for any but the priests to eat, and also gave it to those who were with him?" And he said to them, "The sabbath was made for man, not man for the sabbath; so the Son of man is lord even of the sabbath."

Mk. 2:23–28; reproduced almost word for word in Lk. 6:
1–5; with some modifications in Mt. 12:1–8

Second indictment: several cures Jesus performed on a Sabbath day:

Again he entered the synagogue, and a man was there who had a withered hand. And they watched him, to see whether he would heal him on the sabbath, so that they might accuse him. And he said to the man who had the withered hand, "Come here." And he said to them, "Is it lawful on the sabbath to do good or to do harm, to save life or to kill?" But they were silent. And he looked around at them with anger, grieved at their hardness of heart, and said to the man, "Stretch out your hand." He stretched it out, and his hand was restored.

Mk. 3:1–5; reproduced in Lk. 6:6–10; Mt. 12:9–13 gives
a rather modified version

Luke's account is almost identical. It specifies that it was "the scribes and the Pharisees" who watched Jesus. In Matthew,

. . . they asked him, "Is it lawful to heal on the sabbath?" . . . He said to them, "What man of you, if he has one sheep and it falls into a pit on the sabbath, will not lay hold of it and lift it out? Of how much more value is a man than a sheep! So it is lawful to do good on the sabbath."

The Gospels according to Saint Luke and Saint John cite other cases of healing on the Sabbath: Luke 13:10–17 recounts the cure of "a woman who had had a spirit of infirmity for eighteen years"; Luke 14:1–6 tells of the cure of a man with dropsy at the house of a Pharisee; John 5:5–18 puts the cure of a paralytic on the Sabbath (the cure is mentioned in the Synoptics, but without allusion to the Sabbath). In the discussion that arose about this cure, Jesus had recourse to another argument:

. . . you circumcise a man upon the sabbath. If on the sabbath a man receives circumcision, so that the law of Moses may not be broken, are you angry with me because on the sabbath I made a man's whole body well?

Jn. 7:22–23

It is likewise on the Sabbath that John sets the cure of the man born blind (Jn. 9:16), an episode passed over by the Synoptics.

Applying the principle that only the wealthy can borrow, let us look at these passages as a whole. There appears to have been a well-established tradition on this point. It matters little how many and what kind of cures were performed on the Sabbath, or that a given account appears in Matthew at one place and in Luke at another.

In all honesty, what should we conclude from these texts?

That Jesus "openly broke the Sabbath," as Edmond Stapfer wrote [16] following on and following after Ernest Renan? [17]

No, but that he was accused of it, that the Pharisees—or more precisely some Pharisees, for "There was a division among them" (Jn. 9:16)—accused him of it, and that he, Jesus, defended himself spiritedly, heatedly, haughtily, drawing his arguments sometimes from Scripture, sometimes from the Law, sometimes from custom and common sense.

Now, if Jesus took the trouble to argue, if he declared it lawful for someone to pick a few ears of grain from a field when he was hungry, or to cure sick people on the Sabbath, what does this mean? Doesn't it mean implicitly that Jesus was acknowledging that some acts could be unlawful, and hence that he was not thinking of contesting the principle of the Sabbath rest?

He was thinking so little of this that we read in Matthew 24:20, in the apocalyptic speech, "Pray that your flight may not be in winter or on a sabbath." The Sabbath is not mentioned in the parallel passage in Mark, 13:18, but Father Lagrange nonetheless adjudges "the mention authentic" because it implies that the first Christians were faithful to the Law, "as was the case." [18]

Where did Edmond Stapfer get the notion that Jesus "did not abstain from one of the thirty-nine kinds of work forbidden on the Sabbath"? [19] Not even from Renan's book, his bible. We stand stupe-

[16] Stapfer, op. cit., p. 211.
[17] Renan, op. cit., p. 226.
[18] Father Marie-Joseph Lagrange, O.P., ed. and tr., Évangile selon saint Matthieu, Paris, Gabalda, 1922, p. 462.
[19] Stapfer, op. cit., p. 215.

fied before these groundless assertions. Can we confirm, anyway, that it was forbidden to gather or pick a few ears of grain?

It was forbidden to harvest, which is not the same thing. It is written in the Gemara:

> Bundles which can be taken up with one hand may be handled [on the Sabbath]. . . . and he may break [it] with his hand and eat [thereof], provided that he does not break it with a utensil. [These are the] words of R. Judah.
>
> Shabbath 128a [BT]

Jesus said: "The sabbath was made for man, not man for the sabbath. . . ." But the most liberal of the Pharisee rabbis said as much, and the formula can be found in very similar terms in the Midrash:

> R. Simon b. Menasiah says: . . . This [Ex. 31:14] means: The Sabbath is given to you but you are not surrendered to the Sabbath.[20]

Jesus said: ". . . the Son of man is lord even of the sabbath." All right. This is a reaffirmation of a sovereign authority, on the same order as "something greater than the temple is here" (Mt. 12:6), a royal affirmation which nothing justifies transforming into a nullification of the Sabbath, and which can be seen, from the context, to concern not the commandment itself but its application.

Furthermore, there is proof that Jesus never openly broke the Sabbath: when he appeared before the Sanhedrin, there is no trace of such an accusation, which would certainly not have failed to be produced had it had the slightest foundation.

The conclusion from this coincides with the previous conclusion, and substantiates it: in the case of the Sabbath, as in every other case of the sort, Jesus took a clear position not against the Law, not even against ritual practices, but against the excessive importance that particular Pharisee doctors attributed to them; not even against Phariseeism, but against particular tendencies in Phariseeism, especially the tendency to put the letter before the spirit.

❊　　❊　　❊

All those (and there are many) who are determined to have Jesus breaking with Judaism and rejecting at least some of the legal obligations rely heavily on the passages in Mark and Matthew on handwashing before meals and especially on words in these passages that

[20] [Quotation taken from *Mekilta de-Rabbi Ishmael*, ed. and tr. Jacob Z. Lauterbach, Philadelphia, Jewish Publication Society, 1935, Shabbatta, p. 198.—Tr.]

seem to refer to regulations about food; for the latter were imposed by the Law itself, and the former only by tradition.

In Mark 7:1-17, the scene is Galilee. Pharisees from the area and scribes from Jerusalem criticize Jesus because

. . . some of his disciples ate with hands defiled, that is, unwashed. . . . And he said to them, "Well did Isaiah prophesy of you hypocrites, as it is written,

> 'This people honors me with their lips,
> but their heart is far from me;
> in vain do they worship me,
> teaching as doctrines the precepts of men.'

You leave the commandment of God, and hold fast the tradition of men. . . . Hear me, all of you, and understand: there is nothing outside a man which by going into him can defile him; but the things which come out of a man are what defile him. If any man has ears to hear, let him hear."

Mk. 7:2, 6–8, 14–16 [RSV, including n. a]

In Matthew 15:1–11, Jesus, replying to the doctors and Pharisees, begins by taxing them for "transgress[ing] the commandment of God for the sake of [their] tradition" (15:3). Then he quotes the verses from Isaiah, and concludes in these terms, which differ on one important point from Mark's:

"Hear and understand: not what goes into the mouth defiles a man, but what comes out of the mouth, this defiles a man."

Mt. 15:10–11

From Mark 7:15 and Matthew 15:11, which say that nothing entering a man defiles him, it indeed seems that commentators can deduce —and they are quick to do so—that all the regulations on food in the Law, all its prohibitions, were rejected in one fell swoop. Father Lebreton writes:

A solemn declaration . . . [of] enormous import. . . . . It was no longer a question simply of ritual washings imposed by traditions of old; it was a question of the distinction between pure and impure foods, prescribed by Levitical legislation; that legislation was holy . . . and yet it had only pedagogical value . . . ; beneficial to an immature people, it would have hampered the progress of the Gospel and the freedom of Christians. It ceded to a superior principle,[21] and "That principle," according to a Jewish exegete [Montefiore], "had a decisive grandeur and compass." [22]

[21] "Jesus proclaimed a principle which suppressed legal impurities" (Father Joseph Bonsirven, S.J., Les Enseignements de Jésus-Christ [The Teachings of Jesus Christ], Paris, Beauchesne, 1946, p. 79).
[22] Father Jules Lebreton, S.J., La Vie et l'enseignement de Jésus-Christ, 2 vols., Paris, Beauchesne, 1931, I, 398.

And I too, following Montefiore's example, would willingly accept this radical interpretation if it did not seem excessive to me in terms of the text—that is, if it did not seem to go beyond what the text allows.

First of all, it makes Jesus contradict himself. How so? Would Jesus, who has just retorted to his adversaries' charge that he has not observed the commandments of tradition with the riposte that they do far worse—they do not observe the commandments of the Law— choose that very moment to reject other prescriptions of the Law? It would be hard to believe.

Then there is the explanation given to the disciples; if this was what Jesus was really thinking, why didn't he say so clearly in his explanation?

And when he had entered the house, and left the people, his disciples asked him about the parable. And he said to them, "Then are you also without understanding? Do you not see that whatever goes into a man from outside cannot defile him, since it enters, not his heart but his stomach, and so passes on?" (Thus he declared all foods clean.) And he said, "What comes out of a man is what defiles a man. For from within, out of the heart of man, come evil thoughts, fornication, theft, murder, adultery, coveting, wickedness, deceit, licentiousness, envy, slander, pride, foolishness. All these evil things come from within, and they defile a man."

Mk. 7:17–23

Matthew 15:15–20 is similar, except that it does not have the words "Thus he declared all foods clean," and it ends thus:

"These are what defile a man; but to eat with unwashed hands does not defile a man."

What is the primary idea in this explanation?

That there is no distinction to be made among foods, that there is no need to heed the prescriptions of the Law on this subject, that "legal impurities" are "suppressed"? [23]

Not at all. A single small segment of the account suggests this in its quiet obscurity: "Thus he declared all foods clean." But this is an interpolation of Mark's, not a reflection by Jesus, as Father Lagrange rightly points out.[24]

The primary idea, a very beautiful and noble idea in the direct line of the prophetic tradition, is that the fundamental source of all impurity resides inside man, not outside. It is not so much the hands that

[23] See n. 21, above.
[24] Lagrange, *op. cit.*, p. 306.

need purifying—after all, the question here concerns the ritual washing of hands—as the heart.

Here as elsewhere and as everywhere, Jesus was stating in other terms the golden rule: the primacy of the spiritual. True, it is stated here with a negative emphasis, calculated to scatter all obstacles, but demanded by that obsession with physical purity to which the Pharisees and Essenes had succumbed. It is not surprising if the food regulations, while not in themselves attacked or rejected, were jostled in the scuffle. Doubtless Jesus saw no great harm in it. Was this a breaking with Judaism? No; it was an attempt to unshackle it. "If any man has ears to hear, let him hear." The profound lesson surely had meaning for Israel and its doctors, and it had a broader scope; it has meaning for others also.

❈   ❈   ❈

There is no reason to delay further giving the decisive passages on the subject. They have a clarity, a directness, a sharpness that seem to allow no equivocation.

Jesus said: *God alone is good; observe the commandments of God* (Mk. 10:17–19; Mt. 19:16–19; Lk. 18:18–20).

Jesus said: *The great commandments of the Law are: love of the one God, and love of one's neighbor* (Mk. 12:28–31; Mt. 22:35–40; Lk. 10:25–28).

Finally and above all, Jesus said: *The Law will not pass away; it will attain its fullness in me:*

Do not think that I have come to destroy the Law or the Prophets. I have not come to destroy, but to fulfill. For amen I say to you, till heaven and earth pass away, not one jot or one tittle shall be lost from the Law till all things have been accomplished. Therefore whoever does away with one of these least commandments, and so teaches men, shall be called least in the kingdom of heaven; but whoever carries them out and teaches them, he shall be called great in the kingdom of heaven. For I say to you that unless your justice exceeds that of the Scribes and Pharisees, you shall not enter the kingdom of heaven.

Mt. 5:17–20 [CCD]

This cardinal text is given by Matthew alone, in the Sermon on the Mount, and this, for reasons already noted,[25] invites some reservations. But if the first Gospel is largely tributary from the second in its

[25] See p. 55, above.

narration, in its didactic elements—the teachings of Jesus—it seems incomparably richer and, judging by Papias' evidence,[26] equally old. Moreover, a segment of the text from Matthew—touching on the essential point that the Law will be everlasting—is also found in the third Gospel:

But it is easier for heaven and earth to pass away, than for one dot of the law to become void.

Lk. 16:17

When we remove the parasitic vegetation of glosses that have grown up around them (perhaps the better to smother them?), these passages are perfectly clear. Or rather, they would be, were it not for the aura of mystery that emanates from the initial statement as it has been given by many translators:

I have not come to destroy, but to fulfill.

"Fulfill"—what a magnificent vista this verb opens to the theological imagination! Let us take a look. "The Law will be 'fulfilled' in the double meaning of raised to perfection and superseded," in the words of Fernand Ménégoz.[27] According to Father Lebreton, "To fulfill signifies not only to put into practice but also to consummate." [28] And somewhat more cautiously (in style, that is), Father Bonsirven says about the same thing: "The New Covenant and its economy do not suppress those that came before but 'fulfill' them, as does the fruit into which the flower is transformed." [29]

Indeed! I am disturbed by these subtleties, these acrobatics around a verb, "to fulfill," which in the final analysis is simply a translation of a translation.

We do not know the Aramaic word Jesus used. The observations on this subject furnished by Father Léonce de Grandmaison, following on the expert Gustaf Dalman, are purely conjectural.[30] By a rare coin-

[26] See p. 28, above.

[27] Fernand Ménégoz, "Études critiques: Étude sur la personne et l'oeuvre de Jésus" [Critical Studies: Study on the Person and Works of Jesus], Revue d'Histoire et de Philosophie religieuses (annual), Paris, Presses Universitaires de France, 1944, XXIII, 59 ff.

[28] Lebreton, op. cit., I, 199.

[29] Bonsirven, Les Enseignements de Jésus-Christ, p. 81.

[30] Father Léonce de Grandmaison, S.J., Jésus-Christ, sa personne, son message, ses preuves, 2 vols., Paris, Beauchesne, 1928 [repub. 1946], II, 11 [see, in English, as idem, Jesus Christ, His Person, His Message, His Credentials, tr. Dan Basil Whelan and Ada Lane, 3 vols., London, Sheed & Ward, 1930–1934]; Gustaf Dalman, Jesus-Jeschua [Jesus-Joshua], Leipzig, Hinrichs, 1922, pp. 52–53.

cidence, it happens that the Talmud (Shabbath 116b) cites this Gospel aphorism, but as a kind of joke, and in such a way, in such a text and context, that it could not be taken seriously. This is the authoritative view of Chief Rabbi Maurice Liber, director of Hebrew studies at the École des Hautes Études. Actually, the talmudic passage is open to dispute. Some assert that the Gospel saying which it contains must be understood to read, "I have not come to subtract from the Law of Moses, but to add to it." [31] Others read it as "I have come neither to subtract from the Law of Moses nor to add to it." [32] The context seems to demand the latter interpretation.

Next, there is the original Greek text of the first Gospel. "To fulfill" translates *plerosai*, a verb with a very clear and concrete meaning: to fill, to cram full, to fecundate. It is true that the evangelists often use the verb *pleroo* in the passive to mean "to be fulfilled" or "to be perfected," but it is in the passive. Or else we would have to accept Loisy's comment that the term is "in the evangelist's style," used deliberately to show that "The Gospel provides the fulfillment" of formal prediction.[33] As for the active verb *plerosai*, I see no good reason *not* to stick with the usual meaning, the first meaning, with the idea of "fullness" expressed by all the Greek words that come from the same root: *pleres*, full; *plerountos*, fully; *plerosis*, the act of filling, the state of being full. And I see the best reasons in *favor* of sticking with this meaning. For to express Jesus' thought and will, the evangelist, his interpreter, seems deliberately to have chosen the most concrete and clearest words: *plerosai*, to fill or fecundate, is opposed to *katalusai*, to dissolve, destroy, overthrow. Some Catholic translators, like Canon Crampon and Father Lagrange, have made an effort in this direction by substituting "to perfect" for the usual translation "to fulfill." [34] "To give fullness" seems to me to express the exact meaning of *plerosai* even more forcefully. "The context does not make interpre-

---

[31] Hermann L. Strack and Paul Billerbeck, *Kommentar zum Neuen Testament aus Talmud und Midrasch* [Commentary on the New Testament Based on the Talmud and Midrash], 4 vols., Munich, Beck, 1922–1928, I, 24.

[32] Dalman, *loc. cit.*; and see Joseph Klausner, *Jésus de Nazareth*, tr. Isaac Friedmann, Paris, Payot, 1933. [See the latter, in English, as *idem, Jesus of Nazareth: His Life, Time, and Teaching*, tr. Herbert Danby, New York, Macmillan, 1953, p. 45; repub. Boston, Beacon Press, 1964.–Tr.]

[33] Alfred Loisy, *Les Évangiles synoptiques* [The Synoptic Gospels], 2 vols., Ceffonds, by the au., 1907–1908, I, 563.

[34] [Father Lagrange underlines that *plerosai* does not mean "to fulfill" in the sense of accomplishing prophecies, nor in the sense of accepting what is and adding to it, completing it. Jesus "perfected" the Law, ". . . he rediscovered God's meaning in it . . ." (Lagrange, *op. cit.*, pp. 93–95).—Ed.]

tation easy," says Pierre Lestringant.[35] But what do you want, then? All you need do is give up the tendentious "to fulfill" for it all to become clear: not only do I not overthrow the Law, said Jesus, or empty it of its content, but on the contrary I increase that content, so as to fill the Law full to the brim;

For I tell you, unless your righteousness exceeds that of the scribes and Pharisees, you will never enter the kingdom of heaven.

Mt. 5:20

And then come the memorable injunctions, introduced thus:

You have heard that it was said to the men of old. . . . But I say to you. . . .

Mt. 5:21–22

I say to you: do not stop halfway in obedience to God and His holy commandments; go beyond, always beyond the letter of the commandment, to the spirit that gives it life, from the literal to the inner meaning; ". . . be perfect, as your heavenly Father is perfect" (Mt. 5:48); and may the Law at last be carried into effect, in its fullness:

Ouk elthonn katalusai alla plerosai.
I have not come to overthrow, but to fill.
I have not come to destroy, but to give fullness.[36]

☼   ☼   ☼

Categoric words, clear words, irksome words.

The army of scribes, instantly mobilized, have since strained their wits to twist them, not only by making a subtle interpretation of a convenient translation, but also—an unworthy tactic—by claiming to find proof that Jesus contradicted himself elsewhere.

Where?

From the days of John the Baptist until now the kingdom of heaven has suffered violence, and men of violence take it by force. For all the prophets and the law prophesied until John; and if you are willing to accept it, he is Elijah who is come.

Mt. 11:12–14

---

[35] Lestringant, *op. cit.*, p. 61.
[36] [The lines in English are translations of the Greek (and of the author's French).—Ed.]

The law and the prophets until John; [37] since then the good news of the kingdom of God is preached, and every one enters it violently.

Lk. 16:16

The least that can be said of these passages is that they are obscure, especially when compared with the luminous passages we have just been discussing. But, God be praised, it takes a great deal of obscurity to extinguish so much light.

Taking Luke's sentence "The law and the prophets until John" out of context, Renan states placidly: "Jesus was the first who dared to say that beginning with himself, or rather with John, the Law no longer existed." [38] As if verse 17, already quoted, did not give the lie to such an interpretation:

But it is easier for heaven and earth to pass away, than for one dot of the law to become void.

Among the translators, Segond did not hesitate to introduce the bold conjecture into the wording, not even signaling it to the reader with the customary square brackets or parentheses: "The Law and the prophets abided until John." Many others adopt the notion, but most are at least correct enough to signal their insertion: "The Law and the prophets [have been] until John" (Darby); "The Law and

37 [This is a modification of the RSV version, which actually reads, "The law and the prophets were until John. . . ." Given the omission of the verb in the French edition, and the brackets or parentheses (standing for brackets) around the verbs in the French Bibles from which the author quotes here and below, we deduce that he again translated directly from the Greek for his wording of Luke 16:16.

[It is interesting to note the discrepancies that exist among various standard translations into English also. In addition to the wording in the RSV, we find these versions, for example:

CCD: "Until John came, there were the Law and the Prophets; since then the kingdom of God is being preached, and everyone is forcing his way into it."

JB: "Up to the time of John it was the Law and the Prophets; since then, the kingdom of God has been preached, and by violence everyone is getting in."

KJ: "The Law and the Prophets *were* until John; from that time the gospel of the kingdom of God is preached and every man entereth violently into it."

RK: "The law and the prophets lasted until John's time; since that time, it is the kingdom of heaven that has its preachers, and all who will, press their way into it."

Moreover, as Professor Isaac notes below regarding Segond's translation, the interpolated verbs are not indicated to be such in any of these English versions except KJ.—Ed.]

38 Renan, *op. cit.*, p. 222.

the prophets [lasted] until John" (Oltramare); "Until John (it was) the Law and the prophets" (Crampon); "The Law and the prophets [continue] until John" (Lagrange); "Until John the Law and the prophets [reign]" (Goguel).[39] Yet Goguel's thoughts on this subject seem to have varied. If in his *Life of Jesus Christ*, as implicitly in his translation of the New Testament, he appears to conclude from Luke's text that in Jesus' eyes ". . . the role of the Law and the prophets . . . had been outlived,"[40] later he wrote elsewhere: "The precise meaning of this sentence escapes us, but it does seem to indicate that with John a new period opened: the messianic era which will conclude at the coming of the Kingdom of God."[41]

An unpartisan reading tells us that the central theme which Jesus took up in the two texts, Matthew and Luke, is the Kingdom of God; as Charles Guignebert shows clearly, it is in relation to the Kingdom of God that "the Law and the prophets" are considered here.[42] If we must conjecture, combining Matthew and Luke would seem to give us the most plausible meaning:

The law and the prophets prophesied [the kingdom of God] until John; since then the good news of the kingdom of God is preached [by John]; and if you are willing to accept it, he [John] is Elijah who is to come.

Or:

The law and the prophets [that is, the preparation for the kingdom of God] were until John; since then [there is a new event,] the good news of the kingdom of God is preached.

In essence, this means that the mission of John the Baptist, coming after the Law and the Prophets, marks a decisive stage in Israel's pro-

[39] Louis Segond, ed. and tr., *La Sainte Bible* [The Holy Bible], Paris, Société biblique protestante, 1877 [repub. 1967]; John Nelson Darby, ed. and tr., *Les Livres Saints, connus sous le nom de Nouveau Testament* [The Holy Books, Known by the Name of the New Testament], Paris, Claye, 1875 [Darby's works are still used today by his French Protestant followers; the standard edition in English is *The Collected Writings of J. N. Darby*, ed. William Kelly, 36 vols., London, Morrish, 1867–1902. —Ed. and tr.]; Hugo Oltramare, ed. and tr., *La Sainte Bible: Le Nouveau Testament*, Geneva, 1944; Canon A. Campon, ed. and tr., *La Sainte Bible*, rev. ed., Tournai, Desclée, 1939; Father Marie-Joseph Lagrange, O.P., ed. and tr., *Évangile selon saint Luc*, Paris, Gabalda, 1921; Maurice Goguel and Henri Monnier, eds. and trs., *Le Nouveau Testament*, Paris, Payot, 1929.
[40] Goguel, *op. cit.*, p. 540.
[41] Maurice Goguel, "Christianisme primitif" [Primitive Christianity], in Raoul Gorce and Maxime Mortier, eds., *Histoire générale des religions* [General History of Religions], Paris, Quillet, 1945 [repub. 1958], II, 186.
[42] Charles Guignebert, *Jésus*, Paris, Albin Michel, 1938 [repub. 1947], p. 367. [See, in English, as *idem, Jesus*, tr. S. H. Hooke, New York, Knopf, 1935.—Tr.]

gress toward the Kingdom of God. And the abolition of the Law, far from being envisaged, is explicitly rejected, so that Jesus' formal denial of such an intention stands indestructible:

Think not that I have come to abolish the law and the prophets. . . . till heaven and earth pass away [which does not mean: until John], not an iota, not a dot, will pass from the law. . . .

Mt. 5:17–18

Another comparison drawn for the purpose of countering the solemnity of this declaration is taken from Mark:

Now John's disciples and the Pharisees were fasting; and people came and said to him [Jesus], "Why do John's disciples and the disciples of the Pharisees fast, but your disciples do not fast?" And Jesus said to them, "Can the wedding guests fast while the bridegroom is with them? . . . No one sews a piece of unshrunk cloth on an old garment. . . . And no one puts new wine into old wineskins; if he does, the wine will burst the skins, and the wine is lost, and so are the skins; but new wine is for fresh skins."

Mk. 2:18–22

When the phrase "new wine . . . for fresh skins" is taken out of context, according to the procedure usual among theologians (but condemned by historians), and translated freely by some exegete eager to "de-Judaize" Jesus, it reads thus: "One does not pour the bounteous wine of the Gospel into the old skins of Judaism." [43] Henri Monnier, who refers to the German scholar Adolf Jülicher for this idea, could just as well have turned to Éduard Reuss: "The new wine could not be put in old skins; in the long run, the spirit of the Gospel would not tolerate the forms of the Law, but would necessarily break it"; [44] or to Renan: "When they pushed [Jesus] to the limit, he lifted all the blinds and declared that the Law now had no authority left. . . . One does not repair the old with the new. One does not put new wine in old skins. There, in application, is his act as master and creator." [45] Catholic writers are not left behind: "The old skins of Judaism [were] incapable of holding the new wine of the Gospel," says Louis-Claude Fillion; [46] "The metaphor is clear: the new garment and the new wine are the Gospel; the old garment and the old skins are

[43] Henri Monnier, La Mission historique de Jésus, Paris, Fischbacher, 1906, p. 107.
[44] Éduard Reuss, Histoire évangélique [Gospel History], Paris, Sandoz et Fischbacher, 1876, p. 260.
[45] Renan, loc. cit.
[46] Louis-Claude Fillion, Vie de Notre Seigneur Jésus-Christ [Life of Our Lord Jesus Christ], 22nd ed., Paris, Letouzey, 1929, II, 256.

the old Law," according to Ferdinand Prat; [47] "[Jesus] had early declared the old institutions and the new order incompatible; the old, its cycle definitively run, gives way to the reign of the new," writes Joseph Bonsirven.[48]

But Jesus' whole life and all his own words, including the most solemn, contradict such an interpretation. If we can be sure of anything, it is that the idea of comparing the Torah, the Jewish Law, with an "old skin" into which one could not think of pouring the "new wine" of the Gospel is a near-sacrilege that never crossed Jesus' mind; it needs only to be formulated to be rejected. Jesus said the diametric opposite, without resorting to a parable, in ineradicable words:

I have not come to destroy, but to give fullness.[49]

Mt. 5:17

And he also said, concluding the parables on the Kingdom of Heaven:

Therefore every scribe who has been trained for the kingdom of heaven is like a householder who brings out of his treasure what is new and what is old.

Mt. 13:52

In addition, is it the Law that is in question in the context, so carefully put aside by our exegetes? No; rather the fast prescribed by John or the Pharisee doctors, a pious practice that was not even inscribed in the Law. To apply a passing comparison regarding a nonobligatory and legally unbinding fast to the Law itself, the foundation stone of Judaism, has all the earmarks of a tendentious distortion of Jesus' thought. What was that thought? That it was up to Jesus himself to choose his own course, as master of his own fate, without having to heed either the rigorist tradition of the Pharisees or John's ascetic practices. In speaking of "old wineskins," what was the past that Jesus was rejecting? Pharisee tradition, it would seem; certainly not the Law.

[47] Father Ferdinand Prat, *Jésus-Christ, sa vie, son oeuvre, sa doctrine* [Jesus Christ: His Life, His Work, His Doctrine], 2 vols., Paris, Beauchesne, 1938 [repub. 1953], I, 301.

[48] Bonsirven, *Les Enseignements de Jésus-Christ,* p. 79, with reference to Saint Irenaeus. [A current "interpretation" adds: ". . . the jars stand for Judaism . . . and the water in the jar represents the weak insipid character of the Jewish ceremonial religion" (*Adult Teacher* [Methodist], December, 1967–February, 1968, pp. 69–70; quoted in Gerald Strober, ms. in preparation, New York (Xerox), p. 22).—Ed.]

[49] [The author's translation. See n. 36, above.—Ed.]

Some less partisan authors recognize this: "Without condemning the Law, which he came not to destroy but to complete, Jesus claims his followers' right to independence regarding religious traditions or groups insofar as these disclose purely human characteristics," writes Father Joseph Huby.[50] "It must be noted that what is involved here is not the Law but the fasts of the Pharisees or, on this occasion, if you will, the whole of the Pharisees' observances," says Father Lebreton.[51] It is true that a few pages farther on, forgetting his own testimony, he cedes to current opinion and adopts the broad and arbitrary interpretation hostile to the Law.[52]

*   *   *

I have kept until last what might be called an *a posteriori* proof.

If Jesus had really been the revolutionary against the Law that he has been called; if he had presented himself as a "destroyer of Judaism," as Renan and Stapfer say; if he had let it be understood—in any way—that the whole of the Law was "fulfilled" in his person and was thenceforth "superseded," in Ménégoz' phrase; if he had explained this to his disciples, for "privately to his disciples he explained everything," Mark 4:34 tells us; if he himself, "emancipated from the ritual Law," had "given no place to Judaism in the formation of his disciples, as though the Good News necessarily entailed its abrogation," in the words of Pierre Lestringant; [53] or if at least his thinking evolved to the point where he was convinced "that nothing more could be hoped for from Israel" and that the "dispensation of Judaism should be abrogated," as Goguel esteems [54]—

if all these declarations and all these hypotheses were grounded solidly in the Gospel,

how is it that Jesus' most intimate disciples, the Eleven, and along with them, following them, hundreds and thousands of converted Jews who were the first Christians were totally unaware of it, made not one allusion to it, seemed to know absolutely nothing about it? The Acts of the Apostles record their respect and love for the Law, and even more their devoted attendance at the Temple, the most

[50] Father Joseph Huby, *L'Évangile et les Évangiles* [The Gospel and the Gospels], Paris, Beauchesne, 1929 [repub. 1954], p. 90.
[51] Lebreton, *op. cit.*, I, 141.
[52] *Ibid.*, I, 150, 199.
[53] Lestringant, *op. cit.*, p. 46.
[54] Goguel, *La Vie de Jésus-Christ*, pp. 493, 570.

zealous being James, "the brother of the Lord" and the recognized leader of the Christian community in Jerusalem, and not the least zealous being Saul of Tarsus, called Paul, the former Pharisee who had become "the Apostle to the Gentiles":

And day by day, attending the temple together. . . .

Acts 2:46

Now Peter and John were going up to the temple at the hour of prayer, the ninth hour.

Acts 3:1

And they [the Apostles] were all together in Solomon's Portico.

Acts 5:12

. . . they entered the temple at daybreak and taught.

Acts 5:21

And every day in the temple and at home they did not cease teaching and preaching Jesus as the Christ.

Acts 5:42

At the Council of Jerusalem, a group of converted Pharisees maintained that "It is necessary to circumcise them, and to charge them to keep the law of Moses" (Acts 15:5); they did not win their case, but no word of Jesus' was invoked against their argument by the Apostle Peter any more than by James. Taking up Jesus' words in Matthew 5:19, James wrote: "For whoever keeps the whole law but fails in one point has become guilty of all of it" (Jas. 2:10). James also asked for and obtained a regulation to be imposed on "those who from among the Gentiles are turning to the Lord" that they "abstain from anything that has been contaminated by idols and from immorality and from anything strangled and from blood," because, he said, "Moses for generations past has had his preachers in every city in the synagogues, where he is read aloud every Sabbath" (Acts 15:19–21 [CCD]).

James and the elders said to Paul: "You see, brother, how many thousands there are among the Jews of those who have believed [in Jesus Christ]; they are all zealous for the law . . ." (Acts 21:20 [RSV]). They exhorted him to go with four men who had made a vow, according to Jewish custom, and purify himself with them, in order to show that "you yourself live in observance of the law" (21:24). The Apostle Paul followed their suggestion, "and the next day he purified himself with them and went into the temple . . ." (21:26).

Paul said to the governor, ". . . it is not more than twelve days since I went up to worship [God in the temple] at Jerusalem. . . . according to the Way, which they call a sect, I worship the God of our fathers, believing everything laid down by the law or written in the prophets . . ." (24:11, 14).

And Paul spoke thus to the Jews of Rome: "Brethren, though I had done nothing against the people or the customs of our fathers, yet I was delivered prisoner from Jerusalem into the hands of the Romans" (28:17).

Finally, we can substantiate the evidence in Acts with the witness of Saint Irenaeus: "But they themselves . . . continued in the ancient observances. . . . Thus did the apostles . . . scrupulously act according to the dispensation of the Mosaic law. . . ."[55]

※   ※   ※

I will refrain from saying that I rest my case, for there are cases that are never done being heard; and what text, no matter how clear, could arrest the flight of theological genius? But commentaries pass, and the Word remains.

Yet I would not want the meaning of this exposition to be misunderstood. It was inspired by no ulterior motive, no attachment to outdated Judeo-Christian formulas, no reckless desire to turn back time and reopen established fact to question.

My only purpose has been to demonstrate that Jesus, "born under the law" (Gal. 4:4), lived "under the law," that in this respect he remained a faithful Jew until his human death, and that no one can maintain a contrary opinion without perverting the texts.

[55] Irenaeus, *Against Heresies*, 3:23:15. [Quotation taken from *ibid.*, in *The Ante-Nicene Fathers*, ed. Rev. Alexander Roberts and James Donaldson, rev. ed. Rev. A. Cleveland Cox, 10 vols., New York, Scribner, 1917–1925, I, 436.—Tr.]

PROPOSITION 10

NOTHING WOULD BE MORE FUTILE THAN TO TRY TO SEPA-
RATE FROM JUDAISM THE GOSPEL THAT JESUS
PREACHED IN THE SYNAGOGUES AND IN THE TEMPLE.
THE TRUTH IS THAT THE GOSPEL AND ITS ENTIRE TRA-
DITION ARE DEEPLY ROOTED IN JEWISH TRADITION AND
IN THE ATTEMPTS AT RENOVATION AND PURIFICATION
WHICH HAD BEEN MANIFESTED FOR ALMOST TWO CEN-
TURIES IN PALESTINE.

Like the previous one—like all those that precede and follow it—
this tenth proposition is what it is, says what it says, without ulterior
motives or doctrinal claims. It is a simple statement of fact, accepted
by all men of faith who are at the same time men of learning and of
good faith. "The more that scholars apply themselves to the study of
this religious movement," writes Father Lagrange, "the more they
recognize its Jewish point of departure, which for us in no wise negates
its divine originality." We have nothing to add, lifting our eyes from
the roots of the tree to its high top.

But we refuse to subscribe to Adolf Harnack's assertion: "Jesus
Christ's teaching will at once bring us by steps which, if few, will be
great, to a height where its connexion with Judaism is seen to be only
a loose one." [1] Nor do we subscribe to Paul Fargues's notion: "If
[Jesus'] indebtedness to Hebraism is real, we must concur with Edersheim, Schürer, Stapfer, Bousset, Strack, and others that he borrowed little from the Judaism of his time." [2] Equally remote
from the position of some Jews, who deny that the Gospel has any

---

[1] Adolf Harnack, *L'Essence du christianisme* [The Essence of Christianity],
tr., Paris, Fischbacher, 1907, p. 24. [Quotation taken from *idem, What Is Christianity?*, tr. Rev. Thomas Bailey Saunders, New York, Putnam, 1902, p. 17.—Tr.]
[2] Paul Fargues, *Histoire du christianisme* [History of Christianity], 6 vols.,
Paris, Fischbacher, 1929–1936, I, 43.

originality,[3] and from the position of some Christians, who are inclined to sever it completely from Judaism, we believe, because we have found this at every turn, that every root of Jesus' Gospel is sunk deep in the soil of Jewish tradition, which it is specious to distinguish from "the Judaism of his time," itself far more diversified in its aspirations than is generally accepted.

Not even a whole book on the subject could contain everything there is to be said on it; [4] the ties between the Gospel, or the Gospels, and Judaism are countless. But since the purpose here is only to dislodge a prejudice based on lack of knowledge, we can limit ourselves to a few examples.

The Temptation in the Desert

According to the three Synoptic Gospels, before Jesus took up his ministry, he retired to the desert, where he remained and fasted for forty days (Mk. 1:12–13; Mt. 4:1–2; Lk. 4:1–2).

Forty days—a sacred number. Christian tradition coincides with Jewish tradition on this point. Moses had stayed and fasted forty days on Mount Sinai (Ex. 34:28); Elijah had journeyed forty days— without eating—to Horeb, "the mount of God" (1 Kings 19:8).

The evangelists count three temptations by the Evil One during Jesus' time in the desert. The first time:

And the tempter came and said to him, "If you are the Son of God, command these stones to become loaves of bread."

Mt. 4:3; Lk. 4:3 puts "stone" in the singular:
". . . command this stone . . ."

Jesus answered Satan with one of the most beautiful sayings in the Old Testament:

. . . know that man does not live by bread alone, but that man lives by everything that proceeds out of the mouth of the Lord.

Deut. 8:3 (Mt. 4:4)

[3] An exposition and analysis of the main currents in Jewish opinion will be found in Father Joseph Bonsirven, S.J., *Les Juifs et Jésus* [The Jews and Jesus], Paris, Beauchesne, 1937, particularly Chap. 2, "Jésus juif, uniquement juif" [Jesus: Jewish and Only Jewish].

[4] And many books have already been devoted to the subject. Specifically, the problem of the relationships between Gospel and rabbinical teachings is treated in depth in the German work by Hermann L. Strack and Paul Billerbeck, *Kommentar zum Neuen Testament aus Talmud und Midrasch*, 4 vols., Munich, Beck, 1922–1928; and in the English volume by Claude Montefiore, *Rabbinic Literature and Gospel Teachings*, London, Macmillan, 1930.

The second time, according to Matthew—the third according to Luke—the devil took Jesus to "the holy city" and bade him to throw himself from the pinnacle of the Temple, since it is written:

> For he [God] will give his angels charge of you
> to guard you in all your ways.
> On their hands they will bear you up,
> lest you dash your foot against a stone.
>
> Ps. 91:11–12 (Mt. 4:6)

But Jesus answered him with this other saying from Scripture:

You shall not put the Lord your God to the test. . . .

Deut. 6:16 (Mt. 4:7)

The third time, the devil took Jesus to "a very high mountain, and showed him all the kingdoms of the world and the glory of them." "All these I will give you," he said, "if you will fall down and worship me." But Jesus answered him with yet another commandment of the Old Law: "Begone, Satan!" he said, "for it is written,

You shall fear the Lord your God; you shall serve him, and swear by his name."

Deut. 6:13 (Mt. 4:10)

Such is the Gospel tradition: it was by referring thrice to the Law, to the Word of God gathered by Moses and inscribed in the Book of Deuteronomy, that Jesus victoriously repulsed the Evil One's on-slaught. On the threshold of his ministry, Jesus resolutely placed himself under the aegis of the Law.

The Beatitudes

From faithfully attending synagogue meetings, Jesus' ardent soul was permeated with the pious exaltation imparted by the prophetic calls and by the Psalms. What could be less surprising than that later he quite naturally recall the rhythms of the Psalmist and the tones of the Prophets in preaching his Gospel? It takes nothing away from the supreme beauty of the Beatitudes to observe that they reflect a manner of expression common in the Psalms:

> Blessed is the man
> who walks not in the counsel of the wicked. . . .
>
> Ps. 1:1

Blessed is he whose transgression is forgiven. . . .
Blessed is the man to whom the Lord imputes no iniquity. . . .

Ps. 32:1–2

Blessed is he who considers the poor!
The Lord delivers him in the day of trouble. . . .

Ps. 41:1

Blessed are they who observe justice,
who do righteousness at all times!

Ps. 106:3

Blessed is the man who fears the Lord,
who greatly delights in his commandments!

Ps. 112:1

Blessed are those whose way is blameless. . . .
Blessed are those who keep his testimonies,
who seek him with their whole heart. . . .

Ps. 119:1–2

There is as yet only a kinship in form. But the Beatitudes are related to Jewish tradition not only in letter but in spirit:

For thus says the high and lofty One
who inhabits eternity, whose name is Holy:
"I dwell in the high and holy place,
and also with him who is of a contrite and
humble spirit,
to revive the spirit of the humble,
and to revive the heart of the contrite. . . ."
Is. 57:15

Blessed are the poor in
spirit,[5] for theirs is the
kingdom of heaven.
Mt. 5:3

My soul makes its boast in the Lord;
let the afflicted hear and be glad.
Ps. 34:2

A man's pride will bring him low,
but he who is lowly in spirit will obtain
honor.
Prov. 29:23

. . . for great is the mercy of God;
he makes his secrets known to the humble.
Ecclus. 3:20 [JB, n. h] [6]

[5] Not to be understood as "the simple-minded," but as "those who have the
spirit of poverty" or, according to Father Paul Joüon, as "those who, poor by dint
of circumstance, are so also by free will" (Joüon, ed. and tr., L'Évangile de Notre
Seigneur Jésus-Christ [The Gospel of Our Lord Jesus Christ], Paris, Beauchesne,
1930, p. 20).
[6] [The Hebrew text. The Greek (from which the body of Ecclesiasticus in JB
is translated) reads, ". . . for great though the power of the Lord is, he accepts
the homage of the humble."—Ed.]

Blessed are those who
mourn, for they shall
be comforted.

Mt. 5:4

> . . . because the Lord has anointed me
> to bring good tidings to the afflicted;
> he has sent me to bind up the broken-
> hearted, . . .
> to comfort all who mourn. . . .
> yours shall be everlasting joy.
>
> Is. 61:1, 2, 7
>
> The Lord is near to the brokenhearted,
> and saves the crushed in spirit.
>
> Ps. 34:18
>
> Those that sow in tears shall reap rejoicing.
>
> Ps. 125:5 [CCD]

Blessed are the meek,
for they shall inherit
the earth.

Mt. 5:5

> Yet a little while, and the wicked man shall be
> no more. . . . But the meek [7] shall pos-
> sess the land, they shall delight in
> abounding peace.
>
> Ps. 36:10–11 [CCD]
>
> . . . but to the humble he shows favor.
>
> Prov. 3:34

Blessed are those who
hunger and thirst for
righteousness, for they
shall be satisfied.

Mt. 5:6

> Ho, every one who thirsts,
> come to the waters. . . .
>
> Is. 55:1
>
> Well for the man . . . who conducts his affairs
> with justice; he shall never be moved.
> . . .
>
> Ps. 111:5 6 [CCD]
>
> He who pursues justice and kindness will find
> life, justice,[8] and honor.
>
> Prov. 21:21 [CCD]

Blessed are the merci-
ful, for they shall ob-
tain mercy.

Mt. 5:7

> Forgive your neighbor's injustice; then when
> you pray, your own sins will be forgiven.
>
> Ecclus. 28:2 [CCD]
>
> . . . he who is merciful to others, mercy is
> shown to him by Heaven.
>
> Shabbath 151b [BT]

---

[7] The Hebrew term can also be translated by "humble."

[8] [For conformity with the French version of Proverb 21:21, "justice" has been inserted into the CCD wording here on the authority of JB, which comments in a note: " 'life and honour' Greek; 'life, justice, and honour' Hebr."—Ed.]

Blessed are the pure in
heart, for they shall see
God.

Mt. 5:8

> For the Lord is righteous, he loves righteous
>   deeds;
> the upright shall behold his face.
>
> Ps. 11:7
>
> Who shall ascend the hill of the Lord?
> And who shall stand in his holy place?
> He who has clean hands and a pure
>   heart. . . .
>
> Ps. 24:3–4
>
> Create in me a clean heart, O God. . . .
>
> Ps. 51:10
>
> God is indeed good to Israel,
>   the Lord is good to pure hearts.
>
> Ps. 73:1 [JB]
>
> God loves him whose heart is pure.
>
> Berakoth R. 41 (84b)

Blessed are the peace-
makers, for they shall
be called sons of God.

Mt. 5:9

> For out of Zion shall go forth the law,
>   and the word of the Lord from Jeru-
>   salem. . . .
> nation shall not lift up sword against nation,
>   neither shall they learn war any more.
>
> Is. 2:3–4
>
> . . . seek peace, and pursue it.
> The eyes of the Lord are toward the righ-
>   teous. . . .
>
> Ps. 34:14–15

Blessed are those who
are persecuted for righ-
teousness' sake, for
theirs is the kingdom
of heaven.

Mt. 5:10

> Hearken to me, you who know righteousness,
>   the people in whose hearts is my law;
> fear not the reproach of men,
>   and be not dismayed at their revilings.
>
> Is. 51:7
>
> A man should always strive to be rather of the
>   persecuted than of the persecutors.
>
> Baba Kamma 93a [BT]
>
> Always, everywhere, God is with the perse-
>   cuted.[9]
>
> Eccles.3:15, commentary in the Mid-
>   rash Tanhouma on Emor, chap. 9

Yet Father Bonsirven, whom I have already signaled as one of the
most informed and equitable of Catholic authors on the subject of Judaism, has written these astonishing lines: "If there is a theme in

---

[9] The last two quotations were found in Strack and Billerbeck, *op. cit.*, I, 220.

Jesus' preaching that is little Jewish, or even anti-Jewish, in tone, it is indeed that of the Beatitudes." And in this connection, he censures the Jewish "mania" for "finding rabbinic parallels and antecedents for all of Jesus' sayings." [10] But isn't he letting himself be drawn into an anti-Jewish "mania" here? What could be more appropriate in such a debate than to juxtapose the texts? What could be more informative, more moving for a Christian than this visible kinship between the New Testament and the Old? And in what way is the supreme merit of the Beatitudes diminished if it is clearly demonstrated that they are in the direct lineage of Jewish tradition, at least in its noblest and purest line?

The Teaching of Prayer

Prayer held a place of major importance in the religious life of the Jewish people. Morning and evening, every pious Jew recited the prayer called Shema⁣ᶜ ("Hear") and several verses of the Pentateuch, some taken from Deuteronomy and others from Numbers. Did he by this date also recite the Shemoneh Esreh, the "Eighteen" benedictions, three times a day? We cannot know for certain, but "The ideas expressed in this magnificent prayer were not foreign to pious Jews contemporaneous with Jesus," because "they are contained in the Old Testament." [11] For Father Lagrange, "There is no doubt about the Pharisee origin" of this prayer.[12] In addition, each meal was preceded and followed by a thanksgiving.

These ritual prayers, whose recitation was more or less obligatory, were not the only ones. Pious souls offered prayers constantly. Most of the Psalms are admirable prayers in the form of canticles. "It often happened that doctors of the Law composed [a prayer] themselves for the use of their disciples." [13] It was thus, and according to Jewish custom, that Jesus' disciples addressed themselves to him to learn how to pray:

He [Jesus] was praying in a certain place, and when he ceased, one of his disciples said to him, "Lord, teach us to pray, as John taught his disciples."

Lk. 11:1

[10] Bonsirven, op. cit., p. 109.

[11] Edmond Stapfer, La Palestine au temps de Jésus-Christ, Paris, Fischbacher, 1898, p. 381.

[12] Father Marie-Joseph Lagrange, O.P., Le Judaïsme avant Jésus-Christ, Paris, Gabalda, 1932, p. 470.

[13] Stapfer, op. cit., p. 384.

On the teaching of prayer, the most explicit text is Matthew 6:5–15, contained in the Sermon on the Mount. Again, to show its Jewish roots, reverberations, and parallelisms does not in any way indicate that its intrinsic merits and the efficacity of its perfect simplicity are in dispute.

But when you pray, go into your room and shut the door and pray to your Father. . . .

Mt. 6:6

> So he [Elisha] went in and shut the door upon the two of them, and prayed to the Lord.
>
> 2 Kings 4:33

And in praying do not heap up empty phrases as the Gentiles do; for they think that they will be heard for their many words. Do not be like them, for your Father knows what you need before you ask him.

Mt. 6:7–8

> [Says the Lord:] even though you make many prayers,
> I will not listen. . . .
>
> Is. 1:15
>
> Be not rash with your mouth, nor let your heart be hasty to utter a word before God, for God is in heaven, and you upon earth; therefore let your words be few. For . . . a fool's voice [comes] with many words.
>
> Eccles. 5:2–3

Pray then like this:
  Our Father who art in heaven,
  Hallowed be thy name.
  Thy kingdom come,
  Thy will be done,
  On earth as it is in heaven.

Mt. 6:9–10

> For . . . thou, O Lord, art our Father,
> our Redeemer from of old is thy name.
>
> Is. 63:16
>
> Thou art my Father,
> my God, and the Rock of my salvation.
>
> Ps. 89:26
>
> The Lord will reign for ever,
> thy God, O Zion, to all generations.
>
> Ps. 146:10
>
> Exalted and hallowed be God's great name
> In this world of His creation.
> May His will be fulfilled
> And His sovereignty revealed . . .
> Speedily and soon. . . .
>
> Kaddish [14]
>
> R. Eliezer says: Do Thy will in heaven above, and grant relief [literally: ease of spirit] to them that fear Thee below. . . .
>
> Berakoth 29b [BT] [15]

[14] Present-day form, but this prayer seems to be very old in most of its versions. [Quotation taken from *The Traditional Prayer Book for Sabbath and Festivals*, ed. and tr. David de Sola Pool, New Hyde Park, N. Y., University Books, for the Rabbinical Council of America, 1960, pp. 5 *et seq.*—Tr.]

[15] Found in Joseph Klausner, *Jésus de Nazareth*, tr. Isaac Friedmann, Paris, Payot, 1933, p. 558.

| Give us this day the bread we need to live;[16] And forgive us our debts, As we also have forgiven our debtors; And lead us not into temptation, But deliver us from evil.

Mt. 6:11–13 | . . . give me neither poverty nor riches; feed me with the food that is needful for me. . . .

Prov. 30:8
Forgive your neighbor's injustice; then when you pray, your own sins will be forgiven.

Ecclus. 28:2 [CCD]
. . . bring me not into sin, or into iniquity, or into temptation. . . . And deliver me from evil. . . .

Berakoth 60b [BT] |

Similarities to the Essenes

Was Jesus acquainted with the Essenian brotherhood? Was he in contact with them? Was he in any way influenced by their rule?

Very different answers have been given to these frequently posed questions. Some, like Edmond Stapfer,[17] have gone so far as to maintain—rashly—that Jesus might or even must have been affiliated with the brotherhood. This is a puzzling allegation; for while the Gospels speak of the Pharisees and Sadducees, they do not breathe a word about the Essenes. The name of the Essenes appears nowhere in the New Testament. Thus, we are limited to conjecturing.

Taking the opposite position, Harnack writes: "Neither can he [Jesus] have had any relations with the Essenes, a remarkable order of Jewish monks. . . . His aims and the means which he employed divide him off from them." [18] These peremptory statements are no less surprising and no less unacceptable. We can find both contrasts and similarities between Essenism and the Gospel, between Essenian and

[16] Because the Greek word *epiousios* is known only in this passage and Luke 11:3 of the Gospels, it is very troublesome to translate, and has been argued over since ancient times. Some render it "our bread for the morrow," others "our spiritual bread," and still others "our daily bread," which is the accepted translation but which creates a pleonasm. The translation adopted here, "Give us this day the bread we need to live . . . ," is closer to the Greek (*epi ousia*, bearing on existence, or necessary for existence), and has the advantage of being applicable to both the spiritual and the temporal, which is more in keeping with Jesus' practice. [All but this first clause of the quotation is from RSV.—Tr.]

[17] Stapfer, *op. cit.*, pp. 134–137.

[18] Harnack, *op. cit.*, pp. 46–47. [Quotation taken from *idem, What Is Christianity?*, p. 35.—Tr.]

Gospel practices. The contrasts prevail, which we need not demonstrate here; this has been shown, and shown well, many times. It is
undeniable, however, that similarities do exist; these have been
strongly substantiated by the Dead Sea Scrolls:[19] "The Qumran documents manifest clearly that the primitive Christian Church is rooted,
to a depth that no one could have suspected, in the Jewish [Esseni-
an] sect, and borrowed from it a good part of its organization and its
rites, its doctrines, . . . its mystical and moral ideal." [20] But the principal similarities are already apparent from a comparison of New
Testament passages with long-extant texts on the Essenes: Flavius Josephus' *The Jewish War* and Philo Judaeus' *Every Good Man Is
Free.*[21]

Condemnation of swearing: compare Matthew 5:33–37 with Josephus'
  The Jewish War, 2:135 (=2:8:6). On this point, the Essenian tradition itself issues directly from the Decalogue (Ex. 20:7; Deut.
  5:11), and accords with the teaching in the Book of the Wisdom
  of Ben Sirach (Ecclus. 23:9).

Scorn of earthly riches: compare Mark 10:17–22, 25 (and parallels
  Mt. 19:16–22, 24; Lk. 18:18–23, 25); Matthew 6:24 (Lk. 16:13);
  and Luke 6:20–24; 12:33; 14:33; and 16:19–31 with Josephus' *The
  Jewish War*, 2:122–134 (=2:8:3–6) and Philo's *Every Good Man
  Is Free*, 84 (=12). We should note here that the Essenian rule of
  holding goods in common was adopted by the first Christian community, which was composed wholly of Jews (Acts 4:32–35).

Respect for authority: compare Mark 12:14–17 (Mt. 22:17–21; Lk. 20:
  22–25) with Josephus' *The Jewish War*, 2:140 (=2:8:7).

Rules for missionary travel: compare Mark 6:7–11 (Mt. 10:1, 5, 9–13;
  Lk. 9:1–5) and Luke 10:4–7 with Josephus' *The Jewish War*,
  2:124–126 (=2:8:4).

It seems excessive to conclude from these few parallels that Jesus
was Essenian. Nonetheless, we do have the right at least to deduce
that the Gospel has roots not only in ancient Jewish tradition—the
tradition of the Prophets—but also in a more recent tradition, in the
Judaism of the first century before Christ, a Judaism whose rich spirituality is beginning to be more fully appreciated.

[19] See pp. 41–42, above.
[20] André Dupont-Sommer, "Les Esséniens" [The Essenes], *Évidences*, no. 69,
January, 1958.
[21] The passages from Josephus and Philo cited below were found in Lagrange,
op. cit., pp. 308–317.

✿   ✿   ✿

Were it not for the fear that continuing these comparisons would exhaust patience, it would be easy to multiply the evidence.

For example, after exposing the similarities with Essenism, we could highlight similarities with Phariseeism, which today are not seriously disputed.

When Jesus, at grips with the skepticism of the Sadducees, affirmed his belief in the resurrection of the dead, he was adopting a Pharisee doctrine, and the Pharisee doctors could not help reacting favorably to his words:

Some scribes then spoke up. "Well put, Master," they said. . . .

Lk. 20:39 [JB]

When Jesus, in the Sermon on the Mount, taught:

So whatever you wish that men would do to you, do so to them; for this is the law and the prophets.

Mt. 7:12

we are forcibly reminded of the saying of the Pharisee master Hillel: "What is hateful to you, do not [do] to your neighbour; that is the whole Torah, while the rest is the commentary thereof . . ." (Shabbath 31a [BT]). And the hypocrisy of the Pharisees itself, we have seen,[22] is denounced in the Talmud as in the Gospels.

We could also show how certain of Jesus' messianic statements have their origin in the apocalyptic literature of Judaism, although it is often difficult here to sort out the original Jewish text from the numerous Christian interpolations.

Beginning with the well-known passage from the Book of Daniel, 7:13–14:

> I saw in the night visions,
>   and behold, with the clouds of heaven
>   there came one like a son of man,
>   and he came to the Ancient of Days
>   and was presented before him.
>   And to him was given dominion
>   and glory and kingdom,
>   that all peoples, nations, and languages
>   should serve him;
>   his dominion is an everlasting dominion,
>   which shall not pass away,
>   and his kingdom one
>   that shall not be destroyed.

[22] See pp. 39–40, above.

we end at the Gospel passages:

And then they will see the Son of man coming in clouds with great power and glory. And then he will send out the angels, and gather his elect from the four winds, from the ends of the earth to the ends of heaven.

Mk. 13:26–27; see also Mt. 24:30–31 (Lk. 21:27 contains only the first sentence)

❁   ❁   ❁

Finally, contemplating the wondrous flowering of images, of metaphors, of similes and parables which give the Gospel the grace of an Oriental poem or tale, permeated with the atmosphere of Galilee, how can we not recognize, harmoniously combined and transposed onto a high plane, the evocative word of the Prophets, the literary figures of the ancient or more recent Psalmists, the teaching methods familiar to the Jewish rabbis who were contemporaries of Jesus'?

But if any one strikes you on the right cheek, turn to him the other also. . . . Mt. 5:39	. . . let him give his cheek to the smiter, and be filled with insults. Lam. 3:30
Therefore I tell you, do not be anxious about your life, what you shall eat or what you shall drink. . . . Look at the birds of the air: they neither sow nor reap nor gather into barns, and yet your heavenly Father feeds them. Mt. 6:25–26	. . . for if I should be hungry, O Lord, unto thee will I cry, O God: and thou wilt bestow. For the fowl and the fish thou dost feed. . . . thou givest rain in the desert to cause the grass to spring up, to prepare food in the wilderness for every living thing. . . . Ps. of Sol. 5:10–12 [23]

The messianic feast described in Isaiah 25:6,

On this mountain the Lord of hosts will make for all peoples a feast of fat things . . .

reappears in the Gospel parable of the marriage feast for the king's son:

Tell those who are invited, Behold, I have made ready my dinner, my oxen and my fat calves are killed, and everything is ready; come to the marriage feast.

Mt. 22:4

[23] The Psalms of Solomon, Pharisee in inspiration, were the work of a poet at the end of the first century B.C. who took the pseudonym of Solomon. [Quotation taken from *The Odes and Psalms of Solomon*, ed. and tr. J. Rendel Harris, Cambridge, Eng., Cambridge University Press, 1909, p. 144.—Tr.]

The parable ends:

But when the king came in to look at the guests, he saw there a man who had no wedding garment; and he said to him, "Friend, how did you get in here without a wedding garment?" And he was speechless. Then the king said to the attendants, "Bind him hand and foot, and cast him into the outer darkness. . . ." For many are called, but few are chosen.

Mt. 22:11–14

What a feeling of relationship with this talmudic parable:

This may be compared to a king who summoned his servants to a banquet without appointing a time. The wise ones adorned themselves and sat at the door of the palace, ["for,"] said they, "is anything lacking in a royal palace?" The fools went about their work, saying, "can there be a banquet without preparations?" Suddenly the king desired [the presence of] his servants: the wise entered adorned, while the fools entered soiled. The king rejoiced at the wise but was angry with the fools. "Those who adorned themselves for the banquet," ordered he, "let them sit, eat and drink. But those who did not adorn themselves for the banquet, let them stand and watch." 24

Shabbath 153a [BT]

I think I have said enough to demonstrate that the Gospel preached by Jesus in Palestine comes from good Jewish stock, although this may displease the pharisees among the Gentiles. Like a clear mirror, he reflects Jewish Palestine, indeed the purest Palestinian and Semitic tradition.

24 The parable of the wise and the foolish virgins (Mt. 25:1–13) is likewise related to this talmudic parable.

PART

◇◇

Jesus and His People

This came to the ears of the chief priests and the scribes, and they tried to find some way of doing away with him; they were afraid of him because the people were carried away by his teaching.

MK. 11:18 [JB]

. . . for all the people hung upon his words.

LK. 19:48

PROPOSITION 11

CHRISTIAN WRITERS DELIBERATELY OMIT THE FACT THAT
AT THE TIME OF CHRIST THE DISPERSION OF THE JEWS
HAD BEEN A *fait accompli* FOR SEVERAL CENTURIES.
THE MAJORITY OF THE JEWISH PEOPLE NO LONGER
LIVED IN PALESTINE.

"True as it is that the Messiah 'came unto his own,' it is equally true,
considering their leaders and themselves as a whole, that 'his own received him not'!" writes Father Léonce de Grandmaison.[1] Father A.
Brassac says the same: "The great majority of Jews did not believe in
Jesus' divine mission."[2] And Father François-Marie Braun states:
"Rather than curry popularity . . . by gratifying the desires of the
crowd, [Jesus] will consent to seeing himself rejected by his
people."[3]

These formulas express the nigh-on unanimous conviction of Christianity; tirelessly repeated century after century, the notion has become almost an article of faith. Ministers of religion preach and
teach: it was not only the leaders of Judaism—high priests and
scribes, Sadducees and Pharisees; it was the entire Jewish people, "as
a whole," who spurned Jesus, refused to believe in his messiahship,
his divinity, and finally crucified him. On this count, they incurred
not a partial but a total responsibility. They are the refractory people,
they are the deicide people, they are—many add—the accursed
people.[4]

[1] Father Léonce de Grandmaison, S.J., *Jésus-Christ, sa personne, son message,
ses preuves*, 2 vols., Paris, Beauchesne, 1928, I, 63.
[2] Father A. Brassac, *Nouveau Testament* [New Testament], vol. III of Fathers
Fulcran G. Vigouroux and A. Brassac, *Manuel biblique, ou Cours d'Écriture
sainte à l'usage des séminaires* [Biblical Manual, or Sacred Scripture Course for
Use in Seminaries], ed. Fathers A. Brassac and Louis Bacquez, 4 vols., 12th ed.,
Paris, Roger et Chernoviz, 1906–1909, p. 487.
[3] Father François-Marie Braun, O.P., "Jésus," in Raoul Gorce and Maxime
Mortier, eds., *Histoire générale des religions*, Paris, Quillet, 1945, II, 134.
[4] [In spite of recent efforts on the part of many churches to correct such
theses, these abusive terms are still current; see the Foreword, above, and Part
IV, below.—Ed.]

These common and crushing allegations must be compared, in keeping with the procedure we have committed ourselves to following, first with history and then with Scripture.

           ❉   ❉   ❉

The "whole" of the Jewish people?

History answers: there are solid grounds for saying that they were no longer in Palestine.[5]

For there is a historic fact which is sufficiently well known not to be deliberately thrown in shadow and which is even highly important for the history of primitive Christianity:

the great Dispersion of the Jewish people, that Dispersion perennially offered to Christian thinking—often from the height of the pulpit —as punishment for the crime,[6] took place several centuries before Jesus' time, before the crime.

Yet Father Gaston Fessard has written, "Jesus had predicted it. The people would be dispersed. . . . Some few decades after Jesus' death . . . the people [would be] dispersed to the four corners of the earth." [7]

If there was punishment, then it was anticipatory and in a certain sense, it would be tempting to believe, providential; for there is another incontestable historic fact:

the spread of Christianity took place at first because of the Dispersion of the Jews. The Apostles, the first Christian missionaries and themselves Jews, went from synagogue to synagogue across the ancient world. "Without the synagogue and . . . without the Dispersion of Israel, the establishment of the universal Church would have been impossible, humanly speaking, and the conversion of the pagans would have required a thousand years of miracles." [8]

[5] See Jules Isaac, La Dispersion d'Israël, Algiers, C.C.J.J., 1954.

[6] "The execution of the sentence, the ruin of Jerusalem and the dispersion of the people . . ." (Grandmaison, op. cit., II, 297); "When the Jewish people were punished, and dispersed in the disaster of A.D. 70 . . ." (Father François-Marie Braun, O.P., Où en est le problème de Jésus [Where the Problem of Jesus Is], Paris, Gabalda, 1932, p. 147).

[7] Father Gaston Fessard, Pax Nostra [Our Peace], 8th ed., Paris, Grasset, 1936, p. 201. [And Bishop J. C. Ryle wrote recently in The Presbyterian Journal, "Observe the wandering Jew, scattered over the face of the world. Then preach with conviction that God most surely hates evil and punishes sin" (Ryle, "S[un-day] S[chool] Lesson and Youth Program for December 22 [and] Circle Bible Study for January: Preach Hell," The Presbyterian Journal, December 11, 1963, p. 1).—Ed.]

[8] Alfred Edersheim, quoted in Father Jules Lebreton, S.J., La Vie et l'enseignement de Jésus-Christ, 2 vols., Paris, Beauchesne, 1931, I, 119. [See the

The Dispersion of the Jewish people—an early practice was to call it by its Greek name, the Diaspora—goes back to the eighth and sixth centuries B.C., the centuries that saw successively the destruction of two Hebrew kingdoms: the Kingdom of Israel by Sargon the Assyrian (722) and the Kingdom of Judah by Nebuchadnezzar the Babylonian (586). The principal victims were the ruling and wealthy classes of the two kingdoms.

The first group deported, more numerous since it included the descendants of the ten tribes who had formed the Kingdom of Israel, disappeared rather quickly, leaving no trace; a troubling disappearance for a certain brand of theology, tenaciously seeking even today to rediscover the ten exiled and lost tribes. They were absorbed by the diversified population in whose midst they were settled, demonstrating at least that they were not an "unassimilable" people. As for the populace that remained behind, in Palestine, it also blended with the foreign immigrants the Assyrians brought there; it seems even to have accepted to some degree a blend of beliefs—of the cult of Yahweh with the worship of foreign gods; thus a new people came into being in Palestine, related to the Jews through ethnic and religious traditions but ultimately detested by the Jews because of their impurity.

The second group of deportees—descendants of the two tribes, Judah and Benjamin, who had formed the Kingdom of Judah—was destined for a greater future. Entrenched in their Yahwist faith as in a fortress, they retained their identity in Babylonia and did not allow themselves to be absorbed into their Chaldean surroundings, until the miraculous day when the new ruler of the East, the Persian conqueror Cyrus the Great, accorded them freedom to return to their country of origin (538). Not all the deportees exercised this right, many of them having taken root and prospered in the land of Exile. So it was that from the end of the sixth century onward, there were in effect two Judeas, closely linked to each other: the Judea restored in its ancient Palestinian setting around Jerusalem (where the Temple was rebuilt in 520–515) and the Judea in Exile, flourishing in Babylonia. In both, a religious legalism of strict observance came to prevail; the era of the scribes followed on the era of the Prophets. The fifth century, the century of Pericles for humanism, was the century of Ezra for pietism.

former, in English, as Alfred Edersheim, *The Life and Times of Jesus the Messial*, rev. ed., 2 vols., 35th prtg., New York, Longmans, Green, 1952.—Tr.]

❄   ❄   ❄

To say that there were thenceforth two Judeas, the Palestinian and the Chaldean, is still not accurate. There were at least three principal centers.

For fertile Egypt, full of marvels, had long attracted Israel; before and after disaster befell their country, many Judeans took refuge there, bringing the old Prophet Jeremiah with them. Because the Jews were reputed to be good soldiers, the pharaohs established Jewish military enclaves in Upper Egypt on the Ethiopian border, notably on Elephantine Island, not far from the first waterfalls; a whole collection of papyri issuing from the Jewish settlement on Elephantine has been found.

In the following centuries, under the successive rules of the "Great King" of the Persians, the Greco-Macedonian descendants of Alexander, and finally the Romans, the Dispersion of the Jewish people continued, swelled, spread by degrees throughout the ancient world, from East to West.

Of this multitude scattered afar, the majority held together, and did not melt into the milieu where chance had placed them. At first sight, this seems a surprising phenomenon; but as before, in Babylonia, the explanation is found in the action of the same spiritual forces—the hardiness of a faith that, in this era, was also braced and fortified by the legalism of the scribes, the increasing awareness that the Jews were then developing of their religious vocation, the pride they took in their privilege of election. Almost everywhere they succeeded in forming distinct communities, grouped around their synagogues and barricaded, as it were, in their Law, following the commandment in Scripture: "I am the Lord your God, who have separated you from the peoples. . . . that you should be mine" (Lev. 20:24, 26); [9] living completely apart from the pagan world, which, not understanding them, was suspicious of them and calumniated them; returning scorn for scorn, and withal exercising a strange attraction on anyone tormented by religious anxiety, and trailing in their wake a crowd of proselytes and sympathizers, or "God-fearers." "The masses have long since shown a keen desire to adopt our religious observances," wrote Josephus; "and there is not one city, Greek or barbarian, nor a single nation, to which our custom of abstaining from work on the seventh day has not spread, and where the fasts and the lighting of lamps and

[9] See pp. 5 and 35, above.

many of our prohibitions in the matter of food are not observed." [10]

This was the setting surrounding the Jewish people at the time of Jesus. The probability, if not the certainty, is that the Jews in Palestine were at that point only a minority, the estimates—and they are very rough—ranging from a half-million to one or two million.[11] The Jews of the Diaspora constituted the majority, numbering four or five million or perhaps more.[12] Of these, the largest group, and the most important in terms of economic and intellectual activity, was in Egypt—about a million; 200,000 of these lived in the city of Alexandria alone, and had abandoned the Semitic tongue for Greek. The same was true almost everywhere in the Diaspora, where the Greek translation of the Bible known as the Septuagint had been adopted.

Palestine nonetheless remained the Holy Land of Judaism, and Jerusalem with the Temple its religious capital. Every Jewish adult consented to pay the tax—a didrachma—for the maintenance of the unique Sanctuary. Thousands of pilgrims took themselves to Jerusalem every year to celebrate Passover there and to carry their offerings to the Lord. Yahwism was the solid bond that united the far-flung members of the Jewish Diaspora and linked them all with the head, Jerusalem.

[10] Flavius Josephus, *Against Apion*, 2:282–283 (= 2:39). [Quotation taken from *ibid.*, tr. H. St. J. Thackeray, in *Josephus*, 9 vols., "Loeb Classical Library" series, New York, Putnam, 1926, I, 405–407.—Tr.]

[11] A half-million according to Hans Lietzmann, 700,000 according to Adolf Harnack, and a million at most according to Father Bonsirven. Jean Juster's opinion notwithstanding, we cannot rely on Josephus' figures, which are manifestly exaggerated (as Josephus had a habit of doing).

[12] It is generally accepted that the Jewish population of the Roman Empire represented 7 to 8 percent of the total population.

PROPOSITION 12

THEREFORE, NO ONE HAS ANY RIGHT TO SAY THAT THE JEWISH PEOPLE "AS A WHOLE" REJECTED JESUS. IT IS ENTIRELY PROBABLE THAT THE JEWISH PEOPLE "AS A WHOLE" WERE NOT EVEN AWARE OF HIS EXISTENCE.

Actually, any assertion regarding Jesus' reception by the Jewish people "as a whole" is rash. The state of the documentation does not allow us any certainty. But as we have already noted more than once, such is the doctrinal schooling of theologians, such is their resolve to incriminate a whole people, that they do not hesitate to transgress the sound procedures of historical method and to transform the shakiest conjectures into peremptory statements.

From the conclusions of historic research, it seems undeniable that the Jews of the Diaspora represented the majority and even the great majority of the Jewish people in Jesus' time. Given this, can it be said that these millions of Jews dispersed throughout the ancient world knew Jesus? This means not simply whether they had heard of him, but whether they knew him from direct personal acquaintance, whether they could have listened to him in the Temple often enough, long enough to have been moved by him. There is not one line of Gospel text that allows us to answer the question. And all the evidence points to the negative.

Certainly, on feast days, and especially during Passover, Jerusalem gathered within her walls a great crowd of pilgrims who had assembled from all quarters of the Diaspora, in addition to her resident population—estimated at fifty to a hundred thousand people. Let us suppose that this influx tripled or even quadrupled her population. Among these hundreds of thousands of men traveling in the Holy Land, themselves representing (whatever their number) only a more or less sizable minority in relation to the masses in the Diaspora, how many heard Jesus preach the "Good News"? How often? How many times? Who can answer these questions? [1]

If we hold to the tradition established earliest, and accepted by the three evangelists Mark, Matthew, and Luke in succession, Jesus made only a single brief visit to Jerusalem and its immediate environs, on the eve of a Passover, on the eve of the Passion. But perhaps the visit was longer than the Synoptics reveal.

Let us suppose that Jesus stayed in Jerusalem several months during the previous autumn, as some exegetes believe.[2] At that time of year, pilgrims did not come to Jerusalem, or were there in smaller numbers. The great crowd came for the Passover. How many days and weeks would it have taken for Jesus to touch that crowd, to sway them? We can even ask, was it possible for him to touch them? Most of the Jews of the Diaspora did not know Aramaic, the language Jesus spoke, and it is at least doubtful that Jesus also spoke Greek, the most widespread language in the Diaspora. The Gospels are silent on this point. The only Greeks mentioned are in John 12:20, and we do not see Jesus welcoming them.

Wherever we turn, there is the same lack of light, the same silence. If the Jewish world in the Diaspora, or at least those who represented it at Jerusalem during the feasts, had really been touched by Jesus' teaching, in whatever way, with whatever effect—whether they were offended or attracted—it would be strange that no trace of any sort remained of this for history to perceive. In this mass of pilgrims, there must have been many Hellenizing Jews from the great community at Alexandria; returning home, these pilgrims could not have failed to give their coreligionists a lengthy account of everything they had seen and heard when they were there in the Holy City. Now, in that same period, in Jesus' time, the renowned Jewish philosopher, the wise and pious Philo, lived at Alexandria; his extensive works are rich not only in metaphysical and theological speculation but also in all kinds of information on the history of contemporary Judaism. Philo died some twenty-five years later than Jesus, in the year 54; he

---

1 John alone makes any mention: "Now among those who went to worship at the [Passover] feast were some Greeks" (Jn. 12:20). They asked to see Jesus, the request was transmitted by Philip and Andrew, and it was then that Jesus, avoiding a direct answer, said, "The hour has come for the Son of man to be glorified" (12:23). We will have occasion to return to the significance of this passage. It is generally accepted that the "Greeks" mentioned by Saint John were "God-fearing" Gentiles, that is, Judaizers; *Hellenes* is translated as *Gentiles* in the Vulgate.

2 See, for example, Maurice Goguel, *La Vie de Jésus-Christ*, Paris, Payot, 1932, p. 233.

spoke of the Roman procurator Pontius Pilate, drew a severe picture
of him; but nowhere in all his works is there the smallest allusion to
Jesus.

A first conclusion forces itself on us: in all probability, the Jewish
Diaspora "as a whole" did not know Jesus; they didn't even know
anything about him.

✿   ✿   ✿

There remains the Jewish population of Palestine, still fairly large
though cruelly decimated, especially among its elite, by an almost uninterrupted succession of wars, revolts and revolutions, oppressive
and murderous tyrannies.

Can we say of these, "as a whole," that they knew Jesus, received
his teaching, heard the Gospel in its first preaching, in its divine
purity?

No doubt ruffled the mind of Father de Grandmaison.[3] But why
make a matter of faith out of what is a matter of fact? Even limited in
this way, to Palestine, the fact cannot be established with certainty.
Where could we find the necessary details? The Jewish historians of
the first century, members of the generation that followed immediately after Jesus' own, tell us nothing on this subject. One of them,
Justus of Tiberias, never mentioned Jesus in his writings, although he
was Galilean. Another, Flavius Josephus, devoted only a few lines to
him (see *The Jewish Antiquities*, 18:63–64 [=18:3:3]), and one wonders whether some or all of them might not be pious interpolations;
in its extant form, this passage is not held as authentic by any serious
writer; in addition, it does not contain the slightest indication of time
and place. We are therefore reduced to seeking the indispensable
particulars in the Gospels; but a sacred text is not necessarily an
accurate text. Evangelical tradition, we know, was not firmly established until fairly long after the events; the facts of time and place it
gives us are woefully insufficient, uncertain, and sometimes contradictory.

What was the probable span of Jesus' ministry, from his baptism by
John in the waters of the Jordan to the Cross erected on Golgotha?

---

[3] See p. 89, above.

Hardly a year, if we accept what the Synoptics say; a little more than two years, according to the fourth Gospel—a problem of chronology interminably revived and discussed, which I will not pause over. Most modern exegetes, following several Church Fathers (Clement of Alexandria, Sextus Julius Africanus), conclude in favor of the shorter time indicated in the Synoptics, and the reasons they give seem valid. One year, one single year—and even if there had been two—what is such a brief moment for someone wanting not only to be heard by a whole people but to attract them to himself, to carry them away, to move them to the roots of their being, to re-create them morally, spiritually, to tear them away from all earthly concerns, to lift them, transport them onto a higher plane, to the threshold of the Kingdom of God? One year! One year to fashion a people of saints, one year to revolutionize the human heart. . . . Alas! Buddha preached his doctrine forty-five years; Muhammad took twenty years to rally a few Arab tribes to Islam; the Church needed three hundred years—and how many servitors, how many martyrs—to win spiritual leadership over the pagan world, and more than a thousand years to make Europe Christian (that is, if it can be called Christian . . .).

That the one year, Jesus' single year, was enough to kindle a flame in the world which would never be extinguished thereafter is a miracle; there are none more convincing. But let us come back down to earth, among men: there were twelve of them, chosen companions, who did not leave the Master's side during that one year, to whom he told everything, explained everything, confided everything. And when the time came, the crucial hour, one of these twelve men betrayed him, one—Simon, called Peter, in Aramaic *Cephas*, meaning rock—denied him three times, and the others fled, abandoning him to hatred and death. To mold these deserters into soldiers of Christ, propelled by an invincible faith, required no less than the miracle of miracles, of Jesus' Resurrection from the dead, just as it required the miracle of Jesus' appearance on the road to Damascus for a Saul of Tarsus, the fiercest of the Pharisee persecutors of Christ, to become the Apostle Paul. By these elite souls, which faith had purified and sanctified, judge the others, the thousands of others. Do not say: wretched people! Say: wretched humankind, whose common fate is meanness, traitorousness, faithlessness.

Say as Jesus said, according to the account given in the fourth Gospel:

During his stay in Jerusalem for the Passover many believed in his name when they saw the signs that he gave, but Jesus knew them all and did not trust himself to them; he never needed evidence about any man; he could tell what a man had in him.

Jn. 2:23–25 [JB]

Listen well; Jesus said: "about any man."

☆   ☆   ☆

After the question of time is the question of place.

In one year—or two or even three—did Jesus travel all over Jewish Palestine, and exercise his ministry in all or almost all the cities, villages, and countryside where the Jewish population was numerically dominant; and if not, did the people from those cities, villages, and countryside come to him?

For Calvin, no less absolute in his statements—and his findings against the Jewish people—than Father de Grandmaison, there is no possibility of doubt: "In three years, Christ roamed and encompassed the whole countryside of Judea, to the point where there was no tiny corner that did not benefit by his presence," and, he adds later, "to the point where there is no excuse for the Jews, who, by their indifference, deprived themselves of the grace of salvation which was offered them." [4] No excuse for the Jews, Protestant theologians repeat with one voice, as do Catholic: "They saw Jesus' works and heard his teachings. . . . They have no excuse for their sin." [5]

On the contrary, those who broach the texts without prejudice are forced to doubt.

We must distinguish between the two principal countries in Palestine, Galilee and Judea. The more important was undeniably Judea, the home of Judaism, the religious center because of the Holy City and the Temple, with a population more purely Jewish, less mixed with pagan elements. Now, according to the Synoptics, it was Galilee that was privileged to receive the Master's teaching longer:

Now after John [the Baptist] was arrested, Jesus came into Galilee, preaching the gospel of God. . . . And he went throughout all Galilee, preaching in their synagogues. . . .

Mk. 1:14, 39; see also Mt. 4:23; Lk. 8:1

[4] Quoted in Max Dominicé, *L'Humanité de Jésus d'après Calvin* [Jesus' Humanity in Calvin's View], Paris, Je Sers, 1933, p. 94.
[5] Father Jules Lebreton, S.J., *La Vie et l'enseignement de Jésus-Christ*, 2 vols., Paris, Beauchesne, 1931, II, 355.

Strong evidence for Galilee, even taking account of the fact, mentioned in the Synoptics, that Jesus' reputation attracted a goodly number of Jews to Galilee from the other countries of Palestine and even from Syria (Mk. 3:8; Mt. 4:24–25; Lk. 6:17). His itinerant ministry radiated out—apparently a short distance—from the little town of Capernaum, which Jesus had made his chosen residence, "his own city" (Mt. 9:1). What are the other Galilean towns or villages mentioned in the Gospels? Hardly more than three or four: Chorazin or Corozain (Mt. 11:21; Lk. 10:13) and Magadan or Magdala (Mt. 15:39), in the neighborhood of Capernaum; Nain (only in Lk. 7:11) and Cana, nearer Nazareth (only in Jn. 2:1–11; 4:46); there is mention also of "the district of Dalmanutha" (Mk. 8:10), which is hard to identify, and of Gennesaret (Mt. 14:34; Mk. 6:53), a village or plain on the shore of the lake. These places are few, if we recall that Josephus counted more than two hundred important centers and fifteen fortified towns in Galilee.

Moreover, the period when Jesus preached unhindered does not seem to have lasted long. It was inevitable that Herod Antipas, the tetrarch of Judea, should become alarmed over the rumors circulating about the new prophet. To avoid John the Baptist's tragic fate, Jesus constrained himself to prudence: we see him now crossing the lake in the direction of Bethsaida, drawing away from populous places (Mk. 6:31–32; Mt. 14:13; Lk. 9:10); now moving into Phoenicia, toward Tyre, trying to go unnoticed (Mk. 7:24); again traveling to the north of the Decapolis, at the foot of Mount Hermon, in the district of Caesarea Philippi (Mk. 8:27; Mt. 16:13); then returning to Galilee and his beloved Capernaum, but almost incognito:

They went on from there and passed through Galilee. And he would not have any one know it. . . .

Mk. 9:30

Came the hour of supreme decisions: Jesus left Galilee for Judea, where he knew that the danger was even greater, owing to the Roman and Jewish authorities; walking ahead of the anxious disciples (Mk. 10:32), he went toward an ignominious death. By way of Perea east of the Jordan, and then to Jericho, he proceeded to Jerusalem, arriving a few days before Passover; and almost immediately came the arrest, the Passion, the agony on the cross.

This, in outline, is the Synoptic narrative. If we accept it as accurate, it is clear that the Jewish population of Judea and of Jerusalem did not have time to hear the Gospel: "Who is this?" asked the crowd regarding Jesus' arrival (Mt. 21:10); their curiosity, their excitement, their surprise testify to their ignorance.

If we accept the account in the fourth—Saint John's—Gospel, which lengthens the time of the ministry in Jerusalem, obviously Jesus' audience in Jerusalem would have been that much larger. But even in this case, we do not see that Jesus really spread out into Judea; here again, the hostility he had met with from the beginning forced him to be careful (Jn. 7:1, 10; 11:54); he retired from public view and did not return to Jerusalem until the eve of the Passover, to undergo the Passion.

❉   ❉   ❉

These are the facts as given in the Gospels. Is it excessive to conclude that, even in Palestine, parts of the Jewish population, a segment whose size we have no way of estimating—though it was doubtless larger in Judea than in Galilee—was not able to approach Jesus, to hear the Gospel, to profit by "the grace of salvation which was offered them"? This is at least the probability that we glean from the texts. To conclude this subject where we began it, let us say again, simply: historical honesty does not permit us to go any farther; it precludes any firm assertion.

PROPOSITION 13

BUT WITH RARE EXCEPTIONS, WHEREVER JESUS WENT THE
JEWISH PEOPLE TOOK HIM TO THEIR HEARTS, AS THE
GOSPELS TESTIFY. DID THEY, AT A GIVEN MOMENT, SUD-
DENLY TURN AGAINST HIM? THIS IS A NOTION WHICH
HAS YET TO BE PROVED.

That the Jewish people took Jesus to their hearts, and that their turning against him suddenly has yet to be proved—these statements clash violently with accepted opinion, we know. To Calvin, to Father de Grandmaison, to Father Braun, already quoted, how many others could we add!

"So instead of listening to him . . . , the Jews rebuff him, persecute him, insult him, crucify him": Henri Bois, Dean of the Protestant School of Theology at Montpellier.[1]

"Let us admit frankly that until now . . . we have too often imitated the callousness of the Jews, who were not moved when he appeared in the midst of their darkness": Dom Prosper Guéranger, Abbot of Solesmes.[2]

"Jesus sought out Israel, but the people, especially through the fault of their leaders, rejected him": Father Charles Schaefer.[3]

And in a more recent *History of the Church*, published under the

[1] Henri Bois, *La Personne et l'oeuvre de Jésus* [The Person and Works of Jesus], Neuilly, La Cause, 1926, p. 120.

[2] Dom Prosper Guéranger, O.S.B., *L'Avent* [Advent], vol. I of *L'Année liturgique* (6 vols.), 23rd ed., Tours, Mame, 1934, pp. 117–118, the first Sunday in Advent. [See, in English, as *idem, The Liturgical Year*, tr. Dom Laurence Shepherd, O.S.B., and the Benedictines of Stanbrook, 15 vols., Westminster, Md., Newman, 1948–1949.—Tr.] While Dom Guéranger's great work dates from 1841, it has retained such prestige that after the individual volumes had each gone through many printings, the monks of Solesmes published a new, five-volume edition in 1948–1952. [In addition, an abridged version, edited by Tissot, was published Paris, Desclée, 1955.—Ed.]

[3] Father Charles Schaefer, *Précis d'introduction au Nouveau Testament* [Short Introduction to the New Testament], tr. Grandclaudon, Paris, Salvator, 1939, p. 69.

editorship of the eminent Catholic university professors Augustin
Fliche and Victor Martin, we read, "The original plan of the Lord
. . . [which] aimed to win over Israel . . . failed before the unyielding hostility of the Jews and especially their leaders": Jules Lebreton
and Jacques Zeiller.[4]

Even such an informed exegete as Maurice Goguel does not hesitate to write: "The first part of the Gospel [of Mark] tells of a latent
conflict between Jesus and his people, a conflict that flared every time
contact occurred." [5]

Thus Catholics and Protestants, disputing brothers, find themselves
miraculously at one on this point: "callous," deaf and blind, "hypocritical and rebellious," [6] the Jewish people refused to give Jesus any
hearing, and before crucifying him, they rejected him: "True as it is
that the Messiah 'came unto his own,' it is equally true, considering
their leaders and themselves as a whole, that 'his own received him
not'!" [7]

❀   ❀   ❀

Let us open the Gospels, the only evidence we have at our disposal, "inspired" evidence for a man of faith but also incriminating

[4] Father Jules Lebreton, S.J., and Jacques Zeiller, *L'Église primitive*, vol. I of
Augustin Fliche and Victor Martin, eds., *Histoire de l'Église depuis les origines
jusqu'à nos jours* [History of the Church from Its Origins to Our Day], Paris, Bloud
et Gay, 1934, p. 71. [See, in English, Jules Lebreton, S.J., and Jacques Zeiller, *The
History of the Primitive Church*, tr. E. C. Messenger, 2 vols., New York, Macmillan,
1949.—Tr.]

[5] Maurice Goguel, *Les Sources du récit johannique de la Passion* [The Sources
of the Johannine Account of the Passion], Paris, Leroux, 1923, p. 10. Yet Goguel
recognizes that "Jesus made more of an impression on the people [of Galilee]
than simple curiosity; he had a true attraction for them" (*idem, La Vie de Jésus-
Christ*, Paris, Payot, 1932).

[6] John Nelson Darby, *Étude sur l'Évangile de Jean* [Study on the Gospel of
John], 2nd ed., Vevey, Dépôt des Livres et Traités chrétiens, 1934.

[7] Father Léonce de Grandmaison, S.J., *Jésus-Christ, sa personne, son message,
ses preuves*, 2 vols., Paris, Beauchesne, 1928, I, 63. [Even such a responsible
thinker as Father (now Cardinal) Jean Daniélou has not been able to put aside
these opprobrious notions. Speaking of "the death of Christ and of the responsibility or excuses of the Jews with regard to it," he writes that "In one sense, the
condemnation of Jesus by the Jews goes beyond the level of individual responsibilities." He does qualify that "It is not Israel who crucified Jesus, it is the infidelity of Israel." The distinction is not likely to reorient the reader who has been
told some pages earlier, "Thus, the Jewish people, to whom had belonged the
promises and the covenant, on the day when the object of the promises was
given, rejected him" (Father Jean Daniélou, S.J., and Rabbi Jacob B. Agus, *Dialogue with Israel*, tr. Joan Marie Roth, Baltimore, Helicon, 1968, pp. 84, 85,
70).—Ed.]

evidence, let us not forget. Let us collect the texts and examine them. What do they say, for or against?

Two reservations first: the attitude of the "chiefs," the leaders—high priests, scribes, and Pharisees—and Jesus' arraignment should and will be studied separately; the texts that follow thus relate only to the Jewish people "as a whole," and go no farther than the arrest.

And one observation: the method chosen is dry, and may tire some readers. It is of course easier to argue without quoting the texts, that is, without giving the necessary substantiation; or again to multiply abusive references in the secret hope that no troublemaker would take it into his head to verify them. But in such a discussion any cheating would seem a sacrilege, and we do not hesitate to sacrifice ease of reading to honesty of demonstration.[8]

Jesus in Galilee

For Jesus: Favorable Reception

[Mark:]   [In the synagogue at Capernaum:] And they were astonished at his teaching, for he taught them as one who had authority, and not as the scribes [1:22; see Mt. 7:28–29; Lk. 4:32].

[After an exorcism and cures:] And the whole city was gathered together about the door [1:33].

[Preaching and cures in other places:] . . . Jesus could no longer openly enter a town [because of the crowds] . . . ; and people came to him from every quarter [1:45; see Lk. 5:15].

[Return to Capernaum, the miracle of the paralytic:] And many were gathered together, so that there was no longer room for them, not even about the door; and he was preaching the word to them. . . . And . . . they could not get near him because of the crowd . . . [2:2, 4; see Lk. 5:19].

He went out again beside the sea; and all the crowd gathered about him, and he taught them. . . . And as he sat at table in his [Levi the tax collector's] house, many tax collectors and sinners were sitting with Jesus and his disciples; for there were many who followed him [2:13, 15].

Then he went home; and the crowd came together again, so that they could not even eat [3:19–20].

   [8] [The original French quotes more passages, including some of the Synoptic parallels, than are given below. In the interests of conserving space, we have regretfully relegated these to cross references following the quotations.—Ed.]

Again he began to teach beside the sea. And a very large crowd gathered about him, so that he got into a boat and sat in it on the sea; and the whole crowd was beside the sea on the land [4:1; see Mt. 13:1–2; Lk. 8:4].

And he [Jesus] went with him [Jairus]. And a great crowd followed him and thronged about him [5:24; see Lk. 8:42].

King Herod heard of it [miracles performed by the Apostles]; for Jesus' name had become known [6:14; see Mt. 14:1; Lk. 9:7].

And they went away in the boat to a lonely place by themselves. Now many saw them going, and knew them, and they ran there on foot from all the towns. . . . As he [Jesus] landed he saw a great throng, and he had compassion on them, because they were like sheep without a shepherd; and he began to teach them many things [6:32–34; see Mt. 14:13–14; Lk. 9:10–11].

[Miracle of the multiplication of the loaves:] And those who ate the loaves were five thousand men [6:44; see Mt. 14:21; Lk. 9:14].

[Return from Bethsaida:] And when they got out of the boat, immediately the people recognized him, and ran about the whole neighborhood and began to bring sick people on their pallets to any place where they heard he was. And wherever he came, in villages, cities, or country, they laid the sick in the market places, and besought him . . . [6:54–56; see Mt. 14:35–36].

[After the transfiguration:] And when they came to the disciples, they saw a great crowd about them. . . . And immediately all the crowd, when they saw him [Jesus], were greatly amazed, and ran up to him and greeted him [9:14–15; see Lk. 9:37].

And he left there and went to the region of Judea and beyond the Jordan, and crowds gathered to him again . . . [10:1; see Mt. 19:1–2, below].

[Matthew:] So his fame spread throughout all Syria. . . . And great crowds followed him from Galilee and the Decapolis and Jerusalem and Judea and beyond the Jordan [4:24–25; see Mk. 3:7–8].

[Sermon on the Mount:] Seeing the crowds, he went up on the mountain . . . [5:1; see Lk. 6:17].

When he came down from the mountain, great crowds followed him . . . [8:1].

Now when Jesus saw great crowds around him, he gave orders to go over to the other side [8:18].

[At Capernaum, miracle of the paralytic:] When the crowds saw it, they were afraid, and they glorified God, who had given such authority to men [9:8; see Mk. 2:12; Lk. 5:26].

[Cure of a mute:] . . . and the crowds marveled, saying, "Never was anything like this seen in Israel" [9:33 (and see 12:23)].

[Return from Phoenicia:] And great crowds came to him . . . , and they put them [the sick] at his feet, and he healed them, so that the throng wondered . . . ; and they glorified the God of Israel [15:30–31].

[Second miracle of the multiplication of the loaves:] Then Jesus called his disciples to him and said, "I have compassion on the crowd, because they have been with me now three days, and have nothing to eat. . . ." Those who ate were four thousand men, besides women and children [15:32, 38; see Mk. 8:1, 9].

Now when Jesus had finished these sayings, he went away from Galilee and entered . . . Judea . . . ; and large crowds followed him . . . [19:1–2; see Mk. 10:1, above].

[Luke:] [In Galilee:] And he taught in their synagogues, being glorified by all [4:15].

[At Capernaum:] And the people sought him and came to him, and would have kept him from leaving them . . . [4:42 (and see 5:1); see Mk. 1:27].

Soon afterward he went to a city called Nain, and his disciples and a great crowd went with him [7:11 (and see 7:16)].

Then his mother and his brothers came to him, but they could not reach him for the crowd [8:19; see Mk. 3:31–32; Mt. 12:46].

Now when Jesus returned, the crowd welcomed him, for they were all waiting for him [8:40; see Mk. 5:21].

[Cure of the possessed child:] And all were astonished at the majesty of God. . . . they were all marveling at everything he [Jesus] did . . . [9:43].

Against Jesus: Hostile Reception

[Mark:] [Jesus in the country of the Gerasenes, east of the Lake of Galilee:] And those who had seen it [the drowning of the two thousand swine, which the unclean spirits had taken possession

of] told what had happened to the demoniac and to the swine.
And they began to beg Jesus to depart from their neighborhood [5:16–17; see Mt. 8:33–34].

He . . . came to his own country [Nazareth]. . . . And on
the sabbath he began to teach in the synagogue; and many
who heard him were astonished, saying, "Where did this man
get all this? . . . Is not this the carpenter, the son of Mary
and brother of James and Joses and Judas and Simon . . . ?"
And they took offense at him. And Jesus said to them, "A
prophet is not without honor, except in his own country, and
among his own kin, and in his own house." . . . And he marveled because of their unbelief [6:1–6; see Mt. 13:54–58].

[Matthew:] [Jairus' daughter:] And when Jesus came to the ruler's house,
and saw . . . the crowd making a tumult, he said, "Depart;
for the girl is not dead but sleeping." And they laughed at him
[9:23–24; see Mk. 5:38–40].

[Luke:] [The episodes of the herd of swine (8:36–37) and Jairus'
daughter (8:52–53) are as they appear in Mark and Matthew;
but Luke puts Jesus' arrival in Nazareth at the beginning of
his ministry, and gives a more detailed and rather different account of it:] And all spoke well of him [at first], and wondered at the gracious words which proceeded out of his
mouth; and they said, "Is not this Joseph's son?" And he said
to them, "Doubtless you will quote to me this proverb, 'Physician, heal yourself; what we have heard you did at Capernaum, do here also in your own country.' " And he said to
them, "Truly, I say to you, no prophet is acceptable in his
own country. . . ." [And Jesus drew various examples from
Scripture.] When they heard this, all in the synagogue were
filled with wrath. And they rose up and put him out of the
city, and led him to the brow of the hill . . . that they might
throw him down headlong. But passing through the midst of
them he went away [4:22–30].

From Galilee to Judea

For Jesus

[Mark:] And they were bringing children to him, that he might touch
them. . . . And he took them in his arms and blessed them,
laying his hands upon them [10:13, 16; see Mt. 19:13, 15; Lk.
18:15].

[At the Temple in Jerusalem, after the expulsion of the merchants:] And the chief priests and the scribes . . . feared him, because all the multitude was astonished at his teaching [11:18; see Mt. 21:14–15, below; Lk. 19:47–48, below].

And . . . Jesus taught in the Temple. . . . And the great throng heard him gladly [12:35, 37].

[Matthew:] [Arrival at Jerusalem:] Most of the crowd spread their garments on the road. . . . And the crowds that went before him and that followed him shouted, "Hosanna to the Son of David! . . ." And when he entered Jerusalem, all the city was stirred, saying, "Who is this?" And the crowds said, "This is the prophet Jesus from Nazareth of Galilee" [21:8–11; see Mk. 11:9–11; Lk. 19:36–38].

And the blind and the lame came to him in the temple, and he healed them. . . . the chief priests and the scribes saw the wonderful things that he did, and the children crying out in the temple, "Hosanna to the Son of David!" . . . [21:14–15; see Mk. 11:18, above; Lk. 19:47–48, below].

But when they [the chief priests and the Pharisees] tried to arrest him, they feared the multitudes, because they held him to be a prophet [21:46; see Mk. 12:12; Lk. 20:19].

Then the chief priests and the elders . . . took counsel together in order to arrest Jesus by stealth and kill him. But they said, "Not during the feast, lest there be a tumult among the people" [26:3–5; see Mk. 14:1–2; Lk. 22:2–6].

[Luke:] . . . a woman in the crowd raised her voice and said to him, "Blessed is the womb that bore you, and the breasts that you sucked!" [11:27 (and see 11:14)].

. . . so many thousands of the multitude had gathered together that they trod upon one another . . . [12:1].

[Cure of the infirm woman:] . . . all his adversaries were put to shame; and all the people rejoiced at all the glorious things that were done by him [13:17].

Now great multitudes accompanied him . . . [14:25].

Now the tax collectors and sinners were all drawing near to hear him [15:1].

[Near Jericho:] . . . and hearing a multitude going by, he [a blind man] inquired what this meant. . . . [Jesus cured him,] and all the people, when they saw it, gave praise to God [18:36, 43; see Mk. 10:46; Mt. 20:29, where there are two blind men].

And he [Zacchaeus] sought to see who Jesus was, but could not, on account of the crowd . . . [19:3].

The chief priests and the scribes and the principal men of the people sought to destroy him; but they did not find anything they could do, for all the people hung upon his words [19:47–48; see Mk. 11:18, above; Mt. 21:14–15, above].

And early in the morning all the people came to him in the temple to hear him [21:38].

And the chief priests and the scribes were seeking how to put him to death; for they feared the people. . . . [Judas] sought an opportunity to betray him to them in the absence of the multitude [22:2, 6].

Against Jesus

[Mark:]   [Nothing.]

[Matthew:] [Nothing.]

[Luke:]   [Cure of the mute:] But some of them said, "He casts out demons by Beelzebul, the prince of demons" [11:15; these words are attributed to the scribes in Mk. 3:22 and to the Pharisees in Mt. 12:24].

❁   ❁   ❁

The reading of these texts is of itself conclusive. They leave no doubt that by the evidence of the Gospels, a favorable reception of Jesus was the rule, a hostile reception the exception.

What in sum do the signs of hostility amount to, according to the Synoptics? A little sarcasm at Jairus' house, before the miracle? What does that mean? The living are ill prepared to see death defeated. The occurrence over the drowning of the swine has as little significance; the importance of the herd is enough to show that Jesus had ventured into a semipagan country. There remains only Nazareth: there, and there alone, the three Synoptics show us a Jewish crowd that was incredulous, according to Mark and Matthew, and stirred up against Jesus (though they "wondered" at him at first), according to Luke. But Nazareth was only one village among more than two hundred, and Jesus himself gives us the explanation for his reverse: "A prophet is not without honor, except in his own country"; however bitterly he took it to heart, the exception proved the rule.

For the evidence of the three evangelists is categorical: everywhere else, in Judea as in Galilee, the crowd was won over; they hurried after Jesus, to the shore of the lake before the boat carrying him, in

the city and the village before the house he entered, in the house itself, in the country on the road he walked along; they "hung upon his
words" (Lk. 19:48), eager to see him, touch him, follow him, to the
point of staying with him three days in some remote place, three
days without eating.

Such is the "callousness" of the Jewish people; such are their "insults."

Independent exegetes have professed some skepticism about this
popular enthusiasm, it is true. Charles Guignebert is convinced that
the evangelists exaggerated: "Perhaps—and at the very outside—
[Jesus] attracted a few hundred simple Galileans." "In any case, if
such a movement did take shape at the beginning, it surely did not
last." [9] It is in fact possible, not sure, that there is a measure of exaggeration in the Gospel accounts. But it seems an even greater exaggeration to conclude from one contradictory text—the curse cast at
three Galilean cities (a passage we will study later)—that the whole
Galilean ministry failed, and to throw out as null and void the imposing body of texts just cited, which attest to the popular sympathy
Jesus won in Galilee as well as in Judea. Will it be said that this was
a superficial enthusiasm, due to the miracles more than to the Word?
Naturally this *is* said, by Max Meinertz among the Germans and Fathers Denys Buzy and Jules Lebreton among the French.[10] I truly do
not know whether the Jewish people—that wretched people so much
and so often run down—were more influenced by miraculous cures
than others (is Lourdes in Judea?). But what I know, by means of the
Gospel texts—and we can judge only by them—is that Jesus' teaching made no less strong an impression on them than his miracles:
". . . for all the people hung upon his words."

The miracles no less than the Word gave evidence of God, of God's
grace, in the eyes of the disciples as in the eyes of the crowd:

. . . the whole multitude of the disciples began to rejoice and praise God
with a loud voice for all the mighty works that they had seen. . . .

Lk. 19:37

[9] Charles Guignebert, *Le Christianisme antique* [Early Christianity], Paris,
Albin Michel, 1921 [repub. 1948], p. 57; idem, *Jésus*, Paris, Albin Michel, 1938,
p. 255. [See the former, in English, as idem, *Christianity, Past and Present*, New
York, Macmillan, 1927.—Tr.]
[10] See Max Meinertz, *Die Gleichnisse Jesu* [The Parables of Jesus], "Biblische
Zeitfragen" series, VIII, Münster, Aschendorffsche Berlh., 1916, p. 86; Father
Denys Buzy, *Introduction aux paraboles évangéliques* [Introduction to the Gospel
Parables], Paris, Gabalda, 1932, p. 350; Lebreton and Zeiller, *op. cit.*, p. 305.

So do not hold it against that crowd for having been captivated by the miracles no less than by the Word; or if you do, admit your bias.

As to how deeply the good seed was planted, how can we discern this? Relying like Guignebert on the curse hurled at the three Galilean towns, Maurice Goguel states that "If Jesus' hearers were impressed by his words, they were so . . . only superficially." [11] In his study "Primitive Christianity," he goes farther: "From the outset . . . there was the germ of a misunderstanding between Jesus and the crowd that degenerated into hostility or indifference as soon as the period of troubles began." [12]

On the religious plane and as far as founding is concerned, numbers matter less than individuals. What new religion has ever been seen to begin with a conversion of the masses? Twelve disciples, twelve strong hearts captured—even if one was to fail and betray—along with a cluster of feminine admirers: it was enough to erect, on the firm foundation of Jewish holiness, the high cathedral of the Christian future. In that future, in that future only, would the conversion of the masses be inscribed, whether Israelite or Gentile. For the present, I mean the time of Jesus' preaching, the Jewish crowd was doubtless what a crowd is generally, in all places, in all times: impressionable, fickle, restless, changeable, quick to form an attachment, quick to dissolve it.

Did they lose interest at a given moment? Did they turn away from Jesus? (I do not say: did Jesus turn away from them?—the question is other.) This hypothesis is maintained by some scholars, and it will be discussed later. A more urgent problem arises first.

✿   ✿   ✿

For we have not finished our scrutiny of the Gospels. Up to this point we have quoted only from the Synoptics; and it seems to us—mistakenly, perhaps—that if there were only these, we would have won our case easily. But there is the fourth Gospel, according to Saint John: this is the fortress where the theologians entrench themselves, the "stumbling block," they would say, which a bold thesis must trip over and break on.

The trial seems to be over, the sentence pronounced before we get beyond the Prologue:

[11] Goguel, *La Vie de Jésus-Christ*, p. 318.
[12] Maurice Goguel, "Christianisme primitif," in Raoul Gorce and Maxime Mortier, eds., *Histoire générale des religions*, Paris, Quillet, 1945, II, 186.

He came unto his own, and his own received him not.

Jn. 1:11 [CCD]

—at least if one falls in with the traditional interpretation, that "his own" means "the Jews."

The Greek text can be interpreted in a far more general sense, as Father Lagrange recognizes: "In fact, nothing points to the Jews in particular. Having created the world, the Word was at home in it and men belonged to him." [13] The opinion that "his own" means "men in general" thus has serious supporters. Furthermore, the discrepancy between the Synoptics and John is only apparent. It is quite true that the unbelief of Israel taken "as a whole" is dogma for Saint John, but it is only that—dogma, an article of faith, a spiritual tenet. Under this theological cloak, it is still possible—if one wants to take the trouble —to discern the historic reality; and this, in the final analysis, is found to be exactly the same as in the three other Gospels: namely, violent antagonism from one clique, more or less declared sympathies from the masses. Father Lagrange acknowledges this, with his customary honesty: "It is the crowd, [in Saint John] as in the Synoptics, that is disposed to acclaim Jesus, and the leaders who are opposed to him." [14]

How can these two contradictory aspects—the theological and the historical—coexist in the same text? But short of knowing nothing about this text, how could this surprise us? [15] The work of a gifted and discerning architect, a scholarly edifice with calculated reverberations and mysterious interweavings, the Johannine Gospel is a sacred labyrinth where not everyone who wishes can penetrate, can find his way. Its wording in particular, with regard to the Jews, the Jewish people, introduces intentional peculiarities of such a nature that, if they are not understood or are understood wrong, the meaning of the text is completely distorted, not to say undecipherable. This is a delicate and serious problem, which regrettably too many commentators, and among them the most expert, pass over too

[13] Father Marie-Joseph Lagrange, O.P., ed. and tr., *Évangile selon saint Jean*, Paris, Gabalda, 1924, p. 13.
[14] *Ibid.*, p. cli.
[15] "This Gospel is a work apart," writes Father Th. Calmes. "Gospel history comes to view in it through the development of dogma" (quoted in Father A. Brassac, *Nouveau Testament*, vol. III of Fathers Fulcran G. Vigouroux and A. Brassac, *Manuel biblique, ou Cours d'Écriture sainte à l'usage des séminaires*, ed. Fathers A. Brassac and Louis Bacuez, 4 vols., 12th ed., Paris, Roger et Chernoviz, 1906–1909, p. 183).

quickly.[16] From our point of view, clearly defined in the 1948 Preface of the present work, it is worth the effort to dwell on it lengthily, to emphasize it heavily. In this regard, the observations that follow have major importance.

First observation: Unlike the three other (canonical) evangelists, Saint John, as much a Jew as Jesus, as all Jesus' disciples, all Christ's Apostles, speaks of the Jews rather as if he were speaking of an alien people, alien to Jesus and his disciples, alien to John himself, so much so that this stylistic peculiarity has sometimes been used as an argument to demonstrate that the author of the fourth Gospel could not have been a Jew, and hence could not have been the Jew John.

Nothing strikes the reader more forcefully the moment he goes from the Synoptics to the fourth Gospel. While Mark writes in 14:1,

It was now two days before the Passover . . .

and Luke writes in 22:1,

Now the feast of Unleavened Bread drew near, which is called the Passover,

John writes:

The Passover of the Jews was at hand . . . [2:13].
After this there was a feast of the Jews . . . [5:1].
Now the Passover, the feast of the Jews, was at hand [6:4].
Now the Jews' feast of Tabernacles was at hand [7:2],

and so forth.

The reader is surprised. Curiously enough, in most cases the commentators do not appear to be. With his usual exactness, Father Lagrange notes that the word *Jews* occurs five times each in Matthew and Luke, six times in Mark, and seventy-one times in John. Yet we must get to page 65 of Father Lagrange's commentary to find the following explanation, with reference to Origen, in a footnote: "John adds 'of the Jews' [to "Passover"] because he is writing for Gentiles, but also because he is aware of belonging to a religious group which is not that of the Jews." [17]

---

[16] [In his book *The Jews and the Gospel* (London, Bloomsbury, 1961), Father Gregory Baum makes an extensive study of the problem (pp. 98–131). His thought is elucidated more clearly, however, in his revised edition of the book, issued in paperback under the title *Is the New Testament Anti-Semitic?* (Glen Rock, N. J., Paulist Press, 1965, pp. 172–178).—Ed.]

[17] Lagrange, *op. cit.*, p. 65, n.

Neither of these reasons seems convincing to me.

And indeed Father Lagrange himself, in his commentary on the third Gospel, concludes: "It becomes quite clear that Luke wrote his Gospel for Gentiles. This was also the opinion of the ancients, led by Origen and Jerome." [18] Now, we have just seen that there is nothing in Luke resembling what we see in John. And how much more justified would such a stylistic peculiarity be on the part of Luke, who was not Jewish but Greek!

And yet John "is aware," we are told, "of belonging to a religious group which is not that of the Jews"—as if the term *Jew*, at the very time we are considering, had a uniquely religious meaning. We need only reread Saint Paul to prove this to ourselves:

There is no distinction made here between Jew and Gentile ["who have become Christians" being understood]; all alike have one Lord. . . .

Rom. 10:12 [RK]

Is the chronological gap between Saint Paul and Saint John so great? They were contemporaries, members of the same generation, if their works were not. In the time when tradition has it that John, having reached an extreme old age, drafted his Gospel, say at the very end of the first century, the Christian communities still included a number of Jews, among them John, son of Zebedee, to begin with. And John was not the only one. The bishop of Jerusalem, successor to James, the "brother of the Lord," was the Jew Simeon,[19] also related to Christ.

So we must seek another explanation. I am inclined to find it in a second observation—this one fundamental—which discloses the evangelist's real intention: actually to treat the Jewish people as aliens, and even more as an enemy, to mark their name with a sort of brand, doubtless with a view to burning his bridges behind him and to moving the Christian secession wholly beyond recall. The procedure used is this:

In the fourth Gospel, the term "the Jews" serves indiscriminately to designate sometimes the Jewish people as a whole, sometimes the inhabitants of Judea, and sometimes—and most often—the clique of Jesus' enemies, those the Synoptics designate with the formula "the

[18] *Idem,* ed. and tr., *Évangile selon saint Luc,* Paris, Gabalda, 1921, p. cli.
[19] Martyred under Trajan (Msgr. Louis Duchesne, *Histoire ancienne de l'Église,* 3 vols., 5th ed., Paris, Fontemoing, 1911, I, 120).

chief priests, the scribes, and the Pharisees." "The Jews" thus inevitably takes on *a pejorative meaning*.[20]

The commentators have been forced to acknowledge this. But on the main they do so in passing, without attaching or seeming to attach the slightest importance to it. For Father Lagrange,

What is peculiar to John is that he gives the name of "the Jews" particularly to those who led the attacks against Jesus, that is, to the leaders of the nation, by which he means above all the chief priests and the Pharisees. . . . It is rather natural for this nuance of the word to have been suggested to him by the attitude taken by the leaders of the nation toward Jesus . . . : the religious and political leaders, responsible for the practice of the cult and zealous about the Law, were perfectly qualified to represent the people and could be vested with their name.[21]

André Charue, a Belgian theologian, writes, "On the whole, the Jews in the fourth Gospel become the models and agents of the opposition encountered by the incarnate Word: confronting Christ the Light, they incarnate the darkness of error and sin. And this should not astonish us. . . ."[22]

"This should not astonish us." I indeed understand that "this" does not astonish theologians. But shall we now, with the texts before us, judge what a typical example of "this" leads to, what is simultaneously singular and effective about John's stylistic procedure, and what worth there is in the more or less awkward justifications given by some of the authors cited?

The Jews were looking for him [Jesus] at the feast, and saying, "Where is he?" And there was much muttering about him among the people. While

[20] [After the year 70, the relationship between Christians and Jews deteriorated, and the Christian tendency was to minimize the Romans' responsibility while emphasizing that of the Jews. This may have played a part in the final writing of the Gospels, as Marcel Simon points out in his *Verus Israël* (The True Israel), rev. ed., Paris, Boccard, 1964, p. 147.—Ed.]

[21] Lagrange, . . . *Jean*, p. cxxxii. I reserve the question of how well "the religious and political leaders . . . were perfectly qualified to represent the Jewish people." We will have occasion to return to this apropos Jesus' trial and sentencing to death.

[22] Father André Charue [now Bishop of Namur], *L'Incrédulité des Juifs dans le Nouveau Testament* [The Unbelief of the Jews in the New Testament], Louvain, Gembloux, 1929, p. 224. For other, similarly minimizing comments, see Alexandre Westphal, *Dictionnaire encyclopédique de la Bible* [Encyclopedic Dictionary of the Bible], Paris, Je Sers, 1932–1934, I, 596; Father Louis Bouyer, *Le quatrième Évangile* [The Fourth Gospel], Paris, Je Sers, 1938 [repub. 1955], pp. 147–148; Frédéric Godet, *Commentaire sur l'Évangile de Jean* [Commentary on the Gospel of John], Paris, Fischbacher, 1876, II, 137; Louis-Claude Fillion, *Vie de Notre Seigneur Jésus-Christ*, 22nd ed., Paris, Letouzey, 1929, II, 441; Father Jules Lebreton, S.J., *La Vie et l'enseignement de Jésus-Christ*, 2 vols., Paris, Beauchesne, 1931, I, 382, and II, 138; and Grandmaison, *op. cit.*, I, 170, n. 2.

some said, "He is a good man," others said, "No, he is leading the people astray." Yet for fear of the Jews no one spoke openly of him.

Jn. 7:11–13

A fine text, though it hasn't received any particular attention from commentators. What does it tell us? That opinion on Jesus was very divided in Jerusalem; that he was accused (evidently in educated circles) of "leading the people astray"—and thus that he had popular sympathy; and that in talking about him people "muttered," they did not dare raise their voices, for fear of his powerful enemies.

But disregard for a moment everything that has just been said, and especially the second observation stressed above. Reread the passage rapidly. What is the dominant note? The relentless enmity of "the Jews" against Jesus. What unalerted reader would think of distinguishing among them? Who would get the idea of inserting the implied "Jews" in the phrasing—"the [Jewish] people," and farther on, "some [of the Jews]," "no one [among the Jews]"?

The Jews were looking for him [Jesus] at the feast, and saying, "Where is he?" And there was much muttering about him among the [Jewish] people. While some [of the Jews] said, "He is a good man," others [of the Jews] said, "No, he is leading the [Jewish] people astray." Yet for fear of the Jews no one [among the Jews] spoke openly of him.

An incoherent and absurd text to anyone who has not been informed in advance of the limited, special, and pejorative meaning that the evangelist has the habit of giving the word *Jews*. How do the following analogous formulas strike us?—"Yet for fear of the Athenians" or "the Greeks no one [among the Athenians] spoke openly of Socrates"; or again, "Yet for fear of the French" or "the Catholics no one [among the Parisians or French] spoke openly of Joan of Arc."

Father de Grandmaison and Father Lagrange consider that the use of the word *Jews* in this special sense is "quite natural," according to one, and "rather natural," according to the other; perfectly explainable, they both assure us.

I readily agree: explainable, but in a completely different way; explainable, but on one condition and one only: explainable, if it was *intentional*. [23]

[23] Father Th. Calmes acknowledges that the fourth Gospel "is the most anti-Judaic book of the New Testament" (Calmes, ed. and tr., *Évangile selon saint Jean* [Gospel According to Saint John], Paris, Lecoffre, 1904, p. 60), and Goguel that "Anti-Jewish polemics and above all apologetics are among the major preoccupations" of the evangelist (*Introduction au Nouveau Testament* [Introduction to the New Testament], Paris, Leroux, 1923, II, 541). This is quite obvious. We could multiply comparable quotations.

116 JESUS AND HIS PEOPLE

o   o   o

But what a polemical find, and how far-reaching!

Given that it is nearly impossible for the reader of the fourth Gospel to distinguish between "Jews" and "Jews," between the "Jews" who were Jesus' relentless enemies and the rest, it is likewise nearly impossible for him to read this Gospel, unless he is forewarned against such a stylistic procedure, without feeling an overwhelming aversion to the Jewish people in toto, considered, in Father de Grandmaison's phrase, in "their leaders and . . . as a whole." [24]

And this was why the Jews persecuted Jesus . . . [5:16].

Jesus said to them, "I am the bread of life. . . ." The Jews then murmured at him . . . [6:35, 41].

Jesus then [spoke] to the Jews who had believed in him. . . . They answered him, "Abraham is our father." ". . . we have one Father, even God." Jesus said to them, ". . . You are of your father the devil . . ." [8:31, 39, 41–42, 44].

The Jews said to him, "Now we know that you have a demon. . . ." So they took up stones to throw at him . . . [8:52, 59].

The Jews took up stones again to stone him [10:31].

. . . the Jews sought all the more to kill him . . . [5:18; see also 7:1; 8:40; etc.].

What Christian heart would not be revolted by this infernal hatred! It will be, and all the more because the commentators on John and the multitude of Christian writers following in their wake century after century have been only too happy to take the sacred precedent as authorization and generalize according to the example it sets, and, disregarding all the evangelic and apostolic texts—even Saint John's—that say the contrary, have found it proper to beat down "the Jews" indiscriminately.

Shall we take a few examples from the thousands available? We will select them exclusively from our own time, from the last hundred years, though from Saint John to these the chain is continuous—infer the countless voices of more than fifty generations of Christians.

John Nelson Darby, English theologian and founder of the Plymouth Brethren sect: "The blindness of the Jews and their religious pride were as great as their hatred of the true God. . . . The diabolic character of the Jews [contrasts with] Jesus' divine character." [25]

[24] Grandmaison, op. cit., I, 63.
[25] Darby, op. cit., pp. 112, 123.

Ernest Renan: "The exquisite derision, the clever provocations [of Jesus] always strike home. Eternal stigmata, they have stayed congealed in the wound. That Nessus' cloak [26] of ridicule which the Jew, the son of the Pharisees, has dragged after him in tatters for eighteen centuries was woven by Jesus with divine craft." [27]

Dom Guéranger: "We envy the destiny of these few devoted families who welcome [Jesus] into their homes, exposing themselves by this courageous hospitality to all the rage of the Jews [as if "these few devoted families" were not also Jewish]. . . . We see it, the fury of the Jews is at its peak. . . . Having slaked their rage, [the Jews] will sleep without remorse until the terrible awakening prepared for them. . . . The fury of the Jews against Jesus was already conspiring his death." [28]

Father Lebreton: "Christ warns the Apostles: if they are not better than the Jews [at least this should be, "better than other Jews"], they will be rejected like them. . . . The Jews take umbrage [at Jesus]. . . . The Jews cry "Blasphemy!" and gather stones [to hurl at him]. . . . The Jews pursue their prey hotly. . . . There are of course many friends of Jesus' in the crowd [at the foot of the cross], but they are stricken by the catastrophe and terrified by the Jews." [29]

Louis-Claude Fillion: "Alas! Despite the admirable aggregate of his human virtues and his divine attributes, the Jews, for whom he had become incarnate and been born primarily as a member of their own race, not only scorned and rejected him but cruelly delivered him up to Pontius Pilate so that he would have him die on the cross." [30]

Father André Charue: "Judas, the instrument of Satan and the Jews. . . ." [31]

[26] [A cloak, stained with the poisoned blood of the centaur Nessus, which adhered to Heracles' skin and ate into it, finally killing him in agony.—Tr.]

[27] Ernest Renan, Vie de Jésus, 4th ed., Paris, Michel-Lévy, 1863, p. 224.

[28] Dom Prosper Guéranger, O.S.B., La Passion et la Semaine sainte [The Passion and Holy Week], vol. III of L'Année liturgique, 24th ed., Tours, Mame, 1921, pp. 23, 123, 149.

[29] Lebreton, op. cit., I, 392; II, 34, 35, 44, 425. [In similar terms, an American commentator, Father Pius Parsch, writes: "In the Introit [for Passion Sunday], the Lord is struggling as on the Mount of Olives; he begs for a judicial decision between himself and the unholy Jewish people . . ."; and again, in a commentary for Monday of Passion Week, "The heathen Ninevites did penance upon the preaching of Jesus; the Jews remained hard of heart, even to the point of seeking to kill God's messenger" (The Church's Year of Grace, 5 vols., Collegeville, Minn., Liturgical Press, 1953–1959; quoted in M. E. Yarnitzky, review, Sidic [Rome], October–November, 1967, p. 29).—Ed.]

[30] Louis-Claude Fillion, Histoire d'Israël [History of Israel], Paris, Letouzey, 1927, III, 442.

[31] Charue, op. cit., p. 256.

Father Gaston Fessard: "The Jews rejected Christ in order to save their country." [32]

In Jules Lebreton and Jacques Zeiller's *The Primitive Church*, a work presented as inspired by "scholarly concerns," the account of Jesus' preaching in Jerusalem is based on Saint John, with no indication to the reader of the restrictive meaning in which the use of the term *Jews* must be understood. Like Dom Guéranger, the authors, writing of the Jewish women Martha and Mary, adjudge it quite natural to write: "They know that [Jesus] has retired to Perea to evade the plots of the Jews." [33]

Even Goguel, in several of his works, does not abstain from such censure: "The third part of [Mark's] Gospel . . . ends at the time when the Jews are preparing to form a conspiracy against [Jesus]." Likewise, in another book, he writes: "On each of his returns to Galilee, a conflict arises between him and the Jews." [34]

Dr. Franz Michel Willam: "This colloquy . . . led the Jews to resolve to have Jesus killed." [35]

Giovanni Papini: "Satan whispered to Judas: 'Just think, by delivering Christ to the Jews, you will avenge not only yourself. . . .'" [36]

François Mauriac: "'This is a hard saying,' grumbled the Jews; 'who can listen to it?' [Jn. 6:60] . . . The Jews jeered at this witness that [Jesus] gave of himself. . . . 'Master, the Jews want to stone you. . . .'" [37] Who, reading Mauriac, would conceive of the notion that the disciples themselves were Jews and that so was the Master they were speaking to? On the other hand, when the author speaks of the crowd who flocked around Jesus, who "hung upon his words" (Lk. 19:48), that crowd seems oddly unidentified: nothing indicates to the reader that they too are Jewish. (A man of heart, François Mauriac is distressed today, after Auschwitz, at the persistent virulence of anti-

---

[32] Father Gaston Fessard, S.J., *Pax Nostra*, 8th ed., Paris, Grasset, 1936, p. 207.

[33] Lebreton and Zeiller, *op. cit.*, p. 106.

[34] Maurice Goguel, *Jésus de Nazareth, mythe ou histoire?*, Paris, Leroux, 1925, p. 242; *idem, Les Sources* . . . , pp. 10 *et seq.* [See the former, in English, as *idem, Jesus the Nazarene, Myth or History?*, tr. Frederick Stephens, New York, Appleton, 1926.—Tr.]

[35] François-Michel Willam, *Vie de Jésus-Christ* [Life of Jesus Christ], tr. Gautier, Paris, Salvator, 1935, p. 175.

[36] Giovanni Papini, *Les Témoins de la Passion* [The Witnesses of the Passion], tr., Paris, Grasset, 1938, p. 30.

[37] François Mauriac, *Vie de Jésus*, Paris, Flammarion, 1936 [repub. 1958], pp. 54, 165, 204, and *passim*. [See, in English, as *idem, Life of Jesus*, tr. Julie Kernan, New York, Longmans, Green, 1937.—Tr.]

Semitism; how could he have failed to see that with such a book, he himself was sowing it broadcast!)

Daniel-Rops: "The Hatred of the Jews" (against Jesus) is a heading, followed by: "More serious yet than this dogmatically based difference was the hatred-charged violence that Jesus' universalism evoked in the heart of the Jews. . . . This hatred of the Jews seems providential, the instrument of a divine intention that they could not understand, that of the Redemption itself." [38]

Catechism for the Use of French Dioceses: "The evening of the Resurrection, . . . the Apostles were shut up in a room; they had carefully closed the doors for fear of the Jews." (Based on Jn. 20:19; but nowhere is it stated explicitly that these Apostles and their divine Master were themselves Jews.) [39]

Here is how history—sacred history—is written, and how it has been taught to the Christian people from century to century, from generation to generation, yesterday and today, and alas, how it will doubtlessly be taught tomorrow. I leave it to you to estimate what feelings are consequently instilled in receptive souls, what ravages are perpetrated, often by those who called themselves ministers of God.[40]

[38] Henry Daniel-Rops, *Histoire sainte: Jésus en son temps,* Paris, Fayard, 1945, pp. 352, 355, 357. [See, in English, as *idem, Jesus in His Time,* tr. Ruby W. Millar, rev. ed., New York, Dutton, 1956. This translation, fortunately, reflects many of the revisions in the later editions discussed on pp. 260–261, n. 70, below.—Tr.]

[39] Canons Quinet and Boyer, eds., *Catéchisme à l'usage des diocèses de France* [Catechism for the Use of French Dioceses], version pub. for the Diocese of Bourges, imprimatur Cardinal Verdier, Tours, Mame, 1939 [repub. 1965], pp. 17, 182. [A new edition of this work was brought out in 1967 by the same publishing house under the title *Le Catéchisme national français* (The French National Catechism). As the version for the Diocese of Bourges shows, the comments on John 20:19 which Professor Isaac quotes have been deleted, as have other derogatory expressions regarding the Jews. The revision was carried out by the Paris office of S.I.D.I.C., Service international de documentation judéo-chrétienne (International Judeo-Christian Documentation Service). Archbishop Louis Ferrand, of Tours, went in person to submit the galleys to Rabbi Jacob Kaplan, Chief Rabbi of France.

[It was too late for Professor Isaac to rejoice over the corrections made in this standard catechetical text. Yet it remains distressing that until the year 1967 French children and young people were exposed to the kind of slanted presentation which the author has just quoted.—Ed.]

[40] [A recent example: "The people were pleased with His [Jesus'] heavenly teachings. . . . This made the Jews very jealous and envious. . . . The Jews got one of the Apostles. . . ." The author then poses these questions, "To answer": "1. Why did the people love Jesus? 2. Why did the Jews hate Him?" (Msgr. Rudolph G. Bandas, "Lesson 20: Christ Suffered and Died for Us," installment of "New Catechism Series," *The Wanderer* [St. Paul, Minn.], February 29, 1968, p. 41).—Ed.]

Since the time the Gospels were written, centuries, millennia have passed. The Jewish people are no longer the adversary; they are the victim, lying battered by the side of the road, waiting for the good Samaritan to go by. And perhaps today the Christian future calls for greater gentleness, a more strenuous effort of brotherhood, or better: of purification.

In addition, is it not evident that the stylistic practice in the fourth Gospel, systematically used and imitated, ends by completely distorting historic perspective? And anyone who enters the domain of history—including sacred history, and including the theologian (and theology necessarily starts with history)—is bound to obedience to the imperative law of probity, it too being holy.

❉   ❉   ❉

Now apprised of the difficulties that await us but armed with an Ariadne's thread, let us make bold to enter the Johannine labyrinth.

Providing we do not go astray following the tracks of those who, while called "the Jews," are yet not the Jews, that is, the whole of the Jewish people, but are only "some Jews," "certain Jews," a certain Jewish clique;

with this proviso, but this proviso only,

the classifying of the passages for and against Jesus becomes possible also in the fourth Gospel as in the Synoptics.

For Jesus

Now when he was in Jerusalem at the Passover feast, many believed in his name when they saw the signs which he did [2:23. And the evangelist adds: ". . . but Jesus did not trust himself to them . . . ; for he himself knew what was in man" (2:24); thus it is human nature that is in question here, not the Jewish character].

So when the people saw that Jesus was not there, . . . they themselves got into the boats and went to Capernaum, seeking Jesus [6:24. Later, in the synagogue at Capernaum, a lively discussion ensued between Jesus and "the Jews," but it is permissible to believe that those who asked him, "Then what sign do you do, that we may see, and believe you? . . ." (6:30), were not the five thousand who had just been fed by the miracle of the loaves, and who themselves had said, "This is indeed the prophet who is to come into the world!" (6:14)].

Yet many of the people believed him [Jesus]; they said, "When the Christ appears, will he do more signs than this man has done?" [7:31].

When they heard these words, some of the people said, "This is really the prophet." Others said, "This is the Christ." . . . [Here, however, the opinion of the crowd seems unsettled:] So there was a division among the people over him [7:40–41, 43].

The officers then went back to the chief priests and Pharisees, who said to them, "Why did you not bring him? . . . Are you led astray, you also? Have any of the authorities or of the Pharisees believed in him? But this crowd, who do not know the law, are accursed" [7:45, 47–49; further proof that the mass of the people are for Jesus].

[There is a violent altercation with "the Jews," ending in an attempt to stone Jesus (8:12–59); and yet:] As he spoke thus, many believed in him [8:30].

[After the resurrection of Lazarus:] Many of the Jews therefore, who . . . had seen what he did, believed in him. . . . the chief priests and the Pharisees gathered the council, and said, ". . . If we let him go on thus, every one will believe in him, and the Romans will come and destroy both our holy place and our nation" [11:45, 47–48].

[Some days before the Passion:] When the great crowd of the Jews [41] learned that he was there [at Bethany], they came, not only on account of Jesus but also to see Lazarus. . . . So the chief priests planned to put Lazarus also to death, because on account of him many of the Jews were . . . believing in Jesus [12:9–11].

[Jesus' arrival at Jerusalem:] The Pharisees then said to one another, "You see that you can do nothing; look, the world has gone after him" [12:19].[42]

These Jewish sympathies, largely from the people, must have been real and obvious for Saint John himself to have been forced to mention them, despite his doctrinal bias, reaffirmed in this same chapter 12, at verses 37–40:

Though he had done so many signs before them, yet they did not believe in him; it was that the word spoken by the prophet Isaiah might be fulfilled:
"Lord, who has believed our report . . . ?"
Therefore they could not believe. For Isaiah again said,
"He has blinded their eyes and hardened their heart. . . ."

And immediately after this, we read in verse 42:

Nevertheless many even of the authorities believed in him. . . .

[41] Note here, as in 11:45, that the term *Jews* does not designate Jesus' adversaries. "It seems," says Father Lagrange, "that John wanted to designate simply the natives, as distinct from the pilgrims" (. . . *Jean*, p. 324).
[42] [See also Jn. 3:26; 4:39–41; 6:1–2, 10–13, 15; 7:12; 8:2; and 10:40–42, quoted in the French but omitted from this edition.—Ed.]

Against Jesus

He came unto his own, and his own received him not. [This is an assertion of the same order as "the darkness grasped it not" and "the world knew him not" (1:5, 10)—a doctrinal thesis; that we should not take its meaning otherwise is indicated by the very next words:] But to as many as received him he gave the power of becoming sons of God . . . [1:11–12 (CCD)].

[Altercation in the synagogue at Capernaum:] The Jews then murmured at him. . . . They said, "Is not this Jesus, the son of Joseph, whose father and mother we know? . . ." [6:41–42. Compare this text with those in the Synoptics that relate to Nazareth; "The Jews" here are several of those present who knew Jesus and his family personally. Farther on John comments:] After this many of his disciples drew back and no longer went about with him [6:66].

After this Jesus . . . would not go about in Judea, because the Jews sought to kill him. . . . Yet for fear of the Jews no one spoke openly of him [7:1, 13; the context here, as in the similar passage in 5:16–18, shows clearly that "the Jews" in question are the religious authorities, not the people].

[Violent debate in the Temple; Jesus reproaches "the Jews" for their unbelief and declares they are children of the devil (8:21–51); then:] The Jews said to him, "Now we know that you have a demon." . . . So they took up stones to throw at him . . . [8:52, 59; the context shows us that "the Jews" here are Pharisees, as likewise in 9:18–23].

[After Jesus' triumphal arrival at Jerusalem:] The crowd answered him, "We have heard from the law that the Christ remains for ever. How can you say that the Son of man must be lifted up? Who is this Son of man?" . . . Though he had done so many signs before them, yet they did not believe in him . . . [12:34, 37; see again the comments on Jn. 12, above. After the ovations previously described, it would be hard to understand this attitude from "the crowd" were verses 34 and 37 not considered as intended to introduce verses 38–40, where the doctrinal theme of Israel's unbelief is expressed once again].[43]

In the final analysis, which of all these assaults unleashed against Jesus by "the Jews" should we retain because they can legitimately be laid to the account of the Jewish people taken "as a whole"? Hardly more than in the Synoptics. In Galilee, the scene at the synagogue in Capernaum, which the Synoptics place in Nazareth. In Judea, at Jerusalem, where Jesus' adversaries—chief priests, scribes, and Phari-

[43] [See also Jn. 5:16–18; 7:20, 40–44; and 10:24–39. About the last-cited, the author observes, "The context does not say so, but the nature of the controversy indicates that this time, too, 'the Jews' are Pharisees" (Jules Isaac, *Jésus et Israël*, rev. ed., Paris, Fasquelle, 1959, p. 204).—Ed.]

sees (persistently cast in the role of "the Jews")—are relentless and powerful, the crowd appears sometimes divided in opinion, sometimes and most often in favor of Jesus (Jn. 3:26; 7:12, 31, 49; 11:48; 12:19). Historic reality, stronger than the strongest doctrinal considerations, compelled John's recognition, as it did Mark's, Matthew's, and Luke's. The evidence is before us.

❖   ❖   ❖

Thus do the texts speak. But every historian knows that there is more than one way to make them speak, the most advantageous in certain regards being to refer to them or paraphrase them, without quoting them.

If we believe some scholars, the Jewish people, from the time of the Galilean ministry onward, supposedly turned away from Jesus, and Jesus turned away from them. Edmond Stapfer asserts this in his customarily peremptory fashion:

> There is a moment in the ministry of Jesus Christ, a turning point . . . , which marks the approximate midpoint of his public life, and which is indicated in the four Gospels (Matthew 16, Mark 8, Luke 9, John 6). This is the moment when the people abandon Jesus Christ, and when he loses the popularity he has enjoyed until that time. It is . . . the year 29. . . . The disappointed crowd abandons Jesus forever. . . . The inevitable rupture has come to pass.[44]

We find the same or similar theses, formulated in more or less varying terms, among a great number of writers, Catholic and Protestant.

Alexandre Westphal: "This time the people understand. . . . They are scandalized, they move away."[45]

Maurice Goguel: "Henceforth the fate of Jesus' public ministry is sealed; the failure is total and irremediable. Jesus resigns himself to it, as it were, and gives up all public teaching aimed at winning the crowd."[46]

Father Lebreton: "The people, many of whom have been touched only superficially, are shaken . . . , disconcerted. From now on Jesus . . . will speak in parables. . . ."[47]

---

[44] Edmond Stapfer, *Jésus-Christ pendant son ministère*, vol. II of *Jésus-Christ, sa personne, son autorité, son oeuvre*, Paris, Fischbacher, 1897, pp. xxxii, 254.
[45] Alexandre Westphal, *Jéhovah*, Montauban, by the au., 1924, p. 483.
[46] Goguel, *Jésus de Nazareth* . . . , p. 242.
[47] Lebreton, *op. cit.*, I, 106.

Louis-Claude Fillion: "The divine Master does not adopt this practice [recourse to parables] until he has been morally compelled to do so by an increase of hostility on the part of his enemies and a nascent indifference on the part of the crowds." [48]

Albert Dufourcq: "The great crisis when Jesus broke with the people, in refusing the crown and rejecting revolt, simply brought on an irreparable eruption of the misunderstanding that had grown slowly perhaps from the earliest days. . . . [And soon] popular hostility—patriotic in Galilee, legalistic in Judea and at Jerusalem—redoubled." [49]

In itself, there is nothing improbable in this conjecture, but the statement—and so much conviction in the statement, and so much chronological exactness—troubles me. In vain do I reread the Gospels; nowhere do I perceive that "great crisis when Jesus broke with the people," or "the moment when the people abandon Jesus Christ." Now, according to the authors quoted, this is more than a conjecture; it is an "event," [50] a major event, for which Edmond Stapfer does not hesitate to give a date, and which he declares is fixed by the agreement of the four Gospels: Matthew 16, Mark 8, Luke 9, and John 6. This is most impressive. Let us then turn to the four chapters in the Gospels that are given as references.

What does Mark 8 contain? The second miracle of the loaves, which ends in a separation, not a rupture; the refusal to bring down a sign from heaven, but this refusal is addressed to the Pharisees alone (hadn't Jesus just given "a sign" to the people with the multiplication of the loaves?); the crossing of the lake, when the disciples, not the crowd, show lack of understanding; the conversation on the road to Caesarea Philippi, Jesus teaching the disciples that he will be "rejected by the elders and the chief priests and the scribes" (8:31), and saying not a word about the people, verses 27–28 evidencing his prestige among the masses of the people: " 'Who do men say that I am?' And they told him, 'John the Baptist; and others say, Elijah; and others one of the prophets' "; an address by Jesus to the crowd: "If any man would come after me, let him deny himself . . ." (8:34). But however exacting the demands expressed, however discouraging for those who remain attached to temporal goods (the Jews only?), noth-

---

[48] Fillion, Vie de Notre Seigneur Jésus-Christ, II, 602.

[49] Albert Dufourcq, Histoire ancienne de l'Église [Ancient History of the Church], Paris, Plon, 1929, II, 291, 303.

[50] ". . . this event followed the multiplication of loaves . . ." (Stapfer, op. cit., p. xxxii).

ing allows us to consider these words as signifying a rupture between Jesus and his people. From beginning to end of the chapter cited, there is no indication, absolutely none, that "the people abandon Jesus Christ." The reference to Mark 8 is not valid.

Father André Charue recognizes this: "Going by Mark, we cannot infer a growing unbelief among the people."[51] However, Goguel, whose reasoning is always extremely fine-drawn, derives an argument from Mark 6:46: "And after he had taken leave of them [the crowd, following the first multiplication of loaves], he went into the hills to pray." According to Goguel, each of Jesus' prayers marked "a decisive moment in his ministry"; and while Mark "does not say what happened then," John does: the refusal to accept the title of king, which brought about the rupture between Jesus and his people. A wholly hypothetical structure that has only one flaw: it is built on the head of a pin.

If the reference to Mark 8 (and 6) is not valid, even less so is the citation of Matthew 16, which is very nearly a transcription of Mark 8. How could it establish that "the people abandon Jesus"? Nowhere are the people in question except in Matthew 16:14, which, like Mark 8:27–28, recounts the various opinions on Jesus, all favorable.

And Luke 9? What can we cull from it that supports Stapfer's thesis? Barely the passage on the possessed child, Luke 9:37–43, and in that passage Jesus' words, "O faithless and perverse generation, how long am I to be with you and bear with you?" But it is clear from the context that the term *genea* (=generation), here as in Mark 8:12, definitely does not mean the whole people; Jesus says "faithless generation" as he would say "faithless people," and he is addressing the disciples as well as the crowd, who were promptly won over by the miracle of the cure: ". . . they were all marveling at everything he did . . ." (Lk. 9:43). A singular way of proving that "the people abandon Jesus Christ." Luke 9 is no more valid as a reference than the first two.

There remains John 6. It is not surprising that here—and here only—theologians can find some ammunition. John does make an observation, following the multiplication of the loaves, which does not appear in any of the parallel Synoptic accounts:

When the people saw the sign which he had done, they said, "This is indeed the prophet who is to come into the world!"

---

[51] Charue, *op. cit.*, p. 76.

Perceiving then that they were about to come and take him by force to make him king, Jesus withdrew again to the hills by himself.

Jn. 6:14–15

What don't they derive from this passage! That Jesus, horrified at the "carnal fanaticism" of the Jews, removed himself from them forever (Frédéric Godet); [52] that his refusal to accept the title of king "immediately resulted in the collapse of his influence. At the beginning, he could have been considered a prophet; circumstances propelled him toward the role of Messiah. He refused. For the crowd, this refusal was an admission of impotence, and they turned away from him" (Goguel); [53] that "The absolute incompatibility which reigned between [Jesus'] messianic ideal and that of the Jewish crowds could not have created a deeper abyss between them and him" (Fillion).[54] And we have heard Albert Dufourcq speak of a "great crisis," bringing on "an irreparable" rupture, growing "popular hostility." "They thought him King. He showed himself God. He had to get away from Capernaum, as he had first got away from Jerusalem." [55]

The differences did indeed worsen, according to John 6:25–66, in the synagogue at Capernaum. "The Jews" there seemed incapable of understanding Jesus' words:

". . . I am the living bread which came down from heaven; if any one eats of this bread, he will live for ever; and the bread which I shall give for the life of the world is my flesh." . . .

After this many of his disciples drew back and no longer went about with him.

Jn. 6:51, 66

Frédéric Godet's Gospel *Commentary:* "This gross lack of perception [on the Jews' part] gives their seeking after Jesus a false cast, earthly, sensualist, animal. . . . What a difference between this people who come with their gross carnal aspirations, their earthly appetites, and the spiritual Israel which the Old Testament was ordained to prepare." [56]

Edmond Stapfer's historic interpretation: "These uncomprehended sentences revolt his listeners, and a crisis erupts, a terrible crisis, with

[52] Godet, *op. cit.,* II, 489.
[53] Goguel, *La Vie de Jésus-Christ,* pp. 360–361.
[54] Fillion, *Vie de Notre Seigneur Jésus-Christ,* II, 428.
[55] Albert Dufourcq, *Le Christianisme antique* [Early Christianity], Paris, Hachette, 1939, pp. 42–43.
[56] Godet, *op. cit.,* II, 496.

the people displaying their opposition in turn and adding it to the Pharisees'. . . . Abandonment follows on popularity, hatred on enthusiasm. . . . The disappointed crowd abandons Jesus forever." [57]

These theologian-historians exaggerate. Stapfer's biblical references were improper—save one; his deductions are no less so. We must not forget that on the one hand the accounts furnished in the fourth Gospel are later than those which come to us from the Synoptics, and especially from Mark—posterior to the event by at least sixty years; and on the other, they are wholly cloaked in dogmatic construction (let us recall Father Calmes's statement: "Gospel history comes to view in it [John] through the development of dogma" [58]). Thus one must not use them except with extreme caution, and even more, must guard against any overreaching.

That the marveling crowd should have wanted to proclaim Jesus king of Israel, Messiah-King, after the multiplication or multiplications of loaves is not at all impossible, although on this point the Johannine account collides with silence not just from Mark but from all three Synoptics. Alfred Loisy, like Walter Bauer, thinks that there are no grounds for according this refusal of Jesus' the least "historic value," and that "Its apologetic character is obvious"; the evangelist was leading into Jesus' declaration to Pilate, "My kingdom is not of this world" (Jn. 18:36 [CCD]).[59] People will try to explain this silence; in fact, people do try. Maurice Goguel is one.[60] Another, Father Lagrange, prefers to "recognize" that he "cannot account for Mark's silence on this point." [61] The explanation is necessarily conjectural. As is the statement made by John, owing precisely to this silence of the Synoptics.

That they should have been disappointed, the enthusiastic crowd, to see their prophet withdraw is self-evident, although the Johannine text says nothing of it. That some wavering, followed by defections, should then have occurred in the band of Jesus' admirers is again plausible, although the evangelist mentions it only after the controversy at Capernaum (and much could be said about this on the plane of historic likelihood).

But to aver that from this moment on the crowd "turned away from

---

[57] Stapfer, op. cit., pp. 253–254.
[58] Quoted in Brassac, loc. cit.
[59] Alfred Loisy, Le quatrième Évangile, Paris, by the au., 1903.
[60] Goguel, La Vie de Jésus-Christ, pp. 359–360.
[61] Lagrange, . . . Jean, p. 167.

him," to claim that after Jesus' refusal, after the teaching on the eu-
charist (meant for the disciples far more than for the crowd),[62] "a terrible crisis" erupted and that "The . . . crowd abandon[ed] Jesus
forever"—this can indeed be called unfounded overreaching. At best
it can be maintained, on the basis of Mark and Matthew (but not
Luke), that thereafter, in Galilee, Jesus seemed to avoid the crowd,
but the necessity which confronted him then to evade Herod's notice
suffices to explain this. As soon as he passed into Judea, contact with
the crowd was re-established (Mk. 10:1; Mt. 19:1–2); and as we have
seen, as the table of quotations we drew up demonstrates incontestably, the people did not fail to show their sympathies to the last moment, to the eve of the Passion. Father Lagrange acknowledges this:
"Up to the Passion, the crowd's eager attentiveness to him [Jesus]
did not abate." [63]

It would doubtless be more satisfying from the theological standpoint for the opposition of the Jewish people taken "as a whole" to
have joined the opposition of a clique. But in vain has this been asserted, and taught, as though it were a fact of history,[64] for this does
not succeed in proving it: the texts disagree.

✿   ✿   ✿

Yet the theologians have not had their say. Israel's global unbelief
is too necessary to them. In bludgeon argument, they infer from certain words pronounced by Jesus his admission of failure with the people as well as the doctors, in Galilee as well as Judea.

In Galilee:

Then he began to reproach the towns in which most of his miracles had
been worked, because they refused to repent.

"Alas for you, Chorazin! Alas for you, Bethsaida! For if the miracles done
in you had been done in Tyre and Sidon, they would have repented long
ago in sackcloth and ashes. And still, I tell you that it will not go as hard

[62] Father Lagrange proposes that we "regard the third part of the [Caper-
naum] discourse as delivered under other circumstances; verses 51–58 especially
would have been said to a more intimate audience, composed of disciples who to
this point appeared staunch" (ibid., p. 195).
[63] Idem, "Le but des Paraboles d'après l'Évangile selon saint Marc" [The Purpose of the Parables as Seen Through the Gospel According to Saint Mark],
Revue biblique internationale, January, 1910, p. 10.
[64] "While the crowds defected . . ." (Brassac, op. cit., p. 359); "From this
time onward, the majority of the public at large was hostile to him" (Romano
Guardini, Le Seigneur, tr., 2 vols., Paris, Alsatia, 1946, I, 157). [See the latter, in
English, as idem, The Lord, tr. Elinor Castendyk Briefs, Chicago, Regnery,
1954.—Tr.]

on Judgement day with Tyre and Sidon as with you. And as for you, Capernaum, did you want to be exalted as high as heaven? You shall be thrown down to hell. For if the miracles done in you had been done in Sodom, it would have been standing yet. And still, I tell you that it will not go as hard with the land of Sodom on Judgement day as with you."

> Mt. 11:20–24 [JB]; identical text in Lk. 10:13–15, but placed later, following the instructions to the seventy

In Judea:

"Jerusalem, Jerusalem, you that kill the prophets and stone those who are sent to you! How often have I longed to gather your children, as a hen gathers her chicks under her wings, and you refused! So be it! Your house will be left to you desolate, for, I promise, you shall not see me any more until you say: 'Blessings on him who comes in the name of the Lord!' "

> Mt. 23:37–39 [JB]; almost identical text in Lk. 13:34–35 (the word "desolate" does not occur there), but this time placed earlier than in Mt., when Jesus was "making his way to Jerusalem" (Lk. 13:22)

The first thing we notice is that these two passages, common to Matthew and Luke, are absent from Mark, whom Christian tradition sees as the "interpreter" of Peter,[65] the prince of the Apostles.

Taken out of context, the reproach to the Galilean cities is surprising in that Jesus reserved his severest criticism for Capernaum, though till the end of his stay in Galilee it remained "his city," the one where, it seemed, the crowd gave him the warmest welcome, according to the Synoptics; and also in that he said not a word about Nazareth, where—again according to the Synoptics—he suffered the most serious setback of his Galilean ministry. It is true that the Nazareth episode, which is put *before* the reprimand to the cities in Luke, occurs *after* it in Matthew. But we can assume, with Father Lagrange and many other exegetes, that "This reproach must have been pronounced toward the end of the apostolate in Galilee." [66]

Should we deduce from this that, on the question of place, the fourth Gospel is to be believed over the Synoptics: that it was at Capernaum and not Nazareth, in the Capernaum synagogue and not the Nazareth, that Jesus came up against the strongest resistance? Or, more simply, should we believe that Jesus was only expressing his

---

[65] See, for example, Father Joseph Huby, *L'Évangile et les Évangiles*, Paris, Beauchesne, 1929, p. 29.

[66] Father Marie-Joseph Lagrange, O.P., ed. and tr., *Évangile selon saint Matthieu*, Paris, Gabalda, 1922, p. 224.

disappointment that even at Capernaum, despite the sympathies of the crowd, he did not win the efficacious, rigorous repentance which he felt the approach of the "kingdom of God" required?

Between these possibilities, the second seems to us the more valid to hold. Whatever the sympathies of the Galilean crowd, they doubtless did not succeed in fully satisfying the Master's demands: to repent "in sackcloth and ashes," to renounce all temporal goods (Lk. 14:33), to cut all familial ties (Mt. 10:35–38; Lk. 14:26), to follow Jesus without so much as casting a glance behind (Lk. 9:61–62), to "Leave the dead to bury their own dead . . ." (Lk. 9:60). But what crowd, in any corner of the earth, would have obeyed such directives without prior training? François Mauriac corroborates this from a sincere and contrite heart: "I seek among those close to me, in all the good families where I have entry, for the man or woman who would not have been incensed at such demands." [67]

We can go farther: considering the text in Matthew better, and especially the context, perhaps it is not necessary to resort to any of these conjectures. I will not even pose the question of whether such a reproach, in its prophetic-style vehemence, should be taken literally, whether it is conceivable that "cities," instead of people, are called to submit to God's judgment, the Last Judgment. May we be allowed to hold with Father Lagrange's commentary:

The reproach to the cities [does not make a] distinction between the culpability of the doctors and of others. But the next verse (Mt. 11:25) [68] distinguishes the wise from the simple, who are usually the more numerous, so that the withdrawal of the crowds is not regarded as final. . . . In the context in Matthew, the *cities* are chosen to be upbraided because they are the seat of rabbinical schools rather than because they are sites of easy or evil morals. . . . Moral disorder, even the gravest, is a lesser obstacle to recognition of God's action than intellectual pride. The splendor of the synagogue at Capernaum in the second century indicates an intensely active center of Judaic life which must have had its origins far back.[69]

Which is the same as saying that in stigmatizing the "cities," Jesus was still and always thinking of the "doctors." No, "the withdrawal of the crowds is not regarded as final"; and it cannot be, for according to the evidence of the four Gospels, as we have demonstrated, there was no "withdrawal of the crowds."

[67] Mauriac, *op. cit.*, p. 74.
[68] "I thank you [Father] because you have shown to the unlearned what you have hidden from the wise and learned" [ABS].
[69] Lagrange, . . . *Matthieu*, pp. 224–225.

No more in Judea than in Galilee.

The censure of Jerusalem attests to it no more than the prior reprimand, of the Galilean cities. This invocation comes at the end of a long series of maledictions launched at the "scribes and Pharisees, hypocrites!" (Mt. 23:29); it is obviously these who are the object of the observation of rejection, ". . . and you refused!" These alone, and not the crowd:

. . . for all the people hung upon his words.

Lk. 19:48

❊   ❊   ❊

Theologians, and particularly Protestant theologians, place the emphasis on Jesus' severity with regard to the Jewish people. Why do they not speak of his love, his mercifulness, his compassion for the humble, for "the crowd," for "the lost sheep of Israel," shown many, so many times? [70] Jesus extended his love and mercifulness even to those who declined to welcome him, including the Samaritans:

. . . the Samaritans . . . would not receive him. . . . And when his disciples James and John saw it, they said, "Lord, do you want us to bid fire come down from heaven and consume them?" But he turned and rebuked them. [Several manuscripts and the Vulgate add here:] "You do not know of what manner of spirit you are; for the Son of Man did not come to destroy men's lives, but to save them."

Lk. 9:52–55 [RSV], 55–56 [CCD]

An admirable lesson in Christian charity. Never meditated on enough.

[70] See, for example, Mk. 6:34; 8:1–2; 10:45; and Mt. 9:35–36; 14:14; 15:32.

PROPOSITION 14

IN ANY CASE, NO ONE HAS THE RIGHT TO DECLARE THAT THE JEWISH PEOPLE REJECTED CHRIST OR THE MESSIAH, THAT THEY REJECTED THE SON OF GOD, UNTIL IT IS PROVED THAT JESUS REVEALED HIMSELF AS SUCH TO THE JEWISH PEOPLE "AS A WHOLE" AND WAS REJECTED BY THEM AS SUCH. BUT THE GOSPELS GIVE US GOOD REASON TO DOUBT THAT THIS EVER HAPPENED.

The catechism teaches: "Jesus Christ announced that God was a Father and that he was himself the Son of God, the Messiah or the Savior awaited since the sin of Adam, charged with redeeming men and leading them to heaven." [1]

The Catholic instructor teaches: "Then came the Messiah announced by the prophets (Isaiah, Jeremiah, Ezekiel, and Daniel). But the Jews would not recognize him and crucified him." [2]

Theologians declare: Consider "the messianic vocation of Israel," developing, clarifying, exalted from century to century. Under Rome's burdensome domination, it "attains its point of culmination":

The Messiah can come. His own, who have preserved this immense expectation in their hearts for nineteen centuries, will be there to receive and follow him; they will get themselves killed for him. He comes, and his own receive him not; they kill him. . . .

And when the appointed time has run, the Son of God appears here below, the true Emmanuel; the world is ready to receive him; but it is found that by an inscrutable decree of Providence, the people whose

---

[1] Canons Quinet and Boyer, eds., *Catéchisme à l'usage des diocèses de France,* imprimatur Cardinal Verdier, Tours, Mame, 1939.

[2] Henri Guillemain and Canon François Le Ster, *Histoire de France: Manuel du certificat d'études* [History of France: Manual for the Primary School Diploma], rev. ed., Paris, Éd. de l'École, 1947 [repub. 1957]. [See pp. 254–255, n. 56, below.—Ed.]

special mission it would have been to give Christ to the world deny him, rebel once more. . . .[3]

Or more simply, "Jesus openly proclaimed himself the Messiah, and he was rejected by his nation."[4]

Protestant theology agrees completely with Catholic on this point: "The people who were to find fulfillment in the coming of the Messiah they were awaiting refused that Messiah; and so, since then, they have been fragmented, dispersed, rejected by men, and, in the eyes of the faith, rejected by God."[5]

An "inscrutable" design of Providence, says Father Humeau, visibly anxious not to crush Israel. Others have not had that humane concern: "The opposition of the Jews arose uniquely from their ill will, their pride, and their hypocrisy. They did not want to accept a Messiah who corresponded so little with their proud and earthbound ambitions."[6] "The Jews, proud and materialistic, did not want to receive Jesus Christ, Son of God, Savior of the world!"[7] And we have already heard Frédéric Godet, sounding a Protestant echo, make a case of the Jews' "gross lack of perception," their "gross carnal aspirations," their "earthly appetites."[8]

[3] Father M.-B. Humeau, O.P., in H. Davenson *et al.*, *Le Sens chrétien de l'histoire* [The Christian Meaning of History], Rencontres No. 4, Lyon, L'Abeille, 1945, pp. 98, 104.

[4] Father Ceslas Lavergne, O.P., "Le Christ et l'Évangile de Jésus-Christ" [Christ and the Gospel of Jesus Christ], in M. Brillant and M. Nédoncelle, eds., *Apologétique* [Apologetics], Paris, Bloud et Gay, 1937 [repub. 1948], p. 353. Similarly, in Canon Adrien Texier's *Summary of Apologetics*, we read: "Jesus declared himself 'sent by God' and 'Messiah' many times; but he stressed above all the divinity of his person. It is this assertion that the Jews have always held against him, and he was determined to maintain it at the risk of his life" (*Précis d'apologétique*, 4th ed., Paris, Éd. de l'École, 1945 [repub. 1957], p. 107).

[5] Franz-J. Leenhardt, *L'Antisémitisme et le mystère d'Israël* [Anti-Semitism and the Mystery of Israel], Geneva, Labor et Fides, 1939, p. 26.

[6] Father J.-P. Grausem, S.J., *L'Évangile de saint Matthieu* [The Gospel of Saint Matthew], "Témoignage chrétien" series, Le Puy, Mappus, 1945, p. 9.

[7] Texier, *op. cit.*, p. 295. [The author did not see fit to modify his attitude in a later teaching manual: "The presumption of pride and the desire for a temporal Messiah, nothing else, closed the eyes of the Jews through bad faith" (Canon Adrien Texier, *Jésus-Christ, centre de la vie du chrétien* [Jesus Christ: Center of the Christian's Life], Paris, Éd. de l'École, 1963, p. 132; quoted in Canon François Houtart and Jean Giblet, eds., *Les Juifs dans la catéchèse: Étude des manuels de catéchèse de langue française*, Louvain, Centre de Recherches socio-religieuses and Centre de Recherches catéchétiques, 1969, p. 185).—Ed.]

[8] Frédéric Godet, *Commentaire sur l'Évangile de Jean*, Paris, Fischbacher, 1876, II, 496. [Another echo, a recent one, from the United States: "Why did the Jews in their zeal for the scriptures fail to see Christ? The real reason was they loved themselves more than they loved God. They were moved by earthly glory, honor, and ambition. They were ready to give glory to those who came in their own name and will [sic] join their 'mutual admiration society', but they were

Here is what is being widely said, read, taught. Before subscribing to it, or invoking "an inscrutable decree of Providence," let us not be afraid to examine the facts and the texts once more.

❋   ❋   ❋

The first question that arises is what the messianic hope represented for the Jews who were compatriots and contemporaries of Jesus.

But can we know this? As a general rule, in the realm of beliefs more than in any other, historic realities are difficult to grasp. In the particular case that concerns us, the difficulty is aggravated by the fact that belief in a messiah did not derive from official Judaism and thus did not have a clearly defined form, imposed by the priesthood or the doctors; it was like a galaxy in the sky of Judaism, drawing all eyes, but each saw what he would in it, what he hoped to see. "Problems posed everywhere; firm solutions, accepted by all, nowhere." [9]

At least we must try, with a preliminary definition, to outline the givens of the problem.

The Semitic word *messiah,* a transcription of the Aramaic *meshiha* and the Hebrew *mashiah* or its Greek equivalent *christos,* means "anointed," he who has received unction or anointing—from Yahweh being understood—whether this was the anointing with oil which had been the rite of royal coronation in Israel (see 1 Sam. 9:16) or the symbolic anointing accorded by God to those whom He delegated on earth to carry out His providential designs. Thus in the Old Testament the term *messiah* or *anointed,* most often applied to the king of Israel, was likewise used of the Persian conqueror Cyrus, who brought the Babylonian Captivity to an end: "Thus says the Lord to his anointed, to Cyrus . . ." (Is. 45:1).

At an indeterminate but late date, as the combined result of Israel's tribulations and the immense hopes drawn for so long from the sacred writings, Yahweh's faithful came to give the word *messiah* a new meaning: for most if not all, it was around a "messiah" to come that their ceaselessly renewed hopes crystallized—the great hope for the "reign of God." Could these fervent Yahwists doubt that the future

suspicious of anyone who did not have their selfish motives . . ." (*Gospel of John* [Assembly of God], 1965, pp. 23–24; quoted in Gerald Strober, ms. in preparation, New York (Xerox), p. 53).—Ed.]

[9] Father Marie-Joseph Lagrange, O.P., *Le Messianisme chez les Juifs* [Messianism Among the Jews], Paris, Gabalda, 1909, p. 265.

would see Yahweh's final triumph over all the evil forces, over all the false gods of pagan idolatry? Could these pious Israelites doubt that the chosen people would be associated with this triumph, that after so many trials endured in punishment for their sins but also so many signs of divine love, so many splendid promises, Israel, purified, would know a blissful existence in a world regenerated by God's grace? So with growing impatience they awaited the Anointed of the Lord, the providential messenger, the "Messiah," through whom God would impose His will on the world.

How did they think of him? It is hard to conceive. The Near Eastern imagination, the tortured genius of Israel had worked over this highly exalting theme, had woven many variations of it. We can cull some idea from Jewish writings of that ancient time which have come down to us, canonical works (which figure in the Old Testament) or apocryphal documents (which do not).[10] They reveal an enormous diversity of beliefs relative to the Messiah. But in that diversity we can perceive certain major currents.

✿   ✿   ✿

The most important by far derives from what could be called the classic messianic tradition, the "Davidic" tradition. The initial formulation is found in 2 Samuel 7:12–16, whose theme is paraphrased in Psalm 88 [CCD], where God speaks of David thus:

And I will make him the first-born, highest of the kings of the earth. Forever I will maintain my kindness toward him. . . . I will make his posterity endure forever. . . .

Ps. 88:28–30 [CCD]

Thus was born the messianic hope for a king of the house of David who would be the promised deliverer, the Savior of Israel—a hope continually disappointed by the events but continually revived by the inspired words of the Prophets and Psalmists.[11] The most famous passages are in Isaiah 9 and 11:

For unto us a child is born, unto us a son is given; and the government shall be upon his shoulder. . . . And there shall come forth a

---

[10] With the reservation, made before, that the Catholic canon of the Old Testament is larger than the Protestant, which excludes Tobias, Judith, 1 and 2 Machabees, the Book of Wisdom, and Ecclesiasticus.

[11] See, for example, Jer. 23:5–6; 30:9; 33:15–16; Ezek. 34:23–24; 37:21–28; Hos. 3:5; Amos 9:11; Mic. 5:1–2.

shoot out of the stock of Jesse,[12] and a branch out of his roots shall
bear fruit.

Is. 9:6; 11:1 [KJ]

Transmitted faithfully from generation to generation, the Davidic
theme reappeared (but as we will see later, oddly bracketed with another theme, that of the despised Servant) in the prophecies of
Deutero-Isaiah, who was contemporary with the Exile (Is. 55:3–5).

The centuries passed. The time that would be Jesus of Nazareth's
approached. That the messianic faith in a glorious and just king, a
son of David, persisted in Israelite hearts we have proof, even before
the Gospels witness to it, in a Jewish work which can be dated with
some exactness—it comes from the mid-first century before Christ,
and thus from the generation immediately preceding Jesus': the
Psalms ascribed to Solomon. The Davidic ideal is magnificently expressed in Psalm 17:23–46, an ample song, powerful in inspiration,
strongly marked with the imprint of Phariseeism but no less strongly
tied to a centuries-old tradition. It begins: "Behold, O Lord, and raise
up to them their king, the Son of David, according to the time which
thou seest, O God: and let him reign over Israel thy servant. . . ." [13]

This writing gives the clearest picture we have of the Messiah
awaited by a great number of Jews (and particularly Pharisees), if
not the majority. It is striking to see the same image of the glorious
Messiah reappear at the opening of the Gospel according to Saint
Luke, in the *Benedictus* which the Holy Spirit inspired the elderly
Zechariah to utter (Lk. 1:68–79).

According to all these comparative texts, what were the basic characteristics of the Davidic Messiah, characteristics deeply etched in
the hearts of so many pious sons of Israel?

The Messiah would be—must be—

descended from David, and a new David;

taught by God, instrument of God, beloved to God like a son;

blessed with His grace, pure of all sin, holy and righteous, source
of righteousness and holiness for all;

but also powerful king, gatherer of all the dispersed of Israel, liber-
ating king who would break all the enemies of Israel, glorious king
who would rule over all the peoples of the earth,

[12] Jesse: the father of David; see Ruth 4:17, 22.
[13] [Quotation taken from *The Odes and Psalms of Solomon*, ed. and tr. J. Rendel Harris, Cambridge, Eng., Cambridge University Press, 1909, p. 153.—Tr.]

by the supernatural power which the Lord would have given him, without recourse to force of arms;

king of Israel, universal prince, prince of peace;

divine messenger charged with bringing about the great hope of Israel on earth: the Kingdom of God, the return to the lost paradise.

The human and the divine, the natural and the supernatural, the temporal and the spiritual, the thirst for freedom and the love of God mingled and intertwined closely in these messianic dreams, which cannot be said, barring prejudice, to have been bare of nobility, if not illusions. That in some hearts, some Jewish milieux, the scale tended to weigh toward the human side, what could be more natural, how can one be indignant about it? The burden of the Roman yoke is enough to explain it, to make us understand the exaltation of the extremists, ready to recognize anyone as the Messiah who would promise them he would drive out the oppressor. "Proud and earth-bound ambitions," [14] "narrow nationalism," "murky hope," "gross carnal aspirations," "earthly appetites," "a wholly carnal messianism" [15] —our Christian doctors have no terms strong enough to express their scorn. Why weren't they more docile, these Jews, quicker to submit, to collaborate, to defect? (The light the recent past throws on all this!) What a scandal, what blindness the Jewish resistance! What "carnal grossness" the Jewish hopes for liberation! But then, how about the Machabees, and David himself, and Samson, national heroes and heralds of God? (The awesome honor of being the "people of God," a role impossible to play, humanly speaking.) Do the critics forget that the main source of Israel's patriotism was in the heights of

[14] Grausem, loc. cit.

[15] Godet, op. cit., II, 489, 496. Likewise Father Jules Lebreton, S.J., in La Vie et l'enseignement de Jésus-Christ (2 vols., Paris, Beauchesne, 1931, I, 79) and Father Louis Richard in Israël et la foi chrétienne by Father Henri de Lubac et al. ("Manifeste contre le Nazisme" series, Fribourg, Switz., Éd. de la Librairie de l'Université, 1942, p. 101). [The terms rise just as readily in the United States: ". . . the kingdom He formed—the Church—was a spiritual one, not a temporal one such as the Carnal Jews were hoping for," writes Father Francis B. Casselly, S.J., in Religion: Doctrine and Practice (Chicago, Loyola University Press, 1958, p. 400; quoted in Sister Rose Albert Thering, O.P., The Potential in Religion Textbooks for Developing a Realistic Self-Concept, doctoral dissertation, St. Louis University, 1961).—Ed.]

But let these authors then work out a reconciliation with the expert Father Joseph Bonsirven, S.J., who considers that "In the messianic imagery, the political or materialistic aspect is far from prevailing over the moral and religious aspect" (Le Judaïsme palestinien au temps de Jésus-Christ, sa théologie, 2 vols., Paris, Beauchesne, 1935, I, 467).

faith? Even the pious hearts that wisely resisted the impatience of the
Zealots' fanaticism did not separate their dream of holiness from the
dream of liberation. It was written that the Messiah-King, the new
David, would establish the dominion of righteousness on earth; but
how was such a dominion possible, how was it even conceivable, so
long as the idolatrous pagans profaned the sacred soil? You are welcome, severe critics (of others), to excoriate the "ill will," the "pride,"
the "hypocrisy," the "prejudices" of these opinionated Jews—but recognize, with Zechariah, that their hopes seemed solidly grounded on
Scripture; reread the Prophets,[16] reread the Psalms, reread the same
Zechariah's *Benedictus:*

> Blessed be the Lord, the God of Israel, . . .
> [for he] has raised up for us a power for [lit.: a horn of] salvation
> in the House of his servant David,
> even as he proclaimed,
> by the mouth of his holy prophets from ancient times,
> *that he would save us from our enemies*
> *and from the hands of all who hate us.*
>
> Lk. 1:68–71 [JB; italics added]

☼   ☼   ☼

Yet doesn't this messianic concept—which Christians, enlightened
by the Cross of Golgotha, have finally recognized harbored a cor-
rupting seed—doesn't Scripture itself, the ancient Scripture, offer the
corrective for all those who have "eyes to see" and "ears to hear"?
Didn't the Prophet oppose another image to that of the glorious Messiah, triumphant over the Gentiles and liberator of Israel, the image
of the suffering Messiah, unrecognized, persecuted, "man of sorrows"
(Is. 53:3), crushed to the death in expiation of the sins of his people?
    Who doesn't know the poignant text from Isaiah—Deutero-Isaiah
—53:2–10, which the Church believes itself justified in seeing as a miraculous prefiguring of Jesus Christ's Passion? [17]

---

[16] Jer. 30:8; Ezek. 34:27; Mic. 5:5; Zech. 9:8, for example. Father Charles Journet
[of Switzerland, now Cardinal], citing J. Touzard and Blaise Pascal, explains that
these elements of messianic prophecy were obviously "secondary," "a worn en-
velope for promises of a moral and religious order" (*Destinées d'Israël* [Israel's For-
tunes], Paris, Egloff, 1945, pp. 65–66). Easy to say today (or yesterday); difficult to
perceive twenty centuries ago. And how to explain the persistence of those illusory
promises?
    [17] [A 1951 CCD calls Isaiah 53 "A Prophecy of the Passion of Christ," among
many other tendentious chapter titles, commentaries, and notes. Examples are the
headings for Isaiah 16, 32, and 54: "A Prayer for the Coming of Christ," "The

> For he grew up before him like a young plant,
> and like a root out of dry ground. . . .
>
> Is. 53:2

A supremely important text, to which must be joined, "I hid not my face from shame and spitting" (Is. 50:4–9, quotation at 50:6) and "Behold, my servant shall prosper . . ." (Is. 52:13–15, at 13).

But let us reflect on this: that for the corrective contained in these prophetic passages to have been effective, for the Davidic messianism to have been cleansed of whatever impurity—which is the same as saying, whatever carnality—it contained, for it to have become possible for the Jewish people to recognize in Jesus, even jeered at, even nailed to the Gentiles' cross, the Savior promised by God, one prior condition was requisite, and absolutely:

that in Jesus' time, the messianic interpretation of these passages was received by at least a part—a significant part—of Jewish opinion; that the figure of the suffering Servant, humiliated, "bruised," "stricken," was identified in this opinion with the figure of the Messiah.

Was it? The Damascus Document, the Dead Sea Scrolls, the Testaments of the Twelve Patriarchs have shown us how diverse and difficult to grasp were the messianic conceptions in pre-Christian Judaism. If, as André Dupont-Sommer thinks and Géza Vermès agrees,[18] the Master of Righteousness was recognized as Prophet and Messiah, he was then in effect a "suffering" Messiah, in the image of the Servant of Yahweh evoked by Isaiah.

But this interpretation was held by a small group, a sect, and not by an important minority, even less by a majority of the people.

The question arises, is this possible? Wasn't Deutero-Isaiah part of the biblical canon? Weren't these texts read, commented on in the synagogues? Certainly. But they were not linked to the Messiah, the less so because the glorious Messiah reappears in Isaiah 55:4–5. None of the Jews seem to have thought to make the connection which so many Christians did later, *post eventum*. Even today, doesn't Christian thinking profess divergent opinions on this serious subject?

Reign of Christ," and "The Church of Christ Is the New Jerusalem." (See *New Catholic Edition of the Holy Bible*, Douay-Confraternity tr., New York, Catholic Book Publishing Co., 1951.)—Ed.]

[18] André Dupont-Sommer, *Nouveaux Aperçus sur les manuscrits de la Mer Morte* [New Notes on the Dead Sea Scrolls], Paris, Maisonneuve, 1953, pp. 78–80; *idem*, "Les Esséniens," *Évidences*, no. 63, March, 1957, and no. 69, January, 1958; and Géza Vermès, in *Cahiers sioniens*, March, 1955, p. 55.

The texts cited from Deutero-Isaiah actually correspond very closely with other texts in which the "Servant" of Yahweh is expressly named: Israel (Is. 41:8–9; 44:1–2, 21; 45:4; 49:3).

Adolphe Lods writes, "The inspired [prophet], in tracing the unforgettable image of the 'Servant,' was thinking not of himself nor of the Messiah but . . . of Israel." And: "To my mind, there exists no valid reason to reject the interpretation of his thought explicitly given thus by the author himself. The Servant of Yahweh is Israel." [19] To which Father Lagrange replies: how could the Servant of Yahweh—at least in Isaiah 50, 52, and 53—be Israel, since he pays for Israel? "Israel having been the object of the mission cannot have been responsible for carrying it out. This is the whole point." [20]

The arguments exchanged between the sides are strong and unsettling, if not decisive. Without making bold to arbitrate such a controversy, we would observe that there seems to be agreement among the thinkers on at least the point that is essential to our eyes: at the time of Jesus, before Jesus, there was no sign that the concept of the tortured Messiah existed in Jewish opinion. In the realm of history, Adolphe Lods and Father Lagrange concur. "The idea of a suffering Messiah appears to have been totally foreign to Judaism around the Christian era," says the first.[21] And the second: "As gripping as was the picture of the Servant, Judaism did not think for a moment of attributing expiatory suffering and death to the expected Savior." [22]

[19] Adolphe Lods et al., La Bible, Paris, Fischbacher, 1937, p. 41; likewise in Lods's Les Prophètes d'Israël [The Prophets of Israel], Paris, Albin Michel, 1935 [repub. 1950], p. 277.

[20] Father Marie-Joseph Lagrange, O.P., Le Judaïsme avant Jésus-Christ, Paris, Gabalda, 1932, p. 376.

[21] Adolphe Lods, La Religion d'Israël, Paris, Hachette, 1939, p. 228. See Hans Lietzmann, Histoire de l'Église ancienne [History of the Early Church], tr., 4 vols., Paris, Payot, 1936, I, 54: "The idea of a Messiah who must die by very reason of his vocation was completely foreign to the Jews." We have noted just above that the Dead Sea Scrolls and other documents would create reservations about this statement.

[22] Lagrange, Le Judaïsme avant Jésus-Christ, p. 385. The same conclusions are found in Father Léonce de Grandmaison, S.J., Jésus-Christ, sa personne, son message, ses preuves (2 vols., Paris, Beauchesne, 1928), I, 278; Maurice Goguel, Jésus de Nazareth, mythe ou histoire? (Paris, Leroux, 1925), pp. 199–200; and Jean Héring, Le Royaume de Dieu et sa venue ([The Kingdom of God and Its Coming] Paris, Alcan, 1937), pp. 67–68. For Father François-Marie Braun, O.P., "The notion of a suffering Messiah, called to redeem his people, no longer had any effect on the Jews at the time of Christ" ("Jésus," in Raoul Gorce and Maxime Mortier, eds., Histoire générale des religions, Paris, Quillet, 1945, II, 151). But can he tell us at what time it did have an effect? Father Bonsirven believes that "The messianic exegesis of the prophecy of Isaiah [53] had currency among the Jews" (op. cit., I, 383), but he does not give convincing proof.

Father Lagrange adds: "The Jews should have understood that the Servant was the most religious and most sublime aspect of the Messiah." [23] But he himself demonstrates to us, and convincingly, that it was impossible for them to understand this. As the result of a specific blindness, of an erring intended by God? Not even; quite simply by dint of the messianic tradition as Scripture—yes, the Holy Scriptures—had inspired and established it. "The suffering Messiah would have been a contradiction in terms for everyone." How could they "imagine that the Messiah who could put the pagans to flight with a word from his lips would be obliged to suffer death to save his people?" The Servant "would be unrecognized, repulsed, held guilty, put to death: what could be more opposed to the functions of a prince recognized as king, anointed as such, who would make righteousness reign, who would make himself terrible to the wicked . . . ? Let us acknowledge that one could be mistaken. . . . One could doubt until the oracle had been fulfilled." [24]

It is too little to say, "One could"; one had to be mistaken. Before "the oracle had been fulfilled," before the Passion—or better, before the Resurrection—there seemed to be an unshakable opposition between the two images, both proposed by Scripture, of the glorious Messiah, liberator of Israel, and the tortured Servant.

The Gospels offer us numerous proofs, the most striking being the tenacious lack of understanding with which the disciples—the very disciples—greeted the Master's revelation of his afflicted messiahship in the three Synoptics. [25]

Father Lagrange notes in his Gospel According to Saint Mark: "How could the apostles not have been surprised by a prediction so contrary to public opinion? It was more likely that they would fail to understand here than in any other case." [26] So contrary to public opinion? It would be more correct to say: so contrary to the tradition founded on Scripture.

The predicted event, the inconceivable event, came to pass: Jesus was arrested, scourged, crucified. The disciples, appalled, lost faith and ran away. For despite the Master's repeated teachings, the tradi-

---

[23] Lagrange, Le Judaïsme avant Jésus-Christ, p. 387.
[24] Ibid., pp. 386, 399.
[25] See Mk. 8:31–33 (and parallel Mt. 16:21–23) and 9:30–32 (and parallels Mt. 17:22–23; Lk. 9:43–45). Some of these texts are discussed below, pp. 148 ff., where we will return to this subject.
[26] Father Marie-Joseph Lagrange, O.P., ed. and tr., Évangile selon saint Marc, Paris, Gabalda, 1910, p. 218.

tional image lived on in their minds; and that image was not compatible with the hideous reality; no, it did not seem possible that the Crucified was the Messiah. On the road to Emmaus, two of the disciples sadly affirmed this to their fellow wayfarer, whom they did not recognize as Jesus: "But we had hoped that he was the one to redeem Israel" (Lk. 24:21).

For every Jew, disciple of Jesus or no, the Messiah could not be other than a conqueror: when they had observed the miraculous victory—Jesus' victory over death—then, but only then, did the disciples regain faith. And even then, the old image dissipated only slowly: "Lord, will you at this time restore the kingdom to Israel?" (Acts 1:6).

Such was the supreme question, before the Ascension, of those who would become the Apostles of Christ crucified.

✿   ✿   ✿

With this central problem of messianism in Jesus' time clarified—as well as possible—in its dual and contradictory aspects of glorious and suffering messiahship, we find ourselves before another and complementary problem, which can be formulated thus:

for Palestinian Judaism of that epoch, did the locutions "Son of God" and "Son of man," which we know to have taken on such import in the Gospels, have a clearly messianic meaning, and what kind?

"Son of God"

The first time this expression appears in the Jewish Old Testament, it is to the angels that the term is applied:

When men began to multiply on the face of the ground, and daughters were born to them, the sons of God saw that the daughters of men were fair. . . .

Gen. 6:1–2; see also 6:4

It is found again, used in the same sense, in Job 1:6 and Psalm 88:7 [CCD; 89:6, n. *w*, RSV]. The variant expression in the Psalm, "heavenly beings," shows clearly that there is no question here of filial relationship in the proper sense of the words. Among all the creatures of God, the angels are the elect, in closest communication with God; the expression "sons of God" which is applied to them means nothing more.

While preserving all the distinctions, one can say as much of the numerous biblical texts where Israel itself is characterized as the "Son of God"—for example, in Exodus 4:22, Deuteronomy 14:1, Psalm 82:6–7, Isaiah 1:2–4 and 63:8, Jeremiah 3:19 and 21–22, and Hosea 1:10 and 11:1. It is still in the same sense, of spiritual sonship, of preferential grace bestowed by God, that the term is applied to the king of Israel and above all to the king par excellence, David:

> I will be a father to him and he a son to me. . . .
>
> 2 Sam. 7:14 [JB]

> He shall cry to me, "Thou art my Father,
> my God, and the Rock of my salvation."
>
> Ps. 89:26

But from the fact that the signal halo is conferred this time on David, it tends to take on a messianic meaning. This is affirmed with singular strength of expression in Psalm 2:7:

> [The Lord] said to me, "You are my son,
> today I have begotten you. . . ."

Does the figurative sense give way here to the proper sense, and preferential grace to the mystery of the Incarnation? This is Father Lagrange's opinion,[27] although it is disputed both by the text itself (for "today" placed before "begotten" seems to disallow the proper sense) and by the Apostle Paul speaking in the synagogue at Antioch of Pisidia:

And we bring you the good news that what God promised to the fathers, this he has fulfilled to us their children by raising Jesus; as also it is written in the second psalm,

> "Thou art my Son,
> today I have begotten thee."[28]
>
> Acts 13:32–33

What can be confirmed is that the idea of divine sonship, understood in the proper sense, not only did not have currency in Jewish theology at the time of Jesus but did not even seem conceivable to it,

[27] Idem, Le Judaïsme avant Jésus-Christ, p. 365. Father Jules Lebreton, S.J., is of a contrary opinion (Histoire des origines du dogme de la Trinité, 2 vols., Paris, Beauchesne, 1928, I, 121).

[28] Saint Paul also has occasion to use the same locution in a purely metaphoric sense: "For though you have countless guides in Christ, you do not have many fathers. For I became your father in Christ Jesus through the gospel" (1 Cor. 4:15). [The different wording of Psalm 2:7 in itself and in Acts 13:33 is according to the source (RSV).—Tr.]

so sharply did the concept clash with Judaism's rigidly monotheistic faith and with the notion it had formed of divine transcendence. Such a notion, which had become fundamental, "hardly allows the concept of God as the generative physical principle . . . of an individual human life," Father Lagrange acknowledges.[29]

After the solemn declaration of Psalm 2, it would seem logical for the term "Son of God" to have been applied to the Messiah, but this deduction is not confirmed by historic research: the Messiah is designated "Son of God" neither in the Psalms of Solomon nor in the other works of what is sometimes called "late Judaism," at least in the genuine texts. In Jesus' time, the term "Son of God" was "not at all a synonym of Messiah in current usage." [30]

Surely, it could not be surprising that the Messiah-King claimed the glorious title. But from the received meaning—which was the figurative meaning—to the proper sense, there was a chasm, almost unspannable, unless by a supernatural leap of love and adoration. You whom two millennia of theological teaching have prepared to contemplate the mystery of the Incarnation from the remoteness of centuries, try if you can to imagine, on the level of your daily life, how staggering the revelation would be.

"Son of Man"

For this second title, "Son of man," which contrasts strangely with the first, the problem posed seems yet more difficult to resolve, being "perhaps the most complex of New Testament exegesis." [31]

In the Old Testament, with one exception that we will not fail to underline, the term "Son of Man" does not appear linked with messianic visions or previsions. Exactly synonymous with "man," the most it implies is a particular kind of humility before God:

> . . . who are you that you are afraid of man who dies,
> of the son of man who is made like grass . . . ?

Is. 51:12

> Put not your trust in princes,
> in a son of man, in whom there is no help.[32]

Ps. 146:3

[29] Father Marie-Joseph Lagrange, O.P., in *Revue biblique internationale*, 1914, p. 69.

[30] *Idem*, . . . *Marc*, p. cxlvii; see also Father Lagrange's *Évangile selon saint Matthieu*, Paris, Gabalda, 1922, p. 322.

[31] Grandmaison, *op. cit.*, I, 318, n. 3.

[32] See the term also in Num. 23:19; Job 25:6; 35:8; Ps. 8:4; 80:17; and Ecclus. 17:29.

Very rare in the whole of the Old Testament, the expression "Son of man" is widely used only in the prophecies of Ezekiel, where it occurs ninety-four times, each time the Prophet is summoned by God, and thus serves to accentuate "the contrast between the majesty of God who calls, the frailty of the instrument he is using, and the grandeur of the role which [the latter] must fulfill." [33]

Ninety-four times! Repetition all the more remarkable in that it is almost unique in the Old Testament. For all the pious Jews who, assiduous in attending the synagogue, heard the reading of the Prophets and the commentary each Sabbath, such a designation would thus invincibly evoke the memory of the great Prophet of the Exile.

Yet one time at least [34] (one time against ninety-four, but what do figures matter?—once can suffice), in a period closer to Jesus, the expression "Son of man" recurs—in the Book of Daniel, which appeared during the Machabee era, the second century. This time it is as if cloaked in an aura of mystery, which is conducive to the messianic interpretation. During a dream in which Daniel has first seen four monstrous beasts, then God on His throne in all the glory of His appurtenances of righteousness, a new vision rises:

> I saw in the night visions,
> and behold, with the clouds of heaven
> there came one like a son of man,
> and he came to the Ancient of Days [God]
> and was presented before him.
> And to him was given dominion
> and glory and kingdom,
> that all peoples, nations, and languages
> should serve him;
> his dominion is an everlasting dominion,
> which shall not pass away,
> and his kingdom one
> that shall not be destroyed.
>
> Dan. 7:13–14

"Dominion and glory and kingdom [over] all peoples": we rediscover one of the traditional attributes of the Davidic Messiah. But if one attempts to recognize the Messiah in the "Son of man" of Daniel's

[33] Father Édouard Tobac, Les Prophètes d'Israël [The Prophets of Israel], quoted in Grandmaison, op. cit., I, 318. See Ezekiel, passim, beginning with 2:1.

[34] The expression can also be found in two or three other passages in Daniel, but a special value cannot be attached to them (for example, Dan. 8:17). Note that chapter 7 was written in Aramaic, and that "Son of man" in Aramaic is the ordinary expression for man (Claude Montefiore, The Synoptic Gospels, 2 vols., 2nd ed., rev., London, Macmillan, 1927, I, 65).

vision—which the context does not seem to prescribe—the Prophet conferred a new character on him which certain minds have found striking: that of a heavenly being, walking on "the clouds," drawing near the Most High, consecrated everlastingly. Thereafter, under the influence of Daniel's vision, was the term "Son of man" sometimes associated with the concept of a supernatural Messiah, pre-existing, participating in the glory of God? [35] Some passages of the Gospels would tend to make us believe this; and there are those who would find the proof in an apocalyptic Jewish writing titled the Book of Parables, or Similitudes, which dates mainly from the first century B.C. and constitutes chapters 37–71 of the Ethiopic Book of Enoch:

> And there I saw One who had a head of days,
> And his head was white like wool [this was God],
> And with him was another being whose countenance had the
>   appearance of a man,
> And his face was full of graciousness, like one of the holy angels.
> And I asked the angel who went with me and showed me all
>   the hidden things, concerning that Son of Man, who he
>   was, and whence he was, (and) why he went with the
>   Head of Days? And he answered and said unto me:
> This is the Son of Man who hath righteousness,
> With whom dwelleth righteousness,
> And who revealeth all the treasures of that which is hidden,
> Because the Lord of Spirits hath chosen him,
> And whose lot hath the pre-eminence before the Lord of Spir-
>   its in uprightness for ever.
> And this Son of Man whom thou hast seen
> Shall raise up the kings and the mighty from their seats,
> [And the strong from their thrones]
> And shall loosen the reins of the strong,
> And break the teeth of the sinners.
>
>   46:1–4
>
> And at that hour that Son of Man was named
> In the presence of the Lord of Spirits. . . .
> Yea, before the sun and the signs were created,
> Before the stars of the heaven were made,

[35] It seems unprofitable to us to discuss here the question of whether this notion is pagan in origin, perhaps Chaldeo-Iranian, and anterior to the apocalypses of Daniel and Enoch, as Alfred Loisy, following on Richard Reitzenstein, avers. (See Loisy's *La Naissance du christianisme*, Paris, Nourry, 1933, pp. 95–96.) [See, in English, as *idem, The Birth of the Christian Religion*, tr. L. P. Jacks, New York, Macmillan, 1948.—Tr.] The source of this messianic idea has nothing to do with the usage Jesus made of it.

His name was named before the Lord of Spirits.
He shall be a staff to the righteous. . . ,
And he shall be the light of the Gentiles,
And the hope of those who are troubled of heart. . . .
And for this reason hath he been chosen and hidden
        before Him [the Lord],
Before the creation of the world and for evermore.

                                                    48:2–6

And the sum of judgement was given unto the Son of Man. . . .
And from henceforth there shall be nothing corruptible;
For that Son of Man has appeared,
And has seated himself on the throne of his glory,
And all evil shall pass away before his face,
And the word of that Son of Man shall go forth
And be strong before the Lord of Spirits.[36]

                                                    69:27–29

These texts, were they authentic, would be the most precious link connecting Daniel to Jesus. But are they? Many writers use Enoch without even asking themselves this question; the authenticity of the texts has serious advocates but also adversaries, like Father Lagrange, who after a rigorous examination perceived in them all the marks of a Christian interpolation.[37] Father Bonsirven does not accept "this verdict" [38] but does not refute it. At the very least, doubt exists; and it is singularly reinforced by the fact that the Book of Parables does not figure in the fragmentary manuscripts of the apocrypha attributed to Enoch found in cave 4 at Qumran.[39] Father J. T. Milik concludes from this that the Parables of Enoch must be the work of a Jewish Christian "of the second century of our era." [40]

Furthermore, we cannot forget that the texts at hand are a translation of a translation—Ethiopic translated from Greek, which in turn was translated from the original Aramaic or Hebrew. It can thus

[36] [Quotation taken from "Book of Enoch," ed. and tr. R. H. Charles, in *idem et al.*, eds. and trs., *The Apocrypha and Pseudepigrapha of the Old Testament* (1913), 2 vols., Oxford, Eng., Oxford University Press, 1963–1964, II, 214–216, 235.—Tr.]

[37] Lagrange, *Le Judaïsme avant Jésus-Christ*, pp. 247–254.

[38] Father Joseph Bonsirven, S.J., *Les Enseignements de Jésus-Christ*, Paris, Beauchesne, 1946, p. 60, n. 1. Neither does Jean Héring (*op. cit.*, p. 77, n. 1); this author maintains, moreover, that there is absolute incompatibility between the figure of the Messiah and that of Enoch's "Man" or "Son of Man."

[39] [See Millar Burrows, *More Light on the Dead Sea Scrolls*, New York, Viking, 1958, p. 180.—Ed.]

[40] Father J. T. Milik, *Dix Ans de découvertes dans le désert de Juda* [Ten Years of Discoveries in the Judean Desert], Paris, Cerf, 1957, p. 31.

seem temerarious to rely on them in order to demonstrate that in Jesus' time the expression "Son of man" had taken on a messianic meaning in some Jewish circles. Does the Daniel text alone suffice to establish this? Yes, at most, and with regard to Jesus, Jesus personally. But we could go no farther; the unawareness of the Jews in this respect is clearly affirmed by the fourth Gospel. In the paramount discussion between Jesus and his cross-examiners in Jerusalem, the latter declare:

We have heard from the law that the Christ remains for ever. How can you say that the Son of man must be lifted up? Who is this Son of man?

Jn. 12:34

Whence it is justified to deduce and to conclude that in Jesus' era "Son of man" was certainly not in widespread use to designate the Messiah, "was not known as a messianic title," and "remained obscure for all the Jews." [41] It is not impossible that the locution had taken on a messianic meaning in the small circles of initiates, but it is a defiance of truth to teach, "The name of Son of man was a title of the Messiah-redeemer and -judge in all of prophetic revelation." [42]

☼   ☼   ☼

This long road was necessary before entering Christian ground—I mean, trying with the help of the Gospels (insofar as the Gospels allow) to determine what the Jewish people knew of the messiahship, the sonship of Jesus, and what Jesus revealed of these.

Immediately there comes to mind the decisive text, of the exchange with the disciples on the road to Caesarea Philippi, an exchange whose importance is such that the three Synoptic versions must be given here, despite the repetition:

[Mark:]   And Jesus went on with his disciples, to the [nearby] villages of Caesarea Philippi; and on the way he asked his disciples, "Who do men say that I am?" And they told him, "John the Baptist; and others say, Elijah; and others one of the prophets." And he asked them, "But who do you say that I am?" Peter answered him, "You are the Christ." And he charged them to tell no one about him.
              And he began to teach them that the Son of man must suf-

[41] Father Paul Joüon, ed. and tr., *L'Évangile de Notre Seigneur Jésus-Christ,* Paris, Beauchesne, 1930, Appendix A, p. 603.
[42] Texier, *op. cit.,* p. 166.

fer many things . . . [8:27–31; next come the revelation of the Way of the Cross and Peter's and the other disciples' failure to understand, vv. 32–33].

[Matthew:] Now when Jesus came into the district of Caesarea Philippi, he asked his disciples, "Who do men say that the Son of man is?" And they said, "Some say John the Baptist, others say Elijah, and others Jeremiah or one of the prophets." He said to them, "But who do you say that I am?" Simon Peter replied, "You are the Christ, the Son of the living God." And Jesus answered him, "Blessed are you, Simon Bar-Jona! For flesh and blood has not revealed this to you, but my Father who is in heaven. And I tell you, you are Peter, and on this rock I will build my church, and the powers of death shall not prevail against it. . . ." Then he strictly charged the disciples to tell no one that he was the Christ.

From that time Jesus began to show his disciples that he must go to Jerusalem and suffer many things . . . [16:13–21; next, Peter fails to understand, and Jesus calls him Satan, vv. 22–23, as in Mk. 8:33].

[Luke:] Now it happened that as he was praying alone the disciples were with him; and he asked them, "Who do the people say that I am?" And they answered, "John the Baptist; but others say, Elijah; and others, that one of the old prophets has risen." And he said to them, "But who do you say that I am?" And Peter answered, "The Christ of God." But he charged and commanded them to tell this to no one, saying, "The Son of man must suffer many things . . ." [9:18–22; the disciples' failure to understand is noted later and more briefly, v. 45].

As we see, the three versions correspond exactly on the first point: "Who do men say that I am?" In the three Gospels, the disciples give exactly the same answer: the Baptist, or Elijah, or a risen prophet. None of them says, "The Messiah"; none of them says, "The Son of God," in whichever meaning. Thus, according to the admission of his faithful companions, at the hour when the Galilean period of Jesus' ministry was ending, just before his departure for Jerusalem, Jesus' messiahship, his sonship seem to have been completely unrecognized by the Jewish people or, to be more precise, by that part of the Jewish people (how important a part no one can measure) who had known him, approached him, heard him. . . . A prophet, "a prophet mighty in deed and word" (Lk. 24:19), at the very most a precursor of the Messiah, who, according to one segment of belief, was to be a risen Elijah and, according to Jesus himself, John the Baptist (Mt.

11:14)—this was how Jesus looked in the eyes of those Jewish crowds.

On the second point—"But who do you say that I am?"—there is a significant divergence between Mark and Luke on the one hand and Matthew on the other, Matthew being the only one to add to the title of Messiah, formally bestowed by Peter, the title of Son of God.

But the three Synoptic versions correspond again on a third point: Jesus rigorously forbade his disciples to tell anyone that he was the Messiah (he himself did not accept the acknowledgment except in Matthew 16:17). *Secrecy on the messiahship and its corollary, the incomprehension of the Jewish people, were not only an empirical fact observed by the disciples but a stringent rule imposed by Jesus himself.* And we can find multiple examples of the application of this rule all through the Gospels.

In Mark, Jesus forbids the demons to speak "because they knew him" (1:34) and to call him "the Holy One of God" (1:24) or "the Son of God" (3:11–12). He charges the sick whom he has miraculously cured to "say nothing to any one" (1:43–44; 5:43; 7:36). After the Transfiguration, he warns the three—Peter, James, and John—"to tell no one what they had seen, until the Son of man should have risen from the dead" (9:9).

He does likewise in Matthew 8:4; 9:30; 12:16; and 17:9.

In Luke: "And demons also came out of many, crying, 'You are the Son of God!' But he rebuked them, and would not allow them to speak, because they knew that he was the Christ" (4:41). And after the Transfiguration: "And they kept silence and told no one in those days anything of what they had seen" (9:36).

There is a fourth point on which the three accounts correspond, as we have already had occasion to note: the utter incomprehension with which the disciples greet the revelation of the *Via dolorosa.* Matthew's version of this is all the more striking in that it shows Peter within five verses being consecrated as head of the Church and then repulsed as Satan. Thus the revelation of the suffering messiahship, taught by Jesus himself, remained unrecognized by the faithful disciples, unrecognized by Peter, the prince of Apostles. How then with no revelation, with no teaching, could it have been understood, accepted by the Jewish people "as a whole"? Who can answer the question?

These first observations are such, are so obvious, that one would have just cause to stop there and, without going farther, to conclude:

by the evidence of the Synoptics, except for the very last days—the eve of the Passion—which we will discuss later, the Jewish people "as a whole" did not know Jesus as the Messiah; they did not know him as the true Son of God, if indeed the mystery of the Incarnation was intelligible to them in the first place; they did not know him as Messiah-Son of God for the good reason that Jesus not only never presented himself to them as such but even forbade that these signal titles be bestowed on him.[43]

✿   ✿   ✿

Yet it would be incautious not to forestall overly easy objections. We of course hold as valid the observations made above, rigorously deduced from a principal text, whose importance all exegetes recognize. But we arbitrarily treated that text in isolation. When we consider the Gospels in total—if only the three Synoptics—the problem immediately takes on complications, bristles with redoubtable difficulties, to the point where it becomes almost insoluble.

In fact, side by side with either the account of the conversation on the road to Caesarea Philippi or the various texts where the rule of secrecy about the messiahship is set down, we must observe that other Gospel passages sound another note, move in another direction.

A. Is it only to a prophet—however great—or to the awaited Messiah that the following Synoptic texts apply?

And they were all amazed, so that they questioned among themselves, saying, "What is this? A new teaching! With authority he commands even the unclean spirits, and they obey him."

Mk. 1:27; see Lk. 4:36

And as Jesus passed on from there, two blind men followed him, crying aloud, "Have mercy on us, Son of David."

Mt. 9:27

[After the cure of "a blind and dumb demoniac":] And all the people were amazed, and said, "Can this be the Son of David?"

Mt. 12:23

And behold, a Canaanite woman from that region came out and cried, "Have mercy on me, O Lord, Son of David. . . ."

Mt. 15:22

---

[43] "In the Synoptics, except at the very end, [Jesus] never clearly declared who he was" (Bonsirven, *Les Enseignements de Jésus-Christ*, p. 371).

And . . . as he [Jesus] was leaving Jericho with his disciples and a great multitude, Bartimaeus, a blind beggar, the son of Timaeus, was sitting by the roadside. And when he heard that it was Jesus of Nazareth, he began to cry out and say, "Jesus, Son of David, have mercy on me!"

Mk. 10:46–47; see Mt. 20:29–30, where there are two blind men; Lk. 18:35–38

[Entry into Jerusalem:] And those who went before [Jesus] and those who followed cried out, "Hosanna! . . . Blessed is the kingdom of our father David that is coming! . . ."

Mk. 11:9–10

"Hosanna to the Son of David! . . ."

Mt. 21:9

"Blessed is the King who comes in the name of the Lord! . . ."

Lk. 19:38

B. Are the following declarations, made by Jesus more or less publicly, only about a prophet, however great; or are they about the Messiah, or rather the Son of God, God incarnate and sovereign judge?

". . . But that you may know that the Son of man has authority on earth to forgive sins"—he said to the paralytic—"I say to you, rise, take up your pallet and go home."

Mk. 2:10–11; see Mt. 9:6; Lk. 5:24

". . . the Son of man is lord even of the sabbath."

Mk. 2:28; see Mt. 12:8; Lk. 6:5; said to the Pharisees, but probably in public

". . . For whoever is ashamed of me and of my words in this adulterous and sinful generation, of him will the Son of man also be ashamed, when he comes in the glory of his Father with the holy angels."

Mk. 8:38; see Mt. 16:27, where these statements, worded differently, are addressed to the disciples alone, which is more likely as they come immediately after the exchange of Caesarea Philippi; Lk. 9:26

[Sermon on the Mount:] "You have heard that it was said to the men of old. . . . But I say to you. . . ."

Mt. 5:21–48, *passim*

"Not every one who says to me, 'Lord, Lord,' shall enter the kingdom of heaven, but he who does the will of my Father who is in heaven. On that day many will say to me, 'Lord, Lord, did we not prophesy in your name, and cast out demons in your name, and do many mighty works in your name?' And then will I declare to them, 'I never knew you; depart from me, you evildoers.' . . ."

Mt. 7:21–23

". . . All things have been delivered to me by my Father; and no one knows the Son except the Father, and no one knows the Father except the Son and any one to whom the Son chooses to reveal him. . . ."

> Mt. 11:27; see Lk. 10:22, but in Lk. these statements are
> addressed only to the disciples, the seventy, back from a mission

". . . I tell you, something greater than the temple is here. . . ."

> Mt. 12:6

". . . and behold, something greater than Solomon is here. . . . something greater than Jonah is here. . . ."

> Lk. 11:31–32; see Mt. 12:41–42

"And I tell you, every one who acknowledges me before men, the Son of man also will acknowledge before the angels of God; but he who denies me before men will be denied before the angels of God. . . ."

> Lk. 12:8–9, addressed to the disciples, but in the pres-
> ence of a great crowd (Lk. 12:1); in Mt. 10:32–33, these
> words are addressed to the Twelve only, with this differ-
> ence, that where Lk. says, "the angels of God," Mt. says,
> "my Father who is in heaven"

We could also include Matthew 23:10: "Neither be called masters, for you have one master, the Christ." But the genuineness of this verse seems contestable: "The word [Christ] may have been added by a copyist," according to Father Lagrange.[44] He says as much about Mark 9:41: "For truly, I say to you, whoever gives you a cup of water to drink because you bear the name of Christ. . . ." These words, moreover, are addressed to the disciples alone. Lastly, there is a clear allusion to sonship in the parable of the murdering vineyard tenants (Mk. 12:1–9; Mt. 21:33–41; Lk. 20:9–16), but except in Luke, the words are addressed specially to the Pharisees, and the allusion could not be clear to any but them, as we will see later.[45]

C. Finally, must we not recall John the Baptist's messianic question, "Are you he who is to come . . . ?" and Jesus' strongly affirmative reply?

"Go and tell John what you hear and see: the blind receive their sight and the lame walk, lepers are cleansed and the deaf hear, and the dead are raised up, and the poor have good news preached to them. And blessed is he who takes no offense at me."

> Mt. 11:4–6; see Lk. 7:22–23

[44] Lagrange, . . . Matthieu, p. 441.
[45] See pp. 210 ff., below.

We cannot tell, it is true, whether the question and answer were private or public; but immediately afterward, addressing the crowd (according to Matthew and Luke), Jesus identified John as the Precursor, in terms which make no sense unless Jesus himself was indeed he "who is to come," the Messiah:

"What did you go out in the wilderness to behold? . . . a prophet? Yes, I tell you, and more than a prophet. This is he of whom it is written,

> 'Behold, I send my messenger before thy face,
> who shall prepare thy way before thee.'

Truly, I say to you, among those born of women there has risen no one greater than John the Baptist; yet he who is least in the kingdom of heaven is greater than he. . . . and if you are willing to accept it, he is Elijah who is to come. He who has ears to hear, let him hear. . . ."

> Mt. 11:7–15; almost identical text in Lk. 7:24–28, except that it lacks the last verse, "and if you are willing . . ."

There emerge from these passages, if we accept them (provisionally) as they have come down to us, the following theses.

From the Quotations at A and C

That from the Galilean ministry onward, the Jewish crowd, struck by the miracles that Jesus brought about and even more by the sovereign authority with which he spoke, wondered, at least at times, whether Jesus was not the awaited Messiah, Son of David.

That Jesus' messianic reputation spread from Galilee into Judea and the neighboring lands, since at Capernaum as well as at Jericho and in Phoenicia many of those who implored him did not hesitate to call him "Lord, Son of David!"

That from the Galilean ministry onward, and from his answer to the Baptist's inquiry, Jesus clearly let it be understood that John was "the Precursor" and Jesus himself the Messiah whom the Precursor was to announce—which can equally be deduced from the passage of Isaiah Jesus chose in the synagogue at Nazareth and the commentary he made on it (Lk. 4:18–21).

That the entry into Jerusalem indeed had the character of a messianic demonstration: Jesus was loudly and publicly proclaimed Messiah, Son of David, at least by those who escorted him.

From the Quotations at B

That from the Galilean ministry onward, while he chose to use the modest title "Son of man" to designate himself, Jesus concealed nothing of his supreme grandeur, of his sovereign powers—the power to remit sin, to perfect or give fullness to the Law, to grant or prevent access to the Kingdom of Heaven—all powers which can be said are not specifically messianic but basically divine; thus, that Jesus' messiahship, no less than the mystery of his sonship, could not remain entirely unperceived by the Jewish people.

How can these deductions, drawn from the Synoptic texts quoted, be reconciled with the deductions previously drawn from the same Synoptics concerning the exchange on the road to Caesarea Philippi? On the face of it, are they not at least partly contradictory? If Jesus' messianic reputation was as has just been said, can it be that only the Twelve were ignorant of it? If the declarations just quoted were made by Jesus in public, what is the import of the imperative rule of secrecy on the messiahship formulated by Jesus himself near Caesarea Philippi, and moreover what is the import of Peter's confession? It is of course understandable that this secrecy held only for a time, and that *in extremis,* as he entered Jerusalem on the eve of the Passion, Jesus accepted the idea of a formal messianic demonstration. But how is this suffering messiahship that he chose, with a sublime effort of a will simultaneously human and superhuman, to be reconciled with the connotation of glory—temporal as much as spiritual glory, national and military glory—which was for all Israel attached to the name of David and hence necessarily to his messianic lineage?

        ✧   ✧   ✧

We have as yet considered only the Synoptic Gospels in this investigation. The fourth Gospel reserves more serious difficulties for us.

Actually, in Saint John's so very different and so personal account, there is no trace of the exchange near Caesarea Philippi, no trace of the secrecy about the messiahship imposed by the Master on his disciples; quite to the contrary, and from the beginning of the Gospel, Jesus' messiahship and above all else the ineffable sonship—the sec-

ond element essential and inseparable from the first—appear in a
bright light, in such dazzling clarity that, by violent contrast, the incredulity of the "Jews"—those whom Saint John calls the "Jews,"
meaning some few officials, Pharisees, and doctors—takes on a necessarily satanic cast.

The whole of Saint John cannot be quoted here; yet we should follow the steady development of the striking exposition from chapter to
chapter.

1:29–34, 41–51: Witness by John the Baptist, which we may consider to have been made in public: "Behold, the Lamb of God, who
takes away the sins of the world!" (v. 29). Witness by the first disciples: "We have found the Messiah" (v. 41); witness by Nathanael,
whom Jesus, far from silencing, answers: "Truly, truly, I say to you,
you will see heaven opened, and the angels of God ascending and de-
scending upon the Son of man" (v. 51).

2:16: Jesus drives the merchants from the Temple, "my Father's
house," in Jerusalem.

3:13–21, 27–36: To Nicodemus, Jesus identifies himself as "the Son
of man" and God's "only Son" (vv. 13, 16). New witness by John the
Baptist, alluding to Jesus as "he who comes from heaven" (v. 31).

4:10–26, 39–43: Dialogue between Jesus and the Samaritan woman
at Jacob's well, Jesus saying to her: "I who speak to you am [the
Messiah]" (v. 26). After Jesus has spent two days at Sychar, the Samaritans affirm, ". . . we know that this is indeed the Savior of the
world" (v. 42).

5:17–47: At Jerusalem, following the cure of a paralytic, Jesus con-
tends with his adversaries, and says: " 'My Father is working still,
and I am working.' This was why the Jews sought all the more to kill
him, because he not only broke the sabbath but also called God his
Father, making himself equal with God" (vv. 17–18); and again he
says: "The Father . . . has given all judgment to the Son . . ." (v. 22).

6:14–15, 26–59: In Galilee, after the multiplication of the loaves,
the crowd is about to take him by force to make him king; Jesus with-
draws and goes to Capernaum, where he says to them: "I am the
bread of life" (v. 35); and in the synagogue there, he says: "I am the
living bread which came down from heaven; if any one eats of this
bread, he will live for ever" (v. 51).

8:12–59: Jesus teaching in the Temple, debating with his adversaries: "I am the light of the world" (v. 12); "Truly, truly, before
Abraham was, I am" (v. 58).

9: Cure of the man blind from birth: ". . . the Jews had already agreed that if any one should confess him [Jesus] to be the Christ, he was to be put out of the synagogue" (v. 22). Jesus asks the man, "Do you believe in the Son of man [variant in some manuscripts: the Son of God]?" and then answers, "You have seen him, and it is he who speaks to you" (vv. 35, 37).

10: Allegory of the good shepherd: "I am the door; if any one enters by me, he will be saved" (v. 9). During the Feast of the Dedication, the officials ask, " 'If you are the Christ, tell us plainly.' Jesus answered them, 'I told you, and you do not believe. . . . I and the Father are one' " (vv. 24–25, 30).

11:1–44: Before he raises Lazarus from the dead, Martha says to Jesus: "I believe that you are the Christ, the Son of God, he who is coming into the world" (v. 27).

12:12–15: Jesus enters Jerusalem before the Passion, and finds not the divided "Jews" of 7:11–44 but "a great crowd" who "went out to meet him, crying, 'Hosanna! Blessed is he who comes in the name of the Lord, even the King of Israel!' " (v. 13).

Persuasive, seeing the texts bared thus; and sometimes irksome. There is no doubt: according to Saint John, Jesus was openly designated by the Precursor, recognized by his disciples, declared repeatedly by himself to be Messiah and Son of God, even more often Son of God than Messiah—the one always linked to the other for him, and bearing enormously on the other. He said of himself that he was
the only Son of God,
one with God,
descended from heaven,
pre-existent from all eternity,
light of the world, bread of life,
only supreme judge,
only door to salvation.

Moreover, and still according to Saint John, the Samaritans of Sychar recognized Jesus as the Messiah, Savior of the world; the Jews of Galilee, overcome by the miracle of the multiplication of the loaves, wanted to proclaim him king—that is, Messiah-King (Jesus withdrew, and this is not surprising, since the least tribal chieftain in Galilee had himself proclaimed king); even in Jerusalem, where opinion on him was more divided, opposition more lively, his adversaries stronger and more aggressive, he ultimately found a Jewish crowd which recognized him and acclaimed him as Messiah-King of Israel.

So the divergences previously noted in the Synoptics, which can be called internal, are augmented by even sharper external divergences, between Saint John and one or another part of the Synoptics.

John's evidence agrees with some passages in the Synoptic Gospels, it is true. But in regard to the sonship, the texts are as rare in the other three accounts as they are frequent in Saint John; in regard to divinity, it is a far cry from the few suggestions in the Synoptics to the doctrinal statements lavished by Saint John.

And elsewhere, how many contradictions, at least apparent!

Contradiction between the triple witness of the Precursor, the revelation that he "saw the Spirit descend as a dove from heaven, and it remained on him [Jesus]" (Jn. 1:32), and the uncertain inquiry, "Are you he who is to come, or shall we look for another?" related by Matthew (11:3) and Luke (7:19). On this point, could we not say, contradiction even between Saint John and Saint John; for if the Precursor's witness was so positive as it is written, how to explain that his disciples did not all leave him to follow Jesus?

Contradiction—here chronological—between the disciples' act of faith at the outset, inscribed on the first page of the fourth Gospel, "Rabbi, you are the Son of God! You are the King of Israel!" (Jn. 1:49), and Peter's confession, inscribed in the Synoptic table at the very end of the Galilean ministry and presented, especially by Saint Matthew, as having a unique and fundamental import.

Contradiction between the fidelity to the Davidic tradition observed by the Synoptics and the transcendent messianism of the fourth Gospel; for it is noteworthy that the title "Son of David," which Saint Matthew in particular uses liberally, appears nowhere in the Johannine account, not even at the triumphal entry into Jerusalem. The only allusion to traditional messianism that we extract is the doing of hostile challengers: "Has not the scripture said that the Christ is descended from David, and comes from Bethlehem, the village where David was?" (Jn. 7:42); and the question fell in silence, with no refutation.

Finally and above all, the major contradiction, which seems irresolvable: secrecy on the messiahship, thrice formulated in the Synoptics, and most of the time observed; no secrecy on the messiahship in Saint John—far to the contrary, for it is not possible to demand faith from all, wholehearted adherence, as the Johannine Christ does, without saying for what reason, by what sovereign right.

✿   ✿   ✿

Wanting to surmount these precipitous difficulties, principally the John-Synoptics discrepancies, a sheer cliff where I despaired of finding any purchase, I decided to consult the experts best qualified by their learning and orthodoxy, exegetes or theologians.

The respected manuals *Christus* by Father Huby and *Biblical Manual* by Vigouroux, Bacuez, and Brassac [46] are well known to Catholics in France, clergy or laymen, who are intent on instructing themselves in their religion. It was with these that I began my research, and to these that I owed my first disappointments. But those very disappointments deserve to be recounted.

In *Christus*, a chapter subsection entitled "Jesus" contains more than a hundred references to the Synoptics and exactly three to Saint John—and the discussion of the fourth Gospel is separated from that of the "Gospels" (the Synoptics being understood) by forty-six pages. The division is justified to a degree by the chronology, but it makes it possible to avoid textual comparisons. All we find are the statements that in the fourth Gospel, "The characteristics of the Synoptic Jesus are taken to the extreme"; "The vigor with which Jesus asserted himself also increased, in the same measure" (p. 1022); and "It is impossible to be more dogmatic than the Jesus of the fourth Gospel" (p. 1023)—we have seen this already, in an earlier discussion of our own.[47] But two pages above this statement, the manual has taken care to inform us that far from "attenuating the characteristics of the historic figure which stood out so clearly from the Synoptic catechesis," this Gospel "illuminates" them, "on the contrary, with a powerful light." How a repeated affirmation of messiahship, of sonship, could illuminate with a more powerful light the repeated injunction of secrecy on the messiahship remains unexplained. Lack of space, no doubt.

Thus I hoped to have better luck with the *Biblical Manual*, whose third volume, a big book by Father A. Brassac running 768 pages, is devoted to the Gospels and Jesus. And indeed, with Chapter VII of the first part, the author openly broaches "The Johannine Question," that is, the examination and explanation of the divergences which ap-

[46] Father Joseph Huby, ed., *Christus: Manuel d'histoire des religions* [Christus: Manual of the History of Religions], Paris, Beauchesne, 1946; Fathers Fulcran G. Vigouroux and A. Brassac, *Manuel biblique, ou Cours d'Écriture sainte à l'usage des séminaires*, ed. Fathers A. Brassac and Louis Bacuez, 4 vols., 12th ed., Paris, Roger et Chernoviz, 1906–1909, specifically vol. III, *Nouveau Testament*, 1909, by Father Brassac.

[47] See p. 111, above.

pear between Saint John and the Synoptics, between the Johannine
Christ and the Synoptic Christ. Alas, vainly did I search among the
discrepancies enumerated for the one that preoccupied me so deeply:
it was not there; nor was the exchange near Caesarea Philippi included among the "facts of the greatest interest" omitted by Saint
John. As for the "General Explanation" proposed on pages 181–183,
according to which "There are numerous aspects of the Savior's
makeup, and Saint John depicted the most elevated side," what
good is this for resolving so sharp an antithesis as between yes and
no?

I was ready to abandon the quest, that is, the *Biblical Manual*,
when in the middle of the chapter treating "The Public Life of Jesus
Christ" a paragraph entitled "Jesus' Reserve in Unveiling His Messiahship and His Divinity" struck my eye and revived my hopes:
here, surely, the antithesis would have to be set down, explained, resolved. References to John alternated with references to Matthew at
the bottom of the pages. But was I dreaming? The second as well as
the first were invoked in support of "Jesus' reserve about his
messiahship"—the antithesis disappeared, gave way to perfect agreement. It was imperative to clear up this mystery, to consult the texts
again myself following the lead of the references. Here are the exhibits of the case.

Biblical Manual, III, 357: "To convince the Jews [that he was di-
vine], . . . would it not have been better to persuade them of this
dogma by his works than to have it proclaimed by his disciples?" (It
would be proper to add: or to proclaim it himself.) References: Matthew 12:23; John 4:29; 6:30.

First reference (Mt. 12:23): after a miraculous cure, "And all the
people were amazed, and said, 'Can this be the Son of David?' " But
the "Son of David" is not the "Son of God"; he is the Messiah according to tradition, the Messiah of popular belief. Invalid reference.

Second reference (Jn. 4:29): the Samaritan woman says to her people, "Come, see a man who told me all that I ever did. Can this be
the Christ?" In fact, replying to the woman's avowal, "I know that
Messiah is coming (he who is called Christ)," Jesus has just said, "I
who speak to you am he" (Jn. 4:25–26). Is this "to persuade them of
this dogma" of his divinity "by his works"? Is this "Jesus' Reserve in
Unveiling His Messiahship"? And furthermore, how to believe that
the astounding news, ". . . we know that this is indeed the Savior of

the world" (Jn. 4:42), was not immediately propagated from Sychar throughout Samaria, throughout Palestine? Invalid reference.

Third reference (Jn. 6:30): the crowd says to Jesus, "Then what sign do you do, that we may see, and believe you? What work do you perform?" We know Jesus' answer: "I am the bread of life. . . . For this is the will of my Father, that every one who sees the Son and believes in him should have eternal life . . ." (Jn. 6:35, 40). Is this "to persuade them of this dogma" of his divinity "by his works"—without proclaiming it—or on the contrary to proclaim it without seeking to persuade by his works? Doubly mistaken reference.

And so with the rest. The references on page 358 are of the same quality: not one is valid; three out of four say the opposite of what the *Biblical Manual* would have them say.

Accustomed though I was to such malpractices in all the domains of history, this experience disturbed me. Leaving the manuals aside, I turned to the masters of Catholic exegesis who bear the names Louis-Claude Fillion, then consultant to the Pontifical Biblical Commission, and Fathers Marie-Joseph Lagrange, Léonce de Grandmaison, and Jules Lebreton, whose works are the authorities. Need I say that they led me from disappointment to disappointment?

One of them, Louis-Claude Fillion, hews close to the *Biblical Manual*, and lines up contradictory observations one after another:

During the first stage . . . of his Galilean activity, it is certain that Jesus carefully avoided presenting himself openly as the Messiah. . . . Despite everything, from the beginning of his active life, when he foresaw no danger, the Savior presented himself clearly as the [Messiah] a number of times. . . . During the following stage, . . . he continued to exercise great circumspection in regard to the people for some time; however, he did not hesitate to show himself openly as the Messiah on several occasions.[48]

Two other authorities, eminent among all, Fathers de Grandmaison and Lagrange, go so far as to deny any opposition between Saint John and the Synoptics. According to Father Lagrange:

We see [in the Synoptics] that Jesus did nothing to promote the popular belief [that he was the Messiah], and that indeed he rather recommended secrecy to his disciples. *This is also what we see in John.*[49] . . . Jesus' atti-

---

[48] Louis-Claude Fillion, *Vie de Notre Seigneur Jésus-Christ*, a work granted an award by the Académie Française; 22nd ed., Paris, Letouzey, 1929, II, 132–135.
[49] It is I who italicize this dumbfounding sentence.

tude on the question of messianism, vital for the Jews, was palpably the same in the Synoptics and John. . . . Only in John the Messiah is more persistently the Son of God.[50]

And Father de Grandmaison writes:

It would be vain to oppose the Johannine tradition to the Synoptics on this point. . . . Far from contradicting [the Synoptic tradition, according to which, the author says, "It was only at the last moment . . . that Jesus unreservedly and unguardedly proclaimed before all his mission . . . as Son of God"], the fourth Gospel adds reasons for believing it exact.[51]

What reasons? Father de Grandmaison alleges "the desertion of a number of disciples" in John 6:66, but this is after the Capernaum discourse, which was a clear declaration of sonship; and Jesus' "refusing to answer the Pharisees' direct questions" in John 8:53 and 10:24–40. "Refusing"? Was he really "refusing to answer" when he said, ". . . it is my Father who glorifies me, of whom you say that he is your God. . . . Your father Abraham rejoiced that he was to see my day. . . . before Abraham was, I am" (Jn. 8:54, 56, 58), or when he replied, "I told you [that I am the Christ], and you would not believe. . . . I and the Father are one" (Jn. 10:25, 30)? No, it is "vain" to *deny* opposition between the Johannine and Synoptic traditions on this point: it leaps to the eye.

Only Father Lebreton sketches out a systematic explanation, though with the help of a German theologian, and without broaching the problem of "secrecy on the messiahship," for it is the crowd's "ignorance of the messiahship" to which the disciples testified in Caesarea Philippi that troubles him:

In face of this fact, so clearly attested by the three Synoptics, we wonder how we must interpret the declarations which are assigned earlier dates by the evangelists, particularly by John [and which are actually a hundred times more explicit in the fourth Gospel than in the Synoptics]. For the latter [John], commentators argue from the scene in Caesarea Philippi to challenge his evidence, but this is obviously not enough. [Citing Bernhard Weiss, the author continues:] We cannot understand the scene in Caesarea Philippi . . . to mean that the people did not yet consider Jesus as the Messiah, . . . but to mean that the people no longer held him to be the Messiah. . . . [And Father Lebreton concludes:] The tragic episode at

[50] Father Marie-Joseph Lagrange, O.P., ed. and tr., *Évangile selon saint Jean*, Paris, Gabalda, 1924, pp. cli–clii.

[51] Grandmaison, *op. cit.*, I, 337–338.

Capernaum, as reported by John, is the best introduction to the scene in Caesarea Philippi. Bitterness over vanished illusions rocked faith in the Messiah in the minds of most of the hearers.[52]

An excessively ingenious explanation which "is obviously not enough." The texts lend it no support whatever; have our authors forgotten that Mark and Luke have related similar sayings of the crowd, in almost the same terms, as already having occurred earlier? ". . . it was said by some that John had been raised from the dead, by some that Elijah had appeared, and by others that one of the old prophets had risen" (Lk. 9:7–8; Mk. 6:14–15, and v. 16 also puts the first formula in Herod's mouth).

Supposing that public opinion had changed so profoundly in so short a time, is it credible that nothing of this transpired in the disciples' reply in Caesarea Philippi, a clear and precise reply which is the same in the three Gospels? Besides, such a turn is far from being proved; we believe we have furnished some proof in support of the opposite thesis, that the sympathies of the people remained constant.

The thorny problem posed by the demonstrable divergences between Saint John and the Synoptics thus does not seem to us resolved in any degree. And we will not take up the task of resolving it. It is difficult if not impossible to grasp the historic reality where doctrinal preoccupations intervene or predominate.[53] Now, on this question of messiahship, most often elevated to the higher plane of sonship in the fourth Gospel, Saint John's characteristic dogmatic aims, carried to the extreme, override and obscure all historicity. This is the least that can be said, and it "is obviously enough."

✿   ✿   ✿

There remain the Synoptics, with their internal divergences, these less marked, less numerous by comparison with the external divergences, and in many cases apparently easy to mend.

For it is not forbidden to note that the Davidic invocation widespread in Matthew occurs only once—in Jericho, on the road to Jerusalem—in Mark and Luke. "It must be recognized," writes Father Lagrange, "that Matthew uses it without rigorous historic exactness.

[52] Lebreton, *La Vie et l'enseignement de Jésus-Christ*, I, 425–426; and citing Bernhard Weiss, *Das Leben Jesu* [The Life of Jesus], 2 vols., Berlin, 1902, II, 267.
[53] We judged it possible previously (pp. 111–123, above), but in an entirely different case, that of the welcome given Jesus by the crowd.

. . . This title [Son of David] corresponds better with the thinking of Matthew himself than with the thinking of those who pronounced it at that moment. This is again the same disregard for a precise historic modality." [54] Let us keep in mind this admission that it would be imprudent to seek the slightest historic exactness in the first Gospel.

Nor is it forbidden either to conjecture that a number of Jesus' declarations quoted on pages 152–153 above were addressed to the disciples rather than the crowd—the very divergences of the evangelists on this point allow this to be seen—from which it follows that the rule of secrecy on the messiahship might have been a good deal more strictly observed than is thought.

As for other declarations to which this conjecture cannot be applied, no matter how clear they seem in the Gospel text, they were still only simple suggestions, doubtless more veiled in actuality, more difficult to interpret except to the doctors present; they could have been not understood or have passed unnoticed by the mass of hearers.

A typical example: after the miracle of the cure of the paralytic, when several scribes who were there "said to themselves" that Jesus was "blaspheming" because he attributed to himself the power "to forgive sins," a power belonging to God alone, what did "the crowds" do? They "glorified God, who had given such authority to men" (Mt. 9:2–8).

In this expanse of shifting sands, if there is an isle of firm ground, it is indeed the group of Synoptic texts related to the exchange near Caesarea Philippi, as we have been bent on establishing from the outset. From the historic standpoint, which is our standpoint, they are and remain the major texts. We are happy to find ourselves in agreement with the most orthodox exegetes on this point, though there is a tendency in Catholic instruction to pass over in silence—a sin of omission—Jesus' injunction to his disciples against revealing his messiahship to anyone. But none of the exegetes contests the reality of "secrecy on the messiahship" or, to avoid a formula too closely associated with certain venturesome theories, of what the *Biblical Manual* calls "Jesus' Reserve in Unveiling His Messiahship and His Divinity"; and willy-nilly they maintain that they can integrate the fourth Gospel itself into that reality. None of them contests that Jesus made constant use of the term "Son of man" and never of "Son of God" or "Son of David" to designate himself. But what does this reserve signify?

[54] Lagrange, . . . *Matthieu*, pp. 189, 309.

Why did Jesus, fully aware of his messianic election, choose to avoid revealing it till the final hour? Why did Jesus, fully aware of his divine sonship, call himself "Son of man"? Where is the alleged guilt, the deafness, the blindness of the Jewish people taken "as a whole" if they knew Jesus and if Jesus made himself known to them neither as Messiah nor as Son of God (in the Christian sense of these words)?

Now, it seems indispensable—to orthodox theology—that whatever the case, this guilt of the Jewish people be shown, be confirmed. This has given rise to efforts to interpret the facts and the texts which can be summarized in the three following postulates.

> 1. *Jesus could not do otherwise than clear his path of "illusions" of a "carnal messianism,"* [55] *so widespread then among his countrymen.*

This is the central idea, the master key of systematic apologetics.

[Louis-Claude Fillion:] If Jesus had revealed himself immediately and indiscriminately to everyone as the [Messiah], his work would have run the risk of being seriously compromised because of the woeful character of popular hopes. The Jewish nation as a whole was by no means prepared to profit by knowledge of that secret. . . . Jesus let no opportunity pass to correct any false element in the people's messianic conceptions and to replace these with the true ideal [?].[56]

[Léonce de Grandmaison:] Even the purest sources nourishing Israel's hope were conducive to serious confusion, for lack of authentic interpretation. . . . The best were not safe from these illusions; the whole Gospel account attests to it. . . . Under these conditions, a public, immediate assertion of the title of Messiah, in addition to the dangers to which it would have subjected the person of the Master prematurely, would have had the prime effect of authorizing, to the point of ineradicability, the common mistaken notion of the nature and ordinations of God's reign.[57]

[Jules Lebreton:] The messianic hopes [of the Jewish crowds] were enveloped in misleading illusions so dangerous that the revelation of [the Messiah] could not be made suddenly, by a summary declaration; it had to be preceded by a slow and progressive preparation.[58]

[Marie-Joseph Lagrange:] The word *Messiah* . . . excited hopes for liberation, mixed with less pure desires for domination. . . . The dispositions of the Jews being what they were, to have himself acclaimed as Messiah

---

[55] Lebreton, *La Vie et l'enseignement de Jésus-Christ,* I, 102; Godet, *op. cit.,* II, 496, among many others who use these terms.
[56] Fillion, *op. cit.,* II, 552–553.
[57] Grandmaison, *op. cit.,* I, 314–315.
[58] Lebreton, *La Vie et l'enseignement de Jésus-Christ, loc. cit.*

would have been to unleash revolution and . . . on Jesus' side . . . to expose his true mission and his doctrine to misunderstanding.[59]

The four authors quoted above belong to the Catholic Church. But analogous formulas could readily be found among Protestant authors —for example, Albert Réville:

There was too great a distance between the Messiah who [Jesus] was and wanted to be and the Messiah whom the Jewish people awaited for him to be able to suddenly claim a like honor without moral violence and without the risk of being misunderstood and of provoking political agitation diametrically opposed to the goal he hoped to attain.[60]

2. *This is why Jesus, rejecting every kind of glorious title, wanted to be only "the Son of man," a name whose modesty was cloaked in mystery and which evoked the Danielic vision of participation in heavenly Power even as it underlined the human condition accepted by the Savior.*

[Louis-Claude Fillion:] It ["Son of man"] was thus at bottom a rather vague and even rather obscure name. And this was precisely the reason Jesus . . . used it. . . . This title veiled him and revealed him in the same breath. . . . It excited attention and curiosity, it prompted investigations, questions; it recalled the oracle of Daniel to the serious-minded, and thus led them little by little to see in [Jesus] the promised Messiah, without his needing to show himself openly.[61]

[Léonce de Grandmaison:] In itself, [this name] was a sort of parable, an enigma, . . . serving to stimulate the hearers' attention but not to satisfy their curiosity. While it effectively linked Jesus' person and mission to the highest messianic prerogatives of the Lord and universal Judge, it also accentuated the characteristics of evident frailty, . . . of redemptive suffering, in a word, of humanity, which would mark the career of the Master in reality.[62]

[Marie-Joseph Lagrange:] What did this term "Son of man" mean, then, and why did Jesus apply it to himself? This problem is still much debated today among various schools of thought: how could the Pharisees have resolved it? Some of them, the most learned, were able to recall Daniel's vision and that heavenly being, like a son of man, who came on the clouds. But what did this apparition have in common with Jesus of Nazareth? Nor was it a vision of the Messiah, since Daniel's human visitation came from

[59] Father Marie-Joseph Lagrange, O.P., *L'Évangile de Jésus-Christ*, Paris, Gabalda, 1928, pp. 128, 466.
[60] Albert Réville, *Jésus de Nazareth*, 2 vols., Paris, Fischbacher, 1906, II, 183–184.
[61] Fillion, *op. cit.*, II, 138.
[62] Grandmaison, *op. cit.*, I, 324.

heaven, and the Messiah was to be born of David as a true son of man.
. . . The Pharisees did not discover the secret of this enigma in their books.
Jesus had to resolve it in his person, but he deemed it prudent to prepare
[men's] minds. He was not resorting to equivocation by choosing an expression boldly signaling the human nature which he had put on in reality
and which . . . he would one day reveal as the same term Daniel had used
to manifest his heavenly origin.[63]

It will be noted that Father Lagrange's wording is much more reserved, and in sum reduces this "preparation of minds" to little. And
it is interesting to observe that on this point Maurice Goguel and Joseph Klausner [64] come closer to Fillion and De Grandmaison than to
Lagrange.

   3. *However, it was important for Jesus to make his capacity, his
       office as Messiah known publicly at least once: the entry into Je-
       rusalem on the eve of the Passion had the character of a solemn
       messianic revelation.*

[Louis-Claude Fillion:] When his "hour" approached, [Jesus] removed all
the veils, for he indeed had to make a formal and public attempt to make
his office known. Thus his triumphal entry into the Holy City only a few
days before his death: a triumph which was for him as for the crowds an
imposing messianic demonstration. . . .
   [It was a demonstration] in keeping with the true messianic ideal. . . .
The Messiah in the image held by most of the Jews of that time would
have made his entry . . . mounted on a charger, surrounded with splendid
officers and a large militia advancing to the sound of trumpets, flags unfurled. . . . Jesus entered Jerusalem . . . seated on a young ass, as a
"Prince of peace," as a spiritual king . . . [according to] the Prophet Zechariah's oracle.[65]

[Jules Lebreton:] The previous year, when the Galilean crowd had wanted
to make him king, Jesus had withdrawn (Jn. 6:15); now he did not refuse
this homage: he had to exercise messiahship publicly at least once; in any
event, he would do so in the humblest way. . . . but even at that hour, his
messianism remained wholly religious and not at all political like the hopes
on which the Jews were intoxicated.[66]

[Marie-Joseph Lagrange:] Jesus was truly the promised Messiah. Not being
as the people imagined, he had delayed revealing himself until the moment
when he would no longer run the risk of precipitating them into a senseless
venture at the gates of Jerusalem under the eyes of the Roman authorities.

---

[63] Lagrange, *L'Évangile de Jésus-Christ*, pp. 127–128.
[64] Maurice Goguel, *La Vie de Jésus-Christ*, Paris, Payot, 1932, p. 561; Joseph
Klausner, *Jésus de Nazareth*, tr. Isaac Friedmann, Paris, Payot, 1933, p. 377.
[65] Fillion, *op. cit.*, II, 135; III, 216–217.
[66] Lebreton, *La Vie et l'enseignement de Jésus-Christ*, II, 167, 171.

But it was his duty to present himself as Messiah, so that the Jews could not allege that they could not recognize as such a man who had refused that title. Jesus decided on an entrance which was undeniably messianic, as it fulfilled one of the clearest messianic texts (Zech. 9:9), but which was simultaneously the most modest. . . . He allowed the people to acclaim him; he even elicited the acclamations in a way by taking the role described by a prophet. But this simplicity, which the Prophet had insisted on, was to make it clear that he did not come to establish a temporal kingdom, and that he was not of a kind to challenge the Romans' vigilance unnecessarily.[67]

These three postulates and the elaborations given them call forth some observations.

On Postulate 1: The Impediment of "Carnal Messianism"

There is no denying, and we have indeed shown it here,[68] that a chasm existed between messianism as Jesus embodied it and messianism as the great majority of his Jewish fellow countrymen conceived of it. There is no denying that the Jewish messianic ideal entertained hopes for liberation and grandeur, which, incidentally, issued from "the purest sources"—Scripture itself—and which were symbolized by the glorious name of David. The precautions Jesus took to avoid arousing hopes in vain—the "secrecy on the messiahship"—were thus perfectly understandable and justified. But take heed: the explanation given of it is a double-edged sword, for it is made to account for not only Jesus' "secrecy on the messiahship" but also the ignorance, the incomprehension, the lack of recognition of the Jewish people with regard to Jesus the Messiah.

We are told that "the revelation" of the Christ "had to be preceded by a slow and progressive preparation": certainly. "Jesus let no opportunity pass to correct any false element in the people's messianic conceptions and to replace these with the true ideal": perhaps, although this does not appear clearly in what we know of the Gospel teaching. But what is sure, for "the whole Gospel account attests to it," is that despite this "slow and progressive preparation," which the disciples above all profited by, Jesus did not manage "to correct any false element in the . . . messianic conceptions" of the disciples themselves. On this account, how can we be surprised that the people, infinitely less "prepared," also persisted in their error, and while admir-

[67] Lagrange, . . . Marc, pp. 292, 297.
[68] See pp. 138–142, above.

ing Jesus as "a prophet mighty in deed and word before God" (Lk. 24:19), could not recognize in him the Messiah announced in Scripture?

Was this recognition even possible on the level of pure spirituality? We are allowed to doubt it. What people, whoever they may be, can be asked to empty themselves entirely of themselves, of their history, of their most solidly rooted national traditions, inseparable from their most sacred religious traditions? Let us repeat once more, as we will never repeat it often enough, too often: it is easy, from the vantage point of twenty centuries of commentaries and dogmatic teaching, to score "illusions" of a "carnal messianism" and "the woeful character of popular hopes," less easy to see clearly the events themselves and, elbow to elbow with the Roman soldiers, to discern in the son of the carpenter from Nazareth the Messiah, the Son of David; more— the true "Son of God." The good Pharisee Saul of Tarsus was misled. How many of these severe judges would have been misled themselves?—and I am not sure that they would have subsequently had their "road to Damascus."

On Postulate 2: The Title "Son of Man"

We must tirelessly recall to mind that in the Old Testament, the expression "Son of man," which is very rare except in Ezekiel, is always used as a synonym for *man;* the best exegetes recognize that in Jesus' time such a name was not at all a current messianic title. Moreover, writes Father Lagrange,

Catholic exegetical tradition, in its broad currents from the Fathers to Maldonado,[69] shrank from [giving it a] clearly messianic meaning. . . . Thus it seems to me that when Jesus called himself "Son of man," he meant simply "the man I am," to draw attention to his person without openly and so to speak officially taking the title of Messiah.[70]

Under these circumstances, I ask:

How could this "rather vague and even rather obscure" title have "veiled him and revealed him in the same breath"?

Has one the right to write that the title "effectively linked Jesus' person and mission to the highest messianic prerogatives," or again, that this expression, "vague" in itself, had been "providentially en-

[69] [Juan Maldonado, or Johannes Maldonatus, 1533–1583, was a Spanish Jesuit theologian.—Tr.]

[70] Lagrange, . . . *Marc,* pp. cxlix–cl.

riched by the prophets with a potential for a meaning conformed to authentic messianism"? [71]

Is it the Messiah that this term makes us think of when we read the Prophet Ezekiel?

Since Daniel did not even figure in the biblical canon at that time and was known only to a small number of "the most learned," what chance was there for the Jewish people "as a whole" to associate this term with Daniel's vision?

Another puzzle: if Jesus wanted to suggest to the crowds through his words, demonstrate to them through his acts that he not only was the awaited Messiah, the Son of David, but also had the unheard-of, overwhelming identity for which nothing, absolutely nothing prepared them: Son of God, not in the figurative but in the strict sense —the Christian sense—of unique Son of the Unique God ("Hear, O Israel: The Lord our God, the Lord is one"), how to explain that he chose a title to designate himself which can be said not only was not specifically messianic but also seemed to incorporate precisely the denial of the divine sonship: "Son of man"?

Good Catholic writers themselves acknowledge this difficulty: "The expression in Greek means literally a man born of a man, who has a man as father. We can see what misunderstandings this formula could occasion. Thus the Church did not use it later." [72]

On Postulate 3: The Messianic Entry into Jerusalem

It would seem, in fact, according to the fourfold testimony of the Gospels—for the fourth Gospel finds itself in agreement with the Synoptics—that the entry into Jerusalem, the "ovation of the palm branches," [73] took on the character of a demonstration of messiahship by Jesus' explicit intention.

But here again, I perceive a world of contradictions and improbabilities in the commentaries of our authors.

Why did Jesus, finally raising the veil which he had drawn around himself until then, want this demonstration *in extremis?* ". . . it was his duty," Father Lagrange has explained, "to present himself as Mes-

[71] Father André Charue, *L'Incrédulité des Juifs dans le Nouveau Testament,* Louvain, Gembloux, 1929, p. 110.

[72] Father Jules Renié, *Les Évangiles* [The Gospels], vol. IV of *Manuel d'Écriture sainte* [Manual of Holy Scripture], 2nd ed., Paris, Vitte, 1938, p. 360.

[73] Father Marie-Joseph Lagrange, O.P., ed. and tr., *Évangile selon saint Luc,* Paris, Gabalda, 1921, p. cxxxviii.

siah, so that the Jews could not allege that they could not recognize as such a man who had refused that title." So, in this supreme hour, it was the notion of removing any excuse the Jewish people might have, of making the shame of Jewish incredulity more glaring, that supposedly preoccupied the Man-God, him who had resolved to die ignominiously for his own and all humankind. Unless we believe another explanation given, that Jesus wanted to offer the Jewish people their last chance and to rally the masses to him: "Among the multitudes who were following him were many who were undecided. A brilliant demonstration was therefore necessary to overcome their hesitation, and also to strengthen the faith of those who believed in him." [74] But Jesus could have had no doubts about the violent hostility of the Jewish religious leaders and doctors; did he then hope to rouse the crowds against them? No one thinks of attributing these revolutionary designs to him, and yet what other outcome would there have been for such an incitement of the masses?

The texts tell us nothing of Jesus' intentions, except that he wanted to fulfill Zechariah's prophecy: "Lo, your king comes to you / . . . humble and riding on an ass . . ." (9:9). To strike a contrast with this peaceful, modest display "in keeping with the true messianic ideal," the commentators instantly oppose the sumptuousness, the warrior array which the "false ideal" of "most of the Jews" would demand: a Messiah parading "on a charger," at the head of a "splendid" cortege, "to the sound of trumpets, flags unfurled." Bad caricatures (and drawn in bad faith), which it suffices to confront with the noble image pictured in the seventeenth Psalm of Solomon:

. . . for He [the Messiah] will not trust on horsemen nor on chariot; nor on the bow: nor shall He multiply to himself gold and silver for war. . . .[75]

Ps. of Sol. 17:37

Certainly, Jewish public opinion did expect the Messiah to be a liberator. But had the people no right to expect some miraculous liberation by the Anointed of the Lord, the Son of David, without recourse to arms (which only the Zealots, advocates of armed resistance and terrorism, wanted)? What miracle was impossible to God, the God Who had made the walls of Jericho crumble at the sound of trumpets (Josh. 6:20)? "Illusions" of a "carnal messianism": yes, events, reasoning, and time as well as the Christian faith have con-

---

[74] Fillion, op. cit., III, 210.
[75] [Quotation taken from The Odes and Psalms of Solomon, p. 154.—Tr.]

demned them; but it is only fair to recognize, with Father de Grandmaison, that they were nourished at "the purest sources." Preceding
Zechariah 9:9, there is Zechariah 9:8, which the commentators prefer
not to quote:

> The word of the Lord. . . .
> Then I will encamp at my house as a guard,
>   so that none shall march to and fro;
> no oppressor shall again overrun them. . . .
>
> Zech. 9:1, 8

For the rest, if "most of the Jews" awaited a military "Messiah," a
war chief, then the "ovation of the palm branches" becomes inexplicable. Indeed! Here was Jesus advancing toward the city, in the city,
"seated on a young ass, as a 'Prince of peace,' as a spiritual king," and
the people gave him a triumphal welcome, and the acclamations re-
sounded:

> Hosanna! Blessed is he who comes in the name of the Lord! [76] Blessed is
> the kingdom of our father David that is coming! Hosanna in the highest!
>
> Mk. 11:9–10

> Hosanna to the Son of David! Blessed is he who comes in the name of the
> Lord! Hosanna in the highest!
>
> Mt. 21:9

> Blessed is the King who comes in the name of the Lord! Peace in heaven
> and glory in the highest!
>
> Lk. 19:38

> Hosanna! Blessed is he who comes in the name of the Lord, even the King
> of Israel!
>
> Jn. 12:13

"The farther he advanced," writes Father Lebreton, "the denser the
crowd became, and the more enthusiastic. . . . The stir spread little
by little and seized the whole city. . . . Now the clamor was enormous," and "enthusiasm . . . gripped the entire city and . . .
drowned out Christ's enemies." [77] A "triumphal entry," Louis-Claude
Fillion has likewise said, "an imposing messianic demonstration."

But wouldn't this paint too positive a picture of the Jewish people?
Father Lebreton takes care to explain: "The enthusiasm of the crowd
was little enlightened, nationalistic more than religious," while "even
at that hour" Jesus' "messianism remained wholly religious"; the Jews

[76] Ps. 118:26.
[77] Lebreton, La Vie et l'enseignement de Jésus-Christ, II, 168–170.

"were intoxicated" on "political" hopes, and Jesus was pained at this; he wept over Jerusalem.[78] At which one cannot refrain from objecting: if Jesus was pained at the acclamations that swelled around him —these acclamations being the unique indication of "political intoxication"—why then did he answer the remarks of some Pharisees, "I tell you, if these were silent, the very stones would cry out" (Lk. 19:40)?

"It isn't easy to be a Jew. . . ."

Do you remember this saying of Péguy's in *Our Youth?*[79] No, "It isn't easy to be a Jew" in retrospect, either. Had Jesus not been acclaimed, the commentators would say: "Carnal Jews, they had to have a charger instead of a young ass!" And as he was acclaimed, they say even so: "Carnal Jews, they took a young ass for a charger!" For doctrine demands: the Jews must be "carnal," because they must be guilty, cast out, punished.

They still tell us, Father Lagrange has told us:

Not being as the people imagined, [Jesus] had delayed revealing himself [as Messiah] until the moment when he would no longer run the risk of precipitating them into a senseless venture at the gates of Jerusalem under the eyes of the Roman authorities. . . . [The] simplicity [of his demeanor] . . . was to make it clear that he did not come to establish a temporal kingdom, and that he was not of a kind to challenge the Romans' vigilance unnecessarily.

This commentary lacks clarity in substance and form, as happens with Father Lagrange every time he is in a quandary. For in the end analysis, if "the entire city" acclaimed Jesus as "Son of David," "King of Israel," if we are shown a whole people "intoxicated" with "nationalistic" hopes, wasn't this demonstration "at the gates of Jerusalem," in Jerusalem, "under the eyes of the Roman authorities" a more reckless venture, a more "senseless venture," even than in Galilee? Wasn't it "of a kind to challenge the Romans' vigilance"? The procurator (or governor), Pontius Pilate, whom we will introduce later, had a heavy hand when faced with popular agitation; he did not hesitate to spill blood, and Jesus knew it, according to Luke's testimony:

There were some present at that very time who told him [Jesus] of the Galileans whose blood Pilate had mingled with their sacrifices.

Lk. 13:1

[78] *Ibid.*, II, 169, 171.
[79] Charles Péguy, *Notre Jeunesse* [Our Youth], in *Cahiers de la Quinzaine*, 11th ser., no. 12, July, 1910.

It is true, Father Lagrange seems to have foreseen the objection: more thoughtful than others, he sets about to minimize the event, underlining the "ridiculous" and inoffensive aspect that such a "masquerade," such a "caricature of the ascent to the Capitol" [80] could have had to a Roman. But did the single fact that the Jewish rabbi was mounted on an ass make "this popular explosion"—another phrase from the same author—so harmless? Shall we invoke the *Biblical Manual*, where we read that "The asses of the Near East, more vigorous and elegant than those of our countries, sometimes served as mounts for the highest-ranking personages"? [81] Little matters the mount and its size. No one believes that a Roman, a Pontius Pilate, took the trouble to distinguish between "purely religious" messianism and "carnal" messianism as our Christian doctors do; no one doubts that any publicized messianism, any acclamation of a "King of Israel," a "Son of David," seemed equally dangerous for the *pax romana*, calling equally for repression.

How to resolve the dilemma?

Either the entry into Jerusalem was really a "popular explosion," a "triumphal" demonstration, a specifically messianic triumph—and in this case, it is unlikely that the occupation authorities, the Roman gauleiters, would not have instituted an immediate and brutal repression;

or the demonstration had only a very limited scope, and its character was not clearly messianic—but in this case, if it passed unperceived by the Romans, it could have also by the majority of the Jewish population present in Jerusalem.

How to resolve the dilemma? By weighing the texts.

It is noteworthy that neither Mark nor Luke mentions the intervention of the crowds; it is the disciples, "the whole company of the disciples" (Lk. 19:37 [CCD]), who formed the procession and shouted acclamations. Luke 19:39 notes the protest of "some of the Pharisees" mingled in the crowd: the crowd in this case is present at the demonstration without participating in it.

Matthew, on his side, speaks of "the crowd" and "the crowds" who accompanied Jesus and his disciples. But he adds this detail: "And when he entered Jerusalem, all the city was stirred, saying, 'Who is this?' And the crowds said, 'This is the prophet Jesus from Nazareth of Galilee'" (Mt. 21:10–11). Hence the observers were astir and ques-

[80] Lagrange, *L'Évangile de Jésus-Christ*, p. 427.
[81] Brassac, *op. cit.*, p. 613.

tioning, and nothing in the replies of the demonstrators told them that Jesus was the Messiah.

John is the only one to speak of "a great crowd" (Jn. 12:12), and actually of two, one that had left Bethany with Jesus and one that came from Jerusalem to meet him. John too adds a detail: "His disciples did not understand this at first" (Jn. 12:16)—they did not understand at first why Jesus had decided to enter Jerusalem mounted on an ass; thus Zechariah's messianic prophecy, "Lo, your king comes to you / . . . humble and riding on an ass," did not really have currency, and could not have helped enlighten the people's minds.

But "the crowd," "the crowds," the "great crowd" of Matthew and John are ambiguous and imprecise expressions which can designate some hundreds of people as well as several thousands. Historic probability, which makes the scale weigh on Mark's and Luke's side, also makes it weigh in favor of a small number with regard to Matthew's and John's accounts. A few hundred—what is that in a population influx which counted in the hundreds of thousands on the eve of Passover?

The texts therefore do not in any way establish either that the entry into Jerusalem was a "triumphal" demonstration or that messianic "enthusiasm . . . gripped the entire city." They establish on the contrary that the messianic character of the demonstration seemed to escape the observers. As to the size of the demonstration, they are indecisive; and we are justified in concluding that in all likelihood it must have been very limited, limited enough to have not attracted the attention of the occupation authorities.

✿   ✿   ✿

At the termination of this inquiry and debate, we may return to the initial question: did Jesus reveal himself as the Messiah and the true Son of God to the Jewish people "as a whole"? Is one justified in stating, with Father Bonsirven, that Jesus "presented himself in this dual capacity to his hearers"? [82]

We can answer: no.

No, Jesus did not reveal himself as the Messiah to the mass of the people. "Jesus obviously did not want to be recognized as the Messiah except by his apostles," writes Father Lagrange, "although before

[82] Bonsirven, *Les Enseignements de Jésus-Christ*, p. 2.

his death he accepted the small ovation of the palm branches." [83] And this small ovation, we have just seen, was not enough to reveal him to be the Messiah.

As they are reported in the Gospels, certain words of Jesus' had the effect of suggesting his sonship, his divinity. These hints remained uncomprehended by the largest number, and it could not have been otherwise. It cannot be said that Jesus revealed himself as the true "Son of God" to the Jewish people "as a whole."

Will Jesus' miracles be raised as an objection—casting out demons, curing the sick, the crippled, raising the dead? Again I leave the task of replying to Father Lagrange:

All this was extraordinary, but it did not prove that he was the Messiah [and I would add: even less that he was the "Son of God"]. In the general opinion of the Doctors, miracles had already been the work of the prophets. Elijah and Elisha had even raised the dead.[84]

And Jean Guitton observes, "No miracle, however great, can be held as proof of divinity." [85]

The Jewish people—the masses of the people—thus knew Jesus neither as Messiah nor as Son of God. They knew and admired him as a prophet, a great prophet, the evangelist confirms:

. . . and they glorified God, saying, "A great prophet has arisen among us!" and "God has visited his people!"

Lk. 7:16

And despite the "messianic" entry into Jerusalem, they still thought of him as such on the eve of the Passion, if we believe the Gospel according to Saint Matthew:

When the chief priests and the Pharisees. . . . tried to arrest him, they feared the multitudes, because they held him to be a prophet.

Mt. 21:45–46

[83] Lagrange, . . . Luc, loc. cit.
[84] Idem, L'Évangile de Jésus-Christ, p. 153.
[85] Jean Guitton, Jésus, Paris, Grasset, 1956, p. 338.

CHRIST IS SAID TO HAVE PRONOUNCED A SENTENCE OF CON-
DEMNATION AND ALIENATION ON THE JEWISH PEOPLE.
BUT WHY, IN CONTRADICTION OF HIS OWN GOSPEL OF
LOVE AND FORGIVENESS, SHOULD HE HAVE CONDEMNED
HIS OWN PEOPLE, THE ONLY PEOPLE TO WHOM HE
CHOSE TO SPEAK—HIS OWN PEOPLE, AMONG WHOM
HE FOUND NOT ONLY BITTER ENEMIES BUT FERVENT
DISCIPLES AND ADORING FOLLOWERS? WE HAVE EVERY
REASON TO BELIEVE THAT THE REAL OBJECT OF HIS
CONDEMNATION IS THE REAL SUBJECT OF GUILT,
A CERTAIN PHARISAISM TO BE FOUND IN ALL TIMES
AND IN ALL PEOPLES, IN EVERY RELIGION AND IN
EVERY CHURCH.

Since in all historic probability the Jewish people "as a whole" did
not know Jesus;
   since the Jewish people of Palestine, insofar as they knew him, did
so only as a prophet;
   since they listened to him, followed him, and admired him as such,
   it cannot be legitimately maintained that the Jewish people rejected Jesus, or with all the more reason that they rejected the Messiah, the true Son of God, in Jesus.
   Now another question must be posed: were the Jewish people rejected by Jesus?—and therefore, for every believer (in Christ), by
God?

✿　　✿　　✿

Numerous are the theologians of every confession—Catholic and
Protestant—who unhesitatingly answer this question: yes.
   Numerous are the theologians—Catholic and Protestant—who

claim to discover on almost every page of the Gospels "the reprobation of the Jewish people," the sentence of their "condemnation," their
"perdition," their "rejection," indeed even—in certain of Jesus' words
—a "curse." They implicate not only the leaders, political or religious
heads, chief priests, scribes, and Pharisees, but the nation "as a
whole."

For example:

"Concerning the Jews . . . [the Savior predicted] that they would
be supplanted by the Gentiles; . . . that they would be cast out by
God, that they would begin to suffer the most terrible punishment
from that moment on," writes A. Brassac.[1]

"Thus, from the outset of his public ministry, Jesus gave glimpses of
the downfall of the Jews and the calling of the Gentiles," comments
Father Lebreton.[2]

Father Lagrange himself, so little inclined though he is to speaking
with severity, notes that the fulfillment of God's plan presupposed the
reprobation of the Jews.[3] "The doctrine [of the reprobation of the na-
tion] is not of an individual psychological order, but a design of
God's Providence for the Jewish people."[4]

"It was from the rejection of Israel that the Church would be born,"
specifies the Protestant theologian Hébert Roux. Heir to Calvinist rigidity, the same author does not hesitate to write: "Jesus included in
one condemnation the murderers of the prophets, their sons, the contemporary generation, and the whole Israelite race," a condemnation

---

[1] Father A. Brassac, Nouveau Testament, vol. III of Fathers Fulcran G. Vigouroux and A. Brassac, Manuel biblique, ou Cours d'Écriture sainte à l'usage des
séminaires, ed. Fathers A. Brassac and Louis Bacuez, 4 vols., 12th ed., Paris,
Roger et Chernoviz, 1906–1909, p. 439.

[2] Father Jules Lebreton, S.J., La Vie et l'enseignement de Jésus-Christ, 2 vols.,
Paris, Beauchesne, 1931, I, 257. [So, likewise, these judgments from recent Catholic religious teaching manuals: "They are on the point of killing the son of the
master. Is it surprising that pagans will come take the place of the faithless Jews
in the chosen people . . . ?" (G. Delcuve, Jésus-Christ, notre Sauveur, 3rd ed.,
"Témoins du Christ" series, V, Tournai, Casterman, Ed. de Lumen Vitae, 1960,
p. 125); and: "The rejection of Israel as the privileged people [was] owing to its
hardness of heart and its unquenchable pride" (J. Toussaint, Le Christ, idéal de
vie [The Christ, Life Ideal], "La Vie" series, 5, Namur, La Procure, 1963, p.
168; both quoted in Canon François Houtart and Jean Giblet, eds., Les Juifs
dans la catéchèse: Étude des manuels de catéchèse de langue française, Louvain,
Centre de Recherches socio-religieuses and Centre de Recherches catéchétiques,
1969, pp. 151, 201).—Ed.]

[3] Father Marie-Joseph Lagrange, O.P., ed. and tr., Évangile selon saint Marc,
Paris, Gabalda, 1910, p. 121.

[4] Idem, ed. and tr., Évangile selon saint Jean, Paris, Gabalda, 1924, p. 342.

reinforced by "the curse . . . pronounced against Israel by the Crucified himself." [5]

On the liberal Protestant side, as we have seen, the doctrine of Israel's reprobation and rejection often takes the more subtle form of a
historic thesis that Jesus, evolving his thought, would have come to
the idea of a total break with Judaism. The "Jewish reformer" whom
Jesus was at first would later become "the destroyer of Judaism"; he
would lose "his Jewish faith" to convert to "absolute universalism," asserts Edmond Stapfer.[6]

Maurice Goguel is more categoric on this point: "Jesus proclaimed
the downfall of Israel," "the downfall of the Jewish people . . . definitively unworthy of the salvation which was offered them, or more exactly, incapable of accepting it." [7]

❖   ❖   ❖

Let us see, then, if we can establish Jesus' attitude toward his people, the Jewish people, from the texts.

We have previously learned from them and should recall here:

that Jesus, born a Jew, "born under the law" (Gal. 4:4), lived "under
the law" to his final hour;

that he did not stop teaching in the synagogues and the Temple;

that he was steeped to the marrow in the sap of the Jewish Old
Testament;

that he elicited from the beginning and did not cease to elicit the
sympathies of the Jewish masses, heaping signs of love and compassion on them in return.

They also have this to teach us, and it is not least in importance:

---

[5] Hébert Roux, L'Évangile du Royaume [The Gospel of the Kingdom], Geneva,
Labor et Fides, 1934, pp. 196, 272, 277.

[6] Edmond Stapfer, Jésus-Christ pendant son ministère, vol. II of Jésus-Christ,
sa personne, son autorité, son oeuvre, Paris, Fischbacher, 1897, pp. 203, 257, 258,
260.

[7] Maurice Goguel, "Jésus et les origines de l'universalisme chrétien" [Jesus and
the Origins of Christian Universalism], Revue d'Histoire et de Philosophie religieuses (annual), Paris, Presses Universitaires de France, 1932, pp. 198, 201. [In
similar terms, an American Protestant periodical asserts: "After the parable [of
the wicked husbandmen], he [Jesus] predicted the destruction of the nation. The
destruction was proof that God had rejected His Chosen People and called another people in their place" (Sunday School Young Adult [Southern Baptist Con-
vention], January–March, 1967, p. 40; quoted in Gerald Strober, ms. in preparation, New York (Xerox), p. 63).—Ed.]

it was to Israel alone that Jesus preached the "good news" of the Gospel;

to Israel alone that Jesus dispatched his disciples during his life on earth;

in Israel alone that he recruited them, the Twelve, the Apostles, all of whom were Jewish.

                    ❂   ❂   ❂

A suggestive prologue, which I borrow from the two Gospels most remote, most detached from Judaism in certain respects: the third and the fourth, according to Saint Luke and according to Saint John.

When the evangelist Saint Luke, Gentile in origin (a Greek physician) and writing for the Gentiles, brings us to the threshold of Christ's human life, he celebrates in almost biblical terms the link which unites God and, through Him, Jesus "to Israel," "to Abraham and to his posterity forever" (Lk. 1:54, 55 [CCD]). We have already noted this aspect of the *Magnificat*: [8]

My soul magnifies the Lord. . . . He has given help to Israel, his servant, mindful of his mercy—Even as he spoke to our fathers—to Abraham and to his posterity forever.

Lk. 1:46, 54–55 [CCD]

In the *Nunc dimittis*, the elderly Simeon took the Infant Jesus "up in his arms and blessed God and said,"

> Lord, now lettest thou thy servant depart in peace,
>   according to thy word;
> for mine eyes have seen thy salvation
>   which thou hast prepared in the presence of all peoples,
> a light for revelation to the Gentiles,
>   and for glory to thy people Israel.

Lk. 2:28–32

—which is not at all a way of "opposing the nations to Israel, the people of God," [9] but the traditional way of distinguishing Israel, the people of God, among all the nations.

---

[8] See pp. 16–17, above.

[9] Father Marie-Joseph Lagrange, O.P., ed. and tr., *Évangile selon saint Luc*, Paris, Gabalda, 1921, p. 86.

. . . and Simeon blessed them [the father and mother of the child]
   and said to Mary his mother,
"Behold, this child is set for the fall and rising of many in Israel. . . ."

Lk. 2:34

—which does not mean "for the fall of Israel" or even of "the great
majority of Israelites," as Canon A. Crampon would have it: "Jesus
would be a cause of falling, a stumbling block (Is. 8:14), for the great
majority of Israelites, who, refusing to recognize the Christ in him,
would fall into unfaithfulness and eternal ruination, as Saint Paul observes (Rom. 9:31–33; 1 Cor. 1:23)." [10] The "fall *and* rising of many"
apply equally to the Israelites. Opposition to Jesus is predicted, but
so is his destination: Israel.

When the evangelist Saint John, whose Gospel we know from Dom
Th. Calmes to be "the most anti-Judaic book of the New Testament," [11]
brings us to the threshold of Christ's public life, he makes a point of
certifying through the mouth of the Precursor that Jesus has come for
Israel:

Behold, the Lamb of God. . . . I myself did not know him; but for this I
came baptizing with water, that he might be revealed to Israel.

Jn. 1:29, 31

"A revelation . . . reserved at first for Israel," comments Father Lagrange,[12] but "at first" is not in the Johannine text.

✻   ✻   ✻

Let us now follow Jesus in Galilee, in Judea, on all the roads that
he took. The four evangelists testify, and in this case their testimony
can be accepted without reservations: it was to the Jews that Jesus
addressed himself, and to them alone. The only dubious texts on this
point are Mark 3:7–8, Matthew 4:25, and Luke 6:17, which mention
crowds coming not only from Galilee and Judea but also from Phoenicia, from Idumea, from the Decapolis, and elsewhere. It is possible
that these crowds were not exclusively Jewish, but Jesus reserved his
teaching to the Jews, as is shown by all the other passages. Do we not

[10] Canon A. Crampon, ed. and tr., *La Sainte Bible*, rev. ed., Tournai, Desclée,
1939, p. 66, n. 34.
[11] Father Th. Calmes, O.S.B., ed. and tr., *Évangile selon saint Jean*, Paris, Lecoffre, 1904, p. 60.
[12] Lagrange, . . . *Jean*, p. 42.

see him in Mark 5:19 refuse to allow the exorcised Gerasene to follow
him? And if we extract from the Gospel of John an exception relating
to the Samaritans of Sychar—an exception that harmonizes poorly
with the Synoptic tradition—yet we must note that Jesus had earlier
made a profession of faith in the purest Judaism to the Samaritan
woman:

You [Samaritans] worship what you do not know; we worship what we
know, for salvation is from the Jews.

Jn. 4:22

(I will not examine here the question of how this profession of faith
can occur in a context which seems to announce the imminent end of
traditional Judaism: "Woman, believe me, the hour is coming when
neither on this mountain nor in Jerusalem will you worship the Father" [Jn. 4:21]. We have said elsewhere [13] how easy it is to lose
one's way in the twists and turns of the Johannine labyrinth.)

But here are the essential texts, drawn from the Synoptics.

Let us look first at Matthew 10, a chapter the Crampon Bible enti-
tles "Jesus Chooses His Apostles To Found the Kingdom of God on
Earth." The twelve Apostles chosen, whether they bore Aramaic, Hebrew, or Greek names—like Philip and Andrew, the latter a brother
of Simon called Peter—were all Jews. And Jesus, giving them their
instructions, began in these terms:

Go nowhere among the Gentiles, and enter no town of the Samaritans, but
go rather to the lost sheep of the house of Israel.

Mt. 10:5–6

No exceptions, not even for the Samaritans, contrary to what we
have just read in John 4. This is a point on which official teaching
shows itself very discreet. The *Biblical Manual* confines itself to saying that "Jesus sent the apostles to preach the kingdom of God to the
Jews"; it neglects to mention the exclusiveness, which the reader will
surely not suspect from the indications given elsewhere.[14] Most of the
authoritative writers stress the merely "temporary" nature of the re-
striction formulated: "These instructions obviously did not demarcate
the future expansion of the Gospel; they circumscribed only that temporary mission which, like the preaching of Jesus himself, was directed only at the children of Israel." [15] All right, but the "obvious-

[13] See pp. 111 and 163, above.
[14] Brassac, *op. cit.*, p. 340.
[15] Lebreton, *op. cit.*, I, 352.

ness" that strikes Father Lebreton does not arise out of the text; and that text ends with the following sentence, whose meaning is open to discussion but which, marking an ending, undeniably has a restrictive quality as well and is closely tied to the opening declaration:

. . . for truly, I say to you, you will not have gone through all the towns of Israel, before the Son of man comes.

Mt. 10:23

We read at Matthew 10:18, ". . . you will be dragged before governors and kings for my sake, to bear testimony before them and the Gentiles." Yet according to Father Lagrange, it is likely that the kings in question are Jewish princes, sons of Herod, and the Gentiles those inhabiting Palestine.[16]

And why then did Jesus forbid his disciples to go "among the Gentiles, . . . the Samaritans"? Tradition answers through the mouth of Saint Jerome: "*Ne justam haberent excusationem, dicentes ideo se Dominum rejecisse, quia ad gentes et ad Samaritanos apostolos miserit,*" "So that they [the Jews] would have no good excuse, saying that if they rejected the Lord, it was because he sent the apostles to the Gentiles and the Samaritans." [17] So, whether the subject is the preaching of the Gospel, the apostolate of the Twelve, the entry into Jerusalem, what would be the Lord's constant preoccupation, if we take the word of this venerable exegesis? To prevent his people from having any excuse, any chance of justifying themselves. Alas!

Corresponding with and corroborating Matthew 10:5–6 and 23 is the double echo of the parallel texts in Mark 7:25–30 and Matthew 15:22–28. They show us Jesus in Gentile country, in "the district of Tyre and Sidon"; the Master wants to be incognito, but here he is solicited by a woman of those parts, a pagan. What will his reaction be?

And behold, a Canaanite woman from that region came out and cried, "Have mercy on me, O Lord, Son of David; my daughter is severely possessed by a demon." But he did not answer her a word. And his disciples came and begged him, saying, "Send her away, for she is crying after us." He answered, "I was sent only to the lost sheep of the house of Israel." But she came and knelt before him, saying, "Lord, help me." And he answered,

---

[16] Father Marie-Joseph Lagrange, O.P., ed. and tr., *Évangile selon saint Matthieu*, Paris, Gabalda, 1922, p. 203.

[17] Jerome, *Commentarii in Mattheum* [Commentaries on Matthew], in Father Jacques-Paul Migne, ed., *Patrologia latina* [Latin Fathers], 221 vols., Paris, Garnier, 1844–1864, XXVI, 15–218; quoted in Lagrange, . . . *Matthieu*, p. 197.

"It is not fair to take the children's bread and throw it to the dogs." [18] She said, "Yes, Lord, yet even the dogs eat the crumbs that fall from their master's table." Then Jesus answered her, "O woman, great is your faith! Be it done for you as you desire." And her daughter was healed instantly.

Mt. 15:22–28

In this text as well as the parallel, Mark 7:25–30, Jesus' first impulse was to refuse flatly; this, explains Louis-Claude Fillion, was to test the supplicant, to give this soul "the opportunity to manifest her total faith." [19] Matthew seems to emphasize wantonly the rudeness of the refusal: this, explains Father Lagrange, was "because he wanted to show how blind or prejudiced were the Jews who refused to recognize Jesus as their Messiah. If he had been the man for the pagans, they would have had some poor pretext." [20] Always the same refrain, which we judge unworthy of being taken seriously: "poor pretext."

But let us allow the texts to speak for themselves; their language is clearer, simpler, more convincing.

In one of them, Jesus countered the first entreaty with silence: "But he did not answer her a word." The second time, "begged" by the overtaxed disciples, he declared explicitly, categorically that his mission—his divine mission—was reserved for the Jews: "I was sent only to the lost sheep of the house of Israel." The woman knelt at his feet; a third refusal, formulated in terms so contemptuous of non-Jews—"the dogs"—that they might be called, Father Lagrange writes, "inspired by the pharisee spirit, which Jesus had just condemned." [21]

Yet Matthew's testimony here is confirmed by that of Mark, whose clause "for it is not right to take the children's bread and throw it to the dogs" is preceded by the words "Let the children first be fed" (Mk. 7:27), which are not in Matthew, which seem superfluous, which will rescue the commentators from their distress, for we read: "first." With this "first," it becomes possible to capture the whole Gentile world; "first" makes one see that there will be a sequel (for Gentiles assimilated with "the dogs"); "first" lets it be understood that "The

---

[18] The Greek word is *kunaria*, meaning "domestic dogs," house dogs. According to Paul Vulliaud, *kunarion* sometimes carries a connotation of contempt, and could be translated "mangy dog" (*La Clé traditionnelle des Évangiles*, Paris, Thiébaud, 1936, p. 230).

[19] Louis-Claude Fillion, *Vie de Notre Seigneur Jésus-Christ*, 22nd ed., Paris, Letouzey, 1929, II, 463.

[20] Lagrange, . . . *Matthieu*, p. 310.

[21] *Idem*, . . . *Marc*, p. 196.

time of the Gentiles was not yet come" but that "Their turn would come." [22]

Let us observe simply that Jesus' declarations, so explicit, so clear concerning Israel, are hardly so when the Gentile world is—or is believed to be—involved. And let us note that if the foreigner, the poor supplicant, was finally granted her request, it was due to the spirit of propriety and humility which she evidenced in recognizing Israel's privileged status: "Yes, Lord, yet even the dogs eat the crumbs that fall from their master's table."

How nicely said, how clever, too, and it must be admitted, how flattering for the ear of the devout. What is most surprising is the effect it produced—Jesus, finally touched by such humility, joined to such spirit and such faith, let her speak and let himself be moved: the outsider's child was cured.

Other significant texts could be gleaned from place to place in the Gospels where Jesus is shown as strangely traditionalist in his feelings toward outsiders, in his apparently exclusive attachment to Israel:

And if you salute only your brethren, what more are you doing than others? Do not even the Gentiles do the same? [Understood: You, Israelites, you will do no better than the Gentiles?]

Mt. 5:47, the Sermon on the Mount

But in praying, do not multiply words, as the Gentiles do; for they think that by saying a great deal, they will be heard. So do not be like them. . . .

Mt. 6:7–8 [CCD]

Therefore do not be anxious, saying, "What shall we eat?" or "What shall we drink?" or "What shall we wear?" For the Gentiles seek all these things; and your heavenly Father knows that you need them all.

Mt. 6:31–32; see Lk. 12:29–30 [23]

If he [your brother] refuses to listen to them [the witnesses], tell it to the church; and if he refuses to listen even to the church, let him be to you as a Gentile and a tax collector [that is, less than anything; turn away from him].

Mt. 18:17

At the end of his ministry, on the eve of the Passion, Jesus still kept his eyes fixed on the horizon of Israel. When Peter asked him on the road to Jerusalem, according to Matthew, "Lo, we have left every-

[22] *Ibid.*, p. 195.
[23] Luke uses an expression more difficult to interpret: "all the nations of the world" (understood: which are not the Jews). This comes down to exactly the same thing.

thing and followed you. What then shall we have?"; and when the Apostles were disputing in the upper room, according to Luke, about "which of them was to be regarded as the greatest," what did Jesus say to them?

Truly, I say to you, in the new world, when the Son of man shall sit on his glorious throne, you who have followed me will also sit on twelve thrones, judging the twelve tribes of Israel.

Mt. 19:28

You are those who have continued with me in my trials; as my Father appointed a kingdom for me, so do I appoint for you that you may eat and drink at my table in my kingdom, and sit on thrones judging the twelve tribes of Israel.

Lk. 22:28–30

"Which seems to imply," writes Maurice Goguel, "that in the Kingdom, there will be nothing but Jews."[24] A prospect which is obviously displeasing, but which Father Lagrange seems to admit, at least in his commentary on Matthew, when he writes: "The Savior held himself to the perspective of the moment: he was sent only to them" (the twelve tribes of Israel). And he remarks further, "This is the ideal of the Psalms of Solomon (17:28): 'And he [the Messiah] shall gather together a holy people, whom he shall lead in righteousness, / And he shall judge the tribes of the people that has been sanctified by the Lord his God.'"[25]

Is a countersignature needed below the Gospel signatures? There is none more valid—in every way—than Saint Paul's:

For I say that Christ Jesus has been a minister of the circumcision in order to show God's fidelity in confirming the promises made to our fathers. . . .

Rom. 15:8 [CCD]

And we may call to mind the words transmitted by Clement of Alexandria:

Peter states that the Lord said to the Apostles: "Whoever in Israel is willing to repent and believe in God through my name, his sins will be forgiven him; but after [variant: during] twelve years go throughout the world, lest anyone be able to say: we have not heard."[26]

[24] Goguel, op. cit., p. 196.
[25] Lagrange, . . . Matthieu, p. 382. [Quotation of Psalm of Solomon 17:28 taken from "The Psalms of Solomon," ed. and tr. G. Buchanan Gray, in R. H. Charles et al., eds. and trs., The Apocrypha and Pseudepigrapha of the Old Testament, 2 vols., Oxford, Eng., Oxford University Press, 1963–1964, II, 649.—Tr.]
[26] Clement of Alexandria, Stromateis, 6:5. [See, in English, as idem, The Stromata, or Miscellanies, in The Ante-Nicene Fathers, ed. Rev. Alexander Roberts

"Lest anyone," understood: in Israel. It is clear that these words apply to the Israel in Dispersion.

✿   ✿   ✿

All this, and what was seen before, particularly in the last stage of Christ's human life:

Jesus at Jericho, greeting the tax collector Zacchaeus, "son of Abraham" (Lk. 19:9);

Jesus on the road to Jerusalem, or at Jerusalem the evening of the Last Supper, promising the Twelve that they would be called to judge "the twelve tribes of Israel" (Mt. 19:28; Lk. 22:30);

Jesus entering Jerusalem mounted on a young ass, to fulfill the messianic saying of Zechariah;

Jesus on that solemn entry, allowing himself to be acclaimed king, Son of David, by the cortege of his disciples and followers;

Jesus driving the merchants from the Temple in order to purify "my Father's house" (Jn. 2:16);

Jesus discussing the resurrection of the dead with the Sadducees and drawing his argument from "the book of Moses":

> And . . . have you not read in the book of Moses, in the passage about the bush, how God said to him, "I am the God of Abraham, and the God of Isaac, and the God of Jacob"?
>
> Mk. 12:26; very similar text in Mt. 22:31–32; Lk. 20:37

Jesus replying to the question of the Pharisee scribe:

> The first [of all the Commandments] is, "Hear, O Israel: The Lord our God, the Lord is one. . . ."
>
> Mk. 12:29

Jesus teaching in the Temple until the last hour, and the Jewish crowd, pressing about him, "hung upon his words" (Lk. 19:48);

Jesus having "earnestly desired to eat this passover with" the Twelve (Lk. 22:14), taking the ritual Jewish meal with them, and when it was finished, singing the Hallel Psalms with them according to the rites (Mk. 14:26; Mt. 26:30) on this vigil, the last before the Cross—

does all this correspond with the image proposed to us of a Jesus who was not only "a destroyer of Judaism," having broken with the

and James Donaldson, rev. ed. Rev. A. Cleveland Cox, 10 vols., New York, Scribner, 1917–1925, II, 490.—Tr.]

Law, but who also broke with his people, thenceforth and definitively rejecting them, condemning them?

Let me make myself clear. I have no intention of childishly countering this image with another, no less contestable: no more than I wanted to make Jesus a Jewish "legalist" do I want now to make him a "particularist" Jew. A few barbs cast at Gentiles in passing, to stimulate the Jewish audience better, could never prevail over other words, essential and eternal, over the noble teaching of such perfect and necessary virtue summarized in the parable of the good Samaritan (Lk. 10:30–37).[27]

The exclusivity recommended to the Apostles in Matthew 10:5–6 and professed by Jesus himself in Matthew 15:24 is a more serious thing that is not so easily put aside; but if one accepts the notion that it does not involve the future, it becomes reconcilable with all forms of "universalism," Jewish as well as Christian. Do I deduce from this that Jesus remained faithful to the best Jewish tradition, the tradition which associated the privilege of election with the duty for Israel of dispensing the light of the true faith to all peoples, of "universalizing" the radiance, the glory, and the cult of Yahweh—in sum, that he was a Jewish "universalist"? Not at all. If I am convinced of one thing, it is that Jesus does not lend himself to any Scholastic category, any. Exactly for this reason, when someone tries to persuade me that Jesus' universalism was not only not Jewish but anti-Jewish, that it carried an exception and that this exception was addressed to his own people, the Jewish people, the only one he knew, the only one he wanted to know, then I have doubts, I ask to examine the texts.

¤   ¤   ¤

These texts are numerous. They have an impact, if only because of their number. The contrary would be surprising. For about the time the Gospels were first written down—the second half or last third of the first century—and even more in the later time when their form became definitive, the recruiting of Christian communities in Israel tended to dry up. (Why? This is another and difficult problem which

---

[27] Compare with Luke 4:25–26: ". . . there were many widows in Israel in the days of Elijah . . . ; and Elijah was sent to none of them but only to Zarephath, in the land of Sidon, to a woman who was a widow."

it is not possible to study here.[28]) The Christians suffered intensely from hostile persecution by official Judaism; the last ties that united Christianity to Judaism were on the verge of breaking; Judeo-Christianity, the earliest form of Christianity, fell to the lower status of sect on the way to being branded as a heresy. Under these conditions, there was no longer any need to handle "carnal" Israel gently; on the contrary, it was highly desirable to discredit it in the eyes of the Gentiles, "Jewish unbelief"—let us clarify, so as to avoid any ambiguity: not the primary unbelief toward Jesus of Nazareth exercising his ministry, but the secondary unbelief toward the Christ of the new Church —this unbelief constituting a "scandal" [29] which catechesis was constrained to explain. If the Gospel accounts are to be considered in strict orthodoxy as inspired testimony, doctrine cannot obscure the obvious fact that they are testimony for the prosecution. We have already said this, and we will have other occasions to say it again (and prove it), for on the plane of history that is of cardinal importance. The most Catholic exegesis finds itself obliged to take it into account; Father de Grandmaison writes:

It must not be forgotten that our Synoptics and Mark in particular . . . issued directly from oral catechesis. . . . In that catechesis, one could not have failed to cast in strong relief everything in Jesus' instruction announcing the great "judgment of God" which was accomplished by the substitution of the spiritual Israel that was the Christian Church for the fleshly Israel.

And again:

It is not impossible to think that in the very writing of the Synoptics, the fact, thereafter established, of the universal hardening of the Jewish people made itself felt.[30]

Certainly it makes itself felt. Everything in Jesus' instruction—as it had survived through tradition—which could be interpreted as anticipating the "established fact," the condemnation of that "hardening" of Israel, was carefully garnered by one or another of the evangelists,

[28] On this question, see the chapter entitled "Du judéo-christianisme à l'antagonisme judéo-chrétien" [From Judeo-Christianity to Judeo-Christian Antagonism] in Jules Isaac, *Genèse de l'antisémitisme*, Paris, Calmann-Lévy, 1956, pp. 143–158.
[29] Father Joseph Huby, *L'Évangile et les Évangiles*, Paris, Beauchesne, 1929, p. 96.
[30] Father Léonce de Grandmaison, S.J., *Jésus-Christ, sa personne, son message, ses preuves*, 2 vols., Paris, Beauchesne, 1928, I, 331.

the writing tending to accentuate the "strong relief" even more. These anticipated and anachronistic harsh judgments square poorly, to tell the truth, with the historic realities to which they are related and which the evangelists let us glimpse despite everything, almost despite themselves; they square poorly with the Israelite boundary lines beyond which Jesus did not go and did not want to go. Evaluating the texts therefore becomes an absolute necessity here, the only way it remains possible to discover what really was the position Jesus took regarding his people, Israel.

o   o   o

Among the texts in question, a first group includes those that show us Jesus in direct communication with Gentiles or pagans. These texts are rare owing to the fact—significant in itself—that such communications were quite exceptional. The principal one relates the episode of the centurion at Capernaum, in Matthew 8:5–13 and Luke 7:1–10, when the centurion, declaring himself unworthy to have Jesus "come under my roof," averred that his servant would be healed if Jesus would "only say the word" [RSV]. Jesus replied:

> "I tell you, I have never seen such faith as this in anyone in Israel. Remember this! Many will come from the east and the west and sit down at the table in the Kingdom of Heaven with Abraham, Isaac, and Jacob. But those who should be in the Kingdom will be thrown out into the darkness outside, whje they will cry and gnash their teeth." And Jesus said to the officer, "Go home, and what you believe will be done for you." And the officer's servant was healed that very hour.
>
> Mt. 8:10–13 [ABS]

At first reading, one can indeed find in this text "the salvation of the Gentiles contrasted with the loss of the Jews." [31] There is no doubt of it among most of the orthodox commentators. Father Lebreton writes:

> It is the faithful pagans who will find their places alongside the patriarchs, and the Jews, sons of the kingdom, will be thrown out of the banquet room, into the darkness. Thus, from the outset of his public ministry, Jesus gave glimpses of the downfall of the Jews and the calling of the Gentiles. [32]

---

[31] Lagrange, . . . *Matthieu*, p. 164.

[32] Lebreton, *op. cit.*, I, 257. [The Oberammergau Passion Play expresses the same conviction: "This city I will have no more," reads one line; and the Chorus says: "See, Vashti—see the proud one is cast out! / Showing God's purpose for the Synagogue" (*The Passion Play of Oberammergau*, English version of the offi-

Fillion states:

This prophecy by the Savior, joyful for the Gentiles, tragic for the Jews, casts a bright light on the future of his Church. . . . The "sons of the kingdom" [RSV; "those who should be in the Kingdom," ABS] are the Jews who, by virtue of the divine promises, were born to inherit it. . . . What a punishment for them, then, to be excluded from it en masse, while converted pagans will flock to it from all parts of the world.[33]

And Hébert Roux comments: "A warning to Israel, with which Jesus announces the rejection for the first time." [34]

But to speak thus is to disregard (and why, now?) Luke's text, that Luke whom Father Lagrange considers to "surpass" the other evangelists "as historian," [35] about whom it would be more pertinent to say that precisely because he was not a Jew, he showed less prejudice concerning them.

. . . [Jesus] went to Capernaum. A Roman officer there had a servant who was very dear to him; the man was sick and about to die. When the officer heard about Jesus, he sent to him some Jewish elders to ask him to come and heal his servant. They came to Jesus and begged him earnestly: "This man really deserves your help. He loves our people and he himself built a meeting house for us." So Jesus went with them. He was not far from the house when the officer sent friends to tell him: "Sir, don't trouble yourself. I do not deserve to have you come into my house, neither do I consider myself worthy to come to you in person. Just give the order and my servant will get well. I, too, am a man placed under the authority of superior officers, and I have soldiers under me. I order this one, 'Go!' and he goes; I order that one, 'Come!' and he comes; and I order my slave, 'Do this!' and he does it." Jesus was surprised when he heard this; he turned around and said to the crowd following him, "I have never found such faith as this, I tell you, not even in Israel!" The messengers went back to the officer's house and found his servant well.

Lk. 7:1–10 [ABS]

Can anyone not feel that Luke's text, different from the other in several details, above all rings with a very different tone? Luke's cen-

cial text of the 1970 performances, "revised and newly published," Oberammergau, Community of Oberammergau, 1970, p. 32). Regarding this decennial drama, riddled with anti-Semitism, see p. 258, n. 66, below. The editor is indebted to Mrs. Judith Banki and Dr. Gerald Strober for making quotations from the play available to us. These investigators are responsible for a valuable study published by the American Jewish Committee, Interreligious Affairs Department, *Oberammergau, 1960 and 1970: A Study in Religious Anti-Semitism*, New York, July, 1970.—Ed.]

[33] Fillion, *op. cit.*, II, 291.

[34] Roux, *op. cit.*, p. 104.

[35] Father Marie-Joseph Lagrange, O.P., *L'Évangile de Jésus-Christ*, Paris, Gabalda, 1928, p. xi.

turion is not some pagan taken at random like Matthew's centurion; he is a devoted friend of Israel, to all appearances a "God-fearer," since this subordinate officer did not shrink from the enormous expense that the construction of a "meeting house," a synagogue, represented. Wanting to obtain Jesus' intervention, he refrained from going to find him himself—on this point, Luke contradicts Matthew; he delegated distinguished Jews to him who pleaded his cause, vouching for his Jewish sympathies and his Yahwist zeal. Matthew has Jesus say, "I tell you, I have never seen such faith as this in anyone in Israel," while in Luke his words are "I have never found such faith as this, I tell you, not even in Israel!", which is less categoric, less disagreeable toward Israel, whose privileged role seems to be implicitly acknowledged. Finally and above all, the verses at Matthew 8:11–12, ending "But those who should be in the Kingdom will be thrown out into the darkness outside . . . ," are not in Luke.

Or rather, the verses are there, but at another place—13:23–30—and in another context, and they carry notable differences:

And some one said to him, "Lord, will those who are saved be few?" And he said to them, "Strive to enter by the narrow door; for many, I tell you, will seek to enter and will not be able. . . . Then you will begin to say, 'We ate and drank in your presence, and you taught in our streets.' But he will say, 'I tell you, I do not know where you come from; depart from me, all you workers of iniquity!' There you will weep and gnash your teeth, when you see Abraham and Isaac and Jacob and all the prophets in the kingdom of God and you yourselves thrust out. And men will come from east and west, and from north and south, and sit at table in the kingdom of God. And behold, some are last who will be first, and some are first who will be last."

Lk. 13:23–30 [RSV]

What is the fundamental difference between this text and Matthew's? It is that in Luke, Jesus' harsh judgments are not all-inclusive but limited, directed not at all of Israel, all "those who should be in the Kingdom" [ABS] without distinction, but only at those among them who were "workers of iniquity," despite which Canon Crampon gives Luke 13 the heading "Reprobation of the Jews" in his translation of the Bible.[36]

"Depart from me, all you workers of iniquity!" does not mean "all [of you, as many as there are of] you[,] workers of iniquity" but rather "all [those among] you [who have been] workers of iniquity."

[36] Crampon, op. cit.

And this throws a clear light on the last sentence, which does not say, as some—with such charitable zeal—would make it say, "The last (the Gentiles) will be first, and the first (the Jews) will be last," [37] but ". . . some [particular ones] are last who will be first, and some [particular ones] are first who will be last." The meaning is "very plain," writes Father Lagrange, "and the admonition fearsome. . . . [Jesus said:] try not to be among those who may be lost, be they even my countrymen," [38] be they even "sons of Abraham." An admonition indeed fearsome, an admonition deserved by a certain Jewish pride, but an admonition, and not a "Reprobation of the Jews" as Canon Crampon adjudges.[39] An admonition that corresponds exactly with the warning given by the Precursor to the Pharisees and Sadducees according to Matthew 3:9 and seemingly addressed to the same:

. . . and do not presume to say to yourselves, "We have Abraham as our father"; for I tell you, God is able from these stones to raise up children to Abraham.

Now let us reread Matthew 8:11–12 [ABS]. Verse 11, "Many will come from the east and the west . . . ," harmonizes well with Luke 13:29 [RSV], "And men will come from east and west. . . ." As for verse 12, "But those who should be in the Kingdom will be thrown out into the darkness outside . . . ," it suffices to read "many among" into it: "But [among] those who should be in the Kingdom [many] will be thrown out into the darkness outside . . ." to re-establish the harmony needed between Luke and Matthew in order to discover what were in all likelihood Jesus' words as he spoke them or as they were given in the source common to the two evangelists. As proof, I need only offer Matthew himself, in 13:41–42 [KJ], where Jesus, explaining "the parable of the tares of the field" (Mt. 13:36), says to them:

The Son of man shall send forth his angels, and they shall gather out of his kingdom all things that cause stumbling, and them that do iniquity, and shall cast them into the furnace of fire: there shall be the weeping and the gnashing of teeth.

[37] Father Ferdinand Prat, *Jésus-Christ, sa vie, son oeuvre, sa doctrine*, 2 vols., Paris, Beauchesne, 1938, II, 103.

[38] Lagrange, . . . *Matthieu, loc. cit.*

[39] [Nor a "rejection of the Jews," as JB says in the title it gives Luke 13:22 ff.: "The narrow door; rejection of the Jews, call of the Gentiles."—Ed.]

". . . them that do iniquity":[40] this is the Word, the true one.

With this, the episode of the centurion at Capernaum takes on its real meaning, "very plain" and very evangelic: there is a place for everyone in the Kingdom of God, even for Gentiles, on one condition —that they be worthy of it through their faith, faith in Yahweh, faith in Jesus. It is understandable that Luke, a Christian from the Gentile world, writing for Gentiles, would have conscientiously and loyally recollected the incident. It is also understandable that Matthew, a Jew turned Christian, especially irritated by the Judaic hostility and unbelief, would have remembered it, and that he would have tended to strengthen its elements of rigidity, of severity toward the unbelieving Jews. But to discern the "reprobation," the "rejection" of Israel in this episode is to go farther than is allowed by textual criticism and I would say even respect for the Gospel, in its spirit and its letter.

Now, from the first group of texts that we have singled out, Matthew 8:11–12 is the only one in which these judgments can be discerned, and this only barely and not without predisposition. The Synoptics offer us another important account from the same group, of Jesus and the Syrophoenician woman in Mark 7:25–30 and Matthew 15:22–28, texts which have been examined previously [41] and about which one can say anything but that they announce the downfall of the Jews to the advantage of the Gentiles; for on the contrary, they strongly indicate the privilege of the first and the recognized inferiority of the second:

". . . it is not right to take the children's bread and throw it to the dogs." But she answered him, "Yes, Lord; yet even the dogs under the table eat the children's crumbs."

Mk. 7:27–28

To manage to present this episode as a demonstration "of a change in God's salvific will," as do the Protestant theologians Gunther Dehn and Edmond Stapfer,[42] constitutes a true miracle of exegesis: theological faith moves mountains; better yet, it baptizes them as plains.

Of less importance is the episode of the lepers, occurring in Luke 17:11–19 only:

---

[40] See Matthew 7:23 [KJ]: ". . . depart from me, ye that work iniquity," words inspired by Psalm 6:9 [KJ]: "Depart from me, all ye workers of iniquity. . . ."

[41] See pp. 183–185, above.

[42] Gunther Dehn, Le Fils de Dieu, commentaire à l'Évangile de Marc, Paris, Je Sers, 1936, p. 141; Stapfer, op. cit., p. 258.

Then one of them, when he saw that he was healed, turned back, praising God with a loud voice; and he fell on his face at Jesus' feet, giving him thanks. Now he was a Samaritan. Then said Jesus, "Were not ten cleansed? Where are the nine? Was no one found to return and give praise to God except this foreigner?" And he said to him, "Rise and go your way; your faith has made you well."

Lk. 17:15-19

Salvation—even for a Samaritan—by faith in God and in Jesus is the meaning of the episode, exactly as in the case of the centurion at Capernaum. The ingratitude of the other cured lepers (but how could they have been cured without faith?) is shocking, to be sure; anyway, it serves to bring out better the thankfulness of the Samaritan. Luke retained this incident [43] for the auspicious promise it implied in favor of non-Jewish believers. He refrained from including any condemnation of the Jews, whose name is not even mentioned.

That is all in the Synoptics. The fourth Gospel does not add much. As we have already noted, Gentiles appear only once in John, at 12:20–29; and again, these are Gentiles gravitating around Israel, "God-fearers" like Luke's centurion:

Now among those who went up to worship at the feast were some Greeks. So these came to Philip, who was from Bethsaida in Galilee, and said to him, "Sir, we wish to see Jesus." Philip went and told Andrew; Andrew went with Philip and they told Jesus.

Jn. 12:20-22

The request was not welcomed, contrary to what the *Biblical Manual* says: "Our Lord made strangers welcome." [44] No word of the text suggests it. Father Lagrange acknowledges, "Far from attributing the importance of a decisive point to this advance, Jesus did not even reply to it, and did not address himself specially to the Greeks" [45] in the effusion that followed, the admirable mystical effusion concerning glorification through death, crossed with piercing human anguish. Unless we see a reply—an indirect one—to the Greeks' approach in verse 32:

. . . and I, when I am lifted up from the earth, will draw all men to myself.

All men, Jews as well as pagans. Not a word in all this that signifies reprobation or rejection of Israel. Yet here is the commentary given by a highly regarded Protestant theologian, Henri Bois: "One

[43] Very closely linked to the episode of Naaman the Syrian, cured of leprosy by the Prophet Elisha in 2 Kings 5:1–19.
[44] Brassac, *op. cit.*, p. 671.
[45] Lagrange, . . . *Jean*, p. 328.

day the opportunity arose for Jesus to abandon the Jews, who stubbornly persisted in spurning him, and to turn toward the pagan world, which was calling through the voices of the Greeks. Witness to the opposition that Jesus encountered in his nation, the Greeks wanted to invite him to address pagans, who would appreciate and welcome him better than the Jews." [46] A fine example of theological fantasying, inspired by a centuries-old prejudice; the least one can say of such a commentary is that it greatly outreaches the text in question, that it outreaches the entire text of the Gospels. If indeed "the opportunity arose for Jesus to abandon the Jews," which the evangelist breathes not a word about, Jesus disdained it.

There remains the well-known episode of the Samaritan woman at Jacob's well in John 4:5–42, which we have already discussed, and whose religious value and great beauty I readily appreciate. But in the universe of the Gospel it forms a land apart, or better a sparkling and far-off constellation unconnected with the rest of the world. "The doctrinal cast is so transparent in this episode that we should not be too surprised to find it considered as a symbol created by the evangelist's genius." [47] It can in fact be admitted that the Samaritan woman symbolizes "the sinful and yet religious soul outside of Judaism." It is more difficult to admit (because it is difficult to reconcile with the Synoptic tradition) that Jesus, announcing the hour near at hand "when neither on this mountain [Gerizim] nor in Jerusalem will you worship the Father. . . . when the true worshipers will worship the Father in spirit and truth" (Jn. 4:21, 23), meant to toll the death knell of the traditional Jewish cult; for these words go far, they toll the death knell as well of all ritualism, of all cultic materiality, of all localization of the sacred. Why not admit, more simply, that Jesus was announcing the imminent substitution, already achieved by those who believed in him, of wholly pure adoration in the Kingdom of God for gross earthly adoration? As for the "reprobation," the "rejection" of the Jewish people, the people from whom "salvation is" (Jn. 4:22), these notions appear nowhere in this text, which is simultaneously the most enigmatic and the most doctrinal of the whole Gospel.

So, all in all, the "reprobations" in this first group of texts are reduced to Matthew 8:12. And said Matthew 8:12 cannot be read and

[46] Henri Bois, *La Personne et l'oeuvre de Jésus*, Neuilly, La Cause, 1926, p. 79.
[47] Lagrange, . . . *Jean*, p. 101. However, the author protests against this purely symbolic interpretation.

interpreted correctly except with the aid of Luke 13:28–29 and Matthew himself, 13:41–42.

❂   ❂   ❂

But behind the vanguard advances a second group—a compact battalion—of texts, the collection of parables, disguised adversaries and thereby all the more troubling.

At their head, a fearsome monster, the key text. Not one of the parables, but Jesus' teaching on "the divine aim of the parables," which would supposedly be none other than the "hardening of the Jewish people." There is no theme more discussed by exegetes and theologians, more worked over in theological teaching, more disconcerting for a candid heart. The Synoptics offer us three parallel versions of it. The first problem is that these three versions differ on an essential point, which we italicize for emphasis:

And when he was alone, those who were about him with the twelve asked him concerning the parables. And he said to them, "To you has been given the secret of the kingdom of God, but for those outside everything is in parables; *so that* [48] they may indeed see but not perceive, and may indeed hear but not understand; lest they should turn again, and be forgiven."

Mk. 4:10–12

Then the disciples came and said to him, "Why do you speak to them in parables?" And he answered them, "To you it has been given to know the secrets of the kingdom of heaven, but to them it has not been given. For to him who has will more be given, and he will have abundance; but from him who has not, even what he has will be taken away. This is why I speak to them in parables, *because* [49] seeing they do not see, and hearing they do not hear, nor do they understand. With them indeed is fulfilled the prophecy of Isaiah which says:

'You shall indeed hear but never understand,
and you shall indeed see but never perceive.

[48] [The other English translations consulted carry similar wording: "so that" (ABS, JB), "that" (CCD, KJ), "so" (RK). JB has this note regarding "so that": "The conjunction (Mt avoids it) is equivalent to 'in order that the Scripture might be fulfilled that says. . . .'"—Ed.]

[49] [Again, the other English versions consulted all begin with "because." JB notes: "A deliberate and culpable insensibility which is both the cause and the explanation of the withdrawal of grace. . . . Those who saw so dimly could only be further blinded by the light of full revelation. . . . Jesus, therefore, . . . filters the light through symbols, the resulting half-light is nevertheless a grace from God, an invitation to ask for something better and accept something greater." And RK comments: "Our Lord seems to tone down the language of this prophecy, perhaps for fear it might seem that the failure of the Jews to grasp his message was due to some arbitrary decree of heaven, not to their own fault."—Ed.]

For this people's heart has grown dull,
and their ears are heavy of hearing,
and their eyes they have closed,
lest they should perceive with their eyes,
and hear with their ears,
and understand with their heart,
and turn for me to heal them.'. . ."

Mt. 13:10–15

And when his disciples asked him what this parable meant, he said, "To you it has been given to know the secrets of the kingdom of God; but for others they are in parables, *so that* seeing they may not see, and hearing they may not understand. . . ."

Lk. 8:9–10

The fourth Gospel has no exactly parallel passage on the teaching of the parables; yet John has not failed to include the theme of the providential "hardening" to give more support to his doctrinal thesis of the unbelief of the Jews:

Though he had done so many signs before them, yet they did not believe in him; it was that the word spoken by the prophet Isaiah might be fulfilled:

"Lord, who has believed our report,
and to whom has the arm of the Lord been revealed?"

Therefore they could not believe. For Isaiah again said,

"He has blinded their eyes and hardened their heart,
lest they should see with their eyes and perceive with their heart,
and turn for me to heal them."

Isaiah said this because he saw his glory and spoke of him. Nevertheless many even of the authorities believed in him, but for fear of the Pharisees they did not confess it. . . .

Jn. 12:37–42

We immediately see the distance, the incommensurable distance, that separates John from the Synoptics here. The latter attributed the recollection of Isaiah's prophecy to Jesus. John—knowing exactly what he was doing, for he was not ignorant of the earlier Gospels—took it to himself and deliberately used it to drive home in Christian opinion the scandal that the unbelief of traditional Judaism represented at the end of the first century, when he was writing his Gospel: "This astounding fact, that the Jews rejected their Messiah, must not be an object of scandal, for God had prophesied it. . . . There is no reason to be surprised that the Messiah sent to the Jews was not recognized by them: God's plan was not destroyed but rather fulfilled by this resistance." [50] Little matter that in the time when Jesus was preaching in Israel, unbelief was the reaction of one clique and not of the Jewish people; John did not worry about the anachronism. Moreover, we have already demonstrated that historic reality did not fail to show through his doctrinal formulas and theses. According to the last verse quoted, 42, "It was mainly the chiefs who were involved, those who had the duty of leading the nation to Jesus and who on the contrary turned it away." [51] This emerges more clearly from another passage in John, where Jesus himself said:

For judgment I came into this world, that those who do not see may see, and that those who see may become blind.

Jn. 9:39

—and where the context indicates clearly who "those who see" and "may become blind" were: the learned Pharisee doctors who relentlessly opposed Jesus. Doctors, pundits, notables, it is these who are likewise meant in John 12:37–42.

Furthermore, the question is not what the evangelist said and intended to say. It is of a higher order: what Jesus said and intended to say. We must therefore return to the Synoptics, without failing to recognize the significance of the Johannine references.

But first, to which of the three Synoptic texts should we give credence? Mark and Luke, who have Jesus saying that he spoke to "those outside," to "others" in parables "so that" seeing they might not see; or Matthew, ". . . I speak to them in parables, because seeing they do not see . . ." ?

The difference is great: in the first case, the blindness of the Jews, or more precisely of those of the Jews who were not members of Jesus' entourage, is a consequence; in the second case, it is a cause. The difference cannot be resolved by a voice count—two instances of hina, or "so that," as against one of hoti, or "because"—for it is generally agreed that Luke followed Mark on this point. Mark's hina and Matthew's hoti remain at hand, then. It is not impossible, according to some experts, that hina had a meaning in first-century Greek which was close to that of hoti; but it is possible too that it retained its usual meaning: "so that."

In addition, each of the three quotations of Isaiah 6:9–10 is different: Mark gives the beginning and the end; Luke the beginning only,

[50] Lagrange, . . . Jean, pp. 339–341.
[51] Ibid., p. 339.

thus eliminating the harshest words; Matthew the whole passage, but in the Greek Septuagint translation which the Palestinian Jews, who spoke Aramaic, definitely did not use, and which departs appreciably from the Hebraic text. Under these circumstances, Father Lagrange acknowledges, "We cannot know very exactly what Jesus said." [52] This textual uncertainty alone would seem of a nature to make scrupulous commentators hesitate.

But since it is a question of condemning Israel, "carnal" Israel, the Jewish people, why hesitate? From antiquity to our own day, there has been an almost uninterrupted sequence of doctors, and among the most eminent, who have willingly taken Mark's text—Mark's *hina*—literally, and deduced from it that the teaching in parables

. . . was expressly chosen by Christ himself in order to assure the accomplishment of God's plan for his people, . . . [a plan which implied] the preliminary hardening. . . . Judaism did not convert because it was not to convert, and the evangelical truth was proposed to it in an enigma so that it could not see it or be saved. [53]

Following the Fathers of the Church and its greatest doctors, following Clement of Alexandria and Juan Maldonado, Calvinists and Jansenists gave zealous support to a thesis whose rigor harmonized with their conception of grace. The genius of Pascal gave ready assent to these sharp contrasts between light and shadow:

We shall understand nothing about the works of God unless we accept the principle that he wished some people to be blind to them and others to understand them clearly. . . .

There is sufficient light to enlighten the elect and sufficient darkness to humiliate them. There is sufficient darkness to blind the damned, and sufficient light to condemn them and make them unpardonable. . . . [54]

In more recent times, theologians like Fathers Joseph Knabenbauer and Leopold Fonck continued to maintain that in using parables Christ intended to execute "a providential decree of reprobation": "The grace of instruction had been withdrawn [from the Jews], and they now had to experience in themselves the punishment for their hardness of heart." [55]

[52] Lagrange, . . . *Marc*, p. 99.
[53] Alfred Loisy, *L'Évangile selon saint Marc* [The Gospel According to Saint Mark], Paris, Nourry, 1912, p. 130.
[54] Blaise Pascal, *Opuscules et pensées* [Tracts and Thoughts], ed. Léon Brunschvicg, Paris, Hachette, 1897, paras. 566, 578. [Quotation taken from *idem, Pensées*, ed. and tr. Martin Turnell, New York, Harper, 1962, pp. 232, 233.—Tr.]
[55] Father Leopold Fonck, *Die Parabeln des Herrn im Evangelium* [The Parables of the Lord in the Gospels], 1904; quoted in Lagrange, . . . *Marc*, p. 100.

Not without attenuations, not without arduous efforts to bring Mark and Matthew closer together, to reconcile divine rigor and mercy, many still today continue to profess the thesis of "providential" blindness. In the *Biblical Manual*, A. Brassac distinguishes "two intentions" on Jesus' part:

. . . one prior, by which he desired to be understood by all; the other posterior, by which, seeing that a certain number neglected to apply themselves to his words in order to understand his figures, he wanted their neglect to be punished by incomprehension of the figurative language which he persisted in using.[56]

We prefer Pascal.

And here is Louis-Claude Fillion:

The obstinate unbelief of some, the deliberate indifference of others, the profound ingratitude of all would be punished by the retraction of the gifts of light which they had abused. What good continuing any longer to give "the holy thing," the "pearls" of the Gospel to the unworthy? Refusing them these was rather an act of goodness.[57]

Here we move away from exegesis and stumble into casuistry.

Even so, a countercurrent has opposed this current, and since the most ancient times. "If Jesus had not wanted the Jews to understand and be saved," Saint John Chrysostom was already writing, "he had only to keep silent, he did not need to speak in parables; on the contrary, he wanted to spur them on with the very obscureness of his words."[58] Father Lagrange assures us that Saint Thomas Aquinas inclined in this direction; Father Lagrange especially inclines in this direction himself, refuting the thesis of divine "intention" so vigorously that I cannot restrain myself from quoting him at length:

Contrary to Fathers Knabenbauer and Fonck, we cannot believe that Jesus proposed his parables, or those alone that regard the kingdom of God, in such a way that the Jews could not understand because they were outcasts. It is a misrepresentation to take the parables for enigmas, intended to baffle curiosity. Actually the parables which we have before our eyes are not

[56] Brassac, *op. cit.*, p. 471. [Father Brassac's notions are duplicated in this recent example of catechetic literature: "Those who heard the parables were guilty, and it is their guilt which earned them that kind of teaching, appropriate to their state. . . . The parables were punishment for these evil predispositions" (Father Denys Buzy, *Jésus comme il était* [Jesus as He Was], Paris, Éd. de l'École, 1964, p. 165; quoted in Houtart and Giblet, *op. cit.*, p. 180).—Ed.]

[57] Fillion, *op. cit.*, II, 375.

[58] [For the original texts and parallel French translations of John Chrysostom's eight homilies *Against the Jews*, see *Ioannou tou Krusostomou, ta Eurizkomena Panta: Oeuvres complètes de Saint Jean Chrysostome* (Complete Works of Saint John Chrysostom), ed. J. Bareille, Paris, Louis Vives, 1865, II, 350–513.—Ed.]

enigmas, and they are the easier to understand the less one seeks so many veils and mysteries in them. The Savior's disposition, his spirit, his heart thirsting for men's salvation, the very role of every preacher who preaches in order to convert, everything opposes the dissimulation attributed to him. How could he have invited his listeners to lend their ears, to plumb the meaning of his words, if he had chosen images and comparisons which were incomprehensible without special explanation?

Would such an affectation not have had something odious about it? To what preacher or doctor would one dare impute such conduct?

Could it be that Jesus knew God's designs better than we and that he executed them? But *nothing indicates that the crowd merited his reprobation thenceforth.*[59] Mark said absolutely nothing up to that instant which suggested this. . . . [The crowd] pressed around the Master with growing eagerness to hear him. At that moment Jesus had to climb in a boat to teach them, so enthusiastically did they flock to him, and yet the opinion is urged that he answered this thirst for his words with enigmas they could not have understood, so that they would cooperate in his reprobation, and so that positively they would be punished for their hardness of heart! That the sentiments of this crowd were very mixed is understood, and necessitated reservations in the teaching; but that they were treated as an outcast mass, unworthy of being addressed as all men address other men!

If this was indeed what Mark meant to say, one would be forced to conclude with Loisy that he did not understand Jesus' intentions. . . .[60]

We would prefer to admit that Mark transcribed a little clumsily . . . than to attribute to Jesus a procedure that no zealous preacher, and indeed no man of honor, would want to use in his teaching.[61]

That after this, after letting his heart and his knowledge speak so openly, so clearly, good Father Lagrange should believe himself required to take back with the other hand what he has given with one, to state that the "distinction between two kinds of listeners corresponded with a plan of God, who made the blindness of the Jews the condition of salvation" (for "If they had acquiesced to [Jesus'] preaching, God would have pardoned them, and this healing of the breach would have impeded definitive salvation"),[62] the very mediocrity of such formulas betrays his embarrassment—as usual—and takes nothing away from the strength of his refutation. We hold that refutation as valid, and leaving these theological debates aside,[63] will attempt to clarify the problem with the following observations.

[59] It is I who underscore this sentence, which in my opinion is of major importance.
[60] Lagrange, . . . *Marc*, pp. 102–103.
[61] *Ibid.*, p. 105.
[62] *Ibid.*, pp. 104–105.
[63] Interminable debates. Another attempt at explaining, no less embarrassed, will be found in Father André Charue, *L'Incrédulité des Juifs dans le Nouveau*

The first observation is general; it bears not only on the texts now under consideration but also on all the texts to which the meaning of "reprobation" or "rejection" is attributed: It is not true that the Jewish people—I mean the popular masses, the crowd—displayed "unbelief" or "indifference" or "ingratitude" toward Jesus; much to the contrary, as the four Gospels testify and as we have demonstrated, this people did not cease to shower Jesus with signs of fervent regard and marveling trust. A regard perhaps little enlightened, and of dubious quality, all right, but worthy nonetheless of being repaid in kind—and it was; how could it have been otherwise? How can it be thought that Jesus, the embodiment of love, could have responded to this disorderly but touching eagerness with a premeditated plan calling for blindness, punishment, mass reprobation?

The second observation is equally a statement of fact, a dual statement: It is not true that Jesus inaugurated teaching in parables at a given moment in his ministry as a penalty brought down on the crowd; Jesus used this method from beginning to end, with the disciples as well as with the crowd, with neither the ones nor the others exclusively.[64] And it is not true that the parables were enigmas destined to mislead, to blind the (innocent) listeners; this was an instruction process quite usual with religious teachers in Israel; Jesus used it more excellently, not differently. This is spelled out in full by the evangelist Mark himself, at 4:33: "With many such parables he spoke the word to them, as they were able to hear it. . . ."

What is a parable, really? A more or less developed comparison, a sequence of images, sometimes a kind of allegory, aiming simultaneously to awaken the listeners' curiosity and to make some abstract concept, some exposition of a truth of faith, some moral lesson more accessible to them. The Gospel parables are more or less clear; they are no more and no less clear than the talmudic parables. Some needed explaining, and Jesus reserved this to the disciples alone: what could be more natural, more legitimate? Why is it necessary to make a theological mystery of it? A crowd—no matter what crowd, Jewish or Christian—is like a child, to whom it would be imprudent

---

Testament, Louvain, Gembloux, 1929, p. 143. We might note that Fathers de Grandmaison (*op. cit.,* I, 329) and Prat (*op. cit.,* I, 340) range themselves alongside Father Lagrange.

[64] Before the text under study in Mark 4, parables in 2:19–22; 3:24–27. Parable addressed to the disciples, who as usual did not understand, in 8:15–17. Teaching to the crowd without parables in 8:34 ff.; 12:38 ff.; and likewise in Matthew 23:1 ff.; Luke 9:23 ff.; John *passim.*

to tell everything; at all times, in all countries, a crowd needs guides; the disciples trained by Jesus were to be such guides, who would replace others. If then there were "levels" in evangelical teaching, this gradation is self-explanatory, without there being any need to evoke the monster of "providential" blindness for that purpose.

The third observation treats of the monster itself, that is, texts which have given rise to it. Let us note:

that John, knowing the Synoptic tradition, avoided putting the quotation from Isaiah into Jesus' mouth, and took it to himself;

that Matthew attributed to Jesus a quotation drawn from the Septuagint, which, by the statement of Father Lagrange himself, exceeds the limits of likelihood; [65]

that Luke limited himself to reproducing Mark, attenuating him; hence there remains Mark and his inconceivable *hina*, "so that."

Now, we have already observed, and it is accepted by the most orthodox exegesis, that there may have been some displacements of texts in the writing of the Gospels. Eager to substantiate the scandal of Israel's unbelief before Gentile eyes, the evangelists transposed specific occurrences in order to give this unbelief the larger, the collective scope which new circumstances suggested to them. This is an excellent place to repeat the thought-provoking words of Father de Grandmaison: "It is not impossible to think that in the very writing of the Synoptics, the fact, thereafter established, of the universal hardening of the Jewish people made itself felt." [66] Here, precisely, we can put our finger on the retroactive effect.

And from this, we are justified in concluding:

no, Jesus did not intend that;

no, Jesus could not have said that;

preferable to admit with Father Lagrange "that Mark transcribed a little clumsily," or with Alfred Loisy "that he did not understand Jesus' intentions," or as I suppose that there has been textual displacement.

☼   ☼   ☼

There is hardly a parable in the Gospels in which some scribe, armed with special glasses, has not succeeded in turning up the bacillus of "reprobation." Without pausing over secondary discussions, we

[65] See Lagrange, . . . *Matthieu*, p. 261.
[66] Grandmaison, *op. cit.*, I, 331.

will go directly to the major texts, those on which the teaching of Israel's reprobation is most commonly based.[67] They are three:

the parable of the recalcitrant guests;

the parable of the murdering vineyard tenants;

and what might be called a parable in action, the withered fig tree.

The Parable of the Recalcitrant Guests

The parable of the recalcitrant guests is found in Matthew 22:1–14 and Luke 14:15–24, in rather different forms. In Matthew, it begins:

The kingdom of heaven may be compared to a king who gave a marriage feast for his son, and sent his servants to call those who were invited to the marriage feast; but they would not come.

Mt. 22:2–3

And in Luke:

A man once gave a great banquet, and invited many; and at the time for the banquet he sent his servant to say to those who had been invited, "Come. . . ." But they all alike began to make excuses.

Lk. 14:16–18

Here, as before, we collide with an initial difficulty. The two texts exhibit enough similarities to exclude the hypothesis—often adopted —that there are two distinct parables, but enough differences to make it impossible to call them identical and consequently to "know very exactly what Jesus said," which again should suffice to inspire some reserve among commentators, even the most determined (in their passion for "reprobation").

Let us reread these texts, with the greatest possible candor of heart

---

[67] In one of the works most highly regarded by the Catholic public at this writing, Father Ferdinand Prat's *Jésus-Christ, sa vie, son oeuvre, sa doctrine*, published in 1933 and reissued in 1938 and 1953, the author titles Chapter 2 of volume II "Monday in Holy Week: Reprobation of the Jewish People" (this is "the cursed fig tree"), and Chapter 3 "Tuesday in Holy Week, II: The Parables of Reprobation"; here he adds the parable of the "two sons," which we will mention later. "The Jewish nation as a whole," he writes, "is ripe for reprobation" (p. 223). In a work which is older but which has had a large readership in the Protestant Churches, Henri Bois's *La Personne et l'oeuvre de Jésus*, we read: "Let us reread the parable of the talents and that of the pounds [CCD: gold pieces]. . . . Let us reread the account of the curse of the sterile fig tree, the parable of the evil vineyard tenants. . . . What emerges from these various texts is that in Jesus' eyes, Jesus' murder on the cross is indeed a crime which the Jews freely committed. The Jews are unfaithful to their mission. . . . God will break them" (p. 72).

and mind, as if we were hearing them from the mouth of the Master himself.

One, the parable recounted by Luke, lively and lifelike, sounds quite clear. Is it difficult to perceive the meaning it suggests? Those who will take part in the celestial banquet in the Kingdom of God will not be those who, officially invited, have put their selfish preoccupations before God's call; they will be the poor, the destitute, the disabled, and if there is still space, it will be for vagabonds on the highways, the last of the *ammei ha-aretz*, rather than for the notables, the learned men, the doctors and other great personages. Do we not find a thousand examples in the Gospel tradition of this marked preference of Christ's for the unfortunate and the lowly?

As for the parable recounted by Matthew, the first impression is more mixed: I understand the beginning, says the hearer, and I know these recalcitrant guests, who are too attached to the goods of this world, but what is the meaning of the killings and massacres? And the sequel, which is stranger yet: the (substitute) guests, gathered from the streets hit or miss, and because one is found, only one, who is poorly dressed, who is "without a wedding garment" (what is most surprising is that he is the only one of his kind), he is struck down, thrown into Gehenna!

In Matthew, says Father Lagrange, "We always encounter this same disregard for avoiding improbabilities." [68] Indeed, so much so that one can challenge any listener—if he is not a Christian theologian—to see clearly in such a fog, and in reality one is justified in thinking that Jesus did not exercise the "same disregard for avoiding improbabilities." One of the two parallel texts could have been said, the other not. The most widespread opinion, which is also Father Lagrange's, is that Matthew blended two parables into one, the parable of the guests and that of the wedding garb. According to Father Denys Buzy, it would be three rather than two parables that Matthew combined into one; there would be a parable of the homicidal guests distinct from that of the discourteous guests.[69]

Yet what do orthodoxy's experts say, leaning on a tradition which goes back to the Fathers of the Church? What does the *Biblical Manual* teach? That the two parables, although distinct, would have "the same object: reprobation of the Jews, calling of the pagans." How so?

[68] Lagrange, . . . *Matthieu*, p. 424.
[69] Father Denys Buzy, *Introduction aux paraboles évangéliques*, Paris, Gabalda, 1932, pp. 306–310.

In Luke, the first invited, "according to the context," are "the leaders of the Jewish theocracy," and the last, those brought from "the hedges" and along "the highways," are the Gentiles; as for the others, taken from "the streets and lanes of the city," the commentators are obliged to recognize that they are "the whole of the Jewish people, the poor, the tax collectors, the sinners." No matter; these embarrassing guests disappear in the conclusion which says: "The leaders of the Jewish theocracy will be excluded from the messianic kingdom, and pagans will come be seated in their place." In Matthew, "The marriage feast signifies the mystical union of the Son with the Church"; the invited are the Jews; the servants who are sent to them are first the Prophets, then the Apostles and the disciples, and "We know that the Jews seized . . . and killed several [of them]"; their punishment is predicted, the massacres of A.D. 70 and the burning of Jerusalem. "Since the Jews remained deaf to grace, God called the Gentiles," but "To be admitted to the kingdom of God, it is not enough to be called; one must be clothed in Jesus Christ"; the wedding garment is "the state of grace, without which no one enters heaven." [70] The parable in Matthew is thus complicated with prophecy and allegory; was I not right in saying that it seems to be of use exclusively to theologians? We can wager that the disciples themselves understood none of this.

The same teaching is given by the highly authoritative author Louis-Claude Fillion. He also, distinguishing two parables, assigns them the same object: reprobation of the Jews, calling of the Gentiles. The parable in Luke seems to him in sum to be "the whole history of the divine plan regarding redemption"; "The majestic conclusion—'For I tell you, none of those men who were invited shall taste my banquet'—fell like a bludgeon blow on the head of the guilty. It clearly marks the reprobation of the Jews as a nation." [71] In Matthew,

The invited guests symbolize all the civil and spiritual leaders of the Jewish nation. . . . The Romans would be the terrible instruments of divine vengeance. Several of those who heard this threat then would perhaps perish, crushed or burned alive, in the smoking rubble of the Temple. . . .

The Jews rejected because they did not believe, the Gentiles called in their place but rejected in turn . . . if they are found to be unworthy: such, in brief, is the grave teaching of Our Lord.[72]

[70] Brassac, op. cit., pp. 484–488.
[71] Fillion, op. cit., III, 117.
[72] Ibid., III, 248, 250. The same interpretation is found in Prat, op. cit., II, 227. [So also in CCD and JB. CCD comments thus on Matthew 22:1–14: "Refers, like the parable of the vineyard"—that is, Matthew 21:33–46—"to the rejec-

Let us turn from the commentaries back to the texts, and in them to the only problem that concerns us here: that of the invited guests and their replacements, excluding the question of the wedding garment.

The parable in Luke, according to the context of 14:3, is addressed "to the lawyers and Pharisees" who were seated at table with him. The parable in Matthew is told in the Temple, before "the chief priests and the Pharisees" (22:45). There is every possibility, therefore, that in speaking of the recalcitrant guests Jesus was thinking of the audience before his eyes, and our authors recognize this: the invited guests are, "according to the context, the leaders of the Jewish theocracy." All the same, it is hard to merge the Pharisees, a pious sect, with the guests who were entirely absorbed in preoccupation with their temporal goods; but a parable, if it is only a parable, does not have the exactness of an allegory, in which each term has a well-established symbolic value; and everything tends to indicate that Jesus was not allegorizing so much as his interpreters and their commentators did and had him do subsequently.

This said, on what grounds is Jesus' warning to the priestly caste or the Pharisees extended to "the Jews as a nation"? On what grounds is it claimed that "The Jews [are] rejected . . . , the Gentiles called in their place"? Not a single word in the texts necessarily implies this, and several, notably in Luke, explicitly contradict it. The *Biblical Manual* does not dispute that the substitutes taken from "the streets and lanes of the city" are "the whole of the Jewish people, the poor, the tax collectors, the sinners"; after this all that can be involved is a partial reprobation, not a global. As for the Gentiles, searching Luke in vain to find the passwords directed to them, the *Biblical Manual* is reduced to adding them in parentheses: "Go out to the highways and hedges (outside the city, outside Palestine, outside the Jewish nation),

tion of the Jews." And JB notes: ". . . those sent with invitations are the prophets and the apostles; the invited who ignore them or do them violence are the Jews. . . ." Teaching manuals in the United States follow the same path. "The Gentiles came to take the place of the Jews in Christ's Kingdom," says *Living with Christ,* Book I, a Christian Brothers publication, Winona, Minn., St. Mary's College Press, 1945; rev. ed. 1958, p. 130 (quoted in Sister Rose Albert Thering, O.P., *The Potential in Religion Textbooks for Developing a Realistic Self-Concept,* doctoral dissertation, St. Louis University, 1961). "The Jews are the invited guests who refused the invitation and who were themselves finally rejected," claims *Through Christ Our Lord,* "Quest of Happiness" series, ed. Msgr. Clarence E. Eleoell *et. al.,* Book II, Chicago, Meatzer Bros., 1956, p. 184 (quoted in Thering, *op. cit.*).—Ed.]

and compel people to come in. . . ." [73] But Father Lagrange, who respects the texts, does not hesitate to upset this house of cards:

Some believe they recognize the Gentiles here. . . . But the expression "outside" is not there, and it would be necessary to serve as a support for the allegory. . . . There was a difference in the call to the Jews and the Gentiles which would be very inadequately conveyed by the shades of distinction in verses 21 and 23 between "streets" and "highways." . . . The parable does not seem to contain an allegoric allusion to the Jews. . . . Since this application is not made by the Savior, it is better to leave this point in some uncertainty.[74]

It is above all better not to make Jesus say what he did not say: "The lesson is rich enough," Father Lagrange concludes, to serve the ones and the others—the Jews, the Pharisees, the leaders; and even "Perhaps it would be profitable for religious and priests to apply it to themselves." [75]

Christian language too rare, too rarely heeded. We say nothing more: Jesus' lessons are rich enough to apply to all, to Christians as to Jews.

The same argument holds for Matthew's text, patchwork though it is. The expression "outside," or any other indicative expression of the same sort, is equally absent from it, an absence which makes it rash to attempt—as is often done—to broaden its scope beyond the Jewish framework. To read the "reprobation" of the Jewish people into this text requires prior determination, or dependence on certain details in the transcription whose unlikelihood allows us to believe they were not authentic, and whose symbolism is not even convincing. "The parable showed Israel's leaders that they were headed for ruin in refusing the Savior's invitation." [76] So be it, but this is not universal "reprobation," this is not a "calling" of the Gentiles; and we cannot forget, in connection with the commentary on Matthew 22:6 (". . . the rest [of those originally invited] seized his servants, treated them shamefully, and killed them"), that if official Judaism sometimes persecuted Christians, the Gentile world—Roman paganism—did so a thousand times more.

[73] Brassac, op. cit., p. 1085.
[74] Lagrange, . . . Luc, pp. 405–407.
[75] Ibid., p. 407.
[76] Lagrange, . . . Matthieu, p. 426.

The Parable of the Murdering Vineyard Tenants

The parable of the murdering vineyard tenants is found similarly worded in Mark 12:1–12, Matthew 21:33–46, and Luke 20:9–19. Told on the eve of the Passion, it is the text in the Synoptic Gospels in which Jesus designated himself as Son of God most clearly in public.

This time the three texts are very close to each other. The only noteworthy differences: in Mark and Matthew, Jesus addressed himself directly to Sanhedrists—chief priests, scribes, and elders—and in Luke, he was speaking to the people, though patently for the sake of the same Sanhedrists; each evangelist describes in his own fashion the sending of the messengers and the violence done them; in Mark, the son is cast out of the vineyard after he is killed, in Matthew and Luke, before he is killed; in Matthew, the Sanhedrists are led by Jesus to formulate themselves the treatment the criminal tenants deserve, and their response evidences surprising docility, while in Luke, the people limit their reply to an exclamation; Matthew and Luke add a commentary to the quotation of Psalm 118 which does not appear in Mark.

Shall we say that this dramatic and thereby impressive parable swarms with improbabilities? It is too easy to point them out, and it is superfluous to stress them except to deduce that this is an allegory far more than a parable, "an allegory which borders on a parable," says Father Lagrange, "because there are a number of traits which must not be explained allegorically." [77] But a genre so poorly defined unfortunately and perforce leaves room for a great deal of fantasy and arbitrariness (and vacillation) in its interpretation.

The *Biblical Manual* teaches: "This parable prophesies the abolition of the Sanhedrin and the Jewish priesthood, the reprobation of the Jewish nation, and the conversion of the Gentiles, who will be substituted for the descendants of Abraham in the messianic kingdom." [78] Louis-Claude Fillion: "The messianic vine will pass into other and more faithful hands, those of the Gentiles, whose future conversion and entry into the Church of Christ are thus again

---

[77] *Idem*, . . . *Marc*, p. 311.

[78] Brassac, *op. cit.*, p. 482. [A theme reiterated in the Oberammergau Passion Play, which has Jesus say: "The Old Covenant which my Father made with Abraham, Isaac and Jacob has reached its end" (*The Passion Play of Oberammergau*, p. 41).—Ed.]

predicted." [79] Father Lebreton: "This discourse . . . [teaches] not only the death of Christ and the punishment of the Jews but . . . the history of the people of God represented in this traditional image of a vine." [80] But the same author is more reserved elsewhere: "Jesus took care to limit the terrible responsibility for this murder [of the son] to the leaders. . . . the vine which represents [the people] directly was neither guilty nor threatened." [81] And Father Lagrange's opinion even is not easy to define. Commenting on Mark, he recognizes that "The allegory is not specific, except for the punishment of the tenants," and he marks well "the care Jesus took not to incorporate the still sympathetic crowd in the guilt and punishment of the chiefs." But commenting on Matthew, he limits himself to posing a question mark: "To what degree the people will be associated with the reprobation [of their chiefs], this is not said. . . ." And commenting on Luke, he takes a step forward: "A really very threatening parable, *especially* [italics in the original] for the Sanhedrists . . . , but the people will be associated with their crime, they will be punished like them. . . ." [82] A progressive and significant slipping. [83]

How can we see clearly in this confusion, compounded of intrepid affirmations, more or less admitted uncertainties, flagrant contradictions?

One point at least seems beyond doubt, strongly highlighted by the

[79] Fillion, *op. cit.*, III, 244.

[80] Father Jules Lebreton, S.J., *Histoire des origines du dogme de la Trinité*, 2 vols., Paris, Beauchesne, 1928, I, 244.

[81] *Idem*, *La Vie et l'enseignement de Jésus-Christ*, II, 181.

[82] Lagrange, . . . *Marc*, pp. 309–312; . . . *Matthieu*, p. 418; . . . *Luc*, pp. 507–512.

[83] [The English translations of the Bible consulted exhibit the same abusive tendency. Regarding Mark 12:1–12, CCD notes: "God is the landowner of the parable. He had sent His prophets, and lastly His Son, to the vine-dressers, the Jews." And we have seen the CCD comment on Matthew 22:1–14 (n. 72, just above). JB comments that in Matthew 21:33–46, ". . . the proprietor is God; the vineyard the Chosen People, Israel . . . ; the servants the prophets; the son Jesus, put to death outside the walls of Jerusalem; the murderous farmers the faithless Jews; the nation to which the vineyard will be entrusted, the pagans."

[If scholarly exegesis shows such bias, can popular catechesis be far behind? Let us judge from these examples: "The parable of the wicked husbandmen deals with the failure of Israel—and particularly Israel's religious leaders—to accept God's revelation through the prophets and in Jesus Christ" (*Sunday School Young Adult*, loc. cit.); and: "Thus the people of Israel as a whole, even many of those who followed John the Baptist, willfully rejected the one to whom they owed their true allegiance. Jesus later compared them to wicked husbandmen who knew who He was and said, 'This is the heir; come, let us kill him, and let us seize on His inheritance'" (*Gospel of John* [Assembly of God], 1965, p. 4; both quoted in Strober, *op. cit.*, pp. 63, 55).—Ed.]

stress laid on it by the three evangelists: the parable was addressed to
Sanhedrists, not to the Jewish people.

. . . for they perceived that he had told the parable against them. . . .

Mk. 12:12

. . . they perceived that he was speaking about them.

Mt. 21:45

. . . for they perceived that he had told this parable against them.

Lk. 20:19

It was for them that this was said; it was they whom this implicated.
They were the evildoing, criminal tenants, who received the vine
under leasehold. The vine itself, according to a perennial tradition of
prophetic literature (Is. 3:14; 5:1; Jer. 2:21; Ezek. 15:6; Hos.
10:1), is the image of Israel. Thus the leaders of Israel were guilty,
were criminal, would be punished: this is quite clear.

All the rest is much less so. All the other affirmations are questionable, for they do not find valid support in the texts.

Where is it seen that the Jewish people were incorporated in the
reprobation which struck their leaders, that they were dragged down
in their fall? Absolutely nothing indicates it; "this is not said," Father
Lagrange confesses. Then why say it? [84]

Where is it read that Jesus predicted "the conversion of the Gentiles" and their "entry into the Church of Christ"? Would it be in the
conclusion, that the owner "will . . . give the vineyard to others"
(Mk. 12:9)? The statement was indeed troubling; it made for confusion; and in Luke it provoked the interjection, "God forbid!" But seriously,[85] is it a strong enough reason—after what has been said about
the vine and the tenants—to divert it from its ordinary meaning: that
the leadership of Israel would pass into other hands?

Commentators invoke—and it is a supreme argument of the
"reprobators"—this small sentence added by Matthew, and by Matthew alone:

[84] [This is also the opinion of Protestant theologian Joachim Jeremias; see his
Die Gleichnisse Jesu (The Parables of Jesus), Göttingen, Vandenboeck und Ru-
precht, 1962.—Ed.]

[85] Father Lagrange is so undecided over this point that he attributes the interruption in one text to "voices from among the people" (. . . *Luc*, p. 510) and in
another to the Sanhedrists (. . . *Matthieu*, p. 416). But such an important proposition cannot be supported on such a frail foundation, especially if one considers
as does Father Buzy that Mark's wording, which is the simplest, in all probability
"represents the original text" (Buzy, *op. cit.*, p. 416), whence it follows that the
interruption noted in Luke would be only literary ornamentation.

Therefore I say to you, that the kingdom of God will be taken away from you and will be given to a people yielding its fruits.

Mt. 21:43 [CCD]

A singular sentence, in all respects. Singularly clear. Singularly obscure.

Singularly clear in the sense that Jesus, leaving figurative language aside, declared quite plainly to the Sanhedrists that they would be cast out, replaced; but then, after this direct threat in 21:43, it is surprising to read in 21:45: "When the chief priests and the Pharisees heard his parables, they perceived that he was speaking about them."

Singularly obscure because of the choice of terms used: "the kingdom of God will be taken away from you," as if they were its guardians or owners. It "will be given to a people yielding its fruits." What does "people" mean? If Jesus had wanted to designate the Gentiles, the text would carry the plural of the word which is necessary in such a case, *ethnesi*. With the singular, *ethnei*, it is reasonable to understand a new group selected to replace the old leaders, doubtless the band of Apostles and disciples, as is expressly said in Luke 12:32: "Fear not, little flock, for it is your Father's good pleasure to give you the kingdom."

A new "people of God": all right, but formed originally of Jews, and nothing indicates that they were broken away from the framework of Israel as they were constituted, that they were a spiritual Israel replacing Israel in the flesh. For the downfall of fleshly Israel would have had to be clearly pronounced beforehand, and it was not.

It was not, anywhere. It is seen everywhere, because there is a determination to see it. It is nowhere.

The Withered Fig Tree

In two of the Synoptics, Mark 11:12–14 and 20–23 and Matthew 21:18–22, the fig tree serves as an "object parable" or "object lesson," in the customary expression; it would be more exact to say, an allegory in action. Luke 13:6–9 alone has a parable of a fig tree in the usual sense of the word.

Luke's parable bears only a vague likeness to the episode recounted by Mark and Matthew. The fig tree in the parable is really unproductive; the master is thinking of getting rid of it; on the gardener's request, he gives it a reprieve. The parable contains a sharp warning, a threat of future punishment, nothing more. Whom is the threat addressed to?

Indubitably, replies Christian tradition, to the Jewish people.[86]

Neither the text nor the context authorizes such a categoric judgment. In the preceding verses, Jesus' severity does extend to everyone, Galileans or Jerusalemites, who refused to do penance: ". . . unless you repent you will all likewise perish" (Lk. 13:3, 5). But what Christian heart would not feel itself included in the terrible reprimand as well? What did Jesus see above all in these men he held in his gaze? Their Jewish nationality or their sinful soul? Strange disciples of Christ who would reply: their Jewish nationality! In the parable itself, nothing proves that the whole of the Jewish nation was at issue and that Jesus wanted to brand "Israel's inveterate barrenness," as Father Buzy writes.[87] It is not the fig tree but the vine which is the symbol of Israel in prophetic literature. Why might not the fig tree in the vineyard symbolize just as well that legalistic clique in Israel, rigid and sterile, whom Jesus saw as his principal adversaries and whom he wanted to uproot? Is it even necessary to attach a precise symbolic meaning to the image of the fig tree? There is "no allegory" here, Father Lagrange replies, and hence no well-established symbol, and as for the fate of the fig tree, "We remain uncertain." [88]

It is quite another and exceptional story that Mark and Matthew tell us. The fig tree they evoke is not a fig tree in a parable, an imaginary one; it is a real fig tree that Jesus is said to have spotted at some distance from the road as he was leaving Bethany to go to Jerusalem: some honest fig tree or other, having only leaves and no fruit, it is true, but quite within its rights to have none in this beginning of spring, for, Mark tells us, "It was not the season for figs" (Mk. 11:13). Vainly do the most orthodox exegetes, discountenanced by this remark, strive to demonstrate that it could have, should have had fruit:

Some opt for early figs or fig flowers; others for summer figs which would supposedly have passed the winter on the tree. But [states Father Lagrange, an expert on Palestine,] it is utterly unknown for summer figs in that country to remain on the trees all winter long. As for fig flowers, they appear before the leaves—I have seen them in Jerusalem as early as February 20—but they are not mature until June. It even commonly happens that

[86] See Fillion, op. cit., III, 106, 229; Albert Réville, Jésus de Nazareth, 2 vols., Paris, Fischbacher, 1906, II, 65.

[87] Buzy, op. cit., p. 127.

[88] Lagrange, . . . Luc, pp. 380–381. Father Buzy vigorously sustains the contrary opinion.

they all fall, so that after a few days the fig tree has nothing but leaves left. What would seem utterly unlikely, as the Eastern Fathers, who know the facts, have noted, would be that Jesus seriously looked for figs. And Father Le Camus [says:] "To maintain that according to the evangelists Jesus really wanted to eat figs from a fig tree at Passover is to admit that they ascribed the most extravagant fantasies to him."

Thus, "If ever a fig tree could be guilty [for not bearing figs], this one was surely not at fault." [89]

For what mysterious reason did Jesus pretend to search the tree for some fruit fit to eat, and then, having rightly found none, for what other mysterious reason did he punish it, condemn it to perpetual barrenness? The disciples were the first to wonder, to ask for an explanation. But Jesus gave them only this one: "Truly, I say to you, if you have faith . . . , even if you say to this mountain, 'Be taken up and cast into the sea,' it will be done" (Mt. 21:21). And the mystery remains: "The story of the fig tree," writes Éduard Reuss, "is an indecipherable enigma." [90]

Not for everyone. Following the Fathers of the Church, Saint Jerome, Saint Augustine, orthodox exegesis teaches thus:

Through the beauty of its precocious foliage, this fig tree aroused the hope of finding some refreshing fruit in its boughs. Perceiving none, Our Lord made this tree with its deceptive appearance a figure of Jerusalem and the Jewish people, whose legal justice was only a seeming justice, barren of the fruits of virtue and holiness (Saint Jerome). . . .
The fig tree represents the Jewish nation, showered with divine favors: a verdant tree, but the Savior finds only leaves on it, and no fruit, and it was struck by divine justice in punishment. [91]

So writes Canon Crampon. Says Father Brassac:

Judaism, withered to the root but still standing, attests by its very sterility to the divine curse that has struck it. . . .
This fig tree is the symbol of the Jewish people, in whom the Son of God found only a worthless semblance of religion, and whom he was close to cursing in punishment for their sterility. [92]

Fillion comments: "The fig tree is a symbolic representation of the Jewish nation, which, showered with divine favors for many centuries . . . , was unhappily devoid of fruit, of merit, by its own fault, and

---

[89] *Idem*, . . . *Marc*, p. 293 (internal quotation is from Father Émile Le Camus, *La Vie de Notre Seigneur Jésus-Christ* [The Life of Our Lord Jesus Christ], Paris, 1901, III, 52, n. 1, and *L'Évangile de Jésus-Christ*, p. 433).
[90] Eduard Reuss, *Histoire évangélique*, Paris, Fischbacher, 1876, p. 557.
[91] Crampon, *op. cit.*, notes on Mark 11:13 and Matthew 21:19.
[92] Brassac, *op. cit.*, p. 416 and n. 4.

hid the emptiness and even malice of its works behind a handsome exterior." [93] According to Father Lebreton, "Through this example, the disciples would understand the fate of Jerusalem and the people of God; it is he . . . whom they would recognize in this symbolic act of the Savior's, similar to so many acts of the prophets of old." [94] (The acts of the Prophets of old differed from this one in that they at least had a certain element of credibility, and everything suggests that the disciples on the contrary understood nothing.) "A judgment brought down upon Israel," the Protestant theologian Gunther Dehn states likewise; "this tree which shone with the splendor of its leaves and bore no fruit" was Israel.[95] And we find this traditional opinion still being expressed in the *Jerusalem Bible*, the most scholarly Catholic Bible: "The fate of the fig tree manifestly represents barren Israel and its coming punishment." [96]

The curse of the fig tree is the divine curse that weighs on Israel.[97] Yet, here again, Father Lagrange has serious reservations:

The Savior's action is a parable in action. Consequently, we must recall the nature of a parable; there is no reason to try to discover literally whom the fig tree represents, what the tree's failing is, [and so forth]. . . . Jesus

[93] Fillion, *op. cit.*, III, 229.

[94] Leberton, *La Vie et l'enseignement de Jésus-Christ*, II, 174–175; the author refers to Isaiah 20; Jeremiah 13, 18, and 19; and other prophecies.

[95] Dehn, *op. cit.*, pp. 199–200. [Likewise also this American Protestant commentary: "The fruit of Israel as a fig tree was bitter and corrupt instead of sweet and good. Israel rejected their Messiah when he came and because of their failure they withered away. This has been Israel's condition as a nation for centuries; she has been dried up . . ." (*Romans* [Assembly of God], 1962, p. 80; quoted in Strober, *op. cit.*, p. 64).—Ed.]

[96] Father Pierre Benoît, O.P. tr., in *La Bible de Jérusalem*, Paris, Cerf, 1950 [1968], note on Matthew 21:18–22. It should be observed that the editions of 1955 *et seq.* abridge this comment to ". . . the fig tree represents Israel punished for its fruitlessness." The suppression of "manifestly" is surely owing in part to the vigorous objections raised by Paul Démann in his article "Le Premier Évangile est-il antijuif?" [Is the First Gospel Anti-Jewish?], *Cahiers sioniens*, September, 1951, who refers specifically to that word in his argument against the classic identification of Israel with the fig tree in the *Bible de Jérusalem*. Despite this minor improvement, the note still inculcates the teaching of the guilt of Israel "as a whole."

[Likewise the English JB, whose note at Matthew 21:18–22 reads: " 'It was not the season for figs,' Mark says. But Jesus wished to perform a symbolic action, cf. Jer 18:1+, in which the fig tree represents Israel punished for its fruitlessness." Similarly, RK observes of the Matthew passage: ". . . our Lord did not expect to satisfy his hunger. He knew that the tree was barren, even of unripe fruit, and used it as a parable of the unfaithfulness which he found in the Jewish people." And CCD comments on Mark 11:14: "The fig tree was a symbol of the Jewish nation which, though rich in foliage, bore no fruit."—Ed.]

[97] Many are the authors, Catholic and Protestant, who apply "the curse of the fig tree" to Israel: Msgr. Pierre Batiffol, *L'Enseignement de Jésus* [The Teaching

sought fruit on a tree which had only leaves; the tree was withered. This means: whoever does not offer the Savior the fruits he asks will be severely punished.

[But Father Lagrange adds:] In the [particular] situation, one would naturally think of the Jewish people.

And why so? The "situation" suggests that "one would naturally think" not "of the Jewish people" but of the enemy clique of Jews— pundits, scribes, and Pharisees. Let us allow Father Lagrange to answer Father Lagrange:

The disciples, who had seen so many miracles, wondered whether it was indeed a miracle; and in fact, it cannot be readily classified with the others. This mystery is not resolved for us either. The Fathers saw it as a threatening allegory for the Jewish people who stubbornly refused fruits to the Savior. The explanation is reasonable, but no word of the text suggests it. This must be carefully noted.[98]

Yes, let us note it carefully: in the present case, as in so many others, no word of the text suggests the explanation given, the current and traditional explanation. If the withered fig tree really symbolized the ungrateful Jewish nation, why would Jesus have hidden this from his disciples, to whom "privately . . . he explained everything" (Mk. 4:34)? Yet when they questioned him, what did the Master reply? "Have faith in God" (Mk. 11:22), faith is all-powerful, faith moves mountains. Nothing authorizes our going beyond this.

An explanation which "no word of the text suggests" is a worthless explanation. Its worth lies in its reasonableness, Father Lagrange concedes. Indeed?

Reasonable to compare the Jewish people with a fig tree that has no fruit? ". . . barren of the fruits of virtue and holiness," the tree which in the recent past had put forth so many inspired wise men, uplifting poets, heroes like the Machabees, and which at present was putting forth John the Baptist and his disciples, Jesus of Nazareth and his, the Apostles, Saint Peter, Saint John, soon Saint Paul, the first Christian Church? . . . A peculiar barrenness, a peculiar reasonableness.

Others reply: "The lesson bears less on barrenness than on the un-

of Jesus], Paris, Bloud et Gay, 1905, p. 77; Karl Adam, *Jésus le Christ,* tr. E. Ricard, Paris, Casterman, 1934, p. 130; Father Marius Lepin, ed. and tr., *L'Évangile de Notre Seigneur Jésus-Christ* [The Gospel of Our Lord Jesus Christ], St.-Étienne, Dumas, 1930 [repub. 1944], p. 184, n. 1; Bois, *op. cit.,* p. 72; Prat, *op. cit.,* II, 206, among others.

[98] Lagrange, . . . *Marc,* p. 298; . . . *Matthieu,* p. 406.

justified pretensions, the hypocrisy that merited the curse," writes
Alexandre Westphal; [99] "The fig tree was cursed [less for its barrenness than] because it was a symbol of hypocrisy and falseness," says
Louis-Claude Fillion.[100] Let us admit it. This hypocrisy was explicitly
denounced by Jesus. In whose person? That of the Jewish people?
No; that of pharisaism, a certain kind of pharisaism. If then the fig
tree must at all costs be a symbol, it is a symbol of this Jewish pharisaism, or rather, of all pharisaism, all religious hypocrisy. We must
return to this, always to this: the lessons of Jesus are "rich enough" to
apply to all, to Christians as to Jews.

✿   ✿   ✿

I ask the reader to excuse me as I treat other "reprobation" texts
more briefly. They are too many, and the interpretations given of
them by the "reprobators" are too aberrant to merit minute examination. But if there is a word, a verse which any interpretation can call
to witness, it will not be omitted. We play fair.

The Parable of the Two Sons Sent to the Vineyard (Mt. 21:28–32)

"The two sons obviously represent Judaism and the Gentile world";
"The two sons represent the Jews and the pagans respectively"—such
is the interpretation of Fathers Prat and Lepin.[101] Louis-Claude Fillion is less categoric: "The second of the two sons (the one who answers the father that he will go but does not) represents the great
mass of Jews, but more particularly their spiritual leaders and the
members of the Sanhedrin, whom Jesus was then addressing
directly." [102]

Yet not a word of the text authorizes the designation of the Jewish
people—in contrast to the Gentiles—any more than "the great mass
of Jews." Jesus himself took the trouble to interpret his parable by declaring to the Sanhedrists, "Truly, I say to you, the tax collectors and
the harlots go into the kingdom of God before you" (Mt. 21:31).

[99] Alexandre Westphal, *Dictionnaire encyclopédique de la Bible*, Paris, Je Sers,
1932–1934, article "Figuier" [Fig Tree].
[100] Fillion, *op. cit.*, III, 576.
[101] Prat, *op. cit.*, II, 244; Lepin, *op. cit.*, p. 191, n. 2.
[102] Fillion, *op. cit.*, III, 240.

A "transparent" parable, says Father Lebreton. In line with a theme particularly dear to Jesus, the lesson contrasts repentant sinners with "professional experts in justice." [103]

In regard to Catholic exegesis, then, there seem to be two kinds of evidence: the kind which strikes Fathers Prat and Lepin, but which "no word of the text suggests"; and the kind which strikes Father Lebreton, because it flows from the text and from Jesus' lesson itself.

You choose.

The Parable of the Narrow Door (Lk. 13:23–30)

We studied this parable previously (pages 192–193), and evaluated it there: a fearsome admonition, an admonition deserved by a certain Jewish pride, but an admonition, and not a massive "reprobation," not a reprobation of the entire Jewish nation.[104]

The Parable of the Prodigal Son (Lk. 15:11–32)

The old opinion which held that the two sons represent the Jews and the Gentiles is hardly in favor any more, agrees Father Lagrange.[105]

The Parable of the Rich Man and the Poor Man Lazarus (Lk. 16:19–31)

Let us here admire the artistry of the *Biblical Manual* as it analyzes this parable, writing innocently (?): "There was a rich man, a Jew . . . ," [106] as if the poor man Lazarus was not "a Jew" too. Father Lagrange argues most forcefully that "individual fates alone" are "at stake" here.[107] At the very most, it can be question only of "pharisaic" unbelief.

---

[103] Lebreton, *La Vie et l'enseignement de Jésus-Christ*, II, 178.

[104] [Nor would it seem to justify the CCD note on this passage reading, "Many Gentiles will be called to salvation and take the place destined for the chosen people of Israel"; or the title which JB gives this section of Luke, quoted in n. 39, above.—Ed.]

[105] Lagrange, . . . *Luc*, p. 420.

[106] Brassac, *op. cit.*

[107] Lagrange, . . . *Luc*, p. 449.

The Parable of the Laborers in the Vineyard
(Mt. 20:1–16)

Commentators sometimes deduce from the final verse, "So the last will be first, and the first last," that "The Jews will be excluded from the Church and the kingdom of God while the Gentiles will take first place." [108] But this can be so only in disregard of the parable itself, since all the laborers, first and last, received an equal wage, and not a word is said about exclusion. Far better founded seems the interpretation that the workers hired the first hour represent the Pharisees, the pietistic, and the workers of the eleventh hour repentant sinners. [109]

The Parable of the Pounds [110] or the Man Invested
with Royalty (Lk. 19:11–27)

As the man who aspires to royalty and is invested with it is the figure of Christ, the deduction is drawn that "his citizens" who "hated him" (19:14) are the Jews, and that the last sentence—"But as for these enemies of mine, who did not want me to reign over them, bring them here and slay them before me" (19:27)—is supposedly "a very plain prophecy of the destruction of Jerusalem and the Jewish State, in punishment of the incorrigible unbelief of the great majority of the nation." [111] "The catastrophe thus predicted would erupt in forty years: Christ's enemies by the hundreds of thousands would be massacred in that Temple which was their pride, which they would have turned into their fortress and which would be their tomb." [112]

A remarkable commentary, given John 6:14–15:

[The crowd said:] "This is indeed the prophet who is to come into the world!" Perceiving then that they were about to come and take him by force to make him king, Jesus withdrew again to the hills by himself.

---

[108] Dom Augustin Calmet, O.S.B., *Évangile de saint Matthieu* [Gospel of Saint Matthew], in *idem, Commentaire littéral sur tous les livres de l'Ancien Testament et du Nouveau Testament* [Annotated Commentary on All the Books of the Old and New Testaments], 22 vols., Paris, Éméry, 1707–1716, p. 433.

[109] Buzy, *op. cit.*, p. 233.

[110] ["Pound" in RSV and "gold piece" in CCD render *mina*, a monetary unit "equal to about twenty dollars" (RSV, Lk. 19:13, n. *e*).—Tr.]

[111] Fillion, *op. cit.*, III, 197.

[112] Lebreton, *La Vie et l'enseignement de Jésus-Christ*, II, 158.

And Luke 9:55 [RK], 19:48 [RSV], and 23:34:

The Son of man has come to save men's lives, not to destroy them.

. . . for all the people [listening to him] hung upon his words.

And Jesus said, "Father, forgive them; for they know not what they do."

A better exegete—one is tempted to say, a better Christian—
Father Lagrange teaches that the parable of the pounds "is conceived
strictly as a parable theme, with no intermingling of real and figurative elements." [113] Any allegoric interpretation of Louis-Claude Fillion's sort is thus arbitrary; nothing impels the belief that the
vengeance exercised by the king against his enemies prefigures an alleged "divine vengeance" exercised against the Jews.[114] For the "reprobators," "the incorrigible unbelief of the great majority of the nation" is surely a convenient myth, but it is only a myth: this has been
demonstrated. Their interpretation is therefore fundamentally un-
sound.

✿   ✿   ✿

Moreover, in the order of prophecy, no threat of punishment, however severe, equals a decree of perdition. It is imprudent in every respect to take prophetic outbursts and excesses literally. Considered in
this light and read without bias, many of Jesus' words which a
"reprobatory" theology adopts as weapons prove less damning than it
teaches, than it is happy (for it takes visible pleasure in doing so) to
teach.

For example, let us take the numerous instances when Jesus used
the word *genea*, "generation," in a clearly pejorative sense. Do they
signify the "condemnation" of "the whole Israelite race"? [115]

But to what shall I compare this generation? It is like children sitting in the
market places. . . .

Mt. 11:16–19, quotation at 11:16; see Lk. 7:31–32

Luke is particularly explicit here and replies clearly to the question
asked. The distinction that Jesus chose to make between the people
on the one hand and his adversaries, scribes and Pharisees, on the
other is plainly revealed:

[113] Lagrange, . . . *Luc*, p. 496.
[114] See p. 207, above.
[115] Roux, *op. cit.*, p. 272.

(When they heard this all the people and the tax collectors justified God, having been baptized with the baptism of John; but the Pharisees and the lawyers rejected the purpose of God for themselves, not having been baptized by him.)

"To what then shall I compare the men of this generation . . . ?"

Lk. 7:29–31

After reading this, how can one maintain that the formula "the men of this generation" applies to the whole of the Jewish people? Quite obviously, it applies to "the Pharisees and the lawyers." This is recognized even by André Charue, who invokes the authority of Maldonado; it is likewise recognized by Father Lagrange.[116]

An evil and adulterous generation seeks for a sign; but no sign shall be given to it except the sign of the prophet Jonah. . . . The men of Nineveh will arise at the judgment with this generation and condemn it. . . . The queen of the South will arise at the judgment with this generation and condemn it. . . .

Mt. 12:39–42

Whom was Jesus speaking to, whom was he thinking of?

Once again, the context indicates it clearly: to "some of the scribes and Pharisees," who had just requested of him, "Teacher, we wish to see a sign from you" (12:38). Request and answer recur in Matthew 16:1–4 and Mark 8:11–12, immediately after the second multiplication of loaves: proof that Jesus refused the sign to the leaders only, the Pharisees and Sadducees in Matthew and the Pharisees alone in Mark, and that the formula "An evil and adulterous generation" applies to them only.

It is true that in Luke 11:29–32, a parallel text to Matthew 12:39–42, Jesus was addressing the crowd; however, it was not the crowd who had asked for "a sign" but rather some in the crowd, "to test him" (Lk. 11:16). When Luke is compared with Mark and Matthew, the supposition imposes itself that these "some" were scribes and Pharisees.

The same formula, "this adulterous and sinful generation," is voiced as well in Mark 8:38 [117] and Luke 17:25 [118] against those who rejected Jesus, but it comes after Mark 8:31:

[116] Charue, op. cit., p. 193, n. 1; Lagrange, . . . Luc, p. 226: "The opposition of the Pharisees is taken to task here."

[117] "For whoever is ashamed of me and of my words in this adulterous and sinful generation. . . ."

[118] "But first he [the Son of man] must suffer many things and be rejected by this generation."

And he began to teach them that the Son of man must . . . be rejected by the elders and the chief priests and the scribes. . . .

Mk. 8:31; see Lk. 9:22

Each time we press close to the text, we end with the same clarifications:

O faithless generation. . . . How long am I to bear with you?

Mk. 9:19; see Mt. 17:17; Lk. 9:41

The context of Matthew 17:19–20 shows that Jesus was calling his own disciples to account:

Then the disciples came to Jesus privately and said, "Why could we not cast it [the demon] out?" He said to them, "Because of your little faith. . . ."

The impression arises from the three accounts that the term *genea* here must not be understood in its proper sense, and that the saying "faithless generation" equals simply "faithless people." It encompasses only the listeners, the disciples included.

Truly, I say to you, all this will come upon this generation.

Mt. 23:36

Yes, I tell you, it shall be required of this generation / that [it be accountable for] the blood of all the prophets, shed from the foundation of the world. . . .

Lk. 11:51, 50

These terrifying threats come at the conclusion of the denunciation Jesus hurled at the "scribes and Pharisees, hypocrites!" (Mt. 23:13–36) and "you Pharisees" and "lawyers" (Lk. 11:39–52). An example-setting punishment is predicted for them—"You serpents, you brood of vipers, how are you to escape being sentenced to hell?" (Mt. 23:33)—in the near future, striking the very generation whom Jesus was addressing (in fact, if this is identified with the events of A.D. 70, the overthrow of Jerusalem and the destruction of the Temple, it is the following generation which was struck). But nothing allows it to be written that "Jesus included in one condemnation . . . the contemporary generation, and the whole Israelite race." [119] Customary, traditional generalizations, ill-considered and abusive.

So also, when you see these things taking place, you know that he is near, at the very gates. Truly, I say to you, this generation will not pass away before all these things take place.

Mk. 13:29–30; see Mt. 24:33–34

[119] Roux, *loc. cit.*

So also, when you see these things taking place, you know that the kingdom
of God is near. Truly, I say to you, this generation will not pass away till all
has taken place.

Lk. 21:31–32

The prophecy is perfectly clear; it says quite unequivocally what it
means to say: ". . . this generation [the current generation, contemporary with me] will not pass away before all these things [which
have just been predicted] take place." But for various reasons, this
meaning seems a bit irksome to theologians. So another must be
found.

Is it worth discussing what Father Lagrange calls frankly "all these
loopholes"? [120] The "weighty authorities" who stand behind them cannot prevent them from clashing violently with common sense, the
context, and the related Gospel texts:

But I tell you truly, there are some standing here who will not taste death
before they see the kingdom of God.

Lk. 9:27

. . . for truly, I say to you, you will not have gone through all the towns of
Israel, before the Son of man comes.

Mt. 10:23

✿   ✿   ✿

There remain the ominous predictions about Jerusalem, widely
used by the "reprobators." No trace of them is found in Mark. They
occur only in Matthew and Luke.

For great distress shall be upon the earth and wrath upon this people; . . .
and Jerusalem will be trodden down by the Gentiles, until the times of the
Gentiles are fulfilled.

Lk. 21:23–24

Actually there is nothing in this prediction of misfortune which surpasses in harshness many of the warnings given their people by Israel's Prophets of old, Amos or Isaiah; there is nothing which necessi-
tates the traditional interpretation that the Jews would be cast out to
the advantage of the Gentiles. The clause "until the times of the Gentiles are fulfilled" is one of those oracular formulations whose obscureness gives rise to theological manipulations. "It must be under-

[120] Lagrange, . . . Marc, p. 348; . . . Luc, p. 533.

stood really as the times accorded to the nations (to the Gentiles), insofar as they succeed the Jews, whose times are ended. This is still another way of saying that the vine will be given to others." [121] But Father Lagrange writes better when he is more sure of himself. The Old and New Testaments put one on guard against a tendentious interpretation. The first offers us this answer in the Book of Daniel:

"For how long is [what] the vision [announces] concerning the continual burnt offering, the transgression that makes desolate, and the giving over of the sanctuary and host to be trampled underfoot?" And he said to him [variant: me], "For two thousand and three hundred evenings and mornings; then the sanctuary shall be restored to its rightful state."

Dan. 8:13–14

And the second gives us this answer in the Revelation to John:

. . . for [the court outside the Temple] is given over to the nations, and they will trample over the holy city for forty-two months.

Rev. 11:2

The chronological foresight of these texts is debatable; at the least they show us that "the times of the Gentiles" can be understood as the times of their domination of Jerusalem, and that this domination would be fulfilled at a moment which would not necessarily be the end of the world.

O Jerusalem, Jerusalem, killing the prophets and stoning those who are sent to you! How often would I have gathered your children together as a hen gathers her brood under her wings, and you would not! Behold, your house is forsaken and desolate. For I tell you, you will not see me again, until you say, "Blessed is he who comes in the name of the Lord."

Mt. 23:37–39

Luke gives the identical text, though abridged to "Behold, your house is forsaken"; but he places the passage at 13:34–35, well before the arrival in Jerusalem, at which he alone supplies this moving lamentation of Jesus':

Would that even today you knew the things that make for peace! But now they are hid from your eyes. . . . your enemies . . . will not leave one stone upon another in you; because you did not know the time of your visitation.

Lk. 19:42–44

The threat of punishment is accompanied at this point, especially in Matthew 23:38, by a threat of divine abandonment. "Thereafter,"

[121] *Idem*, . . . *Luc*, p. 529.

writes Father Lagrange, "Jesus took no further interest in Jerusalem; it was abandoned to itself." [122] Father Prat expresses himself more vigorously: "God's vengeance would sweep down pitilessly on this deicide race and would demand an accounting for all the blood spilled wrongfully." [123]

One cannot mistake the gravity of the threat; there is none so crushing in the whole Gospel. But whom was Jesus addressing? Was it the Jewish nation, "the whole Israelite race," that crowd who, marveling at a miracle Jesus had just wrought, glorified God in these words?

"A great prophet has arisen among us!" and "God has visited his people!"

Lk. 7:16

It is enough to refer to the context in Matthew to answer once more: no. The denunciation of Jerusalem is a corporate part of the maledictions hurled at "you scribes and Pharisees, hypocrites!" If Jerusalem drew down divine wrath on itself, then it was because the city was the principal locus of those implacable adversaries of Jesus' —the priestly caste, the pietistic clan, the body of theologians, the conservative ruling oligarchy; in brief, the general staff of Judaism.

Still and all, the certainty of punishment did not exclude "the hope, the certainty of repentance": [124]

For I tell you, you will not see me again, until you say, "Blessed is he who comes in the name of the Lord."

Mt. 23:39

The reproach to the Galilean lake towns (Mt. 11:20–24; Lk. 10:13–15) was discussed and set aside above (pages 128–131). I think, then, that I have not omitted any of the basic texts supposedly denoting "reprobation." But I think too that even if they are considered valid and generally authentic, even if some commentators do not want to grant that one or another writer could have sharpened the points, not one of these texts is "reprobatory" in the sense commonly meant and taught—not one is aimed at the entire Jewish people, "the whole

[122] *Ibid.*, p. 396.

[123] Prat, *op. cit.*, II, 235. [The same positive conviction imbues a recent religious instruction text: "Rejected as a nation by God, [the Jews] would be led astray by false prophets, cast out of Jerusalem, the siege and destruction of which —prefiguring the end of the world—are described in detail, and finally dispersed throughout the whole world" (Canon Adrien Texier, *Jésus-Christ, centre de la vie du chrétien*, Paris, Éd. de l'École, 1963, p. 120; quoted in Houtart and Giblet, *op. cit.*, p. 205).—Ed.]

[124] Lagrange, *L'Évangile de Jésus-Christ*, p. 456.

Israelite race." If the rejection of Israel had actually been pronounced by Jesus in whatever form, how could Saint Paul have written these words in Romans 11:1–2?

I ask, then, has God rejected his people? By no means! . . . God has not rejected his people. . . .

*　　*　　*

In fact, we can counterprove the theory of "reprobation."

To know whom Jesus rejected, whom he reproved, there is no need to go foraging in the obscurity of a given allegoric parable that has been more or less recast and deformed, to turn over a given ambiguous word again and again when it is impossible to know even if it corresponds exactly with the word said (since Jesus spoke Aramaic and he is made to speak Greek), and then, starting from there, from this obscurity, this uncertainty, these deformations, these transpositions, these translations of a translation, to interpret and interpret until at last the desirable answer is reached, the doctrinally desirable answer, even if "no word of the text suggests it," even if it categorically contradicts what we can ascertain of the historic reality.

What Jesus had in mind to pronounce and denounce was pronounced and denounced unambiguously.

Let us go to the major texts, those that speak loud and clear and need no torturing.

At the dawn of the evangelic ministry, beginning with the Sermon on the Mount, who were the targets of the harshest words?

Hypocrites, the outwardly devout: "Thus, when you give alms, sound no trumpet before you, as do the hypocrites . . ." (Mt. 6:3); "And when you pray, you must not be like the hypocrites . . ." (Mt. 6:5); "And when you fast, do not look dismal, like the hypocrites . . ." (Mt. 6:16).

And after the hypocritically devout, who were the targets of Jesus' greatest severity? The rich, those enslaved by money: "You cannot serve God and mammon [money]" (Mt. 6:24; Lk. 16:13); "It is easier for a camel to go through the eye of a needle than for a rich man to enter the kingdom of God" (Mk. 10:25; Mt. 19:24; Lk. 18:25).

As intent—I do not know why—on making the texts say *less* than they do (about the rich) as on making them say *more* than they do (about the Jews), in vain do conventional commentators try to soften these formulations, which go all the way to explicit condemnation:

But woe to you that are rich, for you have received your consolation. Woe
to you that are full now, for you shall hunger.

Lk. 6:24–25

It is because these twin vices, hypocrisy in worship and thirst for
money and honors—without counting another execrable vice, pride of
learning—were too often to be found among the scribes and Pharisees (Luke calls the Pharisees *philarguroi,* "lovers of money," at 16:14)
that Jesus turned his thunder on them and pronounced his most ringing curses:

Woe to you, scribes and Pharisees, hypocrites! for you tithe mint and dill
and cummin, and have neglected the weightier matters of the law, justice
and mercy and faith; these you ought to have done, without neglecting the
others. You blind guides, straining out a gnat and swallowing a camel! . . .
Woe to you, scribes and Pharisees, hypocrites! for you are like white-
washed tombs, which outwardly appear beautiful, but within they are full
of dead men's bones and all uncleanness. So you also outwardly appear
righteous to men, but within you are full of hypocrisy and iniquity.

Mt. 23:23–24, 27–28

Woe to you lawyers! for you have taken away the key of knowledge; you
did not enter yourselves, and you hindered those who were entering.

Lk. 11:52

Surely, these hypocrites, these rich men, these lawyers, these Pharisees whom Jesus scourged and cursed, they were Jews. How could it
be otherwise, since Jesus, a Jew "according to the flesh," did not
know or want to know any but the Jewish world?

But first and foremost, in Jesus' eyes they did not represent all the
Jews, all the Jewish people, all Israel. The necessary distinction is too
often and too explicitly stressed in the Gospels to be mistaken, in
honesty:

When they heard this all the people and the tax collectors justified God,
having been baptized with the baptism of John; but the Pharisees and the
lawyers rejected the purpose of God for themselves, not having been baptized by him.

Lk. 7:29–30

As he [Jesus] said this, all his adversaries were put to shame; and all the
people rejoiced at all the glorious things that were done by him.

Lk. 13:17

The chief priests and scribes heard of this, and looked for some means of
making away with him; they were afraid of him, because all the multitude
was so full of admiration at his teaching.

Mk. 11:18 [RK]

It is not even all the scribes, all the Pharisees: witness the one among them to whom Jesus declared, "You are not far from the kingdom of God" (Mk. 12:34); witness Nicodemus; witness so many others who came to Christ, as we learn from the Acts of the Apostles 15:5; witness the greatest of all, Saul of Tarsus, Saint Paul, "a Hebrew born of Hebrews; as to the law a Pharisee, as to zeal a persecutor of the church, as to righteousness under the law blameless" (Phil. 3:5–6).

Finally and most importantly, were they rejected, condemned, cursed as Jews? Or as falsely devout, hypocritical, greedily rich, "blind guides"?

To ask the question is to answer it. Thus the condemnations Jesus pronounced did not bear only, specially, specifically on the Jews; they bear on all men. The Jewish people here are only a figure, a figure for humanity as a whole. Beyond the Palestinian horizon which Jesus never stepped across, his malediction reaches universal, eternal pharisaism, pharisaism

of all times,

of all countries,

of all religions,

of all Churches.

Even Christian? Even Christian. One might say: particularly Christian.

Father Henri de Lubac writes:

Do not many of us today make profession of Catholicism from the same considerations of comfortableness and social conformism which, twenty centuries ago, would have prompted rejection of the Glad Tidings as a disturbing innovation? [125]

And Jesus himself said expressly:

Not every one who says to me, "Lord, Lord," shall enter the kingdom of heaven, but he who does the will of my Father who is in heaven. On that day many will say to me, "Lord, Lord, did we not prophesy in your name, and cast out demons in your name . . . ?" And then will I declare to them, "I never knew you; depart from me, you evildoers."

Mt. 7:21–23

[125] Father Henri de Lubac, S.J., *Le Drame de l'humanisme athée*, 3rd ed., rev., Paris, Spes, 1945, p. 131. [Quotation taken from *idem, The Drama of Atheist Humanism*, tr. Edith M. Riley, New York, Sheed & Ward, 1949, p. 70.—Tr.]

PART IV

◇◇

The Crime of Deicide

Come now, you rich. . . . You have
condemned and put to death the just,
and he did not resist you.
JAS. 5:1, 6 [CCD]

PROPOSITION 16

FOR EIGHTEEN HUNDRED YEARS IT HAS BEEN GENERALLY
TAUGHT THROUGHOUT THE CHRISTIAN WORLD THAT
THE JEWISH PEOPLE, IN FULL RESPONSIBILITY FOR THE
CRUCIFIXION, COMMITTED THE INEXPIABLE CRIME OF
DEICIDE. NO ACCUSATION COULD BE MORE PERNICIOUS
—AND IN FACT NONE HAS CAUSED MORE INNOCENT
BLOOD TO BE SHED.

Having come to the threshold of the last phase,
   prepared to enter it with such meditation, such a trembling of heart,
   but without withdrawing before the texts,
   let us listen first to the barbaric clamor rising from the depths of the
centuries, the choir of the Christian accusations, the Christian imprecations—that is, emanating from those who call themselves Christians,
for they harmonize ill with the words of charity, mercy, and love
which are the major teachings and the glory of Christ.
   All these cries of death—can there be "Christian" cries of death?
   And even the previous, even the odious Jewish accusations, Jewish
imprecations do not justify them.

❖   ❖   ❖

   Murderers of Jesus, of the Christ-Messiah, murderers of the God-
Man,

DEICIDES!

Such is the accusation hurled at the whole Jewish people, without exception, without any kind of distinction, the blind violence of ignorant
masses being closely linked to the cold reasoning of theologians.
   A capital accusation, to which is tied the theme of capital punishment, the terrifying curse weighing down Israel's shoulders, explain-

233

ing (and justifying in advance) its wretched destiny, its cruel trials, the worst violences committed against it, the rivers of blood flowing from its constantly reopened and inflamed wounds.

In such wise that by an ingenious technique of alternating learned judgments and popular passions, God is made responsible for acts which, seen in human terms, are surely the doing of man's incurable vileness, of that perversity, variously but skillfully exploited from century to century, from generation to generation, which culminated in Auschwitz, in the gas chambers and crematory ovens of Nazi Germany.

One of those Germans, those servile killers, one of those chief murderers (baptized a Christian) said: "I could not have any scruples because they were all Jews."

Hitler's voice? Streicher's voice?

No. *Vox saeculorum.*

❖   ❖   ❖

Stricken with horror, I could not move one step forward before I felt myself taken by the arm, by both arms. At my right, at my left: two theologians, sympathetic, inexorable.

The first said:

We would like to address a reminder to the Jews.

When they make the Church responsible for their immense misfortunes because of having accused them . . . of deicide, they forget that God, Yahweh himself, by choosing them as the unique messianic and God-bearing people, was bound to make them odious and mark them for the hostility of the world and pagan peoples long before the Incarnation, long before the deicide. Let them recall the time of the Pharaohs, Exodus 1:9, or the time of Esther 3:8–9: "There is a certain people scattered abroad and dispersed among the peoples in all the provinces of your kingdom; their laws are different from those of every other people, and they do not keep the king's laws, so that it is not for the king's profit to tolerate them. If it please the king, let it be decreed that they be destroyed. . . ." In Egypt in the thirteenth century before Christ, in Persia in the fifth, there were already pogroms.[1]

What shall I reply? In my own name, in my name as victim?

First of all, let us leave the Church to itself. Let us leave to it the task of seeking for itself what share of responsibility it has had in

---

[1] Father Charles Journet, *Destinées d'Israël*, Paris, Egloff, 1945, pp. 199–200.

such a tragedy, whether it has truly had none, whether it has truly had no hand in the atrocious deviations in which so many of its members, so many of its faithful have found themselves involved,[2] whether it has truly done everything that its duty as the Church of Christ required it to do in order to prevent such deviations, correct them, brand them, punish them. Yes, let us leave the Church to face itself, to face God.

The case of ancient Egypt is historically complex; it goes well beyond the framework of Israel. Victim of great Semitic invasions, Egypt regained its independence at the price of long and bloody battles which necessarily engendered feelings of mistrust and hatred regarding all Semite peoples.

This said, it is quite true that there was a strain of anti-Semitism in the pagan world preceding Christian anti-Semitism, though it is perceptible in history only beginning in the third century B.C.;

it is quite true that this anti-Semitism sometimes unleashed bloody conflicts and pogroms;

it is quite true that a determining cause of this anti-Semitism was Israel's exclusivism, the separatism of Israel dispersed in the pagan world, a separatism essentially religious, dictated by Yahweh, commanded by Scripture,[3] without which Christianity could obviously not have been born; for it is owing to this, to Jewish separatism, that the Yahwist faith, the worship of the one God could be transmitted intact, preserved from all taint from generation to generation until the coming of Christ.

But in what way does the reminder of these historic facts justify you?

Because a pagan anti-Semitism existed whose source is in effect the divine commandment, in what way does Christianity find itself justified for having followed suit (after having itself been a victim of it for a time), and more, for having pushed the virulence, the evil-mindedness, the murderous calumnies and hatred to paroxysm?

Let us complete this "reminder" with another reminder:

while it is true that the pagan world experienced a current of anti-Semitism—though also the countercurrent of proselytism, of Judaizing paganism—it is nonetheless true that the Jews generally

---

[2] Father Journet straightforwardly recognizes "the faults of Christians," though not of the Church, in *ibid.*, p. 201. His generous thought is expressed forcefully on p. 188.

[3] See p. 5, above.

enjoyed a privileged status in that world, particularly in the Roman Empire, which lasted several centuries,

until the day when the Empire became Christian.[4]

The second theologian, who was waiting his turn, came forward. And from the outset I shivered. For he was armed from head to foot with sacred texts, but I soon doubted that there was a man, a soul with God living in it, inside that armor. He looked like a brother of the scribe in the Gospels (and not of the one who was "not far from the kingdom of God"), and entrenched himself in Scripture as in a blockhouse.

Opening his Bible, he turned to Acts, chapter 2, where Peter is addressing the Jews, and he read:

Men of Israel, hear these words: Jesus of Nazareth, a man attested to you by God with mighty works and wonders and signs which God did through him in your midst . . .—this Jesus, delivered up according to the definite plan and foreknowledge of God, you crucified and killed by the hands of lawless men.

Acts 2:22–23

Then, turning the pages quickly with a dry, cold hand, see here, he said, Acts 2:36; 3:15; 4:10, 27; 5:30; 7:52; 10:39; 13:27–28, not forgetting 1 Thessalonians 2:14–16:

. . . for you suffered the same things from your own countrymen as they [the churches of God] did from the Jews, who killed both the Lord Jesus and the prophets, and drove us out, and displease God and oppose all men by hindering us from speaking to the Gentiles. . . . But God's wrath has come upon them at last!

What more do you want? he asked. Are you challenging these texts? Isn't the crime of the Jewish people—the inexpiable crime— explicitly denounced the very morrow of the Crucifixion by the mouth of the Apostles, of Peter, Paul, by Holy Scripture? We, accusers of Christian posterity, are only plumbing a sacred source. And we say: "God is not mocked with impunity." [5] You denied, you crucified His Son; believe in His "wrath," and bow before it.

Such icy conviction emanated from this prosecutor (for God) that I had difficulty collecting myself. Finally, I replied:

Historian I am, and no theologian, but I am inclined to believe

[4] The questions raised here on pp. 234–236 and commented on briefly are studied more closely in Jules Isaac, Genèse de l'antisémitisme, Paris, Calmann-Lévy, 1956.

[5] Jean Bosc, "Le Mystère d'Israël" [The Mystery of Israel], Réforme, November 23, 1946.

that history precedes theology in all respects and that the theological validity of a text remains subordinate to its historic validity. These venerable and sacred texts with which you bombard us are historical evidence first, and as such must be passed through the sieve of critical analysis beforehand—which will be done in due time and place. For the moment, I will observe simply that even if one accepts as literally exact speeches which were reproduced approximately half a century after they were delivered,

one cannot state that any one of them was directed at the Jewish people taken all together. Some were addressed expressly to the ruling caste, to the Sanhedrin (Acts 4:10; 5:30; 7:52), others to the Jews of Jerusalem or residing in Jerusalem (2:22–23, 36; 3:15). This is said plainly and unequivocally in Paul's discourse in the synagogue at Antioch of Pisidia:

For those who live in Jerusalem and their rulers, because they did not recognize him [Jesus]. . . . yet they asked Pilate to have him killed.

Acts 13:27–28

While "the peoples of Israel" are mentioned in Acts 4:27, it is in conjunction with "the Gentiles," and one cannot endow this pious effusion—the prayer of the faithful after the release of the Apostles— with the slightest validity as historic information. Moreover, the section of Peter's discourse in Acts 10:39 must be understood in the same light as similar portions of others of Peter's speeches.

In the second place, none of these texts formulates the capital accusation, of deicide, against the Jewish people. What is spoken of is homicide ("a man . . . you crucified and killed by the hands of lawless men"); not only that, but homicide out of ignorance, and in words which are terms of remission, singularly worthy of meditation; for the Apostle Peter, addressing the Jews of Jerusalem, still called them "brethren," thus setting a high example (which would not be followed):

And now, brethren, I know that you acted in ignorance, as did also your rulers.

Acts 3:17

As for the canonic Epistles, even the Epistles of Paul, they say nothing more. The Epistle of James (why ignore it? why this persistent neglect?) takes umbrage exclusively at the rich: "Come now, you rich. . . . You have condemned and put to death the just . . ." (5:1, 6 [CCD]). According to Paul in 1 Corinthians 2:8, it was "the rulers of this age," temporal or satanic powers,[6] who "crucified the Lord of glory." The Jews denounced in 1 Thessalonians 2:14–16 are manifestly not all the Jewish people but the Pharisee and Jerusalemite clique—of which Saul of Tarsus was previously a zealous member— expressly named in Acts 13:27; "Paul was not thinking of the Jewish people as such, that is quite clear," writes Jacques Maritain.[7] When the "Apostle to the Gentiles" examines all aspects of the problem posed by the unbelief of a "part of Israel" (Rom. 11:25) in his masterful Epistle to the Romans, where does anyone see the faintest allusion to Israel's guilt, to its crime?

Saint Paul speaks of "trespass," of "disobedience," of "blindness," but he goes no farther; and taking care to put the Gentile brothers on guard against any judgment out of pride, he concludes:

For God has consigned all men to disobedience, that he may have mercy upon all.

Rom. 11:32

You exhort me to believe in God's wrath. I believe in it, as in His mercy. But I believe in it for all men.

And I believe too that it is rash, if not impious, to inscribe it automatically in the history of human turpitude.

☼   ☼   ☼

The way cleared, let us follow the course of the centuries now.

From one generation to the next, the tone grows more heated. We know how far religious passion can go, whether it is Jewish or Christian, Catholic or Protestant: in all ages, the relentlessness of hangmen has made the saintliness of martyrs, Christian martyrs, Jewish martyrs. A vehement dialogue developed between adherents to the Ancient Covenant, persecutors at first, and adepts of the New Covenant, persecuted at first. This nascent Christianity, of Jewish stock, preached by Jewish Apostles who went from synagogue to synagogue and initially recruited only among Jews or Judaizers, not without re-

---

[6] Both interpretations have had currency, the first seeming more plausible. The "rulers of this age" would thus be the secular powers, Roman and Jewish authorities. Alfred Loisy holds the contrary opinion in *La Naissance du christianisme,* Paris, Nourry, 1933, p. 18, n. 4.

[7] Jacques Maritain, *La Pensée de saint Paul* [The Thought of Saint Paul], New York, Maison Française, 1941, p. 141, n. 1. [See, in English, as *idem,* ed., *The Living Thoughts of St. Paul,* tr. Harry Lorin Binsse, New York, McKay, 1941, p. 87.—Tr.]

sistance but also not without success—as the Acts of the Apostles witness [8]—broke away from the Mosaic Law in a bold sweep, and passing from a hardly relaxed exclusivism to absolute universalism, turned toward the masses of the Gentile world. In less than a century, it would sever the ties which attached it to Judaism and simultaneously take wing in a flight that nothing would ever stop again, contempt or ridicule, insults or polemics, persecutions or killings—pagan after Jewish; not even its own internal dissensions, the seething of its heresies. It conquered souls, it conquered the Empire: a redoubtable triumph, it was elevated to the rank of the official religion. But the victory, miraculous though it was, did not pacify the wrath that arose against the most detested of the vanquished.

When the Jewish people as a whole proved irreducible, it became necessary, imperatively necessary for the edification of the faithful, that the Jewish people as a whole prove evil, fundamentally evil, unworthy, laden with crimes, opprobrium, and maledictions. And when this became necessary, this became true, with a theological truth which infinitely outdistanced historic truth, and where need be obliterated it. Nothing easier, nothing more human, albeit not more equitable, more Christian (in the Gospel sense of the word). Where Jesus had said, "the chief priests, the scribes, and the Pharisees"—which was already a substitution of the whole for the part—people exaggerated, people said: "the Jews," "the Jewish people." Where Saint Paul had said, "those who live in Jerusalem and their rulers"—which was once more a substitution of the whole for the part—people said, people said again: "the Jews," "the Jewish people." Where only Temple flunkeys, inflamed followers of the powerful, brutish pagan soldiery figured, people repeated obligingly: "the Jews," "the Jewish people," "all the people," "all Israel." Where only a withered fig tree appeared, people declared calmly: "symbol of Israel." And to discredit contending adversaries more positively, people pointed fingers at them to ignorant populaces and said: "God-killers! Deicides!"

---

[8] The crescendo of conversions can be followed in the Acts of the Apostles: "a hundred and twenty" in 1:15; "about three thousand" in 2:41, "And the Lord added to their number day by day those who were being saved," 2:47; "about five thousand" in 4:4; "And more than ever believers were added to the Lord . . . ," 5:14; ". . . and the number of the disciples multiplied greatly in Jerusalem . . . ," 6:7; "So the church throughout all Judea and Galilee and Samaria had peace and was built up; and walking in the fear of the Lord and in the comfort of the Holy Spirit it was multiplied," 9:31; further increases at 13:43, 14:1, and 18:4; "You see, brother, how many thousands there are among the Jews of those who have believed; they are all zealous for the law. . . ," 21:20.

Thus began the elaboration in (if I dare call it so) Christian con-
sciousness of the theme of the Crime, the Infamy, the Curse, the
Punishment of Israel, collective punishment like the Crime itself,
without appeal, encompassing "carnal Israel" in perpetuity, fallen,
outcast Israel, Judas-Israel, Cain-Israel. A theme which interlaced but
did not blend with another theme, turned into a doctrinal thesis, that
of the Witness People. Reserved by God, the Jew Saint Paul had said,
for the fullness of final conversion. Wretched witness "of their own iniquity and of our truth," [9] said Saint Augustine three hundred years
later; marked by God with a sign, as was Cain, which preserved them
and singled them out at the same time, singled them out for the
loathing of the Christian world.

✿   ✿   ✿

"Deicide." At what moment did the defamatory epithet appear, the
brilliant find—itself murderous—which would be made into an indelible brand, generating frenzies and crimes (homicide, genocide)? It is
impossible to say exactly. But we can discern in the roiled stream of
Judeo-Christian polemics the current whence it issued.[10]
    The contents of the Gospels, begun in the mid-first century, carry
visible marks of these polemics; this is particularly true of the first
Gospel, Matthew's, and the fourth, John's. We have pointed these
marks out, and we will have occasion to return to them, for the account of the Passion is relevant in this regard, owing to the obvious
eagerness it exhibits to slide the whole weight of responsibility for the
Crucifixion from Roman onto Jewish shoulders. In the apocryphal
gospels, written in the following era, this eagerness would become a

---

[9] Augustine, *Enarratio in Ps. LVIII* [Discourse on Psalm 58], 1:22, in Father
Jacques-Paul Migne, ed., *Patrologia latina*, 221 vols., Paris, Garnier, 1844–1864,
XXXVI, 705.
    [10] We will use data here furnished by the learned work of Jean Juster, *Les
Juifs dans l'Empire romain*, 2 vols., Paris, Guethner, 1914, vol. I. In addition, be-
fore the present book went to press, we were able to consult two other writings
in which we found valuable information: Rev. James Parkes, *The Conflict of the
Church and the Synagogue: A Study in the Origins of Antisemitism*, London,
Soncino, 1934 [repub. New York, Meridian, 1961]; and especially Marcel Si-
mon's *Verus Israël*, Paris, Boccard, 1948 [rev. ed. 1964], an indispensable work
for anyone who wants to study the origins of Christian anti-Semitism. [Dr.
Parkes's distinguished contribution to the study of various aspects of Jewish-
Christian relations extends over the last thirty years; see also, for example, his
History of the Jews, 6 vols., Philadelphia, Jewish Publication Society of America,
1945. Marcel Simon is honorary Dean of the Faculté des Lettres, University of
Strasbourg.—Ed.]

veritable obsession with their authors, who would stick at no improb-
ability to attain their aim of making the Jews more criminal, more
odious. A man of deeper learning, the great third-century theologian
Origen, battling with the pagan Celsus, was still taking the trouble to
mention Pilate while declaring that Jesus' condemnation was above
all the act of the Jewish authorities; but let him speak theology and
he did not hesitate to simplify, writing: "The Jewish nation . . . has
been condemned by God . . . ," for "they crucified him [Jesus]." [11]
And such language became common usage.

From this to pronouncing the supreme outrage, "deicide," is not far.
The first step was taken in the fourth century. Eusebius, the Church
historian, reporting the Emperor Constantine's letter on the Council
of Nicaea, had him express himself thus:

For their [the Jews'] boast is absurd indeed, that it is not in [Christians']
power without instruction from them to observe these things [Easter].[12] For
how should they be capable of forming a sound judgment, who, since their
parricidal guilt in slaying their Lord, . . . are swayed by every impulse of
the mad spirit that is in them? [13]

"Such was the reward," wrote Eusebius in his *Church History*, "which
the Jews received for their wickedness and impiety against the Christ
of God." [14]

The Church Fathers go much farther. We have already heard Saint
Ephraim call the Jews "circumcised dogs." [15] Saint Jerome—all the
while asking them for Hebrew lessons—denounced the "Judaic serpents" of whom Judas was the model and consigned them to the
hatred of Christians.[16] But the honors go to Saint Gregory of Nyssa
and Saint John Chrysostom, rivals for truculence in sacred invective.

[11] Origen, *Against Celsus*, 2:34; *On the Principles*, 4:1:8. [Quotations
taken from *idem*, *Against Celsus* and *De principiis*, tr. Rev. Frederick Crombie,
in *The Ante-Nicene Fathers*, ed. Rev. Alexander Roberts and James Donaldson,
rev. ed. Rev. A. Cleveland Cox, 10 vols., New York, Scribner, 1917–1925, IV,
445, 356.—Tr.]
[12] In that period, many Christians celebrated Easter at the same time as the
Jews celebrated Passover.
[13] Eusebius of Caesarea, *The Life of Constantine*, 3:18. [Quotation taken from
ibid., tr. Ernest Cushing Richardson, in *A Select Library of the Nicene and Post-
Nicene Fathers of the Christian Church*, second series, ed. Revs. Philip Schaff
and Henry Wace, 14 vols., Grand Rapids, Mich., Eerdmans, 1952–1961, I, 524.
—Tr.]
[14] *Idem, Church History*, 3:6:32. [Quotation taken from *ibid.*, tr. Rev. Arthur
Cushman McGiffert, in *A Select Library* . . . , I, 141.—Tr.]
[15] See p. 21, n. 4.
[16] Simon, *op. cit.*, p. 271; see Jerome, *Psalmus CVIII* [Psalm 108], in Migne,
op. cit., XXVI, 1155 ff.

In a *Homily on the Resurrection* that spilled a potful of abusive attributes on the head of the Jews—"adversaries of grace," "enemies of God," "devil's advocates," "brood of vipers," "sanhedrin of demons"; and I am skipping—Gregory did not fail to fulminate first the principal grievance: "murderers of the Lord," "slayers of the prophets." [17] And what should we say about the sermons delivered at Antioch by Saint John Chrysostom in the years 386–387! Israel "since the deicide" has been given over to "commerce with demons"; the Jews have all the vices of beasts, and "are good for nothing but slaughter"; gluttons, drunkards, sensualists, "living for their belly . . . , they behave no better than pigs and goats in their lewd vulgarities"; how could the faithful not be ashamed to associate "with those who spilled the blood of Jesus Christ"? Their crime leaves them no hope of mending their ways or being pardoned. The synagogue is now "a brothel, a den of thieves, a lair of wild beasts"—and the translation palliates the crudeness of the terms used.[18]

Even Saint Augustine, teaching the catechumens, put all the resources of his orator's genius to work to carve a gripping image of the deicide, calculated to inflame those novice hearts:

The Jews held Him, the Jews insulted Him, the Jews bound Him, they crowned Him with thorns, they dishonored Him by spitting upon Him, they scourged Him, they heaped abuses upon Him, they hung Him upon a tree, they pierced Him with a lance. . . .[19]

Simple vehemence of language? Alas, no. It was translated into law and deeds. Anti-Semitism would be able to bloom and diversify in the eras to come: it found its finished model there in the fourth century. Under the influence of the Fathers of the Church, and notably Saint John Chrysostom, imperial legislation tended to alter to the detriment of the Jews, to take on even the tone of the anti-Jewish polemic. Material violence followed: synagogues were confiscated and burned, sometimes at the instigation of ecclesiastic authorities; and when the

[17] Gregory of Nyssa, *Homily on the Resurrection,* in Father Jacques-Paul Migne, ed., *Patrologia graeca* [Greek Fathers], 165 vols., Paris, Garnier, 1857–1866, XLVI, 685.

[18] John Chrysostom, *Adversus Judaeos* [Against the Jews], 1, 2, in Migne, *Patrologia graeca,* XLVIII, 847, 861; quoted in Simon, *op. cit.,* p. 257.

[19] Augustine, *Sermo ad catechumenos* [Sermon to the Catechumens], in Migne, *Patrologia latina,* XL, 634. See also Bernhard Blumenkranz, *Die Judenpredigt Augustins* [Augustine's Sermons on the Jews], Basel, Helbing & Lichtenhahn, 1946. [Quotation taken from Augustine, *The Creed,* tr. Sister Marie Liguori Ewald, I.H.M., in *Saint Augustine: Treatises on Marriage and Other Subjects,* ed. Roy J. Deferrari, "The Fathers of the Church" series, 60 + vols., New York, Fathers of the Church, 1955, XXVII, 301.—Tr.]

emperor wanted to deal severely with these acts in protection of public order and of a noble tradition of equity, Saint Ambrose threatened him with excommunication.[20]

Among the Christian masses—the more malleable as they tended to grow more ignorant, more crude, more mixed with barbarians—everything combined to mold this anti-Jewish mentality, permeated with a sacred horror of "the deicide people." As the admirable Christian liturgy, so persuasively efficacious, took form, the hymns and prayers, the readings and sermons insistently recalled "the odious crime perpetrated by the Jews." The majesty of the setting, the solemnity of the ceremony, the beauty of the words and voices helped incise in the hearts of the faithful sentiments which would nevermore be blotted out, which would be transmitted from century to century and would ultimately aggregate to form what could be called "the Christian subconscious." Listen to the *Improperia*,[21] the very moving hymn from the liturgy for Good Friday, which has risen and soared over an unfathomable depth of meditation at the hour of adoration since about the ninth century:

O my people, what have I done to thee? or wherein have I aggrieved thee? answer me. Because I led thee out of the land of Egypt, thou has prepared a Cross for thy Saviour. . . .

I gave thee a royal sceptre: and thou didst put a crown of thorns upon my head.

O my people, what have I done to thee? . . . I raised thee up with mighty power: and thou didst hang me upon the gibbet of the Cross.[22]

[20] See Simon, *op. cit.*, p. 266.

[21] In the *Improperia*, or Reproaches, Christ addresses tender plaints to his "people," for whom he has done so much good and who in return have done him such ill. Christ's voice merges with Moses'. [The beginning of the *Improperia* is drawn from Micah 6:3–4.—Ed.]

[22] [*The Missal in Latin and English*, ed. Father J. O'Connell and H. P. R. Finberg, New York, Sheed & Ward, 1953, "Masses of the Season," pp. 383–385. Let us listen also to the Oriental liturgy:

Awake, singer David. . . .
"The people who do not know mercy,
pitilessly pierced the hands of the Son. . . .
Like dogs, they have surrounded him who keeps silence.". . .
Awake, noble Malachy.
Make the wicked people ashamed who crucified Christ. . . .
Awake, prophet Daniel.
Look at Emmanuel whom Gabriel reveals to you, tortured by the children of
    Israel.
Woe to the prevaricating people. . . .

(Chaldean rite, quoted in Sister Marie Despina, "Jews in Oriental Christian Liturgy," *Sidic* [Rome], October–November, 1967, p. 16.)—Ed.]

The Church does indeed know its duty; it has never failed to join mercy to reprobation. "We must have pity on them [the Jews], fast and pray for them," we read in the Didascalia, a liturgical breviary dating from the third century.[23] One must "pray for them," Saint Justin said, Saint Augustine repeated. But there is prayer and prayer. The prayers for the Jews would soon be reduced to the single contemptuous Good Friday prayer, already known to Gregory of Tours in the sixth century, the only one which remained in the liturgy into our own time. "*Oremus et pro perfidis Judaeis* . . ."—"Let us also pray for the perfidious Jews. . . ." And soon, too, it would be specified that for this single *Oremus,* the ritual genuflexion should be omitted.[24]

Let us say quite plainly: better no prayer than a prayer like that. What can human hearts retain of this too skillfully blended mixture of mercy and reprobation? No mercy; and far worse than reprobation —disgust and hatred and horror toward the deicide people. Come an opportunity, whether a crusade, a plague, or a famine, and the anger sustained and accumulated over centuries, strengthened in the credulous minds of the people by absurd calumnies like the accusation of ritual crimes inherited from paganism, exploded—some monk was always there to trigger it—to be followed by the thousand and one medieval pogroms which pious eloquence and theological learning would then be able to raise to the rank of "providential punishment" and "divine vengeance." [25] "By the twentieth century," writes Jean-Jacques Bovet, "the Jews were no longer being accused of slaughtering children. . . ." [26] Wrong, alas. As the first edition of the present work was being published, there were still churchmen in Poland to

---

[23] See Juster, *op. cit.*, I, 311–312.

[24] [In 1949, following Pope Pius XII's authorization to translate *perfidis* as "unbelieving" or "without faith," Jules Isaac had an audience with the Pope. He pointed out that the change was insufficient; he pressed for total suppression of the word and also for the reinstatement of the ritual genuflexion. The latter was restored in 1955; and in 1959, Pope John XXIII eliminated the word *perfidis* from the prayer forever. Finally, Pope Paul VI removed any mention of conversion and the assertion that Jews needed deliverance "from their darkness," and he introduced the reference to the Jews as "the people of Abraham beloved by God" (see "Prayers on Jews Revised by Pontiff," *New York Times*, April 1, 1965, pp. 1, 9).—Ed.]

[25] Louis-Claude Fillion, *Vie de Notre Seigneur Jésus-Christ*, 22nd ed., Paris, Letouzey, 1929, III, 197, 248.

[26] Jean-Jacques Bovet, "L'Étoile" [The Star], *Le Christianisme social*, October–December, 1946, p. 416.

hawk foul calumnies against the Jews and incite credulous populaces
to pogrom.[27]

      ✿   ✿   ✿

I will not stop to follow the high roads and bypaths of history
traced by the sanguinary course of the teaching, whose major theme
remained the accusation of deicide: this would need a book, and

[27] See *La Quinzaine*, January, 1947, p. 30. [Rare is the twentieth-century nation, in fact, which has not turned on its Jewish citizens or neighbors with precisely the accusations which Bovet claims to be bygone. In Eastern Europe, the
Russian city of Kishinev launched a pogrom at Easter in 1903; so did Bialystok
in 1906. Twenty thousand people were killed in 200 Ukrainian pogroms between
1919 and 1921, and Poland itself foreshadowed the Holocaust with a pogrom at
Przytyk in 1936. Again in the Ukraine, its capital city of Kiev was the setting for
the trial in 1911–1914 of Mendel Beiliss on a charge of ritual murder; Beiliss
was found innocent, and emigrated to the United States. (These and other instances are discussed in detail in Lucy S. Dawidowicz, *The Golden Tradition*,
New York, Holt, Rinehart and Winston, 1967, pp. 46–81.) More recently, Jews
have been accused of using human blood for rituals in the Uzbek Republic of the
U.S.S.R.: at Margelan two days after Rosh Hashanah in 1961, and at Tashkent
shortly after Passover, 1962 (reported by Label Katz, president of B'nai B'rith, at
a press conference, Washington, D. C., January 23, 1963).

[The same libel has been circulating in the Arab world along with the infamous and proven forgery, *The Protocols of the Elders of Zion*. In its issue of
June 21, 1967, the popular illustrated weekly *Akher Saa* (Cairo) carried an article
by Ibrahim Saada entitled "The Secret of the Blood Practices Israel Is Enjoined
To Observe." Under the heading "Some of the Ritual Rabbis Perform with Christian Blood," the author writes, "What is the secret of the Jewish dough mixed
with blood? . . . The kidnapping of children in Syria and Lebanon for the purpose of sucking their blood on the Jewish Passover."

[While political motivations presumably underlie Near Eastern anti-Semitism
in part, not even this excuse can be summoned for physical and moral attacks on
Jews in Western countries. A lives of the saints for children, issued at Valencia
with an imprimatur in 1963, teaches that "They [the Jews] remember the passion on Good Friday by stealing a child and crucifying it" (quoted in Fathers
René Laurentin and Joseph Neuner, S.J., *The Declaration on the Relation of the
Church to Non-Christian Religions of Vatican II*, "Vatican II Documents" series,
Glen Rock, N. J., Paulist Press, 1966, p. 55). Numerous scurrilities, laying heavy
stress on the deicide charge, were printed and distributed broadside to the representatives at the Vatican Council in Rome, 1962–1965, and one of the lengthier
—a pseudonymous book—has since appeared in English in the United States, in
1967. (The editor has examined or possesses four such pieces of hate literature,
and others are discussed by Rabbi Arthur Gilbert in *The Vatican Council and the
Jews*, New York, World Publishing, 1968.) These materials were neither sponsored nor sanctioned by any official Church voice, but this may not be said of the
opinion expressed by Bishop Luigi Carli that ". . . Judaism must be held responsible for deicide, reprobated and accursed by God . . ." (see p. 392, n. 10, below).
And one cannot help sensing an undertone of the same injurious tradition in the
words spoken by Pope Paul VI himself on Passion Sunday, 1965 (see p. 263, n. 76,
below).

[Finally, though the United States may claim never to have mounted a po-

surely that book must be written,[28] but the undertaking surpasses the framework I have set for myself.[29] Having marked the point of origin clearly, I will limit myself to showing where it has led: its contemporary existence and virulence. At the most, I think it useful to erect some landmarks so as to make the continuity of the current visible.

I can therefore only mention the anti-Jewish legislation of the Middle Ages, arising from that system of interdicts, exclusions, degradations applied to the Jews which spread across not several years, like its Nazi imitation, but some fifteen centuries: this constitutes a gauge of its dreadful effectiveness. Actually this system, which began to evolve as soon as the Church united with the State, was not developed fully until the eleventh, twelfth, and thirteenth centuries,[30] the era when there was really a Christendom, in that "great light of the Middle Ages" (Gustave Cohen *dixit*),[31] which to be sure also bore some shadows; it is not an accident that the institution of the *rouelle* or disc, of the various ignominious badges imposed on the Jews, coincided with the apogee of pontifical theocracy: before Hitler, Innocent III; before the Nuremberg Laws, the decrees of the Fourth Lateran Council.

But at the root of this anti-Jewish legislation was deicide, as dei-

---

grom, the Jews of this country too have suffered the degradation of "foul calumnies" and death at the hands of "credulous populaces." In August of 1915, Leo Frank was lynched in Atlanta for a murder of which he was later found innocent. Two days before Yom Kippur, 1928, Rabbi Berel Brennglass was accused by the mayor of Massena, New York, of committing the ritual murder of a four-year-old child (see Morton Rosenstock, *Louis Marshall, Defender of Jewish Rights*, Detroit, Wayne State University Press, 1965, pp. 264–267). And a pamphlet published in Birmingham, Alabama, in 1962 lists hundreds of "well-authenticated" cases of "ritual murder" throughout the world in the present century; the copy in the editor's possession carries the date of October, 1964, and the claim, "Republished by Popular Demand."

[So it is that we, like Jules Isaac, must still answer Jean-Jacques Bovet's allegation of more than twenty years ago: "Wrong, alas."—Ed.]

[28] [Since the initial appearance of *Jésus et Israël* in 1948, and frequently under its inspiration, numerous books have been written on this subject. Notable in the United States is Father Edward H. Flannery's *The Anguish of the Jews: Twenty-Three Centuries of Anti-Semitism*, New York, Macmillan, 1965. Father Flannery is the first Roman Catholic priest who has had the courage to write at length about the history of Christian anti-Semitism.—Ed.]

[29] [Jules Isaac undertook such a work, but time was not left him to complete it. He was able to cover only the period up to the year 1000, in *Genèse de l'antisémitisme* (see n. 4, above).—Ed.]

[30] Prior to the Middle Ages, notably in the Carolingian age, the Jews experienced long periods of tranquillity and prosperity. When one speaks of "providential punishment," then, it is well to distinguish between eras.

[31] Gustave Cohen, *La grande Clarté du moyen-âge* [The Great Light of the Middle Ages], New York, Maison Française, 1943.

cide was the origin of the massacres. "The mob of massacrers shouted, 'They killed our Savior—let them convert or let them die!' "[32] These people were only translating into their own unrefined terms a thesis of the medieval Church to which how many Christians—or would-be Christians—might be disposed to subscribe even in our day. Even those who tried out of Christian charity and theological reasoning to curb popular frenzies recognized the merits of the thesis and of the capital accusation on which it rested. Saint Bernard of Clairvaux, a most noble and powerful figure of twelfth-century French Christendom, wrote in a letter addressed both to "the English people" and to "all the clergy and people of Eastern France [the Rhineland] and Bavaria" in 1146:

The Jews are not to be persecuted, killed or even put to flight. . . . The Jews are for us the living words of Scripture, for they remind us always of what our Lord suffered. They are dispersed all over the world so that by expiating their crime they may be everywhere the living witnesses of our redemption.[33]

And the illustrious thirteenth-century doctor, Saint Thomas Aquinas, said in a consultation given the Duchess of Brabant: "It would be licit, according to the law, to hold the Jews in perpetual servitude because of their crime." Saint Thomas was only restating the formula of the great Pope Innocent III: "The Jews," guilty of having "crucified the Lord," have been "subjected to perpetual servitude."[34]

After the relative tolerance of the Renaissance popes, the popes of the Counterreformation reverted to Innocent III's principles, applying them strictly. By his Bull of July 12, 1555, Pope Paul IV re-established the most rigorous anti-Jewish legislation in the Papal States: confinement in the ghetto, obligatory wearing of a distinctive mark (the yellow hat), prohibition from practicing most professions.[35]

---

[32] Father Joseph Bonsirven, S.J., in Father Henri de Lubac, S.J., et al., Israël et la foi chrétienne, "Manifeste contre le Nazisme" series, Fribourg, Switz., Éd. de la Librairie de l'Université, 1942, p. 133.
[33] Bernard of Clairvaux, Lettres, ed. Father P., Lyons, 1838, III, 105. [Quotation taken from Letters of St. Bernard, ed. Bruno Scott James, Chicago, Regnery, 1953, p. 462, para. 6.—Tr.]
[34] Thomas Aquinas, letter to the Duchess of Brabant, in De regimine principium [On the Primary Rule], Turin, Marietti, 1924, p. 117; Innocent III, CXXI [(letter) 121], in Migne, Patrologia latina, CCXV, 694. Quoted in Father Hippolyte Gayraud, L'Antisémitisme de saint Thomas d'Aquin [Anti-Semitism in Saint Thomas Aquinas], Paris, Dentu, 1896, p. 71; Journet, op. cit., p. 260; Father Joseph Bonsirven, S.J., Les Juifs et Jésus, Paris, Beauchesne, 1937, p. 186.
[35] David Lasserre, "L'Antisémitisme de l'Église chrétienne," Cahiers protestants, no. 1, January–February, 1939, p. 9.

A medieval thesis, then, with Counterreformation postscripts? No; just as much a modern thesis, a classic thesis that Jansenism adopted for its own account in the person of Blaise Pascal:

It is an amazing thing . . . to find the Jewish people surviving after so many years, and to see them in a state of wretchedness; but in order to prove the claims of Jesus Christ it was essential that they should both survive and be wretched because they crucified him. . . .[36]

". . . in order to prove the claims of Jesus Christ . . ."? Isn't it most astonishing of all that Jesus Christ should need this proof?

    ❁ ❁ ❁

But the Reformation?

Wouldn't the Reformation, whose primary inspiration was to go back to the purest sources—the Word of Christ—have been led by this very fact to move away from the traditional viewpoint? Not in the least.

Indeed, Luther—as Muhammad before him—began by lavishing fine words and welcomes on the Jews, with the undisguised hope of rallying them to his cause. He published *Christ Was Born a Jew* in 1523; "Please God that the time [of Israel's conversion] be close, as we hope." [37] But ten years had not passed before the reformer, disappointed in his hope, opened fire against them with all the violence of an impulsive, quick-tempered Germanic temperament. The Jews were then but abominable deicides for him, fit for drowning in the Elba if they asked for baptism: about 1531 or 1532, he declared that if he found some pious Jew to baptize, he would lead him out on the bridge over the Elba, attach a stone to his neck, and throw him in the river, saying: "I baptize you in the name of Abraham!" [38] We read in Luther's *Table Talk:* "The destruction of Jerusalem was cruel, lamentable. . . . It was really too much [for God] to see his own people lead his own Son before the gates of the city to crucify him." [39]

---

[36] Blaise Pascal, *Opuscules et pensées*, ed. Léon Brunschvicg, Paris, Hachette, 1897, para. 640. [Quotation taken from *idem, Pensées*, ed. and tr. Martin Turnell, New York, Harper, 1962.—Tr.]

[37] [Martin Luther, *Das Jhesus Christus eyn geborner Jude sey* (Christ Was Born a Jew), Wittenberg, 1523.—Tr.]

[38] Quoted in Reinhold Lewin, *Luthers Stellung zu den Juden* [Luther's Attitude Toward the Jews], Berlin, Trowitzsch, 1911, p. 37.

[39] [Martin Luther, *Tischreden* . . . (Table Talk . . .), Eisleben, Gaubisch, 1566.—Tr.]

And in one of his last writings, entitled *On the Jews and Their Lies,* the filthiest insults—in the style of Saint John Chrysostom—alternate with frenzied summonses to the worst violence:

Venomous beasts, vipers, disgusting scum, cancers, devils incarnate. . . . Rather than touch the pearl and balm of the word of God, you should handle pig excrement. . . . Their [the Jews'] private houses must be destroyed and devastated; they could be lodged in stables. . . . I beseech our magistrates to exercise severe pity toward these wretches in case it might contribute to their salvation. . . . Let them take care to burn their synagogues . . . and whatever escapes the fire must be covered with sand and mud. . . . Let them force them to work. And if all this avails nothing, we will be compelled to expel them like mad dogs in order not to expose ourselves to incurring divine wrath and eternal damnation! [40]

Patience, Luther, Hitler will come. Your wishes will be granted, and more! Let us recognize here the family ties, the blood ties, uniting two great Germans, and let us place Luther in the place he deserves, in the first row of Christian precursors—of Auschwitz.

John Calvin, more in control of himself, did not deviate from doctrinal considerations. But such was the intransigence of the theologian that it took him to the point of denying Christ's merciful pardon:

When Christ, moved with an affection of mercy, asked God for pardon of those who pursued him, this did not at all prevent him from acquiescing in God's righteous judgment, the which he knew to be ordained for the reprobate and obstinate.[41]

And Calvinist rigidity, as we know, did not hesitate to steal a march on God's judgment against "the reprobate and the obstinate"; in 1632, a pastor, Nicolas Antoine, would be strangled in Geneva for apostasy and conversion to Judaism.

      ✿   ✿   ✿

Wrath of God, vengeance of God, Crime and Punishment—choice theme for great preachers. The oratory of a Bossuet gave it an unequaled magnificence, first in the sermon preached at Metz around 1653, *On the Goodness and Stringency of God,* and then, some twenty

---

[40] [*Idem, Von den Jüden und jren Lügen,* Wittenberg, Lufft, 1543. See, in English, as *idem, The Jews and Their Lies,* St. Louis, Christian Nationalist Crusade, n.d.—Tr.]

[41] Jehan Calvin, *Sur la Concordance ou Harmonie composée de trois évangélistes, asçavoir S. Matthieu, S. Marc et S. Luc,* vol. I of *Commentaires de M. Jehan Calvin sur le Nouveau Testament,* Paris, Meyrueis, 1854.

years later, in the second part of his *Discourse on Universal History*, Chapters XX and XXI.[42] Everything is there.

The definition of the crime:

It was the greatest of all crimes: an unprecedented crime, that is, deicide, which also occasioned a vengeance the like of which the world had never seen.

A striking, graphic description of the "vengeance" of God:

At the moment the Emperor Titus laid siege to the city, the Jews were there in crowds to celebrate Passover. . . . Surely you were remembering, O great God, that it was in the Passover season that their fathers had dared to imprison the Savior; you paid them back, O Lord! and in the same Passover season you imprisoned their children, imitators of their obstinacy, in the capital of their country. . . .

Divine justice demanded an infinite number of victims; it wanted to see 1,100,000 struck down . . . : and even after that, pursuing the remains of this disloyal race, he dispersed them over all the earth. For what reason? As magistrates, having had a number of malefactors broken on the wheel, ordered that their torn and sundered limbs be displayed at several places on the major roads, to strike terror in other villains. This comparison horrifies you: the fact remains that God behaved about the same way. . . .

Finally, the serene affirmation of the traditional doctrine:

By this profound plan of God, the Jews still exist in the midst of the nations, where they are dispersed and captive: but they exist stamped by their reprobation, visibly blighted by their unfaithfulness to the promises made to their fathers, banished from the Promised Land, having no land to cultivate even, slaves everywhere they are, without honor, without freedom, without form as a people. They fell into this state thirty-eight years after they crucified Jesus Christ.

Unfortunately, beauty of style dominates solidity of content. I do not know how the *lex talionis* can be reconciled with the Sermon on the Mount, but as Bossuet speaks of tearing and sundering, I owe it to truth to observe that it is history which finds itself torn and sundered in the hands of the vigorous Bishop of Meaux. Not only is the Dispersion anterior to the events of A.D. 70 by a number of centuries, but there was not even a dispersion of the Palestinian Jews at that date: the proof lies in the second Judean war, fought in 132–135 under

---

[42] Jacques-Bénigne Bossuet, *Discours sur l'Histoire universelle*, vol. V of *Oeuvres de Bossuet*, Paris, Méquignon Junior et Leroux, 1846, pt. II, Chap. XXI, pp. 408–409; *idem*, *Sur la Bonté et la rigueur de Dieu* [On the Goodness and Stringency of God], in *Sermons choisis de Bossuet* [Selected Sermons of Bossuet], ed. Ferdinand Brunetière, Paris, Firmin-Didot, 1882, pp. 40 ff.

the Emperor Hadrian.[43] The "visibly blighted" condition of the Jews was the result of the system of debasement which we have discussed. Finally, if the Jews after a certain period had "no land to cultivate" any more, it was because Christian princes, at the instigation of the Church, progressively withdrew from them the right to own land and the means of practicing agriculture (in the eighth century, there were still Jews in southern Gaul who were great landowners).

o   o   o

Prefacing the contemporary era came the torrential revolutions which seemed—in France, at least—to carry away all the barriers, break all the chains, and which, freeing the Jews from all servitude, restored their human dignity and rights as citizens. In this new climate of freedom, to which public subservience adapted not without difficulty—no more easily than secular privileges, prejudices, and debasements; in this world convulsed as if by an earthquake, there is nothing surprising in the fact that the traditional current nonetheless continued to flow (below ground or in the open), that the traditional teaching continued to shape souls. The incriminating thesis lost nothing of its strength and rigor—far from it. All the varieties of anti-Judaism could wax and flourish in the layer of humus deposited by the silt of centuries: the ground was well prepared. And modern techniques of distribution and publicizing would assure it a monstrous growth.

Works by clerics and laymen, by doctors, professors, men of letters and journalists, Catholic or Protestant, the reading material offers us too much to choose from. And our choice will go by preference to the most qualified, the most reputable.

Among nineteenth-century Protestant theologians, John Nelson Darby stands as an innovator; in what terms did he speak of the Jews? "We can see in Cain a type of the Jews, murderers of the Lord: they carry the mark of it on their forehead." [44] We have already pointed out the merciless severity—inherited from Calvin—of a

[43] [Moreover—were further proof needed—the establishment of the State of Israel in 1948 (after the initial publication of the present book) adds to the implausibility of Bossuet's theses.—Ed.]

[44] John Nelson Darby, *Introduction à la Sainte Bible* [Introduction to the Holy Bible].

Frédéric Godet [45] and an Henri Bois.[46] More recent commentators on the Gospels, Gunther Dehn and Hébert Roux are no less implacable prosecutors in their indictment of Israel. "An internal necessity," the first assures us, "impelled the Jewish people to nail Jesus to the cross, because he destroyed their pretensions." "Israel," the second decrees, "is maintained as a people, as a race, for the day of judgment to come. . . . Just as the descendants of Israel were the object of God's special grace and as it was first to them that Jesus came, so they would be the object of a special judgment, they who took 'innocent blood' upon themselves and who would have to make an accounting." [47] I admire these superior spirits who have penetrated God's designs to the point of being initiated into the secret of His judgments.[48]

More recent yet is an article in the foremost French Protestant periodical, *Réforme*, which, after disdainfully brushing aside "the controversies concerning exegesis and history," reminds us in a hard tone that

. . . willingly or unwillingly: this is the key word in the [Jewish] enigma. The Jewish people have fulfilled and are still fulfilling their mission, but it is *unwillingly*. After centuries of abusing the patience of their God without exhausting it, the decisive moment in [their] history arrived. Jesus Christ came on earth. He came to establish the Kingdom of God. . . . Thus he declared himself king of the Jews. The Jews refused to recognize him as their king: they scoffed at him, condemned him, crucified him. In so doing, they trampled underfoot the mission they had received, they said "no" to God. . . . [Dispersed over all the earth and persecuted by reason of the curse brought down on them,] they [nonetheless] continue to fulfill their function as witnesses. They effectively remind all men and the nations where they dwell that God is not mocked with impunity.[49]

[45] See p. 126, above; and in Godet's work (*Commentaire sur l'Évangile de Jean*, Paris, Fischbacher, 1876), see also III, 518.

[46] See pp. 101 and 205; n. 67, above; and in Bois's book (*La Personne et l'oeuvre de Jésus*, Neuilly, La Cause, 1926), see also pp. 110, 120–122.

[47] Gunther Dehn, *Le Fils de Dieu, commentaire à l'Évangile de Marc*, Paris, Je Sers, 1936, p. 148; Hébert Roux, *L'Évangile du Royaume*, Geneva, Labor et Fides, 1934, p. 289.

[48] [More telepathy, this time American: "In the Judgment Day, the scriptures in which they [The Jews] trusted will therefore judge and condemn them" (*Gospel of John* [Assembly of God], 1965, p. 24; quoted in Gerald Strober, ms. in preparation, New York [Xerox], p. 53).—Ed.]

[49] Bosc, *op. cit.*; and see the editorial "Le Point de vue de Réforme" [The Viewpoint of Reform] in the same issue of *Réforme*, November 23, 1946. [This "hard tone" can be heard in some American Protestant voices which are recorded by way of example in Bernhard E. Olson's book *Faith and Prejudice* (New Haven, Yale University Press, 1963, pp. 35, 242). One says: "When the Jews quote God's promise to Abraham, 'I will curse them that curse Thee,'. . . ask them how that

In other words, God uses the Jews as Sparta did its drunken Helots.[50]

Thus is a theological tradition maintained in all its rigidity which in fact has only a very remote relation to exegesis and history and, one could even add, to the Gospel of Christ.

So faith, hope, love abide, these three; but the greatest of these is love.

1 Cor. 13:13

✿   ✿   ✿

Alternating choruses: Catholic voices reply to Protestant.

Lamennais, who at that moment was still Father Lamennais, pre-echoed John Nelson Darby, and his eloquence and orthodoxy seemed to announce a new Bossuet, more hotblooded—and more absolutist:

Universal, perpetual miracle, which will demonstrate to the end of days the inexorable justness and the holiness of God, whom this [Jewish] people dared to deny. . . . Even to our own time all peoples have seen them pass, all have been gripped with horror at their sight; they were marked with a sign more terrible than Cain's; on their forehead an iron hand had written: Deicide! [51]

It is Cain, again Cain (oh, the convenience—and arbitrariness—of that device, the figure of speech!) whom Father Lagrange himself evokes in his interpretation of Matthew 23:35:

So the chosen people, whose election was prefigured by Abel, adopted Cain's attitude against the Messiah, brother born of their blood who had been sent to them. . . . No man is punished except for his faults, but this time the nation would take responsibility for a crime which summed up all the crimes accumulated since the origin of the world, and its punishment, long deferred, would be definitive.[52]

promise could apply to the Jews whom Jesus Himself condemned. Jesus in very strong terms denounced the Jews, and pronounced judgement upon them. . . . This explains why these judgements are falling upon the Jews, from Jesus' time until today; they are receiving just what they measured out to Christians" (Women's Voice, vol. XI, no. 8, March 26, 1953, p. 1). And another: "Because they rejected their Messiah at His first coming, demanding that His blood be on them and their children, the Jews have had an unhappy lot for centuries" (Adult Teacher [Scripture Press], October–December, 1953, p. 116).—Ed.]

50 [The reference is to Plutarch's report that Helots were forced to appear in public drunk on certain occasions as a lesson to Spartan youth.—Tr.]

51 Félicité de Lamennais, Essai sur l'indifférence en matière de religion [Essay on Indifference in Religious Matters], 4 vols., Paris, 1817–1823, vol. III.

52 Father Marie-Joseph Lagrange, O.P., L'Évangile de Jésus-Christ, Paris, Gabalda, 1928, p. 456.

Less well known, but no less effective for the fact, are the manuals for seminary use which have molded generations of priests. Father Jean-Joseph Rivaux's *Church History Course* was widely distributed at the end of the nineteenth century; I extract a few typical sentences:

Divine wrath already pursued this deicide race everywhere. . . . Everything combined finally to hasten that catastrophe which would consummate the destruction of the deicide nation. . . . Thus this deicide nation is experiencing a punishment comparable to the crime which was the original cause of its misfortunes; and the idolatrous soldiery, by crucifying these wretches, repaid them all the outrages they themselves had heaped on the Son of God at Golgotha.[53]

The place of favor of Father Rivaux's work in Catholic teaching passed to Father Léon Marion's *History of the Church*, "the standard manual in most French seminaries," which contains almost identical formulas on the manifestations of God's "justice toward the deicide people."[54] Sooner or later, the traditional epithet flows from the pen (and certainly from the lips) of the Catholic professor; commenting on Luke 23:27–31, where Jesus, carrying the cross, speaks to the "Daughters of Jerusalem," A. Brassac inserts these parentheses: "If it goes so hard with the tree that is still green (that is, with our Lord), what will become of the tree that is already dried up (that is, of the Jewish nation which is committing an infamous deicide)?"[55]

Better yet—or worse—is one of the more recent history texts for use in Catholic primary schools. It states:

The punishment of the deicide (God-murdering) Jews was not long in coming. Thirty-six years after the Savior's death, the Roman Emperor Titus seized Jerusalem and completely destroyed the Temple. The Jews, dispersed throughout the world, have never again been able to form a nation. They have wandered everywhere, considered a cursed race, an object of contempt to other peoples.[56]

[53] Father Jean-Joseph Rivaux, *Cours d'histoire ecclésiastique à l'usage des séminaires* [Church History Course for Use in Seminaries], 3 vols., 10th ed., Grenoble, Baratier, 1895.

[54] Father Léon Marion, *Histoire de l'Église* [History of the Church], 3 vols., 4th ed., Paris, Roger et Chernoviz, 1905–1922, I, 127–128.

[55] Father A. Brassac, *Nouveau Testament*, vol. III of Fathers Fulcran G. Vigouroux and A. Brassac, *Manuel biblique, ou Cours d'Écriture sainte à l'usage des séminaires*, ed. Fathers A. Brassac and Louis Baceuz, 4 vols., 12th ed., Paris, Roger et Chernoviz, 1906–1909, p. 698. [Father Brassac's insertions aside, the wording of Lk. 23:31 here is from RK, which also carries this note: "This verse is generally understood to mean, If crucifixion is the lot of the innocent, what punishment is to be expected by the guilty (that is, the Jews)?"—Tr.]

[56] Henri Guillemain and Canon François Le Ster, *Histoire de France: Manuel du certificat d'études,* rev. ed., Paris, Éd. de l'École, 1947. This text was oblig-

Let us move up a few degrees. Let us come to that great Catholic work by the Reverend Father Dom Prosper Guéranger, *The Liturgical Year*, the volume devoted to *The Passion and Holy Week*. Dom Guéranger gives us brimful measure:

The most general characteristic of the prayers and ritual of this fortnight is profound grief at seeing the Righteous One oppressed by his enemies to the death [ah, what heart would not endorse this! but Dom Guéranger adds:] and strenuous indignation against the deicide people. . . . Sometimes Christ himself reveals the agonies of his soul; sometimes there are frightful imprecations against his tormentors. The punishment of the Jewish nation is displayed in all its horror.

Here, Dom Guéranger does say, "The Church does not seek to stir up fruitless feeling; it wishes primarily to strike salutary dread in the hearts of its children. If they are terrorized by the crime committed in Jerusalem, if they feel that they are guilty of it, their tears will always flow amply. . . ." But the hearer will persuade himself of the Jew's guilt more readily than of his own. Dom Guéranger continues: "These considerations on the justice of the punishment of the impenitent Jews will succeed in destroying the attachment we have to sin. . . ."

ingly communicated to me by Miss M.-M. Davy, of the faculty at the École de Hautes Études. Canon Le Ster very adequately expressed to me his regret at having allowed such locutions to pass into print, and he corrected the text in a new edition, of 1948. [The revised edition was reprinted in 1957 and was still in use in France in 1967.—Ed.] To see how active this tradition continues to be in Catholic teaching, the reader may refer to the inquiry conducted by Paul Démann, *La Catéchèse chrétienne et le peuple de la Bible* [Christian Catechesis and the People of the Bible], Paris, Éd. des *Cahiers sioniens*, 1952.

[See also Canon François Houtart and Jean Giblet, eds., *Les Juifs dans la catéchèse: Étude des manuels de catéchèse de langue française*, Louvain, Centre de Recherches socio-religieuses and Centre de Recherches catéchétiques, 1969. This broad-based study of catechetical materials documents all too painfully "how active" the anti-Jewish "tradition continues to be in Catholic teaching" still today —more than two decades after *Jésus et Israël's* writing. The quotations which the study incorporates, and on which the editor has drawn freely, parrot the misguided commentaries cited by Professor Isaac. Listen to the familiar ruthlessness underlying these words from an instruction text: "But Jews, his [Jesus'] fellow countrymen, refused to let themselves be loved by Jesus. This is why they will be burned like dried-out vine branches. And the temples [*sic*] of these Pharisees will be nothing but ruins" (J. de Lorimier, *Histoire de notre salut*, teacher's manual, Ottawa, Fides, 1962, p. 157). To this the author joins a corresponding sentence in the pupil's text: "But the Jews, his fellow countrymen, men like the one you see [in the picture of an "Old Jew"], refused to let themselves be loved by Jesus" (*ibid.*, student's text, p. 157). And consider again the brutalizing effect on young ears of such words as these: "The Jews remain those who refuse Christ and the people whose ancestors solemnly called for his blood to fall on them" (A. Ravier, *L'Église du Dieu Vivant* [The Church of the Living God], 2nd ed., "Fils de lumière" series, Paris, Gigord, 1962, p. 152; all quoted in Houtart and Giblet, *op. cit.*, pp. 132, 166, 137).—Ed.]

Alas! They will also succeed in destroying any feeling of humanity that defenseless hearts have toward the "deicide" Jews, whose reprobation is sounded page after page, in words of unparalleled vehemence:

The blood that was spilled by the Jewish people on Calvary . . . is the blood of a God. The whole world must know and understand this from the mere sight of the punishment of the murderers. . . . The spectacle of a whole people drenched with malediction in all its generations, for having crucified the Son of God, gives Christians matter for reflection. They learn from it that divine justice is terrible, and that the Father demands an accounting for the blood of His Son down to the last drop from those who have spilled it. Let us hasten to wash in this precious blood the stain of complicity which we have with the Jews. . . .[57]

But how many faithful will be tempted to cry out here, "First let us wash it in Jewish blood!"

The one and the other, the exegete and the theologian, both accusers, each throwing his stone (in the name of Christ), each decreeing himself final judge by proxy for God: "God's vengeance would sweep down pitilessly on this deicide race and would demand an accounting for all the blood spilled wrongfully," writes Father Prat.[58] "Behind the Roman appears the great bearer of guilt, and it is not Judas alone, it is the leaders of that crowd, and it is 'all the people' who cried out, 'His blood be on us and on our children!' " intones Father de Grandmaison.[59] "The deicide of the Jews"—the stock phrase recurs under Louis-Claude Fillion's pen: the crucifying of the Jews in the year 70 "was a horrible spectacle in which it is hard not to see the punishment that the deicide nation had thus called down upon itself."[60] Father Lebreton, like Calvin, takes the occasion of Jesus' very pardon to crush the Jews: "Those for whom he [Jesus] interceded were neither only nor primarily the soldiers. . . . They were the chief offenders, those against whom Jesus' death armed divine justice, those who called down on themselves the curse of the spilled blood: the Jews."[61] "A murderous people," says Father Fessard, who

[57] Dom Prosper Guéranger, O.S.B., *La Passion et la Semaine sainte*, vol. III of *L'Année liturgique* (6 vols.), 24th ed., Tours, Mame, 1921.
[58] Father Ferdinand Prat, *Jésus-Christ, sa vie, son oeuvre, sa doctrine*, 2 vols., Paris, Beauchesne, 1938, II, 235.
[59] Father Léonce de Grandmaison, S.J., *Jésus-Christ, sa personne, son message, ses preuves*, 2 vols., Paris, Beauchesne, 1928.
[60] Fillion, *op. cit.*, vol. III.
[61] Father Jules Lebreton, S.J., *La Vie et l'enseignement de Jésus-Christ*, 2 vols., Paris, Beauchesne, 1931, II, 422.

assigns Israel a "negating mission," defines the Jews as "enemies of everything that is specifically Christian and everything that is human," denounces the transmutation of the divine favor "into infernal falseness and hatred" through the fault of the Jewish people, and like Bossuet, like so many others who have been less concerned with historic truth than with theological rationalization, finds this eloquent —if not charitable—image to describe Israel's wretchedness:

When they accompanied Jesus to Calvary, at the gates of the City, where he would be crucified by the Romans, who among the Jews foresaw that the destiny of the whole people would be to be crucified by the pagans outside the Holy City, and hence to remain, Witness of God, eternally nailed to the crossroad where Humanity's destinies would converge and traverse, in order to show passersby that we are the meaning of History . . . ? [62]

Imprimatur, imprimatur.[63]

If priests—excellent priests; if pastors, professors, learned men express themselves thus, what can we expect from laymen, men of letters, whose works have (perhaps) less authority, certainly greater distribution and readership, and whose imagination, stimulated by faith, knows no bounds? The uneven but visionary and powerful writer Léon Bloy has won an enthusiastic following, especially since his death, through the appeal of a fierce independence, a holy (but grumbling) poverty, an inspired heart. In the strange book *Salvation Is from the Jews* (written in 1892), "the only one that I would dare present to God without any fear," he said, and one in which the sublime and the ignoble admix in equal measure, he sees fit to call up "the unrivaled ignominy" of that Jewish people who have "butchered the Word made flesh" and "the prodigious spectacle of their endless punishment." He writes:

Demoniac people . . . , anathema of a race . . . [who] were always for Christians an object of horror and at the same time the occasion of a myste-

[62] Father Gaston Fessard, S.J., *Pax nostra*, 8th ed., Paris, Grasset, 1936.
[63] The quotations can be multiplied. I open the May 15, 1930, issue of the *Bulletin catholique de la question d'Israël*, where it is said that Israel's rejection of Jesus "is like a sort of second original sin that the deicide people drag through the world. From that time on, the deicide people would be ostracized by society" (Robert John, "Israël: La grande Tragédie de l'histoire du monde et la question juive" [Israel: The Great Tragedy of the History of the World and the Jewish Question], p. 13). Note that this bulletin was published by the missionary priests of Notre-Dame de Sion. But it should also be noted in fairness that after 1948, when Paul Démann took over its direction, this journal was totally transformed. Retitled *Cahiers sioniens*, not only did its appearance change; its soul changed.

rious fear. . . . they had waited more than two thousand years for an occasion to crucify the Word of God.[64]

This is only a prelude, I know; the deep meaning of the book goes far beyond it; but how many readers penetrate the deep meaning, and how many savor this infamous prelude?

In a Giovanni Papini, one may not recognize any kind of true talent, but one cannot contest that his works in translation have a large Catholic audience. Glancing through his *Life of Christ*, I discover as soon as the subject is broached that "The progeny of those god-killers has become the most infamous but the most sacred of all the peoples"; I learn (not without some surprise) that after the destruction of Jerusalem, "The end of the god-killing people, the partial and local ending, had taken place"; and I perceive in Giovanni Papini, as he comments on the destruction of the Holy City, an emulator of Bossuet or Father Rivaux: "The hills made of stone like the heart of the deicides would only send back the echo of their howling, and the mothers' children would fall in pools of warm blood which would compensate in some feeble way for the blood of Christ." [65] One would like to disregard these oratorical platitudes, but they have currency and they insinuate themselves into innocent hearts. And I say that they lead— yes—they lead to Auschwitz.[66]

---

[64] Léon Bloy, *Le Salut par les Juifs* [Salvation Is from the Jews] (1892), Paris, Mercure de France, 1933, pp. 47, 51, 56; 95, 126, 189.

[65] Giovanni Papini, *Histoire du Christ*, tr., Paris, Payot, 1922; a wholly new translation appeared in 1946. [Quotations taken from *idem*, *Life of Christ*, tr. Dorothy Canfield Fisher, New York, Harcourt, 1923, pp. 46, 273. The last passage is not included in the English edition.—Tr.]

[66] [Other such "oratorical platitudes" which turn into complete distortions of the Gospels still have currency, to wit in the Oberammergau Passion Play, which was staged again in 1950, 1960, and 1970. The presentation of the drama dates from the seventeenth century; the Oberammergau villagers vowed in 1633 that if they escaped the plague which beset Europe during the Thirty Years' War (1618–1648), they would enact a Passion play every ten years. The first performance took place in 1634, and the script was rewritten in 1860. The Nazis endorsed the play as "a racially important cultural document." The official German text of the play was not significantly modified in 1970. Translated into English from the "revised and newly published" 1970 version by the Community of Oberammergau, *The Passion Play of Oberammergau* includes such lines as these:

[*Narrated Prologue:*] Even Pilate is moved to sympathy for him
    [Jesus]. . . .
But around the Saviour of all, in wrath is raging
A furious, blinded people which ceaseth not its clamour
Till the unwilling judge
Cries: So take him and crucify him! [p. 97].
All: Pilate must consent—all Jerusalem demands it of him!
Pilate: Can not even this pitiful sight win some compassion from your hearts?

And of how many others will I say as much? Of my old colleagues in academicians' robes Jérôme and Jean Tharaud, entitling the most biased of accounts *When Israel Is King;* [67] of the raving Louis-Ferdinand Céline, dug into a corner of Hitlery during the Second World War; passing by the hanged Julius Streicher and the obstinate Charles Maurras, sentenced to life imprisonment, mentor and oracle for numerous French youth, frenetic virtuoso of incitement to murder.

As for me, because so much stench gives me a desperate desire to breathe a little clean air, I cannot restrain myself from recalling here the memory of hours of anguish, the memory of a poor woman, a Jew, threatened with deportation and consoling a frightened son, a small Emmanuel seven years old, with words that I do not hesitate to characterize as sublime: "Stop, now, Emmanuel. You mustn't cry. God is with us. He was with us when we came here. He will be with us if we have to leave. He will be in the train that will carry us away. He will be with us everywhere, always." A Jew, a simple Jewish woman, as Jesus was "a simple Jew." But the ashes of millions of Jewish martyrs had not yet cooled before the pious tradition of gratuitous insults and accusations was resumed.

How could the friendship that I had until so recently with Daniel-Rops have stood up under the reading of such sentences as I will quote, gathered in 1946 from his *Sacred History: Jesus in His Time*— a work carrying a nihil obstat signed with the respected name of Joseph Huby and an imprimatur, and assured of the largest distribution by the most skillful promotion?

All: Let him die! to the cross with him!
Pilate: So take ye him and crucify him at your peril.
    I will have nothing to do with it [p. 101].
Pilate: I am compelled by your violence to yield to your desire.
    Take him and crucify him [p. 104].
Caiphas: Triumph! The victory is ours! The enemy of the Synagogue is
    destroyed! . . .
People: Up and away! Away to Golgotha! Come and see him upon the cross! O
    joyful day! The enemy of Moses is thrown down. . . . He deserves crucifixion! Happiest Passover! Now is peace returned to Israel! [p. 106].
People: Drive him with violence that we may get on to Calvary. . . .
Priests and People: Do not let him rest. On, drive him with blows! [p. 109].

[And these words were revived in 1950, less than ten years, Dr. Robert Gorham Davis reminds us, after "bulldozers were literally covering with hills of earth the mass graves of Jewish women and children" ("Passion at Oberammergau," *Commentary,* March, 1960, p. 199).—Ed.]
[67] Jérôme and Jean Tharaud, *Quand Israël est roi* [When Israel Is King], Paris, Plon-Nourrit, 1921.

This last wish of the people he had elected ("His blood be on us and on our children!") was granted by God in his justice. Through the span of the centuries, in all the lands where the Jewish race has been dispersed, the blood falls; and eternally, the cry of murder hurled at Pilate's praetorium covers a cry of pain repeated a thousand times. The face of persecuted Israel fills History, but it cannot make one forget that other face sullied with blood and spit, which the Jewish crowd did not pity. It doubtless did not rest with Israel not to kill its God after having failed to recognize him, and, as blood calls mysteriously to blood, it perhaps no more rests with Christian charity to prevent the horror of the pogrom from compensating for the unbearable horror of the Crucifixion in the secret balance sheet of the divine intentions.

Dreadful sentences, impious sentences, themselves of an "unbearable horror," aggravated by a note which says:

Among modern-day Jews . . . , a certain number . . . try to throw off the weight of this heavy responsibility. . . . Understandable feelings, but History will not be contravened . . . and the terrible burden of [Jesus' death] which weighs on Israel's forehead is not among those which it rests with man to throw off.[68]

I will add: sentences taken out of context and thereby sidetracked from their original (and infinitely less cruel) meaning, for the majority of them are translated from German and taken from an essay by an anonymous German Catholic, "The Blood Falls," [69] written some eight years earlier. Daniel-Rops made them his own. Let him bear the "heavy responsibility" for them, or rather (as I hope) let him have the heart to disavow them.[70]

[68] Henry Daniel-Rops, *Histoire sainte: Jésus en son temps*, Paris, Fayard, 1945, pp. 526–527.

[69] Anon., "Le Sang retombe" [The Blood Falls], in Paul Claudel *et al.*, *Les Juifs*, "Présences" series, Paris, Plon, 1937, p. 19. The note which I wrote to Daniel-Rops severing our friendship, after I had read his *Jésus en son temps*, was published under the title "Comment on écrit l'Histoire (sainte)" [How (Sacred) History Is Written] in *Europe*, July 1, 1946.

[70] I have let this paragraph stand as originally published in 1948. It must be added, and this is thoroughly to Daniel-Rops's honor, that after the note I addressed to him breaking our friendship, the sentences incriminated were modified in subsequent editions. The 1951 printing of *Jésus en son temps* carries this notice: "New Edition, Revised and Corrected in July, 1951." [And in the 1962 edition, Daniel-Rops says, on the subject of Jewish responsibility: ". . . the present text (1961) differs from that written in 1945–1946; this change translates the evolution of the author's thought during these fifteen years" (p. 683, n. 1). Concerning this evolution, Jules Isaac wrote: ". . . I have received the new edition of *Jésus en son temps*, radically revised, far better inspired toward Judaism . . ." (*L'Enseignement du mépris*, Paris, Fasquelle, 1962, p. 144; see, in an abridged English edition [i.e., appendixes dropped], as *idem*, *The Teaching of Contempt: Christian Roots of Anti-Semitism*, tr. Helen Weaver, New York, Holt, Rinehart and Winston, 1964). In a later book, Daniel-Rops remarked: "We must cite in a

❁   ❁   ❁

These innumerable voices (there are a thousand others), this concert of outrages, this unparalleled accusation, insistent, persistent, repeated from century to century, perpetually reinforced by that stirring liturgy, that magisterial teaching—we cannot underestimate their effectiveness, their penetration into souls, their ineradicable influence and marks, beginning in childhood and for life.

This is perfectly seen and described by Sören Kierkegaard in his *Training in Christianity:*

> Then tell the child what befell Him [Jesus] in life, how one of the few that were close to Him betrayed Him, that the other few denied Him, and all the rest scoffed at and derided Him, until at last they nailed Him to the cross—as the picture shows—requiring that His blood might be upon them and their children, whereas He prayed for them that this might not come to pass, that the heavenly Father would forgive them their fault. . . . Tell the child that contemporary with this loving One there lived a notorious robber who was condemned to death—for him the people demanded release, they cried, "Viva! Long live Barabbas!" But as for the loving One, they cried, "Crucify, crucify!" . . . What effect do you think this narrative will make upon the child? . . . The child would have decided that when he grew up he would slay all those ungodly men who had dealt thus with the loving One.[71]

Kierkegaard adds: "When the child became a youth, he would not have forgotten the impression of childhood, but he would now understand it differently. . . ." Perhaps, but the first impression will govern his thoughts, often without his being conscious of it.

Desirous of teaching children after adults, Daniel-Rops takes care to tell them: "Rather than hate the people who crucified Jesus, it is better to be grateful to them for all the true and admirable things that they have given humanity."[72] Here are good intentions. A shame that they are obliterated by the massive affirmation, the poisonous ac-

class by itself the moving plea by Jules Isaac, *Jésus et Israel* . . . , to which our final stage [of thinking] owes many elements" (*La Vie quotidienne au temps de Jésus*, Paris, Hachette, 1961, p. 533; see, in English, as *idem, Daily Life in the Time of Jesus*, tr. Patrick O'Brian, New York, Hawthorn, 1962).—Ed.]

Yet it remains very painful that Daniel-Rops could have written such words even a single time—and that time being immediately after Auschwitz.

[71] Sören Kierkegaard *École du Christianisme* tr. P.-H. Tisseau, Paris, Berger-Levrault, 1937. [Quotation taken from *idem, Training in Christianity*, tr. Walter Lowrie, London, Oxford University Press, 1941, pp. 176–177.—Tr.]

[72] Henry Daniel-Rops, *Histoire sainte de mes filleuls* [Sacred History for My Godchildren], Paris, La Colombe, 1946, p. 215. [See, in English, as *idem, The Book of Books: The Story of the Old Testament*, rev. ed., tr. Donal O'Kelly, New York, Kenedy, 1956, pp. 163–164.—Tr.]

cusation they innocently introduce: "the people who crucified Jesus"; nothing more is needed to arouse hatred.

I say to all Christian educators: it is a serious thing, a thing of the greatest seriousness, to infuse hatred—in the name of Christ—in the heart of a child. That these sentiments, inculcated and almost innate (through heredity), thrust their roots deep into the Christian masses I find further proof on a page of Romain Rolland's *Jean-Christophe:*

His grandfather did not like Jews; but as an irony of fate would have it, his two best music students—one become a composer, the other an illustrious virtuoso—were Israelites, and the good man was very unhappy; for there were moments when he would have wanted to embrace those two good musicians; and then, he recalled with sadness that they had put God on the cross; and he did not know how to reconcile those irreconcilable feelings. . . . As for his mother, she was not sure that she was not committing a sin when she went to work [for Jews] as a cook. . . . she bore them no ill will; she was full of pity for those unfortunates, whom God had damned. . . .[73]

Indubitably, there are exceptions to the rule. There is Péguy, for example, who wrote in those last moving pages of his *Appended Note on M. Descartes and Cartesian Philosophy,* in the last hours of his life as a writer (the eve of the 1914 mobilization):

And I will tell my whole thought, for I will say: if God were fully served in his Church (he is served in it with exactitude, but with such miserly exactitude), he would perhaps not need to recall, when he wants to grant a great grace of thought, that there still exist and he still has in his hand the people of his first servants.[74]

The marvelous resonance of that voice, the purifying clarity of that glance, which Death was besetting.

Yet the accusation lives on, even in the most generous declarations made during the last several years to protest against racist theories and practices: "Christ . . . who took His human nature from that people which was to nail Him to the Cross . . . ," wrote Pius XI; [75] "The Jews . . . stoned the prophets and crucified the Son. [But] their guilt . . .

[73] Romain Rolland, *La Révolte,* vol. IV of *Jean-Christophe,* 10 vols., Paris, Ollendorff, 1904–1910, pp. 79–80. [See, among many English editions, as *idem, Revolt,* pt. IV of *Jean-Christophe,* tr. Gilbert Cannan (1910), New York, Modern Library, 1941, Bk. I, p. 401.—Tr.]

[74] Charles Péguy, *Note conjointe sur M. Descartes et la philosophie cartésienne* [Appended Note on M. Descartes and Cartesian Philosophy], in *Oeuvres complètes de Charles Péguy,* Paris, NRF, 1924, IX, 135.

[75] Pius XI, *Mit brennender Sorge* [With Burning Sorrow], encyclical, 1937. [Quotation taken from *The Church in Germany,* Vatican Press tr., Washington, D. C., National Catholic Welfare Conference, 1937.—Tr.]

is in the fact that not Jew nor pagan nor Christian is justified before God." [76]

I know too, I know very well everything that can be presented to counterbalance the somber picture I have painted.[77] But no counterbalancing will unmake the veracity of this picture. The question which arises now is thus not one of rehabilitating Christian charity— God forbid my ever doubting it; the question is one of discovering whether the accusation of deicide, thrown in the face of the Jewish people for more than fifteen centuries, is justified or not.

[76] Declaration of the Reformed Church of Basel, 1938, in *Foi et Vie*, the first of eight issues devoted to Jewish studies (see p. 328, n. 30, below), April, 1947, pp. 213–222. [And Pope Paul VI stated on Passion Sunday in 1965: " [The Gospel for Passion Sunday is] a grave and sad page because it narrates the conflict, the clash between Jesus and the Hebrew people, a people predestined to await the Messiah but who, just at the right moment, not only did not recognize Him but fought Him, abused Him and finally killed Him" (quoted in "Pope Cites Cross as Timely Lesson," *New York Times*, April 5, 1965, p. 33). The Pope said later that he did not mean to imply collective Jewish guilt. This is an unfortunate example of Christian insensitivity resulting from centuries of a religious teaching of contempt.—Ed.]

[77] [Since this was written, even some Catholic theologians have seen the light. It is all to Father Gregory Baum's credit that he relates, in his Introduction to his own book, how he himself had "repeated the long litany of theological legends" about the Jews and "thought [the Jews] a people condemned for murder" until, he says, "I came upon a book which shattered me: *Jésus et Israël*" (*Is the New Testament Anti-Semitic?*, Glen Rock, N. J., Paulist Press, 1965, p. 12). Among other Christian leaders who have issued statements opposing anti-Jewish "theological legends," Bishop L. A. Elchinger, of Strasbourg, hopes for "doctrinal orientations" such that "the Jews of today feel they are recognized" as members of "a religion which has a place in God's plan" (symposium address, Strasbourg, July 20, 1967; in *Amitié judéo-chrétienne de France*, no. 2, April–June, 1968, p. 15). See also pp. 319, n. 16, and 364, n. 107, below.—Ed.]

PROPOSITION 17

NOW, IN THE GOSPELS, JESUS WAS CAREFUL TO NAME IN AD-
VANCE THE PARTIES RESPONSIBLE FOR THE PASSION:
ELDERS, CHIEF PRIESTS, SCRIBES—A COMMON SPECIES
NO MORE LIMITED TO THE JEWS THAN TO ANY OTHER
PEOPLE.

Enough heard from the scribes. Let us listen to Jesus now:

[Mark:]   And he began to teach them that the Son of man must suffer
            many things, and be rejected by the elders and the chief
            priests and the scribes, and be killed, and after three days rise
            again [8:31].

            . . . he was teaching his disciples, saying to them, "The Son
            of man will be delivered into the hands of men, and they will
            kill him; and when he is killed, after three days he will rise"
            [9:31].

            Once more taking the Twelve aside he began to tell them
            what was going to happen to him: "Now we are going up to
            Jerusalem, and the Son of Man is about to be handed over to
            the chief priests and the scribes. They will condemn him to
            death and will hand him over to the pagans, who will mock
            him and spit at him and scourge him and put him to death;
            and after three days he will rise again" [10:32–34 (JB)].

[Matthew:] From that time Jesus began to show his disciples that he must
            go to Jerusalem and suffer many things from the elders and
            chief priests and scribes, and be killed, and on the third day
            be raised [16:21].

            As they were gathering in Galilee, Jesus said to them, "The
            Son of man is to be delivered into the hands of men, and they
            will kill him, and he will be raised on the third day"
            [17:22–23].

            And as Jesus was going up to Jerusalem, he took the twelve
            disciples aside, and on the way he said to them, "Behold, we

are going up to Jerusalem; and the Son of man will be delivered to the chief priests and scribes, and they will condemn him to death, and deliver him to the Gentiles to be mocked and scourged and crucified, and he will be raised on the third day" [20:17–19].

[Luke:]   [Jesus added:] "The Son of man must suffer many things, and be rejected by the elders and chief priests and scribes, and be killed, and on the third day be raised" [9:22].

. . . he said to his disciples, "Let these words sink into your ears; for the Son of man is to be delivered into the hands of men" [9:43–44].

And taking the twelve, he said to them, "Behold, we are going up to Jerusalem, and everything that is written of the Son of man by the prophets will be accomplished. For he will be delivered to the Gentiles, and will be mocked and shamefully treated and spit upon, they will scourge him and kill him, and on the third day he will rise" [18:31–33].

No ambiguity in these texts, which are essential in the eyes of the Christian faith. Three prophetic utterances enunciated by Jesus: one accuses elders, chief priests,[1] and scribes, initially responsible for the Passion Jesus was to suffer; another "men"; and still another "the Gentiles"—the Romans—from whom he would undergo insult, scourging, and death. In all three cases, not one word about Israel, about the Jewish nation, not one which could be interpreted as signifying its participation in the tragedy, its collective responsibility.

Will John 5:18, 7:16–25, 8:28–40, 10:31–32, and other passages be entered in rebuttal?

This is why the Jews sought all the more to kill him, because he not only broke the sabbath but also called God his Father, making himself equal with God [5:18].

So Jesus answered them [the "Jews"], ". . . Why do you seek to kill me?" The people answered, "You have a demon! Who is seeking to kill you?" . . .

Some of the people of Jerusalem therefore said, "Is not this the man whom they seek to kill? . . ." [7:16, 19–20, 25].

---

[1] The term "chief priests" applies here not only to those invested with that supreme office but to all the high dignitaries of the priesthood and those close to them. [In ancient Judaism, there was one high priest appointed for a certain length of time. However, a high priest "who had held the office only for a day retained the title and also sat in the Sanhedrin" (Joseph Klausner, *Jesus of Nazareth: His Life, Time, and Teaching*, tr. Herbert Danby, New York, Macmillan, 1953, p. 340). On the other hand, the hierarchy of the priesthood contained several grades of chief priests besides the high priests.—Ed.]

So Jesus said [to the "Jews"], "When you have lifted up the Son of man, then you will know that I am he . . . ."
". . . I know that you are descendants of Abraham; yet you seek to kill me. . . ."
". . . you seek to kill me, a man who has told you the truth which I heard from God . . ." [8:28, 37, 40].

The Jews took up stones again to stone him. Jesus answered them, "I have shown you many good works from the Father; for which of these do you stone me?" [10:31–32].

An invalid rebuttal. In keeping with good orthodoxy, can it be otherwise? Will the evangelist's words overshadow Christ's words? They will not, for the major reason—and we know it already—that the fourth Gospel frequently gives the word *Jews* a special, limiting (and abusive) meaning. In an earlier chapter,[2] we fully demonstrated that editorial procedure, bearing the mark of the time the Gospel was written—around the year 100. To designate Jesus' adversaries— elders, scribes, and chief priests—the evangelist (in whom tradition recognizes a Jew, moreover: the Apostle John, son of Zebedee) adjudged it good to say quite indiscriminately "the Jews," and in such a contemptuous tone! Forthwith, opprobrium rained down on the entire Jewish nation, now hardened in unbelief. And we know how the whole army of Christian writers since then, from Saint Augustine to François Mauriac inclusively, has passed through that open breach into the thick of the theological fight.

What of it, it's a fair fight. What of it, nobody thought anything much about it. (And you, Jews, pick up your dead.)

❉   ❉   ❉

But why follow Saint John blindly, beyond the boundaries sovereignly established by Jesus?

Here we are led to examine a new problem—or a new aspect of the problem—of responsibility. Is Christian theology justified in making Israel as a whole jointly liable for the fault, the sin, the crime of some? Is it justified in pronouncing a collective condemnation? And in pronouncing thus, does it not commit a legal error, is it not mistaking one collectivity for another?

Its thesis is as follows: a people is committed by its qualified leaders and representatives, in the present case Pharisees and chief

[2] See pp. 112–116, [and n. 20], above.

priests, "the two great parties which contrived Jesus' death." Father Lagrange's opinion is categoric on this point: ". . . the leaders of the nation, by which he [Saint John] means above all the chief priests and the Pharisees. . . . the religious and political leaders, responsible for the practice of the cult and zealous about the Law, were perfectly qualified to represent the people and could be vested with their name ["the Jews"]." [3] With the burden on the people, reciprocally, of bearing the whole weight of the decisions and acts of its chiefs—of their crimes.

A like thesis leads far and deserves examination. [4] From having traversed centuries and rendered some services, it does not follow that it is correct. It is not enough to say at present: Pharisees and chief priests were the qualified representatives of Israel; this must be proved, and it must be proved as well that they are the guilty ones. To elucidate such a problem, we must leave none of its givens in shadow: from the hostility toward Jesus to his influence in Israel, the power exercised, the role he played, and the acceptance by the people.

✿   ✿   ✿

In the first ranks of Jesus' adversaries, commentators generally place the Pharisees and the scribes, as do the Gospels—and on the same level.

We have seen previously what these two groups were. [5]

The scribes, or doctors of the Law, were not all Pharisees; their authority, their prestige profited from the immense respect that all Is-

[3] Father Marie-Joseph Lagrange, O.P., ed. and tr., *Évangile selon saint Jean*, Paris, Gabalda, 1924, p. cxxxii. [A recent American commentary, equally categoric: "The Lord Jesus was officially rejected by the Jewish nation at his trial before Pilate" (*Young Teen Teacher* [United Methodist Church], April–June, 1968, p. 7; quoted in Gerald Strober ms. in preparation New York [Xerox], p. 57). —Ed.]

[4] The question of "German guilt" for the genocide of the Jews has been penetratingly studied by the German philosopher Karl Jaspers, as also by Eugen Kogon in his book *Organized Hell*. But Kogon does not accept the notion of collective responsibility as formulated by the Allied victors (*L'Enfer organisé*, tr., "Pour servir à l'histoire de ce temps" series, Paris, La Jeune Parque, 1947). [See, in English, as idem, *The Theory and Practice of Hell*, tr. Heinz Norden, New York, Farrar, Straus & Young, 1950.—Tr.] One will agree, however, that the responsibility of the Jewish people in the killing of Jesus and that of the German people in the extermination of six million Jews (1,800,000 of them children) are radically different cases.

[5] See p. 39, above.

rael professed for the Law. Those of them who sat in the Sanhedrin alongside the chief priests and elders held a part of the political and judiciary powers, which must also be defined.

The Pharisees, devotees of the written Law and oral tradition—the Torah and the Mishnah—exercised an influence in Israel's religious life which can be called unequaled. But of what order? Bearing less on persons than on customs, legislation, beliefs. Would we call them "religious leaders"? The terms "guides," "teachers," "inspirers" would seem preferable. Again I would attach some reservations, for their very piety, their devout formalism, their extreme concern with purity made them "separate"; avoiding all contact with the ignorant and impure mass of the *ammei ha-aretz*,[6] they formed a sort of caste of "saints," apart from the people.

Scribes and Pharisees had the loftiest image of themselves, certainly; they considered themselves the elite of Israel. Did this alone suffice to fetter the whole of Israel to them forever? After all, the scribes were only an association, the Pharisees only a party, a sect, a group—most influential, true, and most esteemed; but there were others, and of all sorts, and sometimes antagonists. John the Baptist issued from Israel too, before Jesus.

What do we know of their hostility to Jesus? How can we explain it, measure it? We know it only through the Gospels; thus we must take ourselves to the Gospel texts, never forgetting that the Gospels are prosecution evidence, written in a time when Christianity, in the process of de-Judaization, had no enemies more determined than the Pharisee doctors, the vanguard of official Judaism.[7]

The major texts occur mainly in the Synoptics; the controversies reported in the fourth Gospel carry less weight because, as we have seen, doctrinal inspiration prevails in Saint John's writing. The principal grievances of the scribes and Pharisees against Jesus are these:

Usurping God's sovereign power to forgive sins: Mk. 2:5–7 (Mt. 9:2–3; Lk. 5:20–21)

[6] "But this crowd, who do not know the law [and who admire Jesus], are accursed" (Jn. 7:49).

[7] According to Father Joseph Bonsirven, S.J., such observations are a sign of a bias common to most Jewish authors (*Les Juifs et Jésus*, Paris, Beauchesne, 1937, p. 173). But exactly the contrary is true: to omit such an observation is to neglect a fundamental principle of historical criticism, to refuse to acknowledge facts, and consequently to display a blind apriorism. It is of course easier to adopt as an axiom that the Gospels are "clear and irrefutable testimony" (*ibid.*, p. 172). R. Travers Herford speaks more objectively (*Les Pharisiens*, tr. Gabrielle Moyse, Paris, Payot, 1928, p. 246).

Eating and drinking with tax collectors and sinners (or, in Loisy's
  phrase, fraternizing with "the dregs of Judaism"): Mk. 2:16 (Mt.
  9:2; Lk. 5:30, and see 15:2)
Failing to have his disciples fast: Mk. 2:18 (Lk. 5:33)
Breaking the Sabbath: Mk. 2:23–24 (Mt. 12:1–2; Lk. 6:1–2);
  3:1–6 (Mt. 12:10–14; Lk. 6:6–11); Jn. 9:16
Working miracles through powers from Satan: Mk. 3:22 (Mt. 9:34,
  and see 12:24; Lk. 11:15)
Failing to observe the ritual cleansing of hands: Mk. 7:1–5 (Mt.
  15:1–2, 12)
Displaying excessive indulgence toward an adulterous woman: Jn.
  8:3–9
Attacking wealth: Lk. 16:13–14
Exhibiting messianic pretensions in Jerusalem: Lk. 19:39

The most relentless said of him, "He is a blasphemer! He is not a man
of God but of the devil!" In league with the chief priests, they sought
to seize him and have him killed (Mk. 11:18; 14:1; Mt. 21:46; Lk.
19:47), whether by stoning him themselves, Jewish fashion (Jn. 8:59;
10:31), or by delivering him to the Romans (Lk. 20:20).

Rages sustained, driven to paroxysm by vehement retorts from
Jesus, who hardly dealt tactfully with them, accusing them publicly
of pride, hypocrisy, sham, greed, iniquity, blindness, of themselves
having "neglected the weightier matters of the law, justice and mercy
and faith" (Mt. 23:1–39, quotation at 23:23; Mk. 12:38–40; Lk.
11:39–52; 20:45–47); assuring them that "Truly, . . . the tax collectors
and the harlots go into the kingdom of God before you" (Mt. 21:31).

At first sight or first reading of the Gospels, the opposition thus
seems absolute and irreducible.

At closer view, it is less simple.

We can in fact observe

that in his explicit prophecies of his Passion and death, Jesus mentions the scribes, never the Pharisees (Mk. 8:31 and 10:32–34, and
parallels);

that quite obviously, the scribes and Pharisees who hounded Jesus
are "some" among the Pharisees and scribes (it is easy, but arbitrary,
to generalize);

and that conversely, if Jesus' indictment seems to condemn the
scribes and Pharisees en bloc, it is only polemical violence, the vehemence of the angered prophet, scornful of nuances. It would be ab-

surd to take these sublime imprecations literally. Father Lebreton says of the apocalyptic discourse, "Nothing proves apriori that the words [of Jesus] must be interpreted more literally than similar expressions of Isaiah, Jeremiah, Ezekiel, or Joel." [8] Just as much may be said of the reprimand of the "scribes and Pharisees, hypocrites!" Who would dispute this? The scribes and Pharisees were not all vain and blind, not all hypocritical and greedy, not all iniquitous, without mercy and faith;

that in addition, as is apparent in certain texts (for example, Jn. 9:16), a number of the Pharisees who approached Jesus found favor with him;

and that, as other Gospel texts allow us to see, relations between the Pharisees and Jesus were not uniformly hostile:

Pharisees consult Jesus, asking his opinion: Mk. 10:2 (Mt. 19:3); 12:13–17 (Mt. 22:15–22; Lk. 20:20–26), 28–34 (Mt. 22:34–40; Lk. 10:25–37); Lk. 17:20–21; Jn. 3:1–2 (in some instances the evangelists say that Jesus was approached to be tested, but such a proceeding does not imply unremitting antagonism)
Jesus recommends observance of the Pharisees' teachings: Mt. 23:1–3
Jesus is invited to eat with Pharisees: Lk. 7:36; 11:37; 14:1
Pharisees warn Jesus against Herod: Lk. 13:31
A Pharisee opposes Jesus' arrest: Jn. 7:50–51

If these passages are placed side by side with those discussed a moment ago, we see clearly that they express a different reality. What can we properly deduce from this?

First, that the Pharisees were not all committed enemies of Jesus. Some maintained a wait-and-see attitude, hesitant and questioning, not intentionally hostile; some, more or less openly but quite genuinely, approved of him, admired him, believed in him. "Nicodemus and Joseph of Arimathea were only the most prominent of a fairly numerous group"; [9]

again, that the distance between the two teachings—the Pharisee and the Gospel—was not so great or the opposition so sharp, since when he attacked the hypocrisy of the Pharisees Jesus himself took pains to begin with this public declaration: ". . . so practice and observe whatever they tell you . . ." (Mt. 23:3). Father Lagrange, citing

---

[8] Father Jules Lebreton, S.J., *La Vie et l'enseignement de Jésus-Christ*, 2 vols., Paris, Beauchesne, 1931, II, 206.
[9] Lagrange, *op. cit.*, p. 343.

Saint Augustine, comments that "What is involved is only the authority of the Pharisees when they proclaim the Law." [10] When they proclaim it or interpret it. Even if we accept this restricted meaning, it is difficult to present Jesus' teaching as the negation of Pharisee teaching.

The bonds between the Gospel and Phariseeism, which we have already discussed,[11] are undeniable, no less than the Gospel's bonds with Essenism. Let us restrain ourselves from going too far along this path out of an instinctive reaction against the summariness and inexactitude found in tradition; let us leave to others the sophomoric view of Jesus as only a kind of dissident Pharisee teacher. It remains that the Gospel texts, examined impartially, oblige us to reject the traditional interpretation and to conclude:

it is not at all certain that the Pharisee party took a united position against Jesus and conspired to bring about his downfall; Father de Grandmaison acknowledges that among the Pharisees, "An imposing minority had not sinned against the light"; [12] actually, what grounds are there for speaking about "majority" or "minority"?

The only firm fact, going by the Gospels, is that Jesus set against himself and relentlessly fought against that common species of Pharisees and scribes, the undistinguished species (but look around you, don't you recognize it?) of deadly mortarboards, fortified with their theological virtuosity and their pompous authority, puffed up with scholarship and self-satisfaction; certified righteous men, sanctimonious hypocrites, who lent to God at weekly interest but genuflected profusely, who had "their works" and "their poor" as one has an all-inclusive (of hell too) insurance policy; pietistic and puritanical Tartuffes, a baleful standing army pilloried in the Talmud [13] as in the Gospels—all these, and they are surely numerous (in all times, in all places);

but not the others, not the respected and respectable masters of the Pharisee school, successors to Hillel, the Gamaliels, of whom perhaps Jesus and certainly Saint Paul were disciples, that Gamaliel who would say in the midst of the Sanhedrin, according to the Acts of the Apostles:

[10] *Idem*, ed. and tr., *Évangile selon saint Matthieu*, Paris, Gabalda, 1922, p. 437.

[11] See p. 84, above.

[12] Father Léonce de Grandmaison, S.J., *Jésus-Christ, sa personne, son message, ses preuves*, 2 vols., Paris, Beauchesne, 1928, I, 263.

[13] See p. 39, above.

Men of Israel, take care . . . . for if this plan or this undertaking is of men, it will fail; but if it is of God, you will not be able to overthrow them. You might even be found opposing God!

Acts 5:35, 38–39

In the last analysis, nothing allows us to believe and assert that the Pharisee masters, Judaism's true religious guides, the nation's spiritual elite, who alone may rightly be said to have been Israel's qualified representatives in certain respects, fought against Jesus, and even less that they wanted, demanded, and plotted his death.

Moreover, do we not have testimony from a historian of a nature to put us on guard against tendentious accusations, foolhardy generalizations? The only Jewish evidence—valid evidence—that we can erect in the face of Christian evidence—for the prosecution. It relates to a later event, but that event was the trial and execution of James, "the Lord's brother" (Gal. 1:19), head of the Christian church in Jerusalem. Now, what does Josephus say about this? "Those . . . inhabitants of the city [Jerusalem] who were considered the most fairminded and who were strict in observance of the law were offended at this [judgment]." [14] Weren't these "fair-minded" men, "strict" observers of the Law, Pharisees for the most part, pious Israelites of a kind with Hillel and Gamaliel? We have every reason to believe that these were no more set against Jesus than against James.

*   *   *

When Father Lagrange speaks of "the religious and political leaders, responsible for the practice of the cult," he is thinking principally of the chief priests, of that higher clergy, the priestly aristocracy, who in effect formed the leading class in Judea and who through the Temple, through the Sanhedrin, held the majority of religious, political, and judiciary powers, at least those that the imperial master of the hour, the Roman procurator, agreed to allow them.[15]

About these, as about the scribes and Pharisees, we must therefore ask:

[14] Flavius Josephus, *The Jewish Antiquities,* 20:201 (=20:9:1). [Quotation taken from *ibid.,* tr. Louis H. Feldman, in *Josephus,* 9 vols., "Loeb Classical Library" series, Cambridge, Mass., Harvard University Press, 1965, IX, 497.—Tr.]
[15] "After the death of these kings [Herod and Archelaus], the constitution [of Judea] became an aristocracy, and the high priests were entrusted with the leadership of the nation," wrote Josephus in *The Jewish Antiquities,* 20:251 (=20:10:5). [Quotation taken from *ibid.,* tr. Feldman, IX, 523.—Tr.]

first, to what degree and why they took a position against Jesus;

second (if their hostility be proven), to what degree they can be said, in Father Lagrange's phrase, to have been "perfectly qualified to represent the [Jewish] people," it being clear that "official representatives"—another phrase of Father Lagrange's applied to the chief priests [16]—does not necessarily signify "qualified representatives."

The chief priests are introduced rather late in the Gospels, particularly in the Synoptics. The texts mentioning their predisposition to hostility, their murderous designs are fewer than those where the Pharisees and scribes appear. The reason is simple: the chief priests were men of the Temple, of Jerusalem; according to the Synoptics, then, it would have been only at the end of his ministry that Jesus, arriving in Jerusalem, found himself contending with them directly. There is nothing improbable in the notion that the outcome of the conflict came promptly, almost immediately, on the part of an iron-fisted governing body, brutal guardians of the established order. Yet, as we have seen,[17] it is possible to believe that Jesus was not a new-comer to Jerusalem, that he had already visited there, that the leading oligarchy of chief priests thus had gathered information and taken a stand on him. The texts concerning them, and they are clear and in agreement, show no split, no trace of the divergences observed among the Pharisees.[18]

The text references are brief, with the exception of the Johannine passages at 7:31–32, 45–49 and 11:47–53. Even so, they show clearly that in the eyes of that political and authoritative higher clergy, Jesus was a dangerous dreamer, a miracle-worker, a crowd-charmer, a Galilean agitator of a strange breed ("Can anything good come out of Nazareth?"—Jn. 1:46) who seemed to be playing messiah, without his game being very clear to anyone, who dared to attack the authority of the priests even in the Temple itself, and who, disturbing the peace on the eve of the Passover celebrations, risked drawing Roman thunderbolts down on Jerusalem. Did they need any other reasons for eliminating this nuisance?

[16] Lagrange, . . . *Jean*, p. cxxxii.

[17] See p. 95, above.

[18] Mk. 11:18, 27–28 (Mt. 21:23; Lk. 20:2); 12:12, "they" being "the chief priests and the scribes and the elders" named in 11:27 (Mt. 21:45–46; Lk. 20:19); 14:1 (Mt. 26:3; Lk. 22:2); Mt. 21:15–16; Jn. 7:31–32, 45–49; 11:47–53. While the fourth Gospel does not mention the chief priests explicitly prior to 7:31–32, we know that when it says "the Jews," this can be understood to mean the chief priests, the scribes, and the Pharisees.

Let us admire in passing, let us admire for its credibility the dialogue reported in John 11:47–53, the unforgettable words of Caiaphas: "You know nothing at all; you do not understand that it is expedient for you that one man should die . . . and that the whole nation should not perish" (vv. 49–50). Immortal Caiaphas! The echo of your words has reverberated from century to century: didn't we ourselves still hear it with miraculous clarity just before the turn of our own century, in the course of that other famous debate in which French Catholicism, almost unanimous behind its clergy, crushed an innocent Jew? [19] Does the comparison shock you? It involves principles, not persons. One trial throws light on the other, helps to fix responsibilities, bursts the national framework in which people try to enclose them; for nothing resembles yesterday's conformists (Jewish) more than today's conformists (Christian). The same species. The same race.

Caiaphas. I concede to Father Lagrange that Caiaphas is a representative personage, eminently so; it remains to be seen in what sense.

That year, then—which was the year of Jesus' Passion—Caiaphas was high priest, that is, the highest dignitary in Israel, the supreme head of the clergy, leader of the cult, head of the unique sanctuary— the Temple, president of the Great Council, or Sanhedrin, in Jerusalem. What honors and powers gathered around one head, and what responsibilities! Whoever became high priest in Israel retained the post for life. Theoretically, at least. In fact, the high functionary sent from Rome to govern Judea, the procurator, disposed of the high priesthood as he saw fit, as Herod the Great, king of Palestine and a tyrant detested by the Jews, had done before him. The hard and greedy Roman found this profitable, monetarily and politically, for he was paid dear for his favors, and as these could be revoked at any time, the Jewish high priest was in a totally dependent position—so much so that the Roman commandant of Antonia Fortress, which dominated the Temple, kept under lock and key the sumptuous vestments which the high priest could use only three or four times a year, for the high festivals, including Yom Kippur. Was ever a more humiliating servitude devised? [20] Hence the duration of the high priesthood varied arbitrarily according to the will or the caprice of the Roman

---

[19] [Alfred Dreyfus.—Ed.]

[20] It was abolished by the Emperor Tiberius in the year 36 on application from the Jews.

procurator and the obsequiousness, adroitness, subservience of the Jewish high priest: one would see himself dismissed like a valet hardly a year after his installation; another—a Caiaphas—would succeed in holding his place as long as eighteen years (A.D. 18–36), at what a price we can imagine; still, each retained from his turn at the high priesthood—whether brief or long—the title and dignity of high priest, which entailed certain privileges, such as sitting on the Sanhedrin.

But there is another aspect, and a typical one, which needs to be emphasized: the selection by the procurator, the true master of Israel, was made only within narrow limits, among a small number of families, three or four, and always the same. Thus, Caiaphas was the son-in-law of Annas (or Hanan or Anan or Ananos), who had himself been high priest from the year 6 to the year 15 and whose five sons attained to the supreme office in turn. The chief priests, or as some translators write, "the princes among the priests," thus formed a restricted and closed oligarchy, an exclusive caste, jealous of its privileges, both rich and rapacious—to the point of robbing the lower clergy of its share in the tithes; [21] harsh but compliant, despotic but servile, servile toward the all-powerful Roman but despotic toward the Jewish people, at least those of the lower classes, over whom police at its command, well-schooled police, exercised their fists and clubs according to the rules of the art. The ballad of the "wounds," a popular song included in the Talmud, has preserved the memory for us:

> Woe is me because of the house of Boethus; woe is me
> because of their staves!
> Woe is me because of the house of Hanin [Annas], woe is
> me because of their whisperings!
> Woe is me because of the house of Kathros [Kantheras],
> woe is me because of their pens!
> Woe is me because of the house of Ishmael the son of
> Phabi, woe is me because of their fists!
> For they are High Priests and their sons are [Temple]
> treasurers and their sons-in-law are trustees and their
> servants beat the people with staves.
> Pesahim 57a [BT; line breaks added] [22]

[21] Josephus, op. cit., 28:8.

[22] Quoted in Joseph Klausner, Jésus de Nazareth, tr. Isaac Friedmann, Paris, Payot, 1933, p. 489 [and in idem, Jesus of Nazareth . . . , p. 337.—Tr.]. The terms "whisperings" and "pens" in the second and third lines would be allusions to secret denunciations, oral and written. [Klausner points out that the two closing lines may not belong to the song.—Ed.]

It is possible to believe, as we shall see, that this oligarchic caste
—four powerful families in all, brutal, cynical, and ill-famed [23]—bore
the heaviest part of the responsibility for Jesus' arrest and delivery to
the Romans. And it is this caste which our authoritative theologians
and exegetes, for lack of better, baptize as "perfectly qualified" representatives of the Jewish nation. "Perfectly disqualified" would be
more accurate. Vichy in Jerusalem. And worse yet, if we recall that
Vichy could at least claim some democratic basis and exhibited only
a secular (or military) dishonor.

✿   ✿   ✿

There remain the "elders," expressly designated in Jesus' prophecies
(Mk. 8:31; Mt. 16:21; Lk. 9:22), members of the Sanhedrin along with
the chief priests and scribes, but about whom the Gospel texts say almost nothing elsewhere. Mark 11:27 and the parallel passages in Matthew 21:23 and Luke 20:1 mention them in the company of chief
priests and scribes when these came to ask Jesus, "By what authority
are you doing these things . . . ?" Matthew 26:3–4 and Luke 19:47
mention them likewise with chief priests as resolved to seize Jesus in
order to have him killed. John does not name them explicitly anywhere.

How is this silence to be filled? Because Matthew 26:3 says "the
elders of the people" and Luke 19:47 "the principal men of the people," must we see "qualified" representatives in the persons of these
elders? Not in the least. The elders were the notables of Jerusalem,
leaders and representatives not of the people but of the great families,
who, powerful through their wealth, constituted a secular aristocracy
alongside the priestly aristocracy. Both groups were Sadducees, conservative, rigidly protective of the established order, disposed to deal
severely with every innovation, every innovator arising from the
people and stirring them up dangerously. Perhaps too, in the case of
Jesus, these rich personages felt themselves to be the direct butt of
the scathing contempt he expressed with regard to money and the
wealthy: "But woe to you that are rich . . ." (Lk. 6:24); "You cannot
serve God and mammon" (Mt. 6:24).

---

[23] Another broadside in the same tractate reproaches these priestly families for
"defil[ing] the Temple of the Lord," for "desecrating the sacred sacrifices of
Heaven," for displaying a disgusting gluttony, and so forth (Pesahim 57a [BT]).

The attempts to veil these texts are useless; they explode in the midst of the Gospel. Péguy said, "Jesus' horror of the wealthy is terrifying. He loves only poverty and the poor." And again:

The terrifying anger that runs below the surface of the Gospels is not at all anger against nature or against man before grace [I would add: is not at all anger against the nation, against Israel]; it is uniquely anger against *money*, and truly, it must be that no one wanted to see it for this reprobation not to have blazed before everyone's eyes.[24]

But who says that no one wanted to see it, that no one saw it, with Jesus present and speaking, and that this "reprobation" blazing "before everyone's eyes" was not repaid in turn, mercilessly, by a coalition of the rich, "principal men of the people" or "princes among the priests"? Do we not have James's testimony (5:1, 6 [CCD]) on this?

Come now, you rich. . . . You have condemned and put to death the just. . . .

Embarrassing testimony, not to be cited.[25]

However, other testimony from Scripture puts us on guard against hasty generalizations. It gives us the name of one of these wealthy notables, "a respected member of the council": and it is Joseph of Arimathea, "who was also himself looking for the kingdom of God" (Mk. 15:43).

* * *

A specific number of chief priests, elders, and scribes made up the Sanhedrin.

When Jesus announced to the Twelve that he would be "rejected by the elders and the chief priests and the scribes," he was alluding to the Sanhedrin, and it is the Sanhedrin to which the Gospels—the Synoptics, at least—assign the primary role in Jesus' arrest, judgment, and sentencing to death.

What was the Sanhedrin, then? And what were its powers, particu-

[24] Charles Péguy, *Lettres et entretiens* [Letters and Conversations], ed. Marcel Péguy, Paris, Artisans du Livre, 1927 [repub. Paris, Éd. de Paris, 1954], pp. 160, 187.
[25] Father Joseph Chaine dates the Epistle of James in the neighborhood of the year 60 (*L'Épître de saint Jacques* [The Epistle of Saint James], Paris, Gabalda, 1927). Luther, who found it an impediment to his doctrine of salvation by faith alone, called it an "epistle of straw."

larly its legal powers? In our investigations of responsibilities, this is a point which it is essential to determine.

But here history intervenes, and is compelled to make some painful admissions. It confesses honestly that it can provide only probabilities, feeble and scanty, and almost no certainties. There does indeed exist a tractate called Sanhedrin in the Mishnah, which contains a minute description of the composition of the assembly, its functions, its rules of procedure as a criminal court. But then, how rigorously can we go applying to Jesus' time, to Caiaphas' Sanhedrin, a description drawn some 170 years later by writers who doubtless intended to define the tradition but who were hardly concerned with historic considerations?

What we know, what we can reasonably conjecture, boils down to very little.

All the testimony, the most valid of which is that of the Jewish historian Flavius Josephus, indicates that the Sanhedrin was an aristocratic council, dominated by the priestly oligarchy and presided over by the incumbent high priest. The doctors of the Law—the scribes— had been members for about a century. Through them, or at least through some of them, Pharisee trends were represented. Through the chief priests and elders, the preponderant influence remained with the Sadducees.

There is no sure indication of the size or the method of recruiting the membership of the Sanhedrin. It is generally said, following the indications in the Mishnah, to have numbered seventy or seventy-one; this is possible, but nothing proves that it was so at the beginning of the first century. It is supposed that the Sanhedrists recruited by co-option and that their membership was for life; this is only a hypothesis, and another is not ruled out, is not less likely—that the Roman authorities intervened in their selection as in the appointment of the high priest. Father Lebreton, citing George Foot Moore, recognizes "that they were perhaps named by the political authorities, Herod or the Romans . . . ," and that "The most influential members were the leaders of the priests." [26]

Because it was the supreme council of Jerusalem—the Holy City —the Sanhedrin possessed a certain moral authority over all the Jews of Palestine and of the Diaspora. Its actual authority extended only

[26] Lebreton, *op. cit.*, II, 361.

over the narrow confines of the procuratorial territory—essentially
Judea—and was under the procurator's control.

The Sanhedrin was both a government council and a court of justice. How far did its competence reach in criminal matters, and did it
or did it not have the right to pass a sentence of capital punishment
or to have the sentence carried out—by stoning, according to Jewish
custom [27]—in the case of a religious crime? This is the knot of the
problem.[28] Interminable debates, too often dominated by prejudice,
have not succeeded in unknotting it. In the opinion of some historians
—who reject the Gospel accounts in toto—the Sanhedrin had the
most extensive jurisdiction in religious matters, the right of condemning to death and also the right of carrying out the execution;
a number of capital executions in the period from the Crucifixion
to the destruction of the Temple would prove this (the execution of Stephen, Acts 6:12 ff.; 7:58–60; of James, Josephus' *Jewish Antiquities*, 20:200 [20:9:1]; of the daughter of a priest, Sanhedrin 52b).
From this it is deduced that Jesus, having been crucified and not
stoned, was judged and condemned by the Romans, not by the Jews.
In the opinion of other historians, who accept some of the Gospel accounts and compare them with certain talmudic texts, the Sanhedrin
lost the right to pass capital sentences, either (as in the Talmud) forty
years or so before the destruction of the Temple, which occurred in
the year 70, or (by a reasoning process, for lack of documentary evidence) on the establishment of the Roman regime in Judea, which
was in the year 6. Accordingly, Jesus would have been delivered by
the Sanhedrin to Pontius Pilate, the procurator, who alone possessed
the *jus gladii*, the "right of the sword" or power over life and death. A
third group of historians assume that the Gospel accounts correspond
with historic reality; and their thesis is that the Sanhedrin retained
the right to pronounce capital sentences, but under the control and on
condition of the procurator's confirmation, he alone being empowered
to carry out the sentence. This would explain the dual trial, Jewish
and Roman, the double sentencing, its execution by the Romans, the
nailing to the cross.

To tell the truth, if one holds strictly to the demands of sound his-

---

[27] The condemned could also be burned, decapitated, or suffocated, but not
crucified. Crucifixion was a specifically Roman punishment.

[28] [Paul Winter's *On the Trial of Jesus* (in English), Berlin, De Gruyter, 1961,
discusses this point extensively.—Ed.]

toric method, none of the arguments put forth—in any direction—
appears decisive, capable of producing complete certainty. The fact
that the procurator had the *jus gladii*, which is not debatable, does
not necessarily rule out that the Sanhedrin had power over life and
death, particularly where a religious crime was concerned. The capital sentences invoked in support of the first theory are troubling facts,
but it can be maintained, with the help of the texts, that they were ir-
regular. The talmudic texts, however categoric they may seem, are
unreliable and contradict each other. And one is indeed forced to observe that the Gospel texts themselves, however worthy of respect
they may be, display serious divergences. Finally, if the condemnation brought down by the Jewish authorities was valid only after it
was approved by the procurator, it does not follow that a Roman
punishment like crucifixion had to be substituted for the usual Jewish
punishment in such a case, stoning. This is the opinion of Maurice
Goguel:

> It seems indeed that what was taken away [from the Sanhedrin] was not
> the right to pronounce capital sentences but only the right to carry them
> out before they had received the approval of the Roman authorities. If Pi-
> late had only ratified a condemnation passed by the Sanhedrin, as the Gos-
> pel accounts seem to suppose, Jesus would have suffered a Jewish punish-
> ment; he would have been stoned or strangled, he would not have been
> crucified.[29]

For lack of certainties, we are thus reduced to conjectures. The
best-grounded, by analogy, seems to be the following. Thanks to legal
documents found in Egypt, we know today that in certain important
cases, the prefect of Egypt—the Roman governor of that imperial
territory—gave over to local authorities the task of investigating the
matter; we can say that the same should have been true in Judea, and
that consequently the Sanhedrin functioned in certain cases as a court
of judicial inquiry, a grand jury. Such would have been its role in the
matter of Jesus of Nazareth. And that in no measure diminishes its responsibility.

But that in no measure entails responsibility on the part of the Jewish nation. Whom did the Sanhedrin represent? Basically, an oligarchy of priests and the wealthy, itself completely dominated in Jesus'
time by the powerful Annas family, which circled within the Roman
orbit. Now, we know how vital, fierce, indomitable was the patriotism

[29] Maurice Goguel, "Christianisme primitif," in Raoul Gorce and Maxime Mortier, eds., *Histoire générale des religions*, Paris, Quillet, 1945, II, 196.

of the Palestinian Jews, a patriotism solidly grafted onto their faith. And it is this patriot people that commentators want to make jointly liable for the crimes committed by its leaders, supposedly its qualified representatives [30] but in fact creatures of pagan Rome and representatives of a detested caste, whose single concern was to safeguard its powers, its privileges, and its goods!

❊   ❊   ❊

Yet if there is one point on which the Gospel texts are agreed and positive, it is precisely the distinction which must be made between the people—the popular masses—and the oligarchic clan accountable for initiating the proceedings against Jesus. All the evangelists made a point of emphasizing that this clan acted unbeknownst to and despite the people. And it is evident that the leaders of the clan, its most active element, were the chief priests; associated with them were sometimes the scribes—or the Pharisees—and sometimes the elders. But Judas was not confused: when he had made his fatal decision, it was directly to the chief priests—doubtless to Caiaphas or Annas—that he went. Let us reread the texts:

[Mark:]   The chief priests and scribes heard of this, and looked for some means of making away with him; they were afraid of him, because all the multitude was so full of admiration at his teaching [11:18 (RK)].

And they tried to arrest him, but feared the multitude . . . [12:12].

It was now two days before the Passover and the feast of Unleavened Bread. And the chief priests and the scribes were

---

[30] Or its "spiritual leaders," according to Jacques Maritain's theory, leaders with whom all Israel would be jointly responsible "For the people of Israel is a *corpus mysticum*, a holy nation," and for whose error it must pay over centuries—indeed, "forever" (*Raison et raisons* [Reason and Reasons], Paris, Egloff, 1947, p. 232). [Maritain expounds the same argument in his *Ransoming the Time*, tr. Harry Lorin Binsse, New York, Scribner, 1946, pp. 151–155, and his *A Christian Looks at the Jewish Question*, New York, Longmans, Green, 1939, pp. 26–27.—Ed.] The thesis is fundamentally wrong. It does not follow from Israel's identity as a "mystical body" that it was implicated in the crime of a Caiaphas, who had no right whatever to the title of "spiritual leader." Jacques Maritain is careful to particularize that his "concept is only valid from the highest metaphysical and transcendent viewpoint" (*loc. cit.*). But in such a case it is hard to make an absolute distinction between the metaphysical plane and the other, the historical plane. Would the metaphysical thesis itself be conceivable without a historic basis? [Quotations taken from Jacques Maritain, *The Range of Reason*, New York, Scribner, 1952, p. 131.—Tr.]

seeking how to arrest him by stealth, and kill him; for they said, "Not during the feast, lest there be a tumult of the people" [14:1–2].

Then Judas Iscariot, who was one of twelve, went to the chief priests in order to betray him to them [14:10].

[Matthew:] When the chief priests and the Pharisees. . . . tried to arrest him, they feared the multitudes, because they held him to be a prophet [Mt. 21:45–46].

Then the chief priests and the elders of the people gathered in the palace of the high priest, who was called Caiaphas, and took counsel together in order to arrest Jesus by stealth and kill him. But they said, "Not during the feast, lest there be a tumult among the people" [26:3–5].

Then one of the twelve, who was called Judas Iscariot, went to the chief priests and said, "What will you give me if I deliver him to you?" [26:14–15].

[Luke:] And he was teaching daily in the temple. The chief priests and the scribes and the principal men of the people sought to destroy him; but they did not find anything they could do, for all the people hung upon his words [19:47–48].

Now the feast of Unleavened Bread drew near, which is called the Passover. And the chief priests and the scribes were seeking how to put him to death; for they feared the people.

. . . [Judas] went away and conferred with the chief priests and captains [of the Temple] how he might betray him to them. . . . [Then he] sought an opportunity to betray him to them in the absence of the multitude [22:1–6].

While less clearly than in the Synoptics, the opposition between the leading clan and the people comes to light also in the fourth Gospel:

[John:] Yet many of the people believed him. . . . the chief priests and Pharisees sent officers to arrest him.

. . . but no one laid hands on him.

The officers then went back to the chief priests and Pharisees, who said to them, . . . "Are you led astray, you also? Have any of the authorities or of the Pharisees believed in him? But this crowd, who do not know the law, are accursed" [7:31–32, 44–49].

Many of the Jews therefore, who . . . had seen what he did, believed in him. . . . So the chief priests and the Pharisees gathered the council, and said, ". . . If we let him go on thus, every one will believe in him. . . ." So from that day on they took counsel how to put him to death [11:45–48, 53].

Perfect agreement: not only of the four evangelists with each other, but of the event as they describe it with the prediction which Jesus had made to the Twelve. These texts are truly too emphatic to be challengeable.

✿   ✿   ✿

Thus, the first stage of our inquiry into the crime and its responsible authors has already led us to some notable results.

According to the Synoptic Gospels, Jesus expressly predicted that he would be the victim of "the elders and the chief priests and the scribes"; he did not say "the Pharisees"; he never implicated the Jewish people.

According to the four Gospels, the Pharisees and the scribes were not solidly hostile to Jesus. Nothing proves that the elite of Judaism was involved in the murder plot; on the contrary, there are good reasons to doubt it.

According to historical evidence, the dominant influence in Jerusalem and in the Sanhedrin lay with a priestly and secular oligarchy composed of a few great families, the most powerful of which was that of Annas, father-in-law of the high priest Caiaphas. This oligarchy, Sadducee in outlook, cruel and tyrannical in conduct, was itself subjugated to Rome and detested by the people. It was this oligarchy, in all likelihood, which played the determining role. This is likewise the clearly expressed opinion of Father Lebreton: "It was the Sadducees who had played the decisive role in the trial of Christ." [31]

The Jewish nation could not have been identified with this caste in any way. Not only did the people have no part in the intrigue woven against Jesus, but the four evangelists testify that the leaders acted unbeknownst to the people, despite them, and in fear of them.

It is true that we are only on the threshold of the Passion. In the short moment which confines it,[32] it remains to discover whether there was a shift of opinion, whether the attitude of the people changed radically between one day and the next, whether—as it continues to be taught in print, by word, and through pictures—the Jew-

---

[31] In Father Jules Lebreton, S.J., and Jacques Zeiller, *L'Église primitive*, vol. I of Augustin Fliche and Victor Martin, eds., *Histoire de l'Église depuis les origines jusqu'à nos jours*, Paris, Bloud et Gay, 1934, p. 138.

[32] See p. 288, n. 2, below.

ish people joined Jesus' enemies in order to obtain his death, dispar-
age him and grind him down, even on the cross.

But first, some preliminary observations are required on the
knowledge we have of the trial, the condemnation, and the execution
of the judgment.

PROPOSITION 18

JOAN OF ARC WAS ALSO SENTENCED BY A TRIBUNAL OF CHIEF
PRIESTS AND SCRIBES—WHO WERE NOT JEWISH—BUT
ONLY AFTER A LONG TRIAL OF WHICH WE HAVE THE
COMPLETE AND AUTHENTIC TEXT. THIS IS NOT TRUE OF
THE TRIAL OF JESUS, WHICH WAS HURRIED THROUGH,
WHETHER IN THREE HOURS OR IN THREE DAYS, AND IS
KNOWN ONLY BY HEARSAY. NO OFFICIAL TRANSCRIPT,
NO CONTEMPORARY TESTIMONY ON THE EVENT HAS
COME DOWN TO US.

In the order of faith, I agree, there is no comparison possible, even thinkable: the distance between the event and any other event whatever is infinite.

In the order of history, it is a different matter. By his human, fully human life, Jesus belongs to history, to the fullness of history.

Jesus' trial, his sentencing to death, his nailing to the cross are historic events, as such susceptible of being placed face to face with their ilk—or events of the same family—and as such subject to all the rules which are requisite in historic inquiry.

Now, of all known events—of the same family—the closest is not the trial of Socrates; it is the trial of Joan of Arc, which is close by its nature if not by its date: 1431, fourteen hundred years' remove. From the dual standpoint of responsibilities and historic knowledge, the comparison is compelling; it promises to be suggestive.

✿　　✿　　✿

Our knowledge of Joan's trial, only some five hundred years behind us, is almost perfect, owing to the complete and authentic text of the record preserved in our archives, an incomparable and eloquent document.

"A fine trial": meaning a regular trial, in good form, conducted slowly, solemnly, methodically (which does not rule out: perfidiously), according to all the rules of canon procedure and law. A trial for heresy and sorcery before Church judges, and what judges! Eminent in their honors, their titles, their learning, their renown: the representative of the Most Holy Inquisition—that is, of the Holy See —the Lord Bishop of Beauvais (in whose diocese the said Joan had been captured); the abbots of the most important Norman abbeys and canons of Rouen, persons of distinction; doctors from the illustrious University of Paris, then the highest authority recognized in Latin Christendom, arbiters of kings and popes. This court, gathered to judge the peasant girl of Domrémy—a child, less than twenty years old— was almost a council.

Or a great sanhedrin. There is no doubt: these were indeed the same, the same chief priests and the same scribes; and the lead player of the trial, Lord Bishop Pierre Cauchon, was Caiaphas, Caiaphas in person or his spiritual descendant; and all together, they were indeed that "generation"—*genea*—denounced by Jesus, "this adulterous and sinful generation" (Mk. 8:38): a certain species of men, a certain family of spirits, a certain race, equally Aryan or Semite, to be found in all places, in all times, in all of humanity, there, always there to judge, censure, condemn, from the height of its theological arrogance and its priestly throne.

They condemned her, naturally, as they had condemned Jesus. But the irony is that they condemned her in the name of Jesus (the human genius for corruption is incomparable). They declared her a blasphemer against God—"Then the high priest tore his robes, and said, 'He has uttered blasphemy . . .'" (Mt. 26:65), a blasphemer against the saints, contemptuous of God even in His sacraments; a violater of divine law, sacred doctrine, and ecclesiastical sanctions; seditious, cruel, apostate, schismatic, engaged in a thousand fallacies about our faith; and on all these counts rashly guilty toward God and Holy Church. And when Joan, after the public abjuration, had fallen into their traps and been proclaimed "relapsed," the delicate hypocrisy of the clerics "delivered her to the secular arm," that is, the English occupation troops, to be burned alive on the Place du Vieux-Marché in Rouen. And it was a great spectacle, and among the spectators some laughed, others cried.

Certainly, in this shower of ignominies, partisan feeling figured importantly. France in that era was cut in two, torn apart by a civil war which was paralleled by a foreign war and occupation: this is familiar to us. Joan's judges belonged to the Anglo-Burgundian faction. They esteemed themselves no less good Frenchmen for this; nor were they esteemed any less good Catholics:

> For in sum [as a modern man of the Church has the audacity to write], the judges of Joan of Arc were not monsters; they were most proper and well-schooled, deeply respectful of the law and of the established order. It was they who wrote to the Pope: "If we have reached the point where deviners babbling falsely in the name of God, like a certain female [Joan of Arc] taken in the boundaries of the Diocese of Beauvais, are more welcome to the fickle populace than are pastors and doctors, all is lost, religion will perish, faith crumbles, the Church is trampled underfoot, Satan's wickedness will dominate the world." Yes, it is not sure that we would not have been with Joan of Arc's judges against "the fickle populace," or at least with Charles VII, who abandoned her, after all.[1]

Very well. Let us ponder this admirable text. But does anyone not see that it can readily be transposed fourteen centuries and very realistically made the words of Jesus' judges?

> If we have reached the point where magicians and miracle-workers babbling falsely in the name of God, like a certain yokel of Galilee taken in the garden of Gethsemane, are more welcome to the fickle populace than are chief priests and doctors, all is lost, religion will perish, faith crumbles, the Priesthood is trampled underfoot, Satan's wickedness will dominate the world.

In the same way, Father R. L. Bruckberger's commentary on this passage can be transposed:

> For in sum, the judges of Jesus were not monsters; they were most proper and well-schooled, deeply respectful of the Law and of the established order. . . . Yes, it is not sure that we would not have been with Jesus' judges against "the fickle populace," or at least with the people and the Apostles, who abandoned him, after all.

They rehabilitated Joan, it is true. Twenty-five years after having burned her alive, they rehabilitated her. But at the time (and isn't it the time itself which alone is important, in the eyes of God as in the eyes of men?) not one voice in the Church rose against the evil of her condemnation, not one voice protested against the infamy of her martyrdom. Her judges, "most proper and well-schooled," were heaped with honors and rewards. And if in fact a rehabilitation proceeding

[1] Father R. L. Bruckberger, O.P., *La Valeur humaine du saint* [The Human Value of the Holy], "Les Cahiers du Rhône, Série blanche," no. 16, Neuchâtel, La Baconnière, 1943, p. 13.

was opened twenty-five years later, we owe it to historic truth to rec-
 organize that political motives were largely—almost wholly—responsible for this; for the king of France, Charles VII, had become the
most powerful prince in Christendom in the interim, and was in a
position to impose the action on the pope: it was not fitting that it
should be said that he, "most Christian king," had had recourse to the
good offices of a sorceress in his young days.

Let us then record a point, a first point. The official, authentic documents establish beyond any possible challenge that Joan's punishment, that crime, was the work of qualified representatives of French
theological scholarship and the Catholic Church, in close collaboration with the foreign occupying power, the Englishman. Not the king
of France (for whom Joan had sacrificed everything) nor the highest
ecclesiastical authorities—of France or of Rome—nor the people of
France intervened in any way, although time was not lacking to
them: four months from the beginning of the trial to the flaming
stake. Let us now grant (despite the paucity of documentation, which
we have not yet discussed) that Jesus' punishment, that greater crime,
was the work of qualified representatives of Jewish theological
scholarship—the scribes—and of the higher Jewish clergy—the chief
priests—in close collaboration with the foreign occupying power, the
Roman. Trial and execution took only either less than twenty-four
hours or at most three days, depending on whether the official or the
Essenian calendar is followed; [2] in any event, a very short time for
any intervention, of whatever kind. These first observations alone
allow us to measure the responsibilities involved. Why should we
limit responsibility in the first case to the judges, and to them only?
Why in the second case should we extend it inordinately in time and
space to the whole Jewish nation, to eternity?

If you must have a continuum of responsible subjects, then seek it
where it really exists, according to historic as well as evangelic truth:

---

[2] According to the discoveries made in the Qumran caves, the Essenian sect
used a special calendar, considered to be revealed, on which Passover fell three
days earlier than on the official calendar. If Jesus followed the Essenian calendar,
as some have tried to demonstrate, the course of his trial and Passion could have
spread over three days rather than a few hours. See the study by Annie Jaubert,
La Date de la Cène [The Date of the Last Supper], Paris, Gabalda, 1957.

Among recent works in which the problem of Jesus' trial is examined, let us
signal Oscar Cullmann, Dieu et César, Neuchâtel, Delachaux et Niestlé, 1956
[see, in English, as idem, The State in the New Testament, tr., New York, Scribner,
1966], and Paul Winter, On the Trial of Jesus, Berlin, De Gruyter, 1961.

in that fertile lineage which put forth Joan's judges after Jesus', Cauchon after Caiaphas, that imperishable race of the "proper and well-schooled."

✿   ✿   ✿

A second point to elucidate in this engrossing comparison. We have indicated the authentic and solid nature of the documentary foundation on which our knowledge of Joan of Arc's trial rests. And what exactly is the nature of the documentary foundation for our knowledge of Jesus' trial, almost four times more remote in time—nineteen hundred years against five hundred?

Certain apologists reply without hesitation: excellent, unfailingly solid. "Isn't demonstrating that the Jews did not spill Jesus' blood tantamount to attempting to deny the evidence, namely, the clear and irrefutable testimony of the Gospels?" asserts Father Bonsirven,[3] who is a man of formal scholarship. Daniel-Rops, who is only a man of letters, goes farther:

> The four evangelists have reported the decisive events [of the Passion] . . . with a wealth of detail and striking parallelism. Saint John himself, who usually does not return to what the Synoptics have narrated, feels the need to say everything he knows, everything he remembers. From this point onward, one can reconstruct the events hour by hour, and accompany Jesus in what will be his Passion.[4]

On the Protestant side, Edmond Stapfer is even more categoric: "We have the facts, the sources, the accounts of the witnesses. . . . Everything here is clear, visible, cloudless." For those last moments of Jesus' life, the historian is no longer constrained to resort to conjectures; he can "display historic certainties," he disposes of "documents of an unchallengeable authenticity." Doubtless "There is a swarm of small contradictions," but "this is always the case in history. The greater the abundance of documents, the greater the burden on the critic."[5]

---

[3] Father Joseph Bonsirven, S.J., *Les Juifs et Jésus*, Paris, Beauchesne, 1937, p. 172.

[4] Henry Daniel-Rops, *Histoire sainte: Jéus en son temps*, Paris, Fayard, 1945, p. 464.

[5] Edmond Stapfer, *La Mort et la résurrection de Jésus-Christ* [The Death and Resurrection of Jesus Christ], vol. III of *Jésus-Christ, sa personne, son autorité, son oeuvre*, Paris, Fischbacher, 1898, pp. iv, v, 231.

What could be clearer, more reassuring for trusting readers? But in all conscience, the historian must enter a denial of these startling statements. To express the truth of the documentary situation, we need only reverse them:

we do not have "the sources, the accounts of the witnesses";

nothing of what we have "is clear, visible, cloudless," nothing "irrefutable";

we do not dispose of "documents of an unchallengeable authenticity";

and consequently, we cannot in any way reach "historic certainties."

The only acceptable proposition is that in this "abundance" of details, "There is a swarm of . . . contradictions"; it remains to be seen whether they are "small."

Let us speak seriously. When the historic event is a criminal trial, a good part of which unrolled behind closed doors—interrogation, deliberation by the judges—what sure means do we have of knowing it if we do not dispose of some record taken while the court was sitting, in proper and due form (as in the case of Joan of Arc)? Or at the very least, in the case of Jesus finally judged and condemned to death by the Roman procurator Pontius Pilate, some official report from this high functionary, a report about which we would still have to discover whether it is genuine and whether its author did not have good reason to more or less distort the facts related. Do we need to add that we have neither one, neither a court record nor an official report? Moreover, there is every possibility that a report of this kind never existed. "For Pilate," writes Maurice Goguel, "Jesus' sentencing and execution were only . . . a routine preventive police action." [6]

This lack, the absence of an authentic document of this sort has appeared to be so serious, so troubling to Christian apologists that they set to work rather early to fabricate some. Oh, let us not wax indignant! Intellectual honesty is the rarest thing, the least well-distributed thing in the world (from certain indications, one might fear that it is on its way today to disappearing rapidly and totally). In that time, much less even than in our day, people were hardly bothered by scruples in this respect. In Jewish circles there flourished from an early date a particular literature called "pseudepigraphic" because

---

[6] Maurice Goguel, "Christianisme primitif," in Raoul Gorce and Maxime Mortier, eds., Histoire générale des religions, Paris, Quillet, 1945, II, 176.

the authors of these writings (who were anonymous) did not hesitate to usurp the name of some illustrious predecessor—Daniel, Enoch, Solomon, the Twelve Patriarchs. This was only a harmless hoax, actually, which could not fool very many people. Christian writers used the same procedure widely and with not such harmless effect—given the credulity of the people—when they circulated a quantity of pseudepigraphic gospels alongside the four which were most commonly accepted in the churches and which were in the process of becoming canonical. Falsely attributed to Peter, James, Thomas, Philip, Nicodemus, and other holy figures, these writings are today grouped together under the name of "apocryphal gospels." Some smacked of heresy; all included more or less extravagant fables; several, moreover, had a large audience in the Christian world, especially in the Middle Ages.

Apologetic zeal led Christian piety considerably farther into fraud, to the point of enlarging various notable works with opportune "interpolations," for which understand certain additions, certain alterations of the original texts, with the aim of making the author say what he did not say or want to say but what could be of service to the new faith. An example is the paragraph devoted to Jesus in *The Jewish Antiquities* of the historian Flavius Josephus, 18:63–64 (= 18:3:3), a famous falsification, whether partial or total, which we have already spoken of.[7] The Christian faith had no need to resort to these degrading tricks.

Lacking official documents, do we possess some valid testimony, emanating from a qualified person, whose functions—as a member of the Sanhedrin, officer of the Temple or the Roman garrison—we are sure would have allowed him to attend the trial? Testimony valid not only because of the witness' qualification but also—a major point for historic inquiry—because of its date, as close as possible to the event, since memories alter so quickly? No. Despite a Stapfer's venturesome affirmations, no "accounts of the witnesses," no "documents of an unchallengeable authenticity" have come down to us. It is not at all impossible that such testimony could have been gathered, at least orally: a Joseph of Arimathea, a member of the Sanhedrin, could very well have informed the Apostles, at least if he himself was present during the decisive hours. The evangelic tradition may have been able to incorporate such testimony. But this is only hypothesis, pure hypothe-

---

[7] See p. 96, above.

sis. We know nothing about it, literally nothing. And if testimony has
been incorporated, we do not know either what alterations it has undergone.

In a word, we have at our disposal only the four Gospels adopted
by the Church and called canonical to inform us of the history of the
Passion. I profess the greatest respect for these venerable texts,
through which a Message has been revealed to the world which will
never cease to nourish the human heart. In no wise inclined to that
excess of critical spirit, to that exegesis which dissects them until they
are reduced to crumbs or to dust, I am far from those who deny them
any historic value. But also, out of respect for history, for its demand
for probity, I am compelled to acknowledge that the documentary
value of the Gospels, especially when such an event as the Passion is
involved, is terribly hard to determine.

It is an indisputable and undisputed fact that the drafters of the
Gospels intended to serve religion, not history. Catholic writers are
the first to recognize this. The Gospels are not "pure historiographical
works, but teaching works," says Aimé Puech.[8] "The evangelists
wanted not to compose a rigorous history, as we understand the term
today, but to mount a demonstration," observes Joseph Bonsirven.[9]
"The Gospels are not history books. . . . The evangelists were primarily concerned with throwing light on the religious value of Jesus' life
through a selection of scenes which brought their teaching with
them," writes Daniel-Rops.[10] That is indeed the purpose: teaching,
"catechesis," not history. It certainly does not follow that the Gospels
are denuded of historic value. But it necessarily follows that religious
concerns, concerns of "demonstration," prevailed over strictly historic
concerns in the minds of the evangelists. The tradition they gathered
and set down must have been influenced in the direction in which
they were drawn by the rapid evolution of the new faith and the
"demonstration" of the truths of faith.

It is another and likewise indisputable fact that a certain lapse of
time—very difficult to estimate precisely—occurred between the
event and the Gospel narration, a lapse long enough for one or another memory to blur, and for true historic tradition to find itself pit-

[8] Aimé Puech, Histoire de la littérature grecque chrétienne [History of Greek
Christian Literature], 3 vols., Paris, Belles Lettres, 1928–1930, I, 54.
[9] Father Joseph Bonsirven, S.J., Les Enseignements de Jésus-Christ, Paris,
Beauchesne, 1946, p. 11.
[10] Henry Daniel-Rops, Comment connaissons-nous Jésus? [How Do We Know
Jesus?], Paris, Sequana, 1944, p. 61.

ted against a legendary tradition which did not take long to spring up and cover the field of Christian piety with dense brushwood. I recall that Jesus' death is generally situated around the year 30. According to the most favorable hypothesis, the Synoptic Gospels (the oldest of which is the Gospel according to Saint Mark) would date from the 60s and Saint John's Gospel from the 90s. The minimum interval—we say minimum—would thus be thirty to forty years for the former and sixty to seventy years for the fourth Gospel. In normal times and in the first case, that of the Synoptics, thirty or forty years is relatively little: such memories, so moving, could persist. But what was just said must be taken into account: the times when the religion of Christ, the dogma of the Incarnation evolved in the exaltation of a burning faith were not normal. Puech writes:

> There is no doubt that concerning not only the facts relating to Jesus but also the words that the evangelists put in his mouth, a very large share must be attributed to the work of exposition which was carried out during the time of the first Christian generation, sometimes even up to that of the second.[11]

Equally indisputable is the fact that the canonical Gospels, once written down, were not secure from the (inopportune) zeal which led believers, more particularly manuscript copyists, to make certain alterations, additions, or suppressions. We have already indicated some, and we will have occasion to indicate others, whose suspect character is recognized even in the most conventional exegesis. Among other examples, it is admitted that the ending of the Gospel according to Saint Mark, 16:9–20, is not from the same hand as the whole of that Gospel, and is a later addition, the genuine text of Mark stopping at 16:8.[12] We might recall in this connection, as painful as the words are, the accusation made by the pagan polemicist Celsus in the second century in *The True Account*, which we know through Origen's refutation of it in *Against Celsus*, 2:27: ". . . certain

[11] Puech, *op. cit.*, I, 22.
[12] Segond includes Mark 16:9–20 without any comment; Crampon and Goguel and Monnier do draw attention to the fact that the passage is disputed. (See Louis Segond, ed. and tr., *La Sainte Bible*, Paris, Société biblique protestante, 1877; Canon A. Crampon, ed. and tr., *La Sainte Bible*, rev. ed., Tournai, Desclée, 1939; Maurice Goguel and Henri Monnier, eds. and trs., *Le Nouveau Testament*, Paris, Payot, 1929.) [In the English versions consulted, all but CCD add notations to the effect that the passage is omitted from some early manuscripts but appears in others; KJ (n. 12) observes, for example, "The two oldest Greek manuscripts, and some other authorities, omit from ver. 9 to the end. Some other authorities have a different ending to the Gospel." CCD, like Segond, simply incorporates the passage without comment.—Tr.]

of the Christian believers, like persons who in a fit of drunkenness lay violent hands upon themselves, have corrupted the Gospel from its original integrity, to a threefold, and fourfold, and many-fold degree, and have remodelled it, so that they might be able to answer objections."[13] And Celsus was not alone in saying this: among the Christian writers contemporary with him, Irenaeus, Tertullian, and Dionysius of Corinth recognized that "the writings of the Lord" had been unscrupulously falsified.[14]

It is again an indisputable fact—we have underlined it numerous times and we affirm most emphatically that it must be constantly kept in mind—it is a fact of capital importance for religion and for history that in this same period when the Gospel tradition was put down in writing, a gulf was opening between the Synagogue and its emancipated daughter, the Church. Jews rigorously faithful to the ancient Law and Christians who were breaking away from it, who declared it superseded, became adversaries, sometimes (the theologians especially, the doctors) mortal enemies. In the measure that the new religion took form, its doctrine, its credo bore it daily farther away from traditional Judaism, and it hence came up against increasing incredulity and hostility on the part of the Jews. And daily oriented more toward the Gentile world, the Church became aware of how greatly it was to its advantage to detach itself from the Jews (particularly at the time of the war in Judea, 66–70—which accounts of Matthew and Luke seem very close to), to court the good will of the imperial authorities, as though from a presentiment of the future alliance which would underwrite and consolidate in the temporal order three centuries of spiritual conquests. This is why the historian has the right and the duty, the absolute duty, to consider the Gospel accounts as prosecution evidence (against the Jews), with the aggravating circumstance that they are the only evidence available and that all four lie on the same side: we have neither (valid) Jewish testimony nor pagan testimony to present in opposition or in balance.

Now, nowhere is this partisanship of the evangelists more visible,

---

[13] [Quotation taken from Origen, Against Celsus, tr. Rev. Frederick Crombie, in The Ante-Nicene Fathers, ed. Rev. Alexander Roberts and James Donaldson, rev. ed. Rev. A. Cleveland Cox, 10 vols., New York, Scribner, 1917–1925, IV, 443.—Tr.]

[14] See L.-A.-P. Rougier, Celse, ou le conflit de la civilisation antique et du christianisme primitif [Celsus, or the Conflict of the Civilization of Antiquity and Primitive Christianity], Paris, Éd. du Siècle, 1926, p. 234; Charles Guignebert, Le Christ, Paris, Albin Michel, 1943, p. 33.

more strongly marked, nowhere this lack of non-Christian documentation more deplorable than in the story of the Passion. This is easily
understood: it was a perilous undertaking but an imperious necessity
for the Christian narrator to explain and justify the "scandal of the
cross" (Gal. 5:11 [JB]), that ignominious—and incontestably Roman
—punishment, in pagan eyes. Whence there arose an inevitable
warping in the presentation of the facts, which it would seem were
known only confusedly. The four evangelists doubtless did not go so
far in this regard as the writers of the apocrypha—they were wise
enough to avoid certain excesses which were too obviously absurd;
yet it leaps to the eye that all four had the same concern, which was
to reduce the responsibility of the Romans to a minimum in order to
increase the responsibility of the Jews proportionately. Impartial his-
tory-writing recognizes this:

> The tactic . . . appears clearly in the Gospels. Their authors, eager to court
> Rome, patently applied themselves to presenting a version of the Passion
> such that Roman authority, represented by Pilate, would emerge from the
> affair with almost clean hands, while a freely accepted responsibility would
> crush the Jews: "His blood be on us and on our children!" The exigencies
> of theology, which shows the Jewish people rebellious against the divine
> message, thus joined with the interests of political opportunism.[15]

The four evangelists are unequal in partisanship, moreover: in this
regard Matthew far outdistances not only Mark and Luke but perhaps even John. Should this surprise us? There are no fiercer enemies
than brothers; and Matthew was Jewish, thoroughly Jewish, the most
Jewish of the evangelists. "Converts are often the severest judges of
the religion they have left," observes Father Joseph Huby.[16] According to a tradition that seems well grounded, Matthew wrote "in Palestine and for Palestinians," in order to demonstrate through reference
to the Old Testament that Jesus was indeed the Messiah predicted by
the Jewish Scriptures—this, we are told, being a "doctrinal" aim [17]—
and also "to establish that the rejection of the Jews to the profit of the
Gentiles is the consequence and the punishment of a culpable unfaithfulness," this being obviously a "polemical" aim.[18] "No other Gos-

---

[15] Marcel Simon, *Verus Israël*, Paris, Boccard, 1948, p. 147.
[16] Father Joseph Huby, *L'Évangile et les Évangiles*, Paris, Beauchesne, 1929,
p. 92.
[17] Father J. P. Grausem, S.J., *L'Évangile de saint Matthieu*, "Témoignage
chrétien" series, Le Puy, Mappus, 1945, p. 5.
[18] Father Marie-Joseph Lagrange, O.P., ed. and tr., *Évangile selon saint Matthieu*, Paris, Gabalda, 1922, p. xxix.

pel," Father Charles Schaefer assures us, "was so handy a weapon
in the struggle against Jews and pagans." [19] I readily believe it—
"against Jews" above all—but was historic truth served thereby? It
is possible to doubt it. It is not surprising if Matthew is the most partial of the three Synoptic writers, his account of the Passion the most
tendentious, or if the most impartial under the circumstances—or the
least partial—is Luke, the only evangelist who was not Jewish, the
only one who came from the Gentile world.

Is this all? A last observation of fact is necessary, for anyone who
wishes to test the documentary value of the accounts of the Passion in
the Gospels: their many divergences. Commentators guarantee to us
that these divergences are minimal and easily reconciled. We shall
indeed see. There is no other way to judge than by presenting them
simply, objectively, and without tarrying over secondary details.

The Date [20]

First of all, there is a surprising discrepancy in dates.

The evangelists agree only in placing Jesus' sentencing and death
on the *parasceve*, "the day of Preparation" (Mk. 15:42; Mt. 27:62; Lk.
23:54; Jn. 19:31), which means the eve of the Sabbath, and hence a
Friday.

But according to the three Synoptic evangelists, whose narratives
are categoric in this respect, the final meal taken by Jesus with the
Twelve—the eucharistic Last Supper—was the Jewish paschal meal,
the one for which the "passover," that is, the paschal lamb, was sacrificed: "I have earnestly desired to eat this passover with you before I
suffer . . ." (Lk. 22:15).

Now, "the first day of Unleavened Bread, when they sacrificed the
passover lamb" (Mk. 14:12; see Mt. 26:17), was a fixed date on the
Jewish calendar, the fifteenth of the month of Nisan, which according
to Jewish custom began at nightfall, when the first star was visible in
the heavens. According to the Synoptics, Jesus would therefore have
been arrested, judged, sentenced, and executed on one *Nisan 15*, the
first day of the great Feast of Passover, which in itself cannot but
raise serious difficulties, for such a feast was a day of rest, requiring

---

[19] Father Charles Schaefer, *Précis d'introduction au Nouveau Testament*, tr.
Grandclaudon, Paris, Salvator, 1939, p. 72.
[20] See n. 2, above.

of the faithful—and even more of the priests—abstinence from work, meditation, total consecration.

Quite to the contrary, the fourth evangelist—Saint John, according to accepted tradition—says expressly that the last meal Jesus had with the Twelve took place "before the feast of the Passover" (13:1). Nothing in the account he gives permits us to infer that this meal was the Seder, the paschal meal. The continuation of the account shows no less clearly that Jesus' sentencing and death took place the eve of Passover, namely, *Nisan 14:*

They themselves [the chief priests] did not enter the praetorium, so that they might not be defiled, but might eat the passover [which means that they had not eaten it yet; Jn. 18:28].

[Pilate] brought Jesus out. . . . Now it was the day of Preparation of the Passover; it was about the sixth hour [when Jesus appeared before Pilate; Jn. 19:13–14].

If we think of the gravity of the circumstances—for the faithful Eleven—and the intensity of the memory that the Last Supper and the dramatic events following it must have left them, how to explain that two of them, Matthew and John, or let us say even three—since it is understood that Mark was "Peter's interpreter" [21]—were in disagreement on a date, on an event (the Last Supper), which among all others should have etched itself indelibly in their minds and hearts?

From early times, this disagreement aroused violent controversy, or what has been called the "quartodeciman" dispute (has any other religion engendered so many quarrels among men since its birth as has the religion of Christ, alas?), with some Eastern Churches especially holding to the Johannine date of Nisan 14, the others to the Synoptics' Nisan 15. And since that time, exegetes and theologians have not ceased to cudgel their brains to discover some means of reconciling these contradictory statements. Need I say that the various solutions proposed by "harmonistics" are all conjectural, none decisive, however ingenious they may be? Moreover, the discoveries at Qumran, as well as subsequent studies such as those by Annie Jaubert and Paul Winter,[22] make it possible to think that the meal in question was not the Seder but probably a liturgical repast connected with the Essenian calendar rather than the official calendar.

---

[21] See Huby, *op. cit.*, p. 29.
[22] Jaubert, *op. cit.;* Winter, *op. cit.*

The Arrest

The evangelists agree in attributing the initiative in tracking Jesus to the Jewish authorities in Jerusalem, the chief priests, in concert with the scribes (Mk. 14:1; Lk. 20:19; 22:2), the scribes and the elders (Mk. 14:43), the elders (Mt. 26:3, 47), the Pharisees (Jn. 11:57; 18:3). Only Matthew 26:3 and John 11:49 implicate Caiaphas by name. Mark 14:53 and Luke 22:54 speak of the acting high priest, but seem not to know his name.[23]

These authorities hesitated only out of fear of popular tumult, the people being in favor of Jesus. Judas' betrayal decided them to speed up the operation.

Up to this point, there is no notable disparity.

Not so of the event of the arrest itself, though this is the only episode of the Passion where we can believe all the Apostles were eyewitnesses, at least before their flight. And for them what more poignant memory than the arrest, down to the least detail—which was surely not Judas' kiss, that ignominious betrayal by a companion.

Now, the Synoptic and Johannine accounts differ first of all on an important point: the constitution of the police forces assigned to the operation.

What were these forces? Mark 14:43 and Luke 22:47 say "a crowd"; Matthew 26:47 says "a great crowd," armed "with swords and clubs" (this at Mk. 14:43 also); we can suppose that Jewish police, the Temple guard, who were under the high priest's orders, were involved here. Mark and Matthew state expressly that these troops were sent by the chief priests and the scribes and the elders (Matthew omits "the scribes"); the Sanhedrin was obviously involved here. As for the presence at this night operation of chief priests and elders themselves, mentioned only in Luke 22:52, with "captains of the temple," it is quite unlikely.

But with John 18:3, the picture changes: here and here only [24]

[23] Yet Caiaphas is mentioned once in Luke, though early in his Gospel and in this singular fashion: "In the fifteenth year of the reign of Tiberius Caesar, Pontius Pilate being governor of Judea, . . . in the high-priesthood of Annas and Caiaphas, the word of God came to John the son of Zechariah . . ." (3:1–2).

[24] Which does not prevent Daniel-Rops from writing: "According to the account in the four Gospels (Mt. 26:47–56; Mk. 14:43–52; Lk. 22:47–53; Jn. 18:2–12), we can say that Roman soldiers participated in the arrest: it is a question of a *cohort*, a *tribune* . . ." (*Histoire sainte: Jésus en son temps*, p. 486). A good example of improper referencing and faked "harmony."

Roman troops appear alongside the Jewish police, the Roman "cohort," commanded by a high-ranking officer, a "chiliarch"—a commander of a thousand men—or a tribune. That Roman troops led by a superior officer, even if they were only a detachment from the cohort and not the whole cohort, participated in the Gethsemane raid would seem to be a factor that would strike the witnesses sharply and live engraved in their memory. Strange that the Apostle Matthew, if he was the author of the account in the first Gospel; the Apostle Peter, if Mark, author of the second Gospel, was indeed his "interpreter"; and Mark himself, if he was the young man who "ran away naked" from Jesus' captors, leaving his "linen cloth" in their hands (Mk. 14:51–52)—strange that all these eyewitnesses forgot the momentous intervention of the Romans.

Unless they preferred to forget it, unless the forgetfulness was intentional.

If we do accept the Johannine version and the presence of a cohort (or a detachment from the cohort) at Gethsemane, then the question arises of whether it is possible that the Roman authorities would have been content with the modest role of merely assisting Judas and Caiaphas. A troubling question, an embarrassing question. There is doubt, to say the least. Some exegetes, who believe in the historicity of the Roman intervention, deduce from this that Jesus' arrest was the deed of the Romans, of Pilate acting on his own initiative or in liaison with the Jewish authorities. This is a mere conjecture, which obviously collides with received tradition, but this tradition—and we know what sentiments have inspired it—calls forth the most explicit reservations. That the procurator, likely alerted by Caiaphas, made the decision to have the Galilean arrested on grounds of popular agitation with messianic tendencies is a hypothesis which at least has the merit of seeming plausible.

Another curious discrepancy in the accounts of the arrest: the attitude of Judas, the "kiss of Judas."

How could this kiss of Judas be forgotten? According to the accounts in the Synoptics, this was the planned sign by which the traitor would show the police who were following him which person the Master was: "The one I shall kiss is the man; seize him . . ." (Mk. 14:44; Mt. 26:48). The infamous betrayal was accomplished: "And when he [Judas] came, he went up to him [Jesus] at once, and said, 'Master!' And he kissed him. And they laid hands on him and seized him" (Mk. 14:45–46). Matthew 26:50 [JB] adds this simple word from

Jesus, "My friend, do what you are here for," and Luke 22:48 [JB],
"Judas, are you betraying the Son of Man with a kiss?"

What heart could have been more stricken, more ravaged, than
that of John, a "son of thunder," "the disciple whom [Jesus] loved,"
the tender and passionate John?

Yet the only one of the evangelists who does not mention the kiss
of Judas, and in fact the only one whose account excludes it absolutely, is John, at 18:3–8:

> So Judas, procuring a band of soldiers and some officers from the chief
> priests and the Pharisees, went there with lanterns and torches and weap-
> ons. Then Jesus, knowing all that was to befall him, came forward and said
> to them, "Whom do you seek?" They answered him, "Jesus of Nazareth."
> Jesus said to them, "I am he." Judas, who betrayed him, was standing with
> them. When he [Jesus] said to them, "I am he," they drew back and fell
> to the ground. Again he asked them, "Whom do you seek?" And they
> said, "Jesus of Nazareth." Jesus answered, "I told you that I am he. . . ."

There is no place in this account for the planned sign, the kiss of
Judas. Jesus it is who points himself out, twice. Strange that John, an
eyewitness, John, acquainted with the other Gospel accounts, knowing the place that Judas' kiss holds in them, would have deliberately
crossed it out of his own.

Let us hasten to recognize the agreement of the four—it is so rare
—on another episode in the arrest: the sword stroke with which one
of the disciples cut off the ear of the high priest's servant, the right
ear, specify Luke and John. The latter is alone in naming the disciple
in question, Simon Peter, and his victim, Malchus (18:10).

But the continuation differs in the four accounts.

Mark 14:47 notes the act briefly and adds nothing.

Luke 22:51 [CCD] adds: "But Jesus . . . said, 'Bear with them thus
far,' " [25] a cryptic saying which can be understood in two ways: "Bear
with these people, go no farther," or "Bear with these events, they
must go this far."

Matthew 26:52–54 adds: "Then Jesus said to him, 'Put your sword
back into its place; for all who take the sword will perish by the
sword. Do you think that I cannot appeal to my Father, and he will
at once send me more than twelve legions of angels? But how then

---

[25] [The French reads, "*Laissez, jusqu'à ce point,*" literally "Leave [or let], up
to this point," with no pronoun object; similarly, KJ reads, "Suffer ye *them* thus
far," with the italic indicating here, as throughout KJ, that the word is not found
in the Greek.—Tr.]

should the scriptures be fulfilled, [which say] that it must be so?' "

John 18:11 adds: "Jesus said to Peter, 'Put your sword into its sheath; shall I not drink the cup which the Father has given me?' "

Strange, once more, that Mark, "Peter's interpreter," is the only one not to mention the order received by Peter. And how to accept three different versions simultaneously? The shortest, in this case, is doubtless the best. Jesus' reply in Luke, in Father Lagrange's words, bears "a stamp of authenticity by its very obscureness," [26] and by its brevity, let us add. We cannot say as much of Matthew's text (particularly of verses 53–54). If one is genuine, the other is not.

Jesus Before the Jewish Authorities

Here is one of the principal phases of the Passion: the Jewish trial. What do we know of it? How do we know it?

Not one of the Apostles, not one of the evangelists was able to witness it. After the Master's arrest, all the disciples fled (Mk. 14:50; Mt. 26:56). Peter followed at a distance behind the police or soldiers who were leading Jesus off, and succeeded in penetrating into the courtyard of the high priest's palace, alone of the Eleven according to the Synoptics (Mk. 14:54; Mt. 26:58; Lk. 22:54), but in the company of another disciple according to John 18:15, a disciple who would be John himself.

It little matters whether there were one or two disciples in the courtyard. It was not in the courtyard that Jesus was interrogated and the Sanhedrin gathered. At the most, Peter (or Peter and John) would have been able to witness some police brutality, which everybody knows the Jews have a monopoly on. For the rest, which is the essential part, the evangelists speak only by hearsay. As we have already said, it is not impossible that one or another Sanhedrist, Joseph of Arimathea for example, informed them. Merely a hypothesis; the very presence of Joseph of Arimathea is hypothetical.

For the disparities among the evangelists and consequently the historic uncertainties multiply strangely when the accounts reach that most important point: the Jewish trial. If we go by the academic and conventional biographer, "one can . . . accompany Jesus" in his Passion "hour by hour," [27] step by step; but at each step, each minute, we

---

[26] Father Marie-Joseph Lagrange, O.P., ed. and tr., *Évangile selon saint Luc*, Paris, Gabalda, 1921, p. 564.

[27] Daniel-Rops, *Histoire sainte: Jésus en son temps*, p. 464.

are stopped by some discrepancy (the principal ones of which will be suppressed or concealed; that too is an accepted tradition).

First example: After Jesus' arrest, where did the police take him? Reply of the Synoptics: to the high priest—the incumbent high priest, of course—Caiaphas (Mk. 14:53; Mt. 26:57; Lk. 22:54). Matthew alone names him, doubtless because he alone knew his name; Mark's ignorance in this regard is singular, and Luke's even more so, as he has named Caiaphas in 3:2.[28] It was in the courtyard of Caiaphas' palace that Peter's triple denial occurred.

Reply of the fourth Gospel: first to Caiaphas' father-in-law, the former high priest, Annas (Jn. 18:13). It would be in the courtyard of Annas' palace that Peter's first denial took place (Jn. 18:17). Then Jesus, bound, was led to Caiaphas (Jn. 18:24), where Peter, who followed, made two more denials (Jn. 18:25–27). ·

From an early date efforts have been made to "harmonize" John and the Synoptics on this point. The divergence (one of minor importance) narrows if John's verse 24 ("Annas then sent him bound to Caiaphas the high priest") is transposed to follow immediately after verse 13 ("First they led him to Annas . . ."). Such a version is found in one of the oldest manuscripts of the Gospels, the *Syrus Sinaiticus.* But acceptable though it is, this version is exceptional, not found in any of the other manuscripts which are considered authoritative. Father Lagrange admits that the *Syrus Sinaiticus* "was heavily harmonized," [29] or to say it another way, was the subject of alterations intended to make certain discrepancies disappear, which couples with and confirms earlier remarks of ours.[30]

Second example, second point, this one of major importance: Whom did Jesus appear before?

Reply of Mark-Matthew, whose accounts are more than parallel —they are twins, sometimes identical in their terms: Jesus appeared twice before the Sanhedrin. The first time, at night, immediately after the arrest, he was taken to Caiaphas', where the chief priests, elders, and scribes had come (Mk. 14:53; Mt. 26:57). The two evangelists say expressly, "the whole council," or Sanhedrin (Mk. 14:55; Mt. 26:59). Skeptical about this, Father Lagrange does not believe

[28] See n. 23, above.
[29] Father Marie-Joseph Lagrange, O.P., ed. and tr., *Évangile selon saint Jean,* Paris, Gabalda, 1924, p. 459.
[30] See pp. 293–294, above.

that the Gospel text must be taken literally; for him, that first night-time meeting "was not official," for "Custom, codified orally by the doctors, did not allow assizes terminating in a death sentence to be held at night"; what was involved rather was "a volunteer committee of Sanhedrin members to prepare the case for hearing." [31] A volunteer committee? Then Caiaphas must have chosen among the volunteers those he was sure he could rely on to get rid of Jesus, and not the others, the hesitant, the sympathizers, the Joseph of Arimatheas. The second meeting of the Sanhedrin took place at daybreak (Mk. 15:1; Mt. 27:1); figuring in it were "the chief priests, with the elders and scribes, and the whole council," says Mark; "all the chief priests and the elders," says Matthew. It is possible but not certain that this second meeting was plenary.

Reply of Luke: Luke assures us that he has made an investigation, "carefully going over the whole story from the beginning" (1:3 [JB]). He definitely was familiar with Mark's account, from which he often drew inspiration. In the present case he deliberately departs from it, since he mentions only one meeting of the Sanhedrin, in the morning, "When day came" (22:66). The phrasing used is not precise: "When day came, the assembly of the elders of the people gathered together, both chief priests and scribes; and they led him [Jesus] away to their council. . . ."

Reply of John: this one is clear, but what does it say? Not a word alluding to a meeting, partial or plenary, daytime or nighttime, of the Sanhedrin. A brief interrogation of Jesus by Annas, who sends him to Caiaphas, who sends him to Pilate, and that is all. In his devout presumption, the biographer of *Jesus in His Time* assures us that "Saint John himself . . . feels the need to say everything he knows [about the Passion], everything he remembers." [32] Truly? Well, then, about the Jewish trial—about Jesus' appearance before the Sanhedrin —Saint John knows nothing, Saint John says nothing, Saint John hasn't the slightest recollection. Surely this is a fact that deserves to be emphasized, brought into the light of day, drawn out of the semidarkness where apologetics has kept it carefully hidden: *there is no Jewish trial of Jesus in the Gospel of John.*

This is no obstacle; apologists refer to Saint John as though there were one: "Thus, there was a sort of council assembled around

[31] Father Marie-Joseph Lagrange, O.P., *L'Évangile de Jésus-Christ*, Paris, Gabalda, 1928, p. 539.
[32] Daniel-Rops, *Histoire sainte: Jésus en son temps, loc. cit.*

Caiaphas. A chronological difficulty emerges here. . . . In the fourth Gospel, there is question only of a single appearance, at night. . . ." [33]

Such is the "striking parallelism" of the four Gospels on this profoundly important point.

Third example: How did the trial proceed?

Let us leave John aside, since there is really no trace of a Jewish trial in his Gospel. All that is mentioned is Jesus' interrogation by Annas (by Caiaphas, according to the *Syrus Sinaiticus*). In answering the high priest, who questioned him "about his disciples and his teaching" (Jn. 18:19), Jesus confined himself to saying nearly the same thing he said, according to the Synoptics, to those who came to arrest him:

I have spoken openly to the world; I have always taught in synagogues and in the temple, where all Jews come together; I have said nothing secretly. Why do you ask me? Ask those who have heard me, what I said to them; they know what I said.

Jn. 18:20–21

That is all.

In the Synoptics, the Matthew-Mark pair, as ever united, shows two or three significant discrepancies this time. More palpable yet are the divergences separating them from Luke.

According to Mark-Matthew, the interrogation of Jesus took place during the first Sanhedrin session, at night. According to Luke, it occurred during the single morning session.

Mark and Matthew alone mention the prosecution witnesses; Jesus is accused notably of having said, "I will destroy this temple . . ." (Mk. 14:58), "I am able to destroy the temple . . ." (Mt. 26:61)—a distinct difference. Mark, but not Matthew, adds that "Yet not even so did their testimony agree" (Mk. 14:59). The two concur in indicating that Jesus answered these accusations with a disdainful silence:

Then the high priest stood up [in the assembly], and asked Jesus, Hast thou no answer to the accusations these men bring against thee? He was still silent. . . .

Mk. 14:60-61 [RK]; see Mt. 26:62-63

Let us note in passing: it is surprising that the court, which was able to convene and call witnesses in the middle of the night, did not think of summoning Judas to give evidence, beyond doubt the most qualified, the best informed of the witnesses.

[33] *Ibid.*, p. 490.

The crucial point of the interrogation is the direct question posed to Jesus, by the high priest according to Matthew-Mark, by the Sanhedrin according to Luke:

Again the high priest asked him, "Are you the Christ, the Son of the Blessed [that is, God]?"

Mk. 14:61

And the high priest said to him, "I adjure you by the living God, tell us if you are the Christ, the Son of God."

Mt. 26:63

. . . and they led him away to their council, and they said, "If you are the Christ, tell us." . . . [Only after Jesus' reply comes the other question:] "Are you the Son of God, then?"

Lk. 22:66-67, 70

An abrupt question, which cannot be allowed unless it is split up, the way Luke does it: "If you are the Christ, tell us"; "Are you the Son of God, then?" For it would be astonishing, Father Lagrange notes, "had the high priest thought that anyone who called himself [the Christ, that is, the Messiah] was calling himself the Son of God, as if everybody were agreed on this characterization of the Messiah." [34] I will add: it would be even more astonishing had the high priest used the expression "Son of God" without explaining that he meant it not in the Jewish sense, that is, the figurative, but in the literal sense, that is, the Christian.

What was Jesus' reply to this direct question?

[According to Mk. 14:62:] And Jesus said, "I am [he]; and you will see the Son of man sitting at the right hand of Power, and coming with the clouds of heaven."

[According to Mt. 26:64:] Jesus said to him, "You have said so. But I tell you, hereafter you will see the Son of man seated at the right hand of Power, and coming on the clouds of heaven."

[According to Lk. 22:67-70:] But he said to them, "If I tell you [so], you will not believe; and if I ask you, you will not answer. But from now on the Son of man shall be seated at the right hand of the power of God." [In answer to the second question,] "Are you the Son of God, then?" . . . he said to them, "You say that I am [he]."

Jesus' reply is clearly affirmative in Mark. It seems rather evasive in Luke. It is dubious in Matthew, because the "*Su eipas*" of Matthew

---

[34] Father Marie-Joseph Lagrange, O.P., ed. and tr., *Évangile selon saint Marc*, Paris, Gabalda, 1910, p. 401.

—which means only "You have said"—can be understood either in the affirmative sense adopted by apologetics, "You have said so [understood: I am he]," or in the evasive sense, "You [understood: and not I] have said so," [35] in the same way that Luke 22:70 should be read: "You [and not I] say that I am [he]." It seems difficult to deduce from this triple divergence that "Jesus' reply could not have been more precise or clear." [36]

So writes Giuseppe Ricciotti; Catholic historians want with all their might for the answer to have been affirmative. Another makes much of his philologic knowledge: "I will venture to recall that an expletive *oti* can correspond quite simply with our 'Colon, open quotes.' . . . to translate 'You say [so,] I am [he]' is philologically correct." [37] However, Oscar Cullmann, a Protestant historian of quality, is of a completely opposite opinion, quite close to my own:

Orientalists agree in recognizing that the Aramaic words corresponding to "*You* say it" do not signify a clear "yes" in that language but are a way of eluding the question. . . . They mean in sum: "It is *you* who say it, not I." . . . Luke understood the Aramaic words correctly, which is the same as saying that Jesus eluded the question and that he did not at all designate himself as the Messiah. . . . But on the other hand, nor did he disavow the awareness he had of his mission, since he designated himself as the heavenly Son of man. [38]

Thus Jesus' intention must remain open to conjecture—unless the worrisome text at Luke 22:70 is deformed and made to read: "And they all said, 'Are you the Son of God, then?' And he said to them, 'I am he.' " [39]

But does a historian have the right to modify any text, whatever it is?

Strictly speaking, the three Synoptics do not agree except on one statement of Jesus', and one only:

. . . you will see the Son of man $\left\{ \begin{array}{l} \text{sitting} \\ \text{seated} \end{array} \right\}$ at the right hand of Power, and coming $\left\{ \begin{array}{l} \text{with} \\ \text{on} \end{array} \right\}$ the clouds of heaven.

Mk. 14:62; Mt. 26:64

[35] [Other English versions besides RSV show the same ambiguity in Matthew 26:64: "Thou hast said it" (CCD); "The words are your own" (JB); and, nearer to the Greek, "Thou hast said" (KJ).—Tr.]

[36] Joseph Ricciotti, *Vie de Jésus-Christ*, tr. Maurice Vassard, Paris, Payot, 1947, p. 630. [Quotation taken from Giuseppe Ricciotti, *The Life of Christ*, tr. Alba Zizzamia, Milwaukee, Bruce, 1948.—Tr.]

[37] Henri Marrou, in *Esprit*, June, 1949, p. 841.

[38] Cullmann, *op. cit.*, pp. 31–32.

[39] Daniel-Rops, *Histoire sainte: Jésus en son temps*, p. 502.

. . . the Son of man shall be seated at the right hand of the power of God.

Lk. 22:69

Before the Sanhedrin, then, Jesus would have made only one explicit and sovereign assertion, the assertion that the ringing texts of
David's Psalm and Daniel's vision were thenceforth fulfilled, and,
without saying so explicitly, that they were fulfilled in his person. It
was perhaps—perhaps—the claim of this transcendent and suprahu-
man messiahship, closely associated to God, that was the blasphemy
which the high priest immediately accused him of, according to
Mark-Matthew:

But the high priest tore his garments and said, "What further need have we
of witnesses? You have heard the blasphemy. What do you think?"

Mk. 14:63-64 [CCD]

The text at Matthew 26:65-66 is almost identical.[40] However, in Luke
22:71, it is the Sanhedrists who cry, "What further testimony do we
need? We have heard it ourselves from his own lips." And their exclamation is placed after Jesus' second reply, "You say that I am [the
Son of God]."

Need we go any farther? On all other points, agreement among the
texts disappears; it must be gotten by amalgamating, concealing,
truncating, with heavy support from irrelevant references and tendentious translations.

Fourth example: Was Jesus condemned to death by Jewish authorities?

Affirmative reply in Mark 14:64: "And they all condemned him as
deserving death"; and in Matthew 26:66, though less explicit: "He deserves death." And the two evangelists place this condemnation at the
end of the night session, when, as we know already, custom forbade
death sentences.

Silence, absolute silence, from Luke and John. Neither one makes
the slightest allusion to a Jewish sentence condemning Jesus to death.

The four evangelists do not find agreement again except on this
point—that the Jewish authorities delivered Jesus over to Roman jus-

[40] Father Jules Lebreton, S.J., writes in this connection: "The pretensions to
messianic status were not in themselves regarded as blasphemy; what constituted
blasphemy here, for Caiaphas, was the superhuman and truly divine elevation
that Jesus claimed in proclaiming himself Messiah" (*La Vie et l'enseignement de
Jésus-Christ*, 2 vols., Paris, Beauchesne, 1931, II, 380).

tice, to Pontius Pilate. That is enough to implicate their responsibility
—even were it demonstrated, and it cannot be, that Pontius Pilate
had a more important role in the affair than the Gospels say.

Final example: The assaults.

Mark 14:65 [CCD] ascribes these not only to the police flunkies
but also to "some" who seem to be Sanhedrists:

And some began to spit on him, and to blindfold him, and to buffet him,
and to say to him, "Prophesy." And the attendants struck him with blows of
their hands.

Matthew 26:67–68 seems to suppress the flunkies and to deposit all
the odium of that ignominious scene on the Sanhedrists alone:

Then they spat in his face, and struck him; and some slapped him, saying,
"Prophesy to us, you Christ! Who is it that struck you?"

Father Lagrange is of the opinion, nevertheless, that Matthew's second clause applies to "subordinates," to the guards.[41]

Both Matthew and Mark situate the scene of the insults after the
sentencing, in the night session. Luke 22:63-65 situates it likewise
during the night, but before the Sanhedrin session, and ascribes it to
the police alone:

Now the men who were holding Jesus mocked him and beat him; they also
blindfolded him and asked him, "Prophesy! Who is it that struck you?" And
they spoke many other words against him, reviling him.

John mentions but one instance of police brutality (18:22-23 [JB]).
During the high priest's interrogation,

. . . one of the guards . . . gave Jesus a slap in the face, saying, "Is that
the way to answer the high priest?" Jesus replied, "If there is something
wrong in what I said, point it out; but if there is no offence in it, why do
you strike me?"

Such are the texts, and such the discrepancies. Yet whether it is a
question of the ordinary brutalities of the police or their flunkies, as
Luke and John say and as is likely, or even of a transport of hatred
among the oligarchs, whose tradition of violence, as we have seen, is
equally denounced in the Talmud, it matters little: the Jewish people,
who themselves suffered from these tyrannical practices, are in no
wise involved. Not one word of the texts justifies their being implicated.

[41] Lagrange, . . . *Matthieu,* p. 509.

Yet they are, nonetheless, because there are those who want them to be. In everything: the assaults, the arrest, the trial, the judgment. Catholic writers, Protestant writers. The Sanhedrin's judgment "marks in a solemn and decisive way the rupture between the people of God, represented by their spiritual guides, and the messenger from the Eternal, the Christ, son of the living God," writes Hébert Roux.[42] In Giovanni Papini's transformation of the texts, ". . . on the golden face of Christ, the spittle of the Jews covered the first blood of the Passion." [43] Father Lebreton observes, "The rejection of the Messiah, the rupture between God and his people, was consummated there, in that sinister assembly." [44] And under the pen of a great writer, the traditional interpretation is transformed into a vision of gripping realism (but pure imagination):

It is so crowded you can hardly move. This is the recruited public, a foul-smelling assize court to whom the Son of God will make His statement. They have pushed Christ into that, into such a press that He is one with the flesh of His people. All of Israel is a winepress on Him. And it is there, at the end of an insane questioning, in the inextricable medley of witnesses who contradict one another, that the terrible cry will come forth, the intolerable "Blasphemy" which will divide the world in two: Yes. It is true. I am God. It is I. If we could only stop up our ears! [45]

What an offense to truth, this literature, even signed by the great name of Claudel! What an offense to historic truth, first, but also, I believe, to a higher truth! Between this higher truth, wholly enveloped in mystery, and these unbridled imaginings, these fallacious reconstructions, there is absolute incompatibility. Fictionalized history —which is not living history, which is not (a) history—is in itself an equivocal and bastard breed, but when it touches on the sacred, it is sacrilege.

✿   ✿   ✿

We know now, from examining the facts and the texts, what worth there is in the traditional assertions and descriptions relating to the

[42] Hébert Roux, L'Évangile du Royaume, Geneva, Labor et Fides, 1934, p. 314.
[43] Giovanni Papini, Histoire du Christ, tr., Paris, Payot, 1922, p. 343. [Quotation taken from idem, Life of Christ, tr. Dorothy Canfield Fisher, New York, Harcourt, 1923, p. 324.—Tr.]
[44] Lebreton, op. cit., II, 374.
[45] Paul Claudel, Un Poète regarde la Croix, Paris, Gallimard, 1938, p. 35. [Quotation taken from idem, A Poet Before the Cross, tr. Wallace Fowlie, Chicago, Regnery, 1958, pp. 29–30.—Tr.]

first phase of the Passion: Jesus before the Jewish authorities. We
know what uncertainties we come up against, what a paucity of documentary foundation there is, what gaps traverse it. And we say:

whatever the responsibilities involved,

whether Jesus appeared before only the high priests Annas and
Caiaphas, as it is said in the fourth Gospel, or before Caiaphas as-
sisted by the Sanhedrin, as it is said in the Synoptics,

whether the Sanhedrin session was partial or plenary,

and finally whether the Roman authority took the initiative in
pursuing Jesus in league with the Jewish authorities—which obviously is not in the Gospels and remains purely conjectural;

in every case, we can reiterate and generalize our previous statement:

the Jewish people are in no wise involved.

They are in no wise involved in a matter conducted without them,
apart from them, despite them, and against them.

For this reason, we adjudge it useless to dwell on the question any
longer, and hasten to pass on to the second phase of the Passion, the
Roman trial; for it is here, according to received tradition, that the
responsibility of the people was indissolubly linked with that of the
leaders.

PROPOSITION 19

TO ESTABLISH THE RESPONSIBILITY OF THE JEWISH PEOPLE
IN THE ROMAN TRIAL—THE ROMAN DEATH SENTENCE
—THE ROMAN PENALTY, WE MUST ASCRIBE TO CER-
TAIN PASSAGES IN THE GOSPELS A HISTORICAL VALID-
ITY WHICH IS PARTICULARLY DUBIOUS; WE MUST OVER-
LOOK THEIR DISCREPANCIES, THEIR IMPROBABILITIES,
AND GIVE THEM AN INTERPRETATION WHICH IS NO LESS
BIASED AND ARBITRARY FOR BEING TRADITIONAL.

Let us make this point before entering the praetorium, the residence and court of the procurator.

Jesus' hurried arrest, his immediate arraignment before the Jewish authorities took place in the deep of the night and at daybreak. We know why; the evangelists have told us:

FOR FEAR OF THE PEOPLE.

And we know why the authorities were afraid of the people— because even in Jerusalem, Jesus' words had won over the people:

. . . all the multitude was so full of admiration at his teaching.

Mk. 11:18 [RK]

. . . the multitudes . . . held him to be a prophet.

Mt. 21:46

. . . for all the people [listening to him] hung upon his words.

Lk. 19:48

"If we let him go on thus, every one will believe in him. . . ."

Jn. 11:48

But here is Jesus captured—by Jewish police and/or Roman soldiers. His faithful companions, the Eleven, have fled, apart from Peter (according to the Synoptics) or Peter and John (according to John). Peter himself—Simon called Cephas, the Rock—has denied his Master three times. Abandoned by his own, Jesus is alone, in the power of his enemies, who hand him over to the Romans, without it being explained to us why except by the postscript in John 18:31.

Let us not forget that the event took place on a Nisan 15 according to the Synoptics, the first day of Passover, or a Nisan 14 according to the fourth Gospel, the eve of Passover. In any event, whether we are at the first day or the eve of Passover, on such a day all pious Israelites, and even more the priests and chief priests, should have been absorbed in the celebration or preparation of the feast; anything that distracted them would be sacrilege. The regulations in this connection were strict: no trials, much less capital trials, on the Sabbath or a feast day; no capital trial on the eve of the Sabbath or a feast day.[1] The ranking priests, the prominent people of Israel rabidly hostile to Jesus, by night and by day on a Nisan 14 or 15, thus evidenced incredible contempt for the most revered customs.

During those few hours of night and dawn—from Jesus' arrest to his appearance before Pilate—who knows what was said or done in the city, what was known, felt by one group or the other, the masses of the people or the Jewish elite? Nothing, we know nothing, absolutely nothing. Everything that has been written on this subject is only groundless hypothesis, imagining, literature. Did the news of Jesus' arrest seep out? This is not impossible: in such a swarm of people,[2] the smallest rumor circulates—and is distorted—easily. What would be improbable is that the people knew Jesus' declarations to his judges (according to the Synoptics, since Jesus refused to make any statement in the fourth Gospel), that they knew his sovereign claims, adjudged blasphemous; I find proof of this in the very gibes the passersby threw at the Crucified: "Aha! You who would destroy the temple and rebuild it in three days . . ." (Mk. 15:29): so this is what people were telling each other in the streets. What would also be improbable is that from one day to the next, in a few hours, the sentiments of admiration and love felt by the crowd changed into murderous hate, to the point where they abandoned all devotional duties and joined with the detested pagans and their Jewish acolytes to harrow Jesus.

That Jesus' prestige might have suddenly dropped, perhaps even

---

[1] Sanhedrin 35a [BT]; see Father Marie-Joseph Lagrange, O.P., ed. and tr., *Évangile selon saint Jean*, Paris, Gabalda, 1924, p. 471.

[2] A good number of the pilgrims, however, must have camped outside the city, in the nearby countryside.

been destroyed in a fell swoop by reason of his arrest, of his delivery to the Romans, this is possible. Let us recall the glorious messianic prophecy: ". . . and with the breath of his lips he shall slay the wicked" (Is. 11:4).

Alas! Instead of that glory, that power, that sacred invincibility, this prostration! The more grandiose the hope that the patriot and pious crowd had placed in Jesus, this inspiring prophet whom some perhaps had begun to whisper would be the Messiah, the "liberator of Israel," the deeper, the more bitter their disillusionment must have been when they knew he was falling, brought low, overcome without resistance, delivered like a miscreant into the hands of the occupation forces, of the despicable and impure pagan. Was this not the despairing state of mind of the disciples themselves?

But from this to making common cause with the pagans, to snatching the condemnation of the Jew from them, to howling for his death with the flunkies of the Annases and the Caiaphases, there was an abyss, uncrossable.

The fact remains that at the early hour—"probably at the break of day, toward six o'clock in the morning"[3]—when Jesus, bound, was delivered to Pilate by the Jewish authorities, the crowd does not appear in any of the Gospel accounts.

But it appears in the apocryphal gospel of Giovanni Papini: "And the High Priests, Scribes and Elders set out for the Palace of the Procurator, followed by the guards leading Jesus with ropes and by the yelling horde which grew larger as they went along the street." The "yelling horde" went well in the picture; so no problem, Papini invented it.[4]

Claudelian paraphrase which, for all its superiority as literature to the Papinian, is nonetheless tendentious: "Here is Jesus given over to the Universe by Judaism."[5]

"Jesus given over to the Universe by Judaism": a historic symbolism

---

[3] Lagrange, op. cit., p. 469.

[4] Giovanni Papini, Histoire du Christ, tr., Paris, Payot, 1922, p. 344. [Quotation taken from idem, Life of Christ, tr. Dorothy Canfield Fisher, New York, Harcourt, 1923, p. 325.—Tr.

[Equally inventive are some American writings, such as this one: "I see no wrong in this man Christ,/Pilate addressed the maddened horde . . ." (The Christian in the World [United Church of Christ], 1963, p. 76; quoted in Gerald Strober, ms. in preparation, New York [Xerox], p. 88).—Ed.]

[5] Paul Claudel, Un Poète regarde la Croix, Paris, Gallimard, 1938, p. 38. [Quotation taken from idem, A Poet Before the Cross, tr. Wallace Fowlie, Chicago, Regnery, 1958, p. 33.—Tr.]

dear to Léon Bloy. But Caiaphas was not Judaism, and Pilate was not the Universe. Let us use capitals, us too, and say:

"Jesus given over to the Occupation Force by the Priesthood, Money, the Doctors' Pride." Which is no less symbolic, and of a truer symbolism.

                        o   o   o

From the moment Jesus was delivered to the Romans, Pontius Pilate, the Roman procurator, came to the fore. No one can dispute that thenceforth Jesus' fate and life were entirely in his hands. Everything depended on the decision that he would make, he, the master of Judea. It is therefore necessary to investigate this personage, who is known in history, and not only in the Gospels.

By the year 29 or 30—in which the Passion is generally situated— three or four years had already passed since Pontius Pilate, a Roman of equestrian rank, had received the important appointment (in the year 26) as procurator or governor of Judea from the Emperor Tiberius, from which it can be deduced that in all probability Jesus must not have been completely unknown to him, especially if we allow that a part of the evangelic ministry was exercised at Jerusalem and in Judea.

Aside from Jesus' trial, we can evaluate the administration of Pontius Pilate—and the man—only from a few episodes, five in all, related by Flavius Josephus, Philo Judaeus, and the evangelist Luke. The last episode alone is susceptible of precise dating: "after ten years of tenure in Judea," writes Josephus in *The Jewish Antiquities,* 18:89 (= 18:4:2), and this would be the year 36, shortly before Tiberius' death, which was in 37.

The first of these episodes—the matter of the standards showing the image of Caesar—doubtless goes back to Pilate's entry into office. Colliding head on with the most solidly anchored religious sense in Jewish souls, horror of idolatry, Pilate had standards bearing Caesar's image brought into Jerusalem by night. Immediate reaction, uprising:

Hastening after Pilate to Caesarea, the Jews implored him to remove the standards from Jerusalem and to uphold the laws of their ancestors. . . . Pilate, after threatening to cut them down, if they refused to admit Caesar's images, signalled to the soldiers to draw their swords. Thereupon the Jews, as [if] by concerted action, flung themselves in a body on the ground, extended their necks, and exclaimed that they were ready rather to die than to transgress the law. Overcome with astonishment at such intense religious zeal, Pilate gave orders for the immediate removal of the standards from Jerusalem.[6]

Second affair, second uprising, which ended worse (for the Jews) —the expropriation of the sacred treasure for use on public works:

On a later occasion [Josephus again recounts] he [Pilate] provoked a fresh uproar by expending upon the construction of an aqueduct the sacred treasure known as *Corbanas*. . . . Indignant at this proceeding, the populace formed a ring around the tribunal of Pilate, then on a visit to Jerusalem, and besieged him with angry clamour. He, foreseeing the tumult, had interspersed among the crowd a troop of his soldiers, armed but disguised in civilian dress, with orders not to use their swords, but to beat any rioters with clubs. He now from his tribunal gave the agreed signal. Large numbers of the Jews perished, some from the blows which they received, others trodden to death by their companions in the ensuing flight. Cowed by the fate of the victims, the multitude was reduced to silence.[7]

Third episode, to which Luke 13:1 alludes—a massacre of Galileans ordered by Pilate: "There were some present at that very time who told him of the Galileans whose blood Pilate had mingled with their sacrifices." It is not immaterial to note that this massacre took place during Jesus' ministry, quite likely only a short time before his Passion.

The incident of the gold shields is better known, through a letter from Herod Agrippa to the Emperor Gaius (Caligula) which is quoted by Philo of Alexandria. The issue this time is divine homage rendered to Tiberius by the procurator in the heart of Jerusalem:

He [Pilate], not so much to honour Tiberius as to annoy the multitude, dedicated in Herod's palace in the holy city some shields coated with gold. . . . But when the multitude understood the matter . . . , having put at their head the king's four sons, . . . they appealed to Pilate to redress the infringement of their traditions. . . . When he, naturally inflexible, a blend of self-will and relentlessness, stubbornly refused they clamoured, ". . . having chosen our envoys [we] may petition our lord [the Emperor Tiberius]." It was this final point which particularly exasperated him, for he feared that if they actually sent an embassy they would also expose the rest of his conduct as governor by stating in full the briberies, the insults, the robberies, the outrages and wanton injuries, the executions without trial constantly repeated, the ceaseless and supremely grievous cruelty. So with

---

[6] Flavius Josephus, *The Jewish War*, 2:171–174 (=2:9:2–3). [Quotation taken from *ibid.*, tr. H. St. J. Thackeray, in *Josephus*, 9 vols., "Loeb Classical Library" series, New York, Putnam, 1927, II, 389–391.—Tr.]

[7] *Ibid.*, 2:175–177 (=2:9:4). [Quotation taken from *ibid.*, tr. Thackeray, II, 391–393.—Tr.]

all his vindictiveness and furious temper, he was in a difficult position. He had not the courage to take down what had been dedicated nor did he wish to do anything which would please his subjects.[8]

The Emperor, apprised of the incident, is said to have sent a reprimand to Pilate with the order to withdraw the gold shields from Jerusalem, and they were consecrated in the Temple of Augustus in Caesarea.

The last episode—and the bloodiest—is the incident at Gerizim, the mountain sacred to the Samaritans. Some agitator or pseudo-prophet had assembled a crowd at the foot of the mountain, having led them to expect a miracle: the discovery of sacred vessels hidden by Moses.

But before they could ascend, Pilate blocked their projected route up the mountain with a detachment of cavalry and heavy-armed infantry, who in an encounter with the firstcomers in the village [of Tirathana] slew some in a pitched battle and put the others to flight. Many prisoners were taken, of whom Pilate put to death the principal leaders and those who were most influential among the fugitives.

Thereupon a complaint was brought by the Council of Samaria to Vitellius, governor of Syria, "For, they said, it was not as rebels against the Romans but as refugees from the persecution of Pilate that they had met in Tirathana."[9] The incident turned out badly for Pilate, who received orders to go explain himself in Rome (36). He did not return, and according to Eusebius, he ultimately committed suicide. Philo ranks him among the persecutors of Jews whom God punished with a violent death.

None of these texts is favorable to Pilate. Thus, spokesmen for orthodoxy attempt to minimize them.

"These Jewish accounts," according to Father Lagrange, "reflect a desperate nationalism"—a "fanatical" nationalism, echoes Daniel-Rops. "Pilate did not like the Jews," Father Lagrange continues, "but his conduct toward them was that of a rigid administrator, not of a cruel or plundering man."[10] What do they know about it? This goes a long way in making assertions without proof, and in giving the lie to

[8] Philo Judaeus, *On the Embassy to Gaius*, 299–303 (=38). [Quotation taken from *ibid.*, tr. F. H. Colson, in *Philo*, 10 vols., "Loeb Classical Library" series, Cambridge, Mass., Harvard University Press, 1962, X, 151–153.—Tr.]

[9] Flavius Josephus, *The Jewish Antiquities*, 18:87–88 (=18:4:1–2). [Quotations taken from *ibid.*, tr. Louis H. Feldman, in *Josephus*, 9 vols., "Loeb Classical Library" series, Cambridge, Mass., Harvard University Press, 1965, IX, 63.—Tr.]

[10] Father Marie-Joseph Lagrange, O.P., *L'Évangile de Jésus-Christ*, Paris, Gabalda, 1928, p. 549; Henry Daniel-Rops, *Histoire sainte: Jésus en son temps*, Paris, Fayard, 1945, p. 510.

Philo, Josephus, and Saint Luke besides, a contradiction that has no foundation except the utterly dogged determination to make the incredible Pilate of evangelic tradition credible.

It is quite true that Philo and Josephus were Jewish writers, their evidence prosecution evidence which cannot be accepted without reservations, which cannot be impugned without grounds either; for these authors, who are far from disreputable (didn't Saint Jerome call Josephus "the Greek Titus Livius"?), who were not "fanatics" (elsewhere, Father Lagrange credits Josephus with a "rather honest impartiality" [11]), generally extracted information from good sources. The third evangelist, Luke, who cannot be said to have been either a Jewish writer or a prosecution witness (against Pilate), agrees with them. Pilate's recall is certainly not an invented fact. And if this high functionary left an evil reputation among those under his administration, there must have been some serious reasons for it.

Anyone who wishes to sketch the portrait of the all too highly renowned procurator thus has the right to utilize the texts cited, on condition that he utilizes them prudently. "Pilate did not like the Jews," Father Lagrange says rightly; he took delight in hazing them, offending them, especially in their religious convictions, the more irritating in his eyes in that they were totally incomprehensible to him, as to so many other pagans, Roman or Greek, whose skeptical humanism abhorred Jewish exclusivism and the exacerbated sensitivity of that fervent and intolerant faith. This was the perennial source of pagan anti-Semitism (at least on a certain cultural and social level): Pilate was anti-Semitic. And for the rest, what would be called an iron-fisted administrator, advocate of strong measures, vigilant, wily, stubborn and hard, certainly unhesitant to spill blood—Jewish blood —to repress or prevent any disturbance, even a religious one, above all a religious one (in that land of Judea or Samaria, could we conceive of a disturbance which was not religious? and worse yet in neighboring Galilee, Herod's country—"Can anything good come out of Nazareth?"). About the injustices, the abuses, the depredations Philo speaks of, we know nothing, either pro or con, unless it is that these were common practice in a like case. As for the procurator's "supremely grievous cruelty," it is adequately demonstrated by the fact that of five known actions of his government, three ended in mas-

---

[11] Father Marie-Joseph Lagrange, O.P., *Le Messianisme chez les Juifs*, Paris, Gabalda, 1909, p. 2.

sacre, and the count would be four had not Pilate been struck in
the first episode by the attitude of the crowd—unanimous in accepting death—and presumably retreated before the horror of inaugurat-
ing his functions with such a crime.

We are therefore led to conclude, within the boundaries of historic
probability, that in the hands of the procurator Pontius Pilate the life
of a man, even more of a Jew, even more of a Galilean Jew suspected
of messianic agitation, could not have weighed very heavy.

❊   ❊   ❊

The distance between the Pilate of history and the Pilate of the
Gospels is great, and we see clearly what it demonstrates to us.

If the Jewish accounts are prosecution evidence against Pilate, how
much more are the Gospel accounts of the Passion prosecution evidence against the Jews, exonerating evidence in favor of Pilate, of the
Roman authority. Opposite rabid, vindictive, hate-filled, bloodthirsty
Jews appears a new-style Pilate, indulgent, understanding, accommodating, edifying even, quasi-Christian in advance, *"jam pro conscien-
tia sua christianus"*—"already Christian in his conscience," Tertullian
will say in the second century.[12] "This unfortunate personage early
excited the sympathy of Christian legend," Louis-Claude Fillion
confesses; [13] surely, and first of all that of the evangelists.

The major theme, orchestrated by the four canonical Gospels, taken
up more exaggeratedly by the apocryphal gospels, is the following:
Pontius Pilate, completely disposed to recognize Jesus' innocence,
made vain attempts to save him but had his hand forced by the Jews.
Therefore, it makes no difference that Christ was tried and condemned
by Pilate, scourged and crucified by the Romans; the real guilty ones,
the only ones responsible for the Crucifixion are the Jews. "Let the
Jews not say: We did not kill Christ. . . ." [14]

[12] Tertullian, *Apology*, 21:24.
[13] Louis-Claude Fillion, *Vie de Notre Seigneur Jésus-Christ*, 22nd ed., Paris,
Letouzey, 1929, III, 467.
[14] Roman Breviary, Office for Good Friday Night, Sixth Lesson, drawn from
Saint Augustine's tract on the Psalms. [Dr. Bernhard E. Olson writes: "The myth
of sole Jewish guilt and of Roman innocence has grown to such proportions in
the Near Eastern part of the world that the Coptic Orthodox Church has canonized Pilate as a saint! This St. Pilate, who Luke tells us 'mingled with their sacrifices' the blood of the Galileans (Luke 13:1), is honored by the Coptic and Assyrian Churches on June 25th" ("Anti-Semitism: A Lively Skeleton," *Christian
Advocate* [Methodist Publishing House], April 22, 1965). Western Christians,
whose churches have not canonized the Roman procurator, bend their efforts to

"The Jews killed Christ."

But what Jews?

Caiaphas and his friends, the priesthood, the clan of the "proper and well-schooled"?[15] Or the mass of the Jewish people, all Israel?

We already know the answer of Christian tradition—a tradition which I am assured from the Catholic side does not have "a normative character," which is not (thank God!) a doctrinal principle or an article of faith, but a tradition all the same, against which I do not know that official Catholic voices have ever been raised.[16]

What does Scripture say? Alas, the obscurations, the contradictions that swarm in the evangelic texts, and that we must now scrutinize with a magnifying glass. For if the general trend is the same in the four Gospels—which is equivalent to saying that all four are tendentious—the account of the Roman trial exhibits as many discrepancies from one Gospel to another, if not more, as the account of the Jewish trial.

When it is a question of extracting (or trying to extract) *scriptural truth*, evangelic truth, facing so many Christian and principally Catholic authors who incessantly overreach it and distort it, what other

demonstrating "Pilate's humanitarian instinct" (*Christ* [Assembly of God], n.d., p. 52; quoted in Strober, *loc. cit.*). One writer asserts: "He [Pilate] long resisted; he fought step by step; he fell back only by degrees. If that prolonged resistance does not excuse him, we nonetheless see it as an extenuating circumstance" (Father Denys Buzy, *Jésus comme il était*, Paris, Éd. de l'École, 1964, p. 354; quoted in Canon François Houtart and Jean Giblet, eds., *Les Juifs dans la catéchèse: Étude des manuels de catéchèse de langue française*, Louvain, Centre de Recherches socio-religieuses et Centre de Recherches catéchètiques, 1969, p. 141). Another commentator avers: "Pilate obviously did not want to pass judgement on Jesus. He repeatedly tried to find some alternate way. The Jews were insistent, however, and Pilate finally yielded" (*Young People* [Southern Baptist Convention], April–June, 1968, p. 9; quoted in Strober, *op. cit.*, p. 86).—Ed.]

[15] Father Bruckberger's phrase; see p. 287, above.

[16] [Not until the year 1965, when the Second Vatican Ecumenical Council repudiated this thesis in these words: ". . . what happened in His passion cannot be blamed upon all the Jews then living, without distinction, nor upon the Jews of today." The statement is contained in the conciliar Declaration on the Relationship of the Church to Non-Christian Religions, as translated in Father Walter M. Abbott, S.J., ed., *The Documents of Vatican II*, New York, Guild Press, America Press, and Association Press, 1966, p. 666. The cautiousness of the wording in this Statement on the Jews has been widely noted and discussed, and need not be repeated here, except in one particular: the omission of the term *deicide*, the key word which had been explicitly signaled and rejected in a 1964 draft of the text. This grave omission and its potential consequences have been touched upon in the Foreword. That the Council made this deletion would have been a source of deep grief to Jules Isaac had he lived to see the Declaration promulgated. Yet it is the consensus of all those who knew him, including this editor, that he would have acknowledged the final version—despite its inadequacies—as the breaking of a two-thousand-year deadlock in Christian-Jewish relations.—Ed.]

method can one follow except to quote the biblical texts intact, to compare them with each other and with the few historic data at one's disposal, and to juxtapose the imaginative commentaries on them by these good authors, whom our severest critics carefully refrain from criticizing?

❖   ❖   ❖

First phase of the Roman trial: accusations against Jesus (by "the Jews"), interrogation of Jesus (by Pilate).
First, the texts.

And as soon as it was morning the chief priests, with the elders and scribes, and the whole council held a consultation; and they bound Jesus and led him away and delivered him to Pilate. And Pilate asked him, "Are you the King of the Jews?" And he [Jesus] answered him, "You have said so." And the chief priests accused him of many things. And Pilate again asked him, "Have you no answer to make? See how many charges they bring against you." But Jesus made no further answer, so that Pilate wondered.

Mk. 15:1–5

When morning came, all the chief priests and the elders of the people took counsel against Jesus to put him to death; and they bound him and led him away and delivered him to Pilate the governor. . . .
  Now Jesus stood before the governor; and the governor asked him, "Are you the King of the Jews?" Jesus said to him, "You have said so." But when he was accused by the chief priests and elders, he made no answer. Then Pilate said to him, "Do you not hear how many things they testify against you?" But he gave him no answer, not even to a single charge; so that the governor wondered greatly.

Mt. 27:1–2, 11–14; the account of Judas' suicide is inter-
polated at vv. 3–10

Then the whole company of them arose, and brought him [Jesus] before Pilate. And they began to accuse him, saying, "We found this man perverting our nation, and forbidding us to give tribute to Caesar, and saying that he himself is Christ a king." And Pilate asked him, "Are you the King of the Jews?" And he answered him, "You have said so." And Pilate said to the chief priests and the multitudes, "I find no crime in this man." But they were urgent, saying, "He stirs up the people, teaching throughout all Judea, from Galilee even to this place."
  When Pilate heard this, he asked whether the man was a Galilean. And when he learned that he belonged to Herod's jurisdiction, he sent him over to Herod, who was himself in Jerusalem at that time.

Lk. 23:1–7

Then they led Jesus from the house of Caiaphas to the praetorium. It was early. They themselves did not enter the praetorium, so that they might not be defiled, but might eat the passover. So Pilate went out to them and said, "What accusation do you bring against this man?" They answered him, "If this man were not an evildoer, we would not have handed him over." Pilate said to them, "Take him yourselves and judge him by your own law." The Jews said to him, "It is not lawful for us to put any man to death." This was to fulfil the word which Jesus had spoken to show by what death he was to die.

Pilate entered the praetorium again and called Jesus, and said to him, "Are you the King of the Jews?" Jesus answered, "Do you say this of your own accord, or did others say it to you about me?" Pilate answered, "Am I a Jew? Your own nation and the chief priests have handed you over to me; what have you done?" Jesus answered, "My kingship is not of this world; if my kingship were of this world, my servants would fight, that I might not be handed over to the Jews; but my kingship is not from the world." Pilate said to him, "So you are a king?" Jesus answered, "You say that I am a king. For this I was born, and for this I have come into the world, to bear witness to the truth. Every one who is of the truth hears my voice." Pilate said to him, "What is truth?"

After he had said this, he went out to the Jews again, and told them, "I find no crime in him. . . ."

Jn. 18:28–38

When these texts have been closely read and reread, the following observations seem to be required.

As usual, the sharpest discrepancies exist between the Synoptic group and the fourth Gospel. As usual, in the Synoptic group, the separation between Mark-Matthew on one hand and Luke on the other is noticeable; the texts of Mark and Matthew are very close to identical.

Concerning when and how the evangelists learned of what had happened in the Roman court, we know nothing. But we know how formalistic Roman justice was, even in its severities and brutality. Here it seems oddly out of keeping with itself.

It is impossible not to be surprised that at the summons of the Jewish authorities, as soon as they appeared with their prisoner, the procurator responded in all docility; that instead of having the accused thrown in prison and putting his hearing off until later, after an examination of the matter, he consented to interrogate him without delay, indeed more—according to the Johannine account, he consented to leave the praetorium, re-enter it, leave it again in order to speak with "the chief priests" (Jn. 19:6, 15), on the pretext that they

wanted to avoid any impure contact on such a day, the eve of Passover (Jn. 18:28).

No less surprising is the fact that with the exception of Luke 23:2,
the evangelists give no precise indication of the accusations brought
by the Jewish authorities against Jesus. Why those vague formulations in Mark 15:3–4 and Matthew 27:12–13? Why that awkwardness,
that evasion in John 18:29–30, when Pilate asks the direct question,
"What accusation do you bring against this man?" and one or more
chief priests answer, "If this man were not an evildoer, we would not
have handed him over"?

Now, it emerges clearly from Pilate's interrogation, from the question posed to Jesus in identical terms in the four Gospels ("Are you
the King of the Jews?"), that the principal charge brought against
Jesus was that of messianic agitation. Jesus is accused of laying claim
to the title of Messiah-King, which was a crime in the eyes of the Romans, absolutely not in the eyes of the Jews. However modest the
"ovation of the palm branches" [17] might have been, it doubtless did
not go unnoticed by the procurator. But in such a case the Roman
police, Roman justice were self-sufficient. What could the role of the
Jewish authorities have been, then? That of informers, of zealous
aides.

Jesus' reply and attitude differ profoundly between the Synoptic
Gospels on one hand and the fourth Gospel on the other.

In the three Synoptic Gospels, Jesus says but two words: "*Su legeis,*"
"You have said [so]," meaning "It is you who have said so." According to Mark-Matthew, he refused to reply to any other question and
cloaked himself in absolute silence, "so that Pilate wondered" (Mk.
15:5; Mt. 27:14 is almost identical).

In the fourth Gospel, Jesus answers the procurator's question with
another question: "Do you say this of your own accord, or did others
say it to you about me?" This contradicts Luke 23:2, according to
which Sanhedrists have just accused Jesus explicitly of calling himself
Messiah-King, "Christ a king." This contradicts Mark-Matthew more
sharply yet, for in these Pilate and Jesus engage in a veritable dialogue
inside the praetorium. When Pilate repeats his question, Jesus says
finally, "You say that I am a king."

Did Jesus speak or refuse to speak? One has to choose. It cannot be
yes and no at the same time.

[17] Father Marie-Joseph Lagrange, O.P., ed. and tr., *Évangile selon saint Luc,*
Paris, Gabalda, 1921, p. cxxxviii.

In the one and the other version, Synoptic and Johannine, Jesus'
reply is not free from ambiguity, since it allows of two different interpretations. Actually, "*Su legeis*," like the earlier "*Su eipas*" before the
high priest (Mt. 26:64), can be translated either "You have said so [18]
[understood: I am he]" or "You [understood: and not I] have said
so."

Orthodox exegesis would have it that we must opt for the positive
—the first—sense. The *Jerusalem Bible,* for example, comments in a
note on Matthew 27:11, "By these words Jesus acknowledges as correct, at least in a sense, what he would never have said on his own
initiative" [JB].[19] *There* is subtlety.

If, then, Jesus openly recognized himself as Messiah-King, thus providing "the necessary witness on his mission, on his person," [20] how
do we explain Pilate's statement that follows immediately in Luke
23:4, "I find no crime in this man"? This is, Father Lagrange confesses, a "somewhat disconcerting short cut." [21]

So likewise in the Johannine account. After Jesus' justificatory declaration "My kingship is not of this world . . ." (Jn. 18:36), which Pilate patently does not understand at all since he returns to the
charge: "So you are a king [all the same]?" (Jn. 18:37), is Jesus' reply
so precise, so categoric as tradition and current translations would
have it: "Thou sayest it; I am a king" [CCD]? [22] The Greek text, "*Su
legeis oti basileus eimi*," meaning word for word "You say that I am
king," can obviously be interpreted in two ways like the "*Su legeis*" of
the Synoptics: one positive, "Thou sayest it; I am a king" [CCD], the

---

[18] [Again, the "so" is interpolated by the translators, as indicated by the
brackets around it three paragraphs above. It was pointed out earlier (see pp. 305–
306) that the same is true of the translation of "*Su eipas*."—Tr.]

[19] Father Pierre Benoît, O.P., tr., in *La Bible de Jérusalem*, Paris, Cerf, 1955.
[As indicated, this same wording is found in the English JB.—Tr.]

[20] Father Jules Lebreton, S.J., *La Vie et l'enseignement de Jésus-Christ*, 2
vols., Paris, Beauchesne, 1931, II, 393. Father Lagrange expresses himself more
cautiously in his commentary on Mark: "It seems that it would indeed be the
positive meaning, with this reservation: that [Jesus] would not have said it if
[he] had not been questioned" (Lagrange, ed. and tr., *Évangile selon saint Marc*,
Paris, Gabalda, 1910, p. 412).

[21] Lagrange, . . . *Luc*, p. 577.

[22] This is the way Crampon and Segond translate it. [JB enlarges it thus: " 'It
is you who say it,' answered Jesus. 'Yes, I am a king!' "—Ed.] Daniel-Rops aug-
ments: "Yes, you have said it, I am a king." Goguel and Monnier translate correctly and untendentiously: "You say that I am a king." (See Canon A. Crampon,
ed. and tr., *La Sainte Bible*, rev. ed., Tournai, Desclée, 1939; Louis Segond, ed.
and tr., *La Sainte Bible*, Paris, Société biblique protestante, 1877; Daniel-Rops,
op. cit., p. 511; Maurice Goguel and Henri Monnier, eds. and trs., *Le Nouveau
Testament*, Paris, Payot, 1929.)

other enigmatic, "You [understood: and not I] say that I am a king"
[RSV]. Here the presumption seems to be in favor of the second formulation, for rereading the Johannine text will show that "You say that
I am a king" counterpoints the next sentence, "[Understood: I say
that] For this I was born, and for this I have come into the world,
to bear witness to the truth. . . ." Thus and thus only—granted
the authenticity of the dialogue—is Pilate's conclusion, "Not guilty,"
explicable.

But how do we decipher so many enigmas? How do we find our
bearings in this terrible Game of Death, where the cards have been
jumbled, as though wantonly?

Only one clear factor, the trend common to the four Gospels: to reduce the responsibility of the Romans to a minimum, and to heighten
the responsibility of the Jews to the maximum, not without a revealing clumsiness. There is a marked gradation in this regard from the
Mark-Matthew pair to Luke to John. In Mark 15:5 and Matthew
27:14, Pilate merely "wondered" at Jesus' silence. In Luke 23:4, Pilate
explicitly declares him not guilty, which is rather "disconcerting" to
Father Lagrange. More "disconcerting" yet is the attitude of this singular magistrate in John 18:31 and following: first he tries to dodge;
next comes the Pilate-Jesus dialogue, and then the governor's explicit
declaration, "I find no crime in him . . ." (Jn. 18:38).

A final and important observation: the Jewish people play no role,
have no place in the first phase of the Roman trial.

Mark and Matthew make no mention of them.

John 18:35 has Pilate say in the course of the interrogation, "Your
own nation and the chief priests have handed you over to me. . . ."
"'Your own nation,'" comments the highly traditionalist Louis-
Claude Fillion, "that is, its official representatives, the members of the
Sanhedrin," [23] but the evangelist has implicated only Annas and Caiaphas, to the exclusion of the Sanhedrin. "Yes," Father Lagrange comments, "it was the chief priests and indeed the whole people who
handed Jesus over." [24] But what correspondence does this affirmation
have with the facts? Pilate's words can only be an editorial rendering,
a Johannine rendering, with a doctrinal bent, as lacking in any semblance of likelihood as the next sentence, attributed to the Jew Jesus:
". . . if my kingship were of this world, my servants [my followers,

---

[23] Fillion, op. cit., III, 447, n. 2.
[24] Lagrange, . . . Jean, p. 475.

Jews] would fight, that I might not be handed over to the Jews . . ." (Jn. 18:36).

Luke alone mentions the presence of "the multitudes" during the interrogation: "And Pilate said to the chief priests and the multitudes . . ." (23:4). It is possible, if things happened as the evangelists recount, that a throng formed before the praetorium, around the chief priests and their police. For the moment, this crowd remains passive, is there only as a backdrop. Let us wait.

         ✿   ✿   ✿

Second phase (peripheral to the Roman trial): Jesus before Herod.

There is no need to tarry over this second phase, which is unknown to Mark, Matthew, and John. It appears only in the Gospel of Luke, where it is rather peculiarly intercalated in the Roman trial, which is thus cut in two.

The evangelist Luke has retained the Herodian episode, it would seem, only as a means of imputing to a part-Jewish prince (Idumean in origin, Jewish by religion) and his soldiers the scene of jeering and insults that the tradition accepted by the other—canonical— evangelists imputes to the Romans. "The similarity is undeniable," says Father Lagrange; "on both sides, soldiers, mockeries, the principal one being a garment absurd in its bogus splendor." [25]

In the eyes of the Romans, in Roman public opinion, the detail might have its importance. For us, it has little bearing: whether one does or does not grant the historicity of Luke's account—the jeers and insults of Herod and his guards—the responsibility of the Jews, of the Jewish people, does not figure in it as either increased or diminished.

         ✿   ✿   ✿

Third phase: Jesus and Barabbas, the condemnation of Jesus, wrenched from Pilate by pressure from the Jews.

It has come, the fatal, the doubly fatal hour. "It was then [according to Saint Augustine] that the Jews truly assumed responsibility for the crucifying of their Messiah." [26]

---

[25] *Idem,* . . . *Luc,* pp. 579–580.

[26] Father Ceslas Lavergne, O.P., *Synopse des quatre Évangiles* [Synopsis of the Four Gospels], Paris, Gabalda, 1942 [in print 1968], pp. 234–235, n. 282.

"And the Jews, not only the notables, but all of the people, with a common voice and by a kind of plebiscite. . . ."[27]

Let us begin then by reading the texts, venerable, awesome.

Now at the feast he [the governor] used to release for them one prisoner whom they asked. And among the rebels in prison, who had committed murder in the insurrection, there was a man called Barabbas. And the crowd came up and began to ask Pilate to do as he was wont to do for them. And he answered them, "Do you want me to release for you the King of the Jews?" For he perceived that it was out of envy that the chief priests had delivered him up. But the chief priests stirred up the crowd to have him release for them Barabbas instead. And Pilate again said to them, "Then what shall I do with the man whom you call the King of the Jews?" And they cried out again, "Crucify him." And Pilate said to them, "Why, what evil has he done?" But they shouted all the more, "Crucify him." So Pilate, wishing to satisfy the crowd, released for them Barabbas; and having scourged Jesus, he delivered him to be crucified.

Mk. 15:6–15

Now at the feast the governor was accustomed to release for the crowd any one prisoner whom they wanted. And they had then a notorious prisoner, called Barabbas. So when they had gathered, Pilate said to them, "Whom do you want me to release for you, Barabbas or Jesus who is called Christ?" For he knew that it was out of envy that they had delivered him up. Besides, while he was sitting on the judgment seat, his wife sent word to him, "Have nothing to do with that righteous man, for I have suffered much over him today in a dream." Now the chief priests and the elders persuaded the people to ask for Barabbas and destroy Jesus. The governor again said to them, "Which of the two do you want me to release for you?" And they said, "Barabbas." Pilate said to them, "Then what shall I do with Jesus who is called Christ?" They all said, "Let him be crucified." And he said, "Why, what evil has he done?" But they shouted all the more, "Let him be crucified."

So when Pilate saw that he was gaining nothing, but rather that a riot was beginning, he took water and washed his hands before the crowd, saying, "I am innocent of this man's blood; see to it yourselves." And all the people answered, "His blood be on us and on our children!" Then he released for them Barabbas, and having scourged Jesus, delivered him to be crucified.

Mt. 27:15–26

[After Herod had sent Jesus back to Pilate,] Pilate then called together the chief priests and the rulers and the people, and said to them, "You brought me this man as one who was perverting the people; and after examining him before you, behold, I did not find this man guilty of any of your

<hr>

[27] Claudel, op. cit., p. 40. [Quotation taken from idem, A Poet Before the Cross, p. 34.—Tr.]

charges against him; neither did Herod, for he sent him back to us. Behold, nothing deserving death has been done by him; I will therefore chastise him and release him." Now he was obliged to release one man to them at the festival.[28]

But they all cried out together, "Away with this man, and release to us Barabbas"—a man who had been thrown into prison for an insurrection started in the city, and for murder. Pilate addressed them once more, desiring to release Jesus; but they shouted out, "Crucify, crucify him!" A third time he said to them, "Why, what evil has he done? I have found in him no crime deserving death; I will therefore chastise him and release him." But they were urgent, demanding with loud cries that he should be crucified. And their voices prevailed. So Pilate gave sentence that their demand should be granted. He released the man who had been thrown into prison for insurrection and murder, whom they asked for; but Jesus he delivered up to their will.

Lk. 23:13–25 [incorporating n. m]

". . . But you have a custom that I should release one man for you at the Passover; will you have me release for you the King of the Jews?" They cried out again, "Not this man, but Barabbas!" Now Barabbas was a robber.

Then Pilate took Jesus and scourged him. . . .[29] Pilate went out again, and said to them, "Behold, I am bringing him out to you, that you may know that I find no crime in him." So Jesus came out, wearing the crown of thorns and the purple robe. Pilate said to them, "Here is the man!" When the chief priests and the officers saw him, they cried out, "Crucify him, crucify him!" Pilate said to them, "Take him yourselves and crucify him, for I find no crime in him." The Jews answered him, "We have a law, and by that law he ought to die, because he has made himself the Son of God." When Pilate heard these words, he was the more afraid; he entered the praetorium again and said to Jesus, "Where are you from?" But Jesus gave no answer. Pilate therefore said to him, "You will not speak to me? Do you not know that I have power to release you, and power to crucify you?" Jesus answered him, "You would have no power over me unless it had been given you from above; therefore he who delivered me to you has the greater sin."

Upon this Pilate sought to release him, but the Jews cried out, "If you release this man, you are not Caesar's friend; every one who makes himself a king sets himself against Caesar." When Pilate heard these words, he brought Jesus out and sat down on the judgment seat at a place called The Pavement, and in Hebrew, Gabbatha. Now it was the day of Preparation of the Passover; it was about the sixth hour. He said to the Jews, "Here is your King!" They cried out, "Away with him, away with him, crucify him!"

[28] This verse, 17, is missing from many manuscripts. According to Father Lagrange, "It must not be authentic" (. . . Luc, p. 581). In other words, this would be one of those interpolations we have spoken of (see pp. 293–294, above) intended to "harmonize" the Gospel accounts of the Passion.

[29] The verses elided here, 2–3, describe the scene of the soldiers beating and insulting Jesus, which Mark and Matthew place after the sentencing.

Pilate said to them, "Shall I crucify your King?" The chief priests answered, "We have no king but Caesar." Then he handed him over to them to be crucified.

Jn. 18:39–19:1, 4–16

After the texts, and before studying the texts, let us take a selection of "Christian" commentaries, the continuation of a millennial tradition which we have previously evoked, and whose major source of inspiration, an inexhaustible source, is the atrocious verse 25 in Matthew 27: "His blood be on us and on our children!"

Protestant voices:[30]

[John Calvin:] The ill-considered zeal [of the Jews] precipitates them to this point, that committing an irreparable breach, they add at the same time a solemn imprecation, by which they cut themselves off from all hope

---

[30] There have been more charitable ones, to be sure, but when these lines were first written, such voices were rare, and hardly had an audience. I wish to pay homage here to David Lasserre, the author of an excellent article, "L'Antisémitisme de l'Église chrétienne," which appeared in *Cahiers protestants* (Lausanne), no. 1, January–February, 1939; and to Jean-Jacques Bovet, whose noble and generously inspired article "L'Étoile" in *Le Christianisme social*, October–December, 1946, replies to my article in *Europe*, July 1, 1946, "Comment on écrit l'Histoire (sainte)."

And it should be recognized that since the first edition of this book appeared, a liberal effort has been made on the Protestant side, notably through the activities of Fadley Lovsky: the review *Foi et Vie* published eight issues of Jewish studies (the third—October–November, 1949—was devoted to *Jésus et Israël*, and included Lovsky's essay "Dimensions de l'antisémitisme" [Dimensions of Anti-Semitism]). In addition, a commentary by him on the Ten Points of Seelisberg (see pp. 404–405, below) entitled "Quelles précautions faut-il prendre pour parler des Juifs aux enfants?" [What Precautions Must Be Taken in Speaking About the Jews to Children?], *Journal des Écoles du Dimanche* (Paris, Fédération Protestante de France), June, 1948, was sent to all Sunday School instructors of the Reformed Church of France. [Moreover, Professor Lovsky, the editor of *Foi et Vie*, did not himself subscribe to the 1938 Declaration of the Reformed Church of Basel published later in his journal (see p. 263, n. 76, above); and in a letter to the editor dated October 9, 1969, he comments that the document was subsequently revised.

[Thus the small Protestant community in France (800,000 members), long before the Catholic majority, was moving to correct Christian anti-Jewish traditions, especially in religious teaching materials. The Catholic hierarchy took a decisive and all-encompassing step in this field in 1967, with the publication of the revised *Catéchisme national français* (see p. 119, n. 39, above). A special note, included in the standard text for all adaptations, reads in part: "It will be well, in this case [of Catholic children "in contact with companions of other religions"], to teach the children to regard these companions with friendship, as close to them. . . . Where Jewish children are involved, [the catechist] will be very attentive to *rectifying the false opinions* that the [Catholic] children may hear about them . . ." (italics in the original). The note was published, with the "Fond obligatoire" (Compulsory Fundamentals) for all versions of the *Catéchisme*, in *Catéchèse* (Paris, Centre national d'Enseignement religieux), supplement to no. 29, October, 1967, p. 150.—Ed.]

of salvation. . . . Who is there then who would not say that the whole race is utterly cut off from the kingdom of God? But owing to their baseness and disloyalty, the Lord has shown the firmness of his promise all the more magnificently and visibly. And in order to give it to be understood that it was not in vain that he contracted an alliance with Abraham, he exempts those whom he freely elected from this collective damnation.[31]

[Edmond Stapfer:] A dreadful wish, which has been only too amply fulfilled. The curse that has weighed on the Jews for so many centuries is not near to disappearing. We are done with religious intolerance. . . . But the Jew bears an indelible stigma. Anti-Semitism, that odious thing, is always being revived century after century.[32] [And all the more readily, when one furnishes it with weapons in proclaiming that ". . . the Jew bears an indelible stigma" and that a "curse" weighs on all the Jews.]

[Hébert Roux:] Terrible words, which showed how far Israel's blindness and hardness could go. The pagans acted in ignorance and unawareness. Israel knew that Christ was to come and, seeing him, did not believe; this is why Israel itself uttered its own damnation.[33] [Commentary of the Apostle Peter: "And now, brethren, I know that you acted in ignorance . . ." (Acts 3:17).]

[Gunther Dehn:] The total responsibility that the people assumed is strikingly described by Mark. . . . It is the people who are expressly responsible for the condemnation to death.[34]

[Alexandre Westphal:] We can wonder what sincere Israelites feel who read these words today, after nineteen centuries of still continuing ill fortune have brought them a sinister fulfillment.[35]

Can we not wonder also what sincere Christians feel in observing the obvious fact that a "Christian" hostility, nourished by that "evangelic" tradition, has not been absent from that "sinister fulfillment"? Who says this? A Protestant minister, Freddy Dürrleman:

[31] Jehan Calvin, *Sur la Concordance ou Harmonie composée de trois évangélistes, asçavoir S. Matthieu, S. Marc et S. Luc*, vol. I of *Commentaires de M. Jehan Calvin sur le Nouveau Testament*, Paris, Meyrueis, 1854, p. 700.

[32] Edmond Stapfer, *La Mort et la résurrection de Jésus-Christ*, vol. III of *Jésus-Christ, sa personne, son autorité, son oeuvre*, Paris, Fischbacher, 1898, p. 199.

[33] Hébert Roux, *L'Évangile du Royaume*, Geneva, Labor et Fides, pp. 320–321.

[34] Gunther Dehn, *Le Fils de Dieu, commentaire à l'Évangile de Marc*, Paris, Je Sers, 1936, p. 257. [The same misconception finds expression in an American Protestant periodical in these words: "[Pilate] suggested that He [Jesus] be scourged and released. But the Jews would not be let off [sic] that easily, and Pilate did not wish to antagonize them" ("Student Questions: What They Ask Us," *Scope*, Junior Edition [Peoria], vol. VIII, no. 27, March 31, 1968, n.p.). —Ed.]

[35] Alexandre Westphal, *Jéhovah*, Montauban, by the au., 1924, p. 492.

That anti-Semitism has fed from the beginning on many other foods, granted; that numerous enemies of Israel today make no connection between their hatred and the hatred vowed in the past against Christ by the official representatives of Judaism, agreed. But has not the deep and almost instinctive aversion to the Jews over so many centuries proceeded from the tumultuous outrage provoked by the unthinking and at the same time savage cry of their ancestors about Christ: "His blood be on us and on our children!"? [36]

"Few words of Scripture have done more harm than these," writes a liberal-minded exegete, who adds brutally: "and they were nothing but an invention of the writer's!" [37]

Catholic voices:

[Dom Guéranger:] The voices which were singing "Hosanna" to the son of David a few days ago now sound only savage yells [as if it were proved that they were the same voices!]. . . . Israel is like a tiger; the sight of blood rouses its thirst; it is happy only when it welters in it. . . . And all the people reply [to Pilate] with this frightful wish, "His blood be on us and on our children!" This was the moment when the sign of parricide became imprinted on the forehead of the ungrateful and sacrilegious people, as on Cain's in days past; nineteen centuries of servitude, misery, and contempt have not erased it. . . . [38]

What a frightful judgment Judas brought on himself. . . . God heard him and remembered it. [39] [For these clerics are not afraid of attributing their human, their inhuman feelings to God.]

[36] Freddy Dürrleman, *Jésus*, Neuilly, La Cause, 1928, p. 102. ["By far the most gruesome example of this kind of thought patterning," writes Gerald Strober, "is found in (of all things!) an exposition of Romans 9–11 published for adult study: 'The Jew paid a price for his apostasy in Old Testament days. The Jewish nation rejected Jesus the Messiah and said, his blood be upon us and on our children (Math. 27:25). . . . In the meanwhile world Jewry was subject to bloody purges in many nations. Hitler in this century, was the bloodiest persecutor of all, for he reduced the Jewish population by some six million. What an awful price to pay —"His blood be upon us, and on our children" ' " (Strober, *op. cit.*, p. 65; internal quotation is from *Senior Bible Quarterly* [National Baptist Convention], January–March, 1967, pp. 32–33).—Ed.]

[37] Charles Guignebert, *Jésus*, Paris, Albin Michel, 1938, p. 575.

[38] Dom Prosper Guéranger, O.S.B., *La Passion et la Semaine sainte*, vol. III of *L'Année liturgique* (6 vols.), 24th ed., Tours, Mame, 1921, pp. 505–509.

[39] *Ibid.*, p. 202. [And C. A. Rijk, writing in *Sidic* (Rome), October–November, 1967, p. 30, points out the continuing injuriousness of the following sentences drawn from the same work by Dom Guéranger (1924 ed., pp. 202, 309); ". . . if God finally abandoned them [the Jews] to his divine justice it was only after having exhausted the riches of his mercy and pardon. Such love had borne no fruit; and the ungrateful people, with mounting irritation against their benefactor, cried out in a burst of hatred: 'May his blood be upon us and our children!' " And: ". . . the vengeance of Christ will envelop the city that bought him, that betrayed him, that crucified him. Then will the blood of the Jew flow to such an extent that, on meeting the flames which will devour Jerusalem, its torrent will quench them. . . . Thus shall the Lord take revenge on a parrici [dal] people." —Ed.]

[Louis-Claude Fillion:] The baleful crowd who were violently demanding Jesus' death pronounced an execrable wish, whose full weight was not long in falling upon them. The anathema they thus hurled against themselves and the coming generations materialized fully, forty years later, when the Romans seized Jerusalem and set everything awash in fire and blood. They crucified so many unfortunate inhabitants of the city that soon, according to Josephus' account, wood was lacking to make crosses. This was a horrible spectacle, in which it is hard not to see the punishment that the deicide nation had thus called down on itself.[40]

[Father Joseph Huby:] [The Gospel of Matthew] more than any other writing points up the bitterness of the conflict between Jesus and the leaders of the people, princes among the priests, scribes and Pharisees, pulling the Jewish masses in their wake and implicating them in their unfaithfulness: "His blood be on us and on our children!" But this scandal of Jewish unbelief could not annul God's salvific plan. In the place of culpable Israel others would come from the four corners of the earth to sit at the table of the Father of the family.[41]

[Father Lebreton:] The curse of the spilled blood: the Jews, blinded by passion, calling the full burden down on them and their children, would indeed feel it.[42] And in the fate of this people there is a lesson for all humanity. . . . This blood, which was to have given them life, cries for vengeance against them, more loudly than the blood of Abel. Faced with these punishments, Christ wept in vain; he saw as he died that his torments and his death would be a source of life for the entire world, but for the people he loved most here below, for his people, the cause of a terrible punishment, and his mercy was broken against that obstinate determination.[43]

[Léon Bloy:] Didn't this demoniacal people howl . . . , "His blood be on us and on our children!"? [44] [And elsewhere:] At the culminating point of the Passion, when a hundred thousand desperate Jews cried out for them to crucify him. . . .[45]

[Paul Claudel:] And the Jews, not only the notables, but all of the people, with a common voice and by a kind of plebiscite, the very ones who just

[40] Fillion, op. cit., III, 459.

[41] Father Joseph Huby, L'Évangile et les Évangiles, Paris, Beauchesne, 1929, p. 96.

[42] [An American Catholic commentary says likewise: "However, when the mob saw this, the chief priests took up a cry that put a curse on themselves and on the Jews for all time: 'His blood be upon us and our children'" (Living with Christ, Book II, a Christian Brothers publication, Winona, Minn., St. Mary's College Press, 1947; rev. ed., 1958, p. 247; quoted in Thering, op. cit.).—Ed.]

[43] Lebreton, op. cit., II, 417.

[44] Léon Bloy, Le Salut par les Juifs, Paris, Mercure de France, 1933, p. 95.

[45] Idem, quoted in Stanislas Fumet, Mission de Léon Bloy [Mission of Léon Bloy], Paris, Desclée de Brouwer, 1935, p. 244. [A current commentator says it more simply but with equal wrath: "The Jewish people have denied and crucified Jesus" (Buzy, op. cit., p. 165; quoted in Houtart and Giblet, op. cit., p. 151).—Ed.]

now led Jesus in triumph but whose temporal hopes this man in white once again disappointed, cry out, as they stamp their feet, in a voice which still today makes the ceilings of our cathedrals shake: *Non hunc sed Barabbam!* With Barabbas at least you know whom you are dealing with. We've had enough with Jesus. *Tolle! tolle!* Our nation spews Him out! Take Him away! Let us see Him no more! We can't deal with Him any more! Let Him leave us in peace! Let us clear the atmosphere of Him! It is not a question of *guilty* or *not guilty.* We simply don't want anything more to do with Him. We assume all the consequences. *Let His Blood fall on our heads and on our children's!* Are you satisfied now? What more do you need? [46]

[Giovanni Papini:] The Romans were simple material instruments. The Jews and the Jews alone conceived and desired the deicide. . . .[47]

François Mauriac, more tender-hearted, condemns the Jews to only a temporary curse: "The unhappy people cried, 'His blood be on us and on our children!' It was, and it is still, but not as an eternal curse: Israel's place at the right of the Son of David remains." But the same author has written earlier: "In the drama of Calvary, ordained from all eternity, it was not fitting that the Romans have any other role than that of executioner. Israel would use them to immolate its victim, but the victim belonged first to them." [48]

". . . it was not fitting that the Romans have any other role than that of executioner." It was not fitting. . . . To whom?

We have already quoted Daniel-Rops,[49] "This last wish of the people he had elected . . . was granted by God in his justice," and those sentences of an "unbearable horror" which he borrowed word for word from an essay by a German Catholic:

It doubtless did not rest with Israel not to kill its God after having failed to recognize him, and, as blood calls mysteriously to blood, it perhaps no more rests with Christian charity to prevent the horror of the pogrom from compensating for the unbearable horror of the Crucifixion in the secret balance sheet of the divine intentions.

[46] Claudel, *op. cit.,* p. 40. [Quotation taken from *idem, A Poet Before the Cross,* p. 34.—Tr.] But after this paraphrase, cruel in its deliberate coarseness, one must read in the same book the beautiful and noble pages in Chapter 2, "The Seven Last Words," containing the section titled "The First Word: *Father, forgive them; they do not know what it is they are doing*" (pp. 66, 87 [and pp. 61, 81.—Tr.]).

[47] Giovanni Papini, *Les Témoins de la Passion,* tr., Paris, Grasset, 1938, pp. 186–187.

[48] François Mauriac, *Vie de Jésus,* Paris, Flammarion, 1936, pp. 266, 222–223.

[49] See p. 260, above.

Let us also cull these sentences:

By what mysterious law of reversion and similarity have these abuses and persecutions beaten down for twenty centuries on the race who, more than the savage soldiers or Pilate, had taken the infamy of it on themselves, and who would demand responsibility for spilling [Jesus'] blood, as if it were an honor?

. . . The face of persecuted Israel fills History, but it cannot make one forget that other face sullied with blood and spit, which the Jewish crowd did not pity.

. . . Not able to execute Jesus because of prohibitions laid down by the protective power, the Jews schemed, with the tenacity and cunning we have observed them exercise under other circumstances, to make the Romans undertake the imposition of their sentence.[50]

In Father Bonsirven's opinion, there would be some vacillation in the traditional teaching:

These two exegeses [Saint Thomas Aquinas' and Saint John Chrysostom's] continue to have currency among Catholics: we still encounter the severer interpretation in modern commentaries; on the other hand, a number of contemporary commentators observe that the Jews' words mean quite simply that they assume the responsibility for Pilate's sentence.[51]

"Quite simply."

The distinction between these two interpretations does not seem very clear. What is clear is that "the severer interpretation" prevails, among an overwhelming majority.[52]

[50] Daniel-Rops, *op. cit.*, pp. 527, 523, 526–527, 529. These words were suppressed or modified in later editions of the book. See p. 260, n. 70, above. [But other authors, writing far more recently, have clung to the reprobation theme—with the assistance of Daniel-Rops, the Daniel-Rops of the 1945 *Jésus en son temps*. Under the heading "Why the Jews Refused Jesus," G. Maréchal intones: "This dreadful error of Israel is understandable, replies Daniel-Rops . . . (for the various prophecies could have been interpreted differently). . . . The Jews' hearts were hardened, and they dreamed only of rejecting Jesus in putting him to death" (*Le don de la vie* [The Gift of Life], 8th ed., "Notre foi et notre vie" series, Paris, Belin, 1962, pp. 107–108; quoted in Houtart and Giblet, *op. cit.*, pp. 196–197).—Ed.]

[51] Father Joseph Bonsirven, S.J., *Les Juifs et Jésus*, Paris, Beauchesne, 1937, pp. 184–185.

[52] Of the charitable minority, the best representative (to tell the truth, I do not know many others) seems to me to be Father Louis Richard (see Father Henri de Lubac *et al.*, *Israël et la foi chrétienne*, "Manifeste contre le Nazisme" series, Fribourg, Switz., Éd. de la Librairie de l'Université, 1942, pp. 105–106). I must point out again that, on the Catholic side as on the Protestant (see n. 30, above), a great effort has been made since 1948. The major credit for this lies with Paul Démann, former editor of *Cahiers sioniens*, and his colleague Renée Bloch, departed before her time; see pp. 255, n. 56, and 257, n. 63, above. The inquiry into catechetical literature cited in n. 56 was followed up by a complementary inquiry relating to liturgical formation: Paul Démann and Renée Bloch, "Formation

But here is the opinion, maturely considered, of a wise theologian, Father Journet:

Israel's offense is a collective offense, committed above all by Israel's chiefs and leaders, "the princes among the priests and the elders of the people" (Mt. 27:1), "the chief priests, with the elders and scribes, and the whole Sanhedrin" (Mk. 15:1),[53] but in which the mass of the crowd assembled in Jerusalem for the Passover celebrations nonetheless participated in an appalling way, without knowing precisely what it was all about. . . .

In actuality, Jesus' blood is a cause of catastrophe for the people who spilled it. And at the same time, for this same people, it has already been and continues ever to be a cause of partial conversion; and it will one day be a cause of total conversion. Such is the basis of traditional exegesis.[54]

But let us not forget: human or inhuman, Catholic or Protestant, all the commentators are agreed in asserting that there, before Pilate, in that unique hour, which struck once for all and counts more heavily for humanity than any other hour on earth, the Jewish people, whole and entire, took on themselves explicitly and expressly the responsibility for the innocent Blood.[55] Complete responsibility, responsibility

---

liturgique et attitude chrétienne envers les Juifs" [Liturgical Formation and Christian Attitude Toward the Jews], *Cahiers sioniens*, no. 2–3, June–September, 1953. This latter investigation has proved to be particularly efficacious.

[53] [The biblical quotations are translated directly from Father Journet's wording, with reference to RSV.—Tr.]

[54] Father Charles Journet, *Destinées d'Israël*, Paris, Egloff, 1945, pp. 134–135, 195. [Since the Second Vatican Ecumenical Council, this traditional basis has undergone changes. Monsignor John M. Oesterreicher, addressing a symposium titled "Vatican II and the Jews," stated: "To my knowledge, there is in the Church today no drive, no organized effort to proselytize Jews, and none is contemplated for tomorrow. . . . Though the Church will always profess Jesus as the Savior of all men; though she will never abandon her vision of a humanity united in faith and love . . .—she cannot treat the worshippers of the Holy One, blessed be He, as if they dwelt 'in the land of death's dark shadow' (Mt. 4:16 NEB; Is. 9:1). . . . [There has been] an unmistakable change in the Church's attitude and speech that makes me predict that the time for organized missions among Jews is gone" ("The New Encounter of Christians and Jews," symposium address, Incarnate Word College, San Antonio, Tex., March 5, 1967 [mimeo.], pp. 11–12).—Ed.]

[55] [An opinion to be found just as readily among commentators writing in English. In Protestant readings, a teaching instruction drawn from 1954 "denominational curriculum material" reads: "In treating the trial before the governor, present Pilate as an irresolute judge who let himself be driven by a bloody mob to condemn the innocent. The Jews' sin was the greater." The curriculum material continues: "Severely bruised and with blood streaming from His body, Jesus was presented to the Jews by Pilate with the pitying appeal, 'Behold the Man.' . . . The hard-hearted unbelieving Jews could not even thus be moved to pity" (quoted in Bernhard E. Olson, *Faith and Prejudice*, New Haven, Yale University Press, 1963, pp. 218–220). And Cecil Northcott writes: "'Let him be crucified. Crucify him, crucify him!' The mob chanted the dread words. Pilate saw the cruel hatred in their faces as they shouted aloud for the death of Jesus. 'But why

as a nation. It remains to be explored just how far the texts and the facts they allow us to glimpse substantiate the dreadful weight of such an assertion.

❂   ❂   ❂

In the first place, one is struck by the agreement—at least the apparent agreement—of the four evangelists on what is the basis of the question: Jewish responsibility.

With few variations, the four accounts follow an identical blueprint: Pontius Pilate, an accommodating procurator, inclined to release Jesus; the Jews, savage and relentless, preferring a Barabbas to a Jesus; and Pilate finally bowing to their pressure, their threats, their blackmail: Barabbas freed, Jesus crucified.

"Striking parallelism." [56]

But only superficially striking. For the historian reading and rereading these four texts, it is quite apparent that only one actual fact emerges clearly: Jesus was scourged, then crucified at the command of the Roman procurator. I will not go so far as to say, like certain exegetes: all the rest is embroidery, tendentious, polemica. But I have grounds for saying, with a firm conviction that I am not exceeding the rights and duties of historic criticism: all the rest is subject to caution.

The four evangelists testify that the Roman pronounced the death sentence under pressure from the Jews, and they testify unquestion-

---

crucify him?' asked Pilate . . ." (*People of the Bible*, Philadelphia, Westminster, 1967, p. 114).

[Catholic authors build like images. According to Monsignor Rudolph G. Bandas' simplification, "Pilate said: 'I cannot find any reason for punishing Him.' But the Jews shouted louder and louder, 'Crucify Him' " ("Lesson 20: Christ Suffered and Died for Us," installment of "New Catechism Series," *The Wanderer* [St. Paul, Minn.], February 29, 1968, p. 41). And Father John J. Walsh, S.J., observes, "Even the Roman governor himself, although he was nominally supreme in Jerusalem, had been cowed into doing against his will the bidding of these wily and resourceful men [the leaders of the Jewish nation]" (*This Is Catholicism*, Garden City, N. Y., Doubleday, 1959; rprntd. in *idem*, "This Is Catholicism: The Jewish Leaders," *The Criterion* [Indianapolis], September 6, 1963).

[While quotations like these may seem unpersuasive to fair-minded Christians, their impact on American thinking is unfortunately proven. A sociological study concluded in 1965 gives the findings of a survey conducted among a white nationally representative sample of almost 2,000 people. In their book relating these findings, Gertrude J. Selznick and Stephen Steinberg report that 50 percent of the Christians interviewed named the Jews as the group "most responsible for killing Christ" (*The Tenacity of Prejudice: Anti-Semitism in Contemporary America*, New York, Harper & Row, 1969, p. 11).—Ed.]

[56] Daniel-Rops, *op. cit.*, p. 464.

ingly, emphatically, quite concurrently. But as their testimony is prosecution testimony, partisan and passionate, and is as well indirect
and after the event, it is impossible—speaking honestly—to accept it
without reservations.

Moreover, is it possible to say "the four"? This figure has no meaning unless it is correct to consider the four accounts as fully independent of one another. Who would venture to affirm this? The contrary
opinion is backed by the strongest circumstantial evidence. It is infinitely probable that Matthew and Luke and indeed John himself
knew Mark's account, which is the earliest, and that they drew
greater or lesser inspiration from it. This leaps to the eye with regard
to the first Gospel, Matthew's, whose text is an almost literal repro-
duction of Mark's, with a few emendations and additions that tend
most often to increase Jewish responsibility or to demonstrate the fulfillment of the Scriptures (Jewish Scriptures). As for Luke and John,
everything indicates that they were familiar with Mark's text; if they
followed it less closely, less exclusively, if they had recourse to other
sources, they were nonetheless derivative from Mark. These observations made, the concurrence among the evangelists no longer seems
so impressive. In this case and in figures, let us say that $4 = 1 +
1/20 + 1/2 + 1/2$, not much more.

There is agreement only on the substratum, the basic theme. Taking Mark's account as their point of departure, each of the three other
evangelists followed his natural bent, so to speak, his inclinations, his
personal interests and his personal line of inquiry.

Hence there are multiple divergences, as previously, which do not
all seem to be secondary or minimal.

Example: the crowd, that crowd indispensable for the indictment
of the whole Jewish people, does appear in Mark 15:8, Matthew
27:15, and Luke 23:13. It is totally absent from John's account, where
only "the chief priests and the officers" enter onto the scene (19:6)—
an absence which obstructs the thesis of collective responsibility.
Apologetics therefore passes over it in silence.

Similarly, there is an irreconcilable disagreement among the accounts on the time sequence of the Passion, whose pace supposedly
was singularly rapid according to Mark 15:25, since ". . . it was the
third hour [nine o'clock in the morning], when they crucified him,"
less rapid according to John 19:14, since ". . . it was about the sixth
hour" (noon) when the sentencing occurred.[57]

[57] See p. 288, n. 2, above.

Matthew (27:24–25) is alone in knowing and telling that the Roman procurator Pilate washed his hands, solemnly, in accordance with Jewish custom, to absolve himself of responsibility for the innocent blood which he saw himself compelled to spill. Alone too in noting that "all the people" cried, "His blood be on us and on our children!" Mark, Luke, and John know nothing, say nothing about either the famous washing of hands or the terrifying exclamation.

Matthew (27:19) is likewise alone in knowing that while Pilate was in court, he received a message from his wife which was favorable to Jesus.

According to Mark 15:7, Barabbas had supposedly participated in an insurrection during which there was manslaughter. Matthew 27:16 calls him "a notorious prisoner." Luke 23:19, inflating Mark, charges him with both sedition and murder. So this is the Barabbas of the Synoptics: a notorious agitator, "a kind of national hero," says Father Lagrange.[58] But there remains the fourth Gospel, John 18:40: "Now Barabbas was a robber."

Daniel-Rops provides this elegant amalgam of canonical and apocryphal texts: "Now there was a famous bandit in prison named Barabbas, guilty of murder during an insurrection." [59]

The suggestive gradation observed in the first phase of the trial recurs in this phase. The gradation is already quite noticeable from Mark to Matthew 27:24–25, according to which Pilate expressly absolves himself of responsibility (with the washing of hands) and "all the [Jewish] people," on the contrary, assume it, as if pleased to. In Luke, Pilate declares Jesus innocent three times and shows intentions of releasing him (23:14–16, 20, 22). John goes yet farther. He does not hesitate to prolong the procurator's strange comings and goings into and out of the praetorium. After the interlude of the scourging come the pitiable exhibition: "Here is the man!" (19:5); another exchange between Pilate and "the Jews"; Pilate's uneasiness when he learns that Jesus calls himself "the Son of God"; another exchange between Pilate and Jesus; a new attempt by Pilate to release Jesus; blackmail by "the Jews," who "cried out, 'If you release this man, you are not Caesar's friend . . .'" (19:12), before which the vacillating procurator finally

[58] Father Marie-Joseph Lagrange, O.P., ed. and tr., *Évangile selon saint Matthieu*, Paris, Gabalda, 1922, p. 519.
[59] Daniel-Rops, *op. cit.*, p. 514. The author's source for the apocryphal additives would likely be the so-called Gospel of Nicodemus, which quotes the specious *Acta Pilati*, where Pilate says: "I have a famous murderer in prison named Barabbas."

cedes: "Then he handed him over to them to be crucified" (19:16).

Real competition to see who will make the Jews more odious. As varied, rich, and moving as the writer of the fourth Gospel is, the honors go to Matthew—or at least to the writer of verse 25 in chapter 27; he shot the poisoned arrow, permanently embedded, with a sure hand.

✿   ✿   ✿

What could commentators not say, what have they not said, taking a stand on the ground of historic credibility? But this is dangerous ground, I know: truth can sometimes be incredible. I am only more at ease for observing that the character of Pontius Pilate, especially in Matthew and John, crosses the line into incredibility; "a farcical judge," in Loisy's phrase.[60]

Incredible, this omnipotent procurator who, in his perplexity, asks his subjects the Jews, his creatures the chief priests, what he should indeed do with the prisoner Jesus (Mk. 15:12; Mt. 27:22).

Incredible, this massacrer of Jews and Samaritans, suddenly seized with scruples about a Galilean Jew suspected of messianic agitation, who actually reaches the point of seeking pity for him from the Jews: "Why, what evil has he done?" (Mk. 15:14; Mt. 27:23).

Incredible, this Roman functionary who, to absolve himself of responsibility—before the God of Israel, no doubt—resorts to the symbolic Jewish ritual of washing the hands (Mt. 27:24).

Incredible, this canny politician who takes it into his head that day to plead the cause of a poor beggar of a prophet against the native oligarchy whom it was Roman practice to rely on, and whom he did rely on: it was through Annas and Caiaphas that a Pilate controlled Judea.

Incredible, this representative of Rome, having the prime duty and concern of enforcing respect for Roman majesty, who, in deference to some pietistic Jews, comes and goes from his court chambers to the street where they are assembled.

Incredible, this iron-fisted governor, ready to repress bloodily any insurrection or threat of insurrection, who, to please the (Jewish) crowd, consents to free a "notorious" agitator, imprisoned on charges

[60] Alfred Loisy, *La Naissance du christianisme*, Paris, Nourry, 1933, p. 105, n. 1.

of sedition and murder (and why, with Barabbas freed, does it follow that Jesus must be crucified?).

Incredible, this magistrate, the maker of the law in his province, who seems ignorant of it, saying to the chief priests questioning him: "Take him yourselves and crucify him . . ." (Jn. 19:6).

Incredible, this skeptical pagan, who is impressed with the accusation that the Jews cast against Jesus—according to John 19:7–8—that ". . . he has made himself the Son of God" (in the Christian sense, of itself beyond the reach of a pagan as well as a Jew).

Incredible, this Roman justice, so formalistic, which seems to have forgone all the customary forms, all its rules of procedure for Jesus' trial.

But more incredible yet, a thousand times more incredible, this Jewish crowd, "all the [Jewish] people," this pious and patriotic people, suddenly seized with rage against Jesus, to the point of going and thronging around Pilate, the abhorred Roman, to compel him to take the prophet so admired the day before, a man of the people, one of their own, and have him put on a cross by Roman soldiers according to Roman practice. Can you imagine the French crowd, "all the [French] people," demonstrating in Paris in 1942 before the German commandant's headquarters, howling, "Shoot him! Shoot him!" so that Herr General Heinrich von Stülpnagel would order the execution of one or another notorious Communist, Gabriel Péri for example? [61] Oh, they could have unearthed the few hundreds or thousands of Frenchmen necessary for an operation of this sort, we know whom; but all the people of Paris, all the French people, and back then, demonstrating before Pontius Pilate, "all the [Jewish] people"? Come, now!

✿   ✿   ✿

Let us advance. Let us consider our texts more closely, principally the Synoptics, where I have indicated the role they attribute to the crowd, and among them principally Matthew, where we have seen the use—the abuse—that Christian tradition and literature have made, continue to make, of the ominous verse 25 of chapter 27. At

[61] [General von Stülpnagel was the commandant of the Paris District during the German Occupation of France in World War II.—Tr. Gabriel Péri, a member of the French Chamber of Deputies, was a renowned figure in the Resistance and was ultimately caught and shot for his underground activities.—Ed.]

every step, we stumble over palpable instances of dubious historicity.
Everything conspires to awaken mistrust.

The custom of freeing a prisoner each Feast of Passover, the practice the crowd asked for?

Nowhere outside the Gospels of Mark, Matthew, and John is any
allusion made to this. Nowhere among Jewish writers, even in the co-
pious works of Flavius Josephus, which go so deeply into detail on
events and customs. It is noteworthy that the (relatively) best historian of the three Synoptic evangelists, Luke, does not mention it;
Luke 23:17 is interpolated, as we have said.[62] When Mark and Matthew speak of it, they betray their hesitancy even in the uncertainty
of their composition form, leaving the impression of an awkwardly
grafted postscript:

[In the preceding verses, only Sanhedrists, chief priests, have been involved:] Now at the feast he used to release for them one prisoner whom
they asked. And . . . there was a man called Barabbas. And the crowd
came up and began to ask Pilate to do as he was wont to do for them.

Mk. 15:6–8

Now at the feast the governor was accustomed to release for the crowd any
one prisoner whom they wanted. And they [?] had then a notorious prisoner, called Barabbas. So when they [?] had gathered, Pilate said to
them. . . .

Mt. 27:15–17

It is useless for us to join in the interminable (and fruitless) legalistic debate aimed solely at determining whether Pilate applied the
abolitio privata or the *indulgentia*, some—like Father Lagrange—
inclining toward the *abolitio*, others toward the *indulgentia*, there
being no possibility of establishing with certainty whether the procurator of Judea disposed of these sovereign rights at that time.

In support of the Gospel accounts, modern commentators call especially on a Greco-Egyptian papyrus dating from the years 86–88,
hence fairly close to the Passion; it is a report on an audience with C.
Septimius Vegetus, prefect of Egypt, during which the prefect
declared to one Phibion: "You deserve to be scourged, but I grant
your pardon in consideration of the crowd." A highly enigmatic sentence, says Father Lagrange, ". . . but the remission of punishment in
consideration of the public seems certain." [63] Yes, the comparison is

[62] See n. 28, above.
[63] Lagrange, . . . *Marc*, p. 414.

rather striking, at least in appearance. For nothing in this latter case indicates that it was question of a custom, a recognized right of the crowd, a right such that the Roman magistrate could see himself constrained against his will to release a prisoner indicted for insurrection and murder: it is far from this Phibion of the Greco-Egyptian papyrus to the Barabbas of the Gospels.

Barabbas?

It is time we summoned this illustrious unknown, a famous agitator according to the Synoptics, a robber according to the fourth Gospel, an "infamous robber" and "killer" elaborates a millennial tradition. "Infamous" we know nothing about. But odder indeed than he is generally considered, surrounded with more mystery, and we can even wonder if he ever existed.

How many people, even the most assiduous readers of the Bible, know the curious fact—the troubling coincidence—that Barabbas, according to the evangelist Matthew, or at least according to a number of manuscripts of Matthew, was also himself called Jesus?

Whom do you want me to release for you, Jesus Barabbas or Jesus who is called Christ? [64]

Mt. 27:17

While not quite daring to introduce the reading "Jesus Barabbas" into the Gospel text, Father Lagrange cannot refrain from believing in its genuineness: "One cannot assume that so salient a reading is the result of an error by the copyists: either the name entered several manuscripts of Matthew through the apocrypha, or it is genuine." [65] In the first half of the third century, Origen, surprised to read "Jesus Barabbas" in numerous manuscripts, proposed the hypothesis that perhaps a dishonest addition was involved. But the hypothesis seems groundless, and much rather applies to the suppression of the name. Thus the thesis of genuineness remains.

This is not all. The very name *Barabbas* has a singular ring. It is sometimes transcribed *Bar-Rabba*, which becomes *Bar-Rabban* with certain authors, and means "son of a rabbi," "son of a master." But this arbitrary transcription, which is based on hardly anything more than an allusion of Saint Jerome's to the apocryphal Gospel according

[64] [Note *k* on Matthew 27:17 in RSV reads: "Other ancient authorities read *Jesus Barabbas*." Thus, the translation here is the RSV, with "Jesus" inserted before "Barabbas."—Tr.]
[65] Lagrange, . . . *Matthieu*, pp. 520–521.

to the Hebrews, has the main advantage of avoiding the normal transcription and translation, which are bothersome: for Barabbas or Bar-
abba means "son of Abba," and as "Abba" was used sometimes as a
proper name and sometimes as a common noun with the meaning "father," "son of Abba" can also signify "son of the Father." The name
Bar-Abba seems to have been fairly widespread among the Jews. This
notwithstanding, its appearance in the present case, with the meaning
it inevitably evokes, is again a surprising and troubling coincidence.
What! This man the Jewish crowd clamors to have freed, this man
was called "Jesus, son of the Father" according to the first Gospel
(and perhaps also, let us venture to hypothesize, according to the
second [66])? I leave to be imagined all the conjectures, all the theories,
more or less ingenious (and rash), that have been and continue to be
built on such a coincidence. These are only and can only be intellectual exercises, without solid foundation, not deserving to be tarried
over. Better that we limit ourselves to observing the strangeness of
the mystery we find ourselves immersed in, owing very likely to the
fact that Christian tradition was early subjected to the demands of
catechesis, apologetics, and anti-Jewish polemics. From this an amalgam formed in which, for lack of information from another source, the
portion of historic truths is absolutely undiscernible with regard to
the account of the Passion. But why silence the suspicion that imposes itself on my mind and heart, almost in spite of me, letting me
glimpse—like a Precambrian substructure rising out of a geological
fault—some primitive tradition according to which it was really
Jesus, the true, the one and only Jesus, for whom an anxious Jewish
crowd implored pardon?

Perhaps this fleeting light has worth only for me: I have no illusions in this regard, restraining myself from attributing a clarifying
value to it which it cannot have. Yet I prefer it to the laboriously contrived explanation which some have attempted—among them Salo-
mon Reinach and Alfred Loisy—an explanation which is almost as
tendentious as the Gospel narrative for which it claims to furnish the
key. It relates to the connection which has long been made between
the Barabbas episode in the Gospels and the story of poor, crazy Kar-

---

[66] Mark 15:7: ". . . there was a man called [or surnamed] Barabbas." Some
exegetes have proposed the hypothesis that the original text should be: ". . .
there was a man, Jesus, called [surnamed] Barabbas." "Jesus" would supposedly
have been suppressed later. But as no manuscript bears any trace of this, the hypothesis remains very risky.

abas recounted by Philo in his *Against Flaccus*, 36–39 (=6). Incontestably, the Romans did treat Jesus like a buffoon king: in this respect there is a visible kinship between the Gospel accounts and Philo's, as well as others which evoke other similar masquerades—the Sacae among the Persians, the saturnalia in Rome. But none of this makes "Karabas" equal "Barabbas."

The famous scene which counterpoints Pilate's washing of hands with the cry of "all the [Jewish] people": "His blood be on us and on our children!"?

We have already spoken of this. Not enough, if we think of all the harm that has come from it.

We have said that those excessively well-known verses, excessively well-conceived for striking the popular imagination, are peculiar to Matthew, Matthew's alone, to the exclusion of Mark, "Peter's interpreter," of Luke, the best "historian" among the evangelists according to Father Lagrange, of John, whose account of the Passion, we are assured, would be inspired in large part by personal recollections. For this episode—as for the one of the message to Pilate from his wife—Matthew is linked only with the apocryphal gospels; and he is entitled to be given or denied credit the same as they. How to explain the silence of the other evangelists? Do we not have the right to say again here what was said earlier about Judas' kiss? Must we not believe that if such reverses, on such a day, had really, *really* taken place, they would have remained deeply etched in their memories? And that it would be incumbent on every narrator to recall them?

We have already pointed out how incredible Pilate's gesture was. Doubly incredible, not only because of his singular concern with absolving himself of responsibility, but because of his even more singular recourse to a fundamentally Jewish rite. What are we to think of this Roman procurator who expresses himself and acts in the manner of a Jewish sacrificer or teacher, as if the Old Testament were familiar to him, as familiar as it was to the evangelist Matthew?

[Expiation of a murder whose author is unknown:] And all the elders of that city nearest to the slain man shall wash their hands over the heifer whose neck was broken in the valley; and they shall testify, "Our hands did not shed this blood. . . . Forgive, O Lord, thy people Israel, . . . and set not the guilt of innocent blood in the midst of thy people Israel. . . ."

Deut. 21:6–8

The only thing missing is the heifer. "I am innocent of this man's blood," says Pilate as he washes his hands.

"To wash one's hands in innocence" is a typically Jewish formula, found in Psalms 26:6 and 73:13, as is also the reply, "His blood be on . . .":

> And David said to him, "Your blood be upon your head. . . ."
>
> 2 Sam. 1:16; see also 3:28–29

> On me be the guilt [for the blood spilled], . . . and on my father's house. . . .
>
> 2 Sam. 14:9

> "My blood be upon the inhabitants of Chaldea,"
> let Jerusalem say.
>
> Jer. 51:35

These are the texts which inspired this evangelist, whom no one would deny is the most thoroughly steeped in the Old Testament; these are the texts which Matthew 27:24–25 issued from.

Fruitlessly does Father Lagrange, trying to dispel evident misgivings, aver that the pagans—Greeks and Romans—also knew of this form of protesting innocence: they knew of the purification of hands after a murder, which is not at all the same thing. The learned exegete honestly quotes Origen, who with extreme (and very embarrassing) frankness confesses that "Pilate used a Jewish custom; doing this, he did not act in the Roman way." There follows an attempt at explanation which reveals some discomfiture: "Origen was correct in saying that such an act was absolutely contrary to the procedure in Roman courts, where the judge assumed responsibility for his acts." There we have clarity. Father Lagrange continues:

> Pilate thought he could allow himself to do what his superstitious [?] terror suggested to him, not so as to conform to the customs of the Jews, which he despised, but because they ought to understand such clear symbolism readily, and he hoped they would come to the aid of his troubled conscience by taking everything on themselves.[67]

There we have less clarity, in substance and form. This psychiatrist's diagnosis inspires no confidence in me. But I hold on to the admission that Pilate's gesture was "absolutely contrary to the procedure in Roman courts"; it is enough: I am justified in concluding from it that in all likelihood the gesture was never made. All this stage-setting is

---

[67] Lagrange, . . . Matthieu, p. 523.

worthy of the apocrypha, where in fact it is to be found, exaggerated to absurdity.[68]

The Jews' reply, "His blood be on us and on our children!", is assuredly less paradoxical for being linked to ancient Hebraic traditions and formulas. This does not make it seem any less incredible, as we have said, in its very atrociousness, in the rage it expresses. Says Father Lagrange:

There are examples of swearing on the most cherished heads . . . but it is quite another thing to perpetuate a condemnation by involving one's children in it. Could any instances of this be found? This one is understandable only if the Jews were persuaded that Jesus had blasphemed by giving himself the title of Son of God. Thus they estimated that they had nothing to fear in provoking the wrath of heaven.[69]

Which is the same as saying—and deserves to be said explicitly— that the Jews (at least, those who shouted those terrible words) believed in the reality, in the enormity of the blasphemy, that they therefore sinned out of ignorance, as the Apostle Peter declares in Acts 3:17; and not only they—the crowd—but also their leaders, ". . . for if they had [understood], they would not have crucified the Lord of glory" (1 Cor. 2:8). But think about this: aside from the leaders, chief priests, and some other Sanhedrists, how many Jews could have known exactly the nature of the blasphemy charged—which we are not sure, as seen earlier, was the assertion of sonship, in a meaning which was extraordinary and, I repeat, almost inaccessible on the face of it to the human mind, at any rate to the Jewish mind?

Then where could their feelings have come from—their ferocity, their fury, their thirst for murder, to the point of involving (absolutely unnecessarily) "the most cherished heads," those of their own children? Incredible, incomprehensible, unreal.

Moreover, the dreadful cry is only a response, and on that score it automatically ceases to exist along with Pilate's washing of hands and protestation of innocence, which it supposedly answers. It answers to something else entirely, in fact: the evangelist's utter determination, in Father Lagrange's excellent phrase, "to show how the Jewish people . . . fully assumed responsibility for the death of their Christ." [70]

Never has the tendentiousness of an account, never has concern for

---

[68] Father Léon Vaganay, ed., *Évangile de Pierre* [Gospel of Peter], Paris, Gabalda, 1930, p. 202.
[69] Lagrange, . . . *Matthieu*, p. 524.
[70] *Ibid.*, p. 522.

"demonstration" [71] emerged with more clarity, a clarity that blazes and climaxes in verses 24–25, and fathers conviction in any open mind.

No, Pilate did not wash his hands in the Jewish manner.

No, Pilate did not protest his innocence.

No, the Jewish crowd did not cry out, "His blood be on us and on our children!"

The case is clear. That is, it is for all men of good faith. I would be so bold as to say: it is before God, too. Is there any need to recall how vigorously God's spokesmen Jeremiah and particularly Ezekiel, reacting against certain barbarian tendencies in primitive Yahwism, had declared that responsibility for sin or crime is not transmitted from one generation to another?

[The Lord says:] What do you mean by repeating this proverb concerning the land of Israel, "The fathers have eaten sour grapes, and the children's teeth are set on edge"? As I live, says the Lord God, this proverb shall no more be used by you in Israel. Behold, all souls are mine; the soul of the father as well as the soul of the son is mine: the soul that sins shall die. . . .

The son shall not suffer for the iniquity of the father, nor the father suffer for the iniquity of the son. . . .

Therefore I will judge you, O house of Israel, every one according to his ways. . . .

Ezek. 18:2–4, 20, 30

A certain teaching, a certain tradition refuses to bow, even before God; we have already taken up several examples. Its proponents do not want "the holy declarations of Ezekiel," or more exactly God's word through the mouth of Ezekiel, to nullify "the reality of the mystery of collective wrongs" [72] proclaimed in Deuteronomy 5:9–10 (yes, after the commandment of the Decalogue which forbids bowing down before "graven images"):

. . . I the Lord your God am a jealous God, visiting the iniquity of the fathers upon the children to the third and fourth generation of those who hate me, but showing steadfast love to thousands of those who love me and keep my commandments.

How to reconcile these two "revelations"? (It already appears in the second that the restrictive penalty for God's enemies is offset by infinite love for His faithful.)

They "are not irreconcilable," Father Journet explains,

[71] Father Bonsirven's term; see p. 292, above.
[72] Journet, *op. cit.*, p. 136.

. . . because on the one hand, the wrong of the ancient rulers or leaders could indeed prepare, for men of their own and future times, a web of deleterious attractions and life conditions harmful to private as much as to public religion; but on the other hand, these attractions and life conditions, not being really determinants, that is, causes of invincible moral error, would pass into the state of wrongs only in the exact measure that they are nonetheless accepted internally by the conscience of each individual person.[73]

And that is how an eminent theologian, one of the most fair-minded of all, strives to reconcile the irreconcilable.

✿   ✿   ✿

Not all has been said, however. And indeed the essential remains to be said.

In Matthew 27:25, there are the words "all the people," which have been a gold mine in the Christian anti-Jewish tradition and which consequently deserve examining. There is "the crowd" in Mark 15:8–15, "the people" in Luke 23:13. There is neither "people" nor "crowd" in John.

Thus in the last analysis, in the last stage of this long exploration, we are led here to formulate the capital question:

does anyone have the right to say, teach, proclaim on every occasion (as they do) that the Jewish people "as a whole" joined with their leaders, that the people themselves cried out with one voice demanding Jesus' death, forced the procurator Pilate to pronounce the death sentence, that they therefore largely participated in the supreme crime, that they are fully responsible "as a whole" for the Crucifixion?

We know, furthermore—through the quotations given, which are merely samples from a limitless literature—that the question does not occur to the vast majority of exegetes, theologians, Christian writers, Catholic or Protestant. "Let the Jews not say: We did not kill Christ. . . ." [74] "All the people," "pas o laos," wrote Matthew at 27:25.

[73] Ibid., loc. cit.

[74] Roman Breviary, Office for Good Friday Night, Sixth Lesson. [The Byzantine liturgy echoes: "Where lies the folly of the Hebrews? Where lies their infidelity? How long will you wander? How long will you be bastards? . . . Truly you are all the sons of darkness" (Third Hymn of Compline, Saturday of Lazarus, Eve of Palm Sunday; quoted in Sister Marie Despina, "Jews in Oriental Christian Liturgy," Sidic [Rome], October–November, 1967, p. 15).

[American commentators also take up the refrain, as Sister Rose Albert Thering, O.P., points out in The Potential in Religion Textbooks for Developing a Realistic Self-Concept (doctoral dissertation, St. Louis University, 1961). According

It is enough. Witness this commentary from the most highly qualified
Catholic exegete, Father Lagrange:

Up to this point, it has been a question only of the crowd or the leaders.
Now it is the nation, *o laos*, which will declare itself, the same people
whom Jesus was to save (1:21: ". . . you shall call his name Jesus, for he
will save his people from their sins") and whose sick he had cured (4:23).
This is the only time they come on the scene as the subject.[75]

It would be easy to answer: the only time in Matthew, for it is
written in Luke 19:48: ". . . and all the people [*o laos apas*] hung
upon his words."

But where are we? Utterly beyond reality. For if with the wave of
a wand "the people" mentioned in Matthew 27:20 become "all the
people" (in the sense of all the nation, the whole of the people) in
27:25, this cannot be in reality, obviously, but in the abstract, in the
imagination of the writer, obeying his profoundest feeling, as Albert
Réville properly points out.[76] And as the commentators—obeying the
same tendencies—have exercised their imaginations on this imaginary theme for nigh on twenty centuries, any sense of reality about it
has been literally abolished from minds fashioned by so long and
profitable and fascinating a tradition.

It is not a historic theme that we have to discuss presently but a
stained-glass window picture. An awkward task. But we are obliged
to pursue it nonetheless, however thick the crust of legend we must
cut through to reach what alone is important: the truth.

A preliminary observation needs to be made in this regard, one we

to John Laux, "The worst deed of the Jewish people, the murder of the Messias,
resulted in the greatest blessings for mankind" (*Church History*, rev. ed., Chicago,
Benziger, 1945, p. 9). And Father William F. Ferrell, S.J., writes: "Why did the
Jews commit the great sin of putting God Himself to death? It was because our
Lord told them the Truth, because He preached a divine doctrine that displeased
them, and because He told them to give up their wicked ways" (*Loyalty*, "Essen-
tials of Religion" series, Book II, Chicago, Loyola University Press, 1949, p. 38;
both quoted in Thering, *op. cit.*). A French catechetic manual says similarly: "Israel has crimes on its conscience; it killed the prophets; it is hardening now instead of returning to its first commitments; it will go so far as to kill God's own
Son" (G. Delcuve, *Jésus-Christ, notre Sauveur*, 3rd ed., "Témoins du Christ" series, V, Tournai, Casterman, Éd. de Lumen Vitale, 1960, p. 112; quoted in Houtart
and Giblet, *op. cit.*, p. 154).—Ed.]

[75] Lagrange, . . . *Matthieu, loc. cit.*; and see Journet, *op. cit.*, p. 135.

[76] "This is a translation into objective fact of the idea, dear to the Jewish-
Christian evangelist, that in letting itself be led astray by its religious chiefs . . .
the Jewish nation drew down on itself the frightful misfortunes which were to
strike it some thirty years later" (Albert Réville, *Jésus de Nazareth*, 2 vols., Paris,
Fischbacher, 1906, II, 363).

have made before, one we must take up again: the evangelists' accounts do not agree.

It is indeed a fact to be pondered that there is no trace of "the crowd," of "the people" in the fourth Gospel. "It is not a question here of the people," notes Father Lagrange, "but of partisan or paid men," [77] specifically *uperetai*—underlings or officers of the chief priests. It was these, gathered around the chief priests, who demonstrated before the praetorium like well-schooled police and cried out, "Crucify him, crucify him!" (Jn. 19:6). Now, the fourth evangelist wrote long after the others; he knew the accounts of the others; if he departed from them on this point, it was perhaps not without reason: "the chief priests and the officers," baptized "the Jews," seemed to him personages who more than adequately represented official Judaism.

There is not perfect agreement among the three Synoptics themselves. In Luke 23:13, it is Pilate who takes the initiative, after Herod has sent Jesus back to him, and "called together the chief priests and the rulers and the people," a summoning about which the other evangelists say nothing, about which the least one can say is that it seems peculiar, for "Pilate did not have to consult the people but only their Council [the author means: the Sanhedrin, which is not "the Council of the people"] before passing a death sentence." [78] Obviously the people are there only for form, or for principle's sake, to take their part of a responsibility which it was decided to assign them. If not, how do we explain Pilate's words to them in the following verse— "You brought me this man as one who was perverting the people . . ." (Lk. 23:14), words which quite clearly are not addressed to the people?

There remain the tandem accounts of Mark and Matthew, whose hesitant and awkward style we have already noted as evidencing a poorly grafted postscript (see page 340, above). In Mark 15:8, "the crowd" come to the praetorium of themselves, without being summoned, and of themselves, as is customary (according to 15:6), ask the procurator to free a prisoner; but as Father Lagrange very rightly remarks, "If they were not thinking of Jesus' release, why did they appear at that particular moment [when Jesus' fate was in the balance] and at that early hour? Thus it seems that their good impulse was in

---

[77] Lagrange, . . . *Jean*, p. 481.
[78] *Idem*, . . . *Luc*, pp. 580–581.

favor of the Galilean." [79] In Matthew 27:17, the crowd gather without our being told explicitly whether they have come of themselves, or been summoned, or been herded together by the chief priests; the word *crowd* itself is not uttered (it is at 27:15): "So when they had gathered," we read, "Pilate said to them, 'Whom do you want me to release for you, Jesus Barabbas or Jesus who is called Christ?' " [80] In both Gospels, "the chief priests" according to Mark 15:11 or "the chief priests and the elders" according to Matthew 27:20 work on the crowd, arouse them against Jesus, incite them to call for Barabbas— which quite obviously forces us to suppose that the crowd which was involved was not immense. Docilely "the crowd," "the people" call for Barabbas and set about making a furious clamor for Jesus to be put on the cross. Finally, according to Matthew 27:25, it is "all the people" who cry, "His blood be on us and on our children!"

In sum, of the four versions, three appear difficult to reconcile. There are only two, Mark's and Matthew's, where the role of the crowd is—rather awkwardly—explained and stressed; actually, there is just one, Mark's, on which Matthew depends heavily. And in this single account, the role attributed to the crowd seems as dubious in its historicity as does the Passover custom by reason of which the evangelist brings the crowd onto the scene.

Logically, and in accordance with the rules of historic method, the four accounts which do not agree cannot be all accepted at a time, unless they are "harmonized." We have to choose. And particularly to choose between—

Mark's testimony, of the chief priests and the crowd, whom at a given moment and for the occasion (and to the greatest advantage of traditional theology) Matthew baptizes "all the people,"

or John's testimony, of the chief priests and their "officers."

If we consider the speed with which the events unfolded and the people's obviously favorable attitude toward Jesus up to that moment, we are tempted to give preference to John on this specific point. There are the strongest reasons for believing that all this occurred, apparently in an amicable fashion, between the Roman procurator and his creatures, the Jewish high priests—the sinister trio of Pilate, Annas, and Caiaphas—without it being possible to discern which side the initiative came from, the Jewish or the Roman. Little does it matter, moreover, in our humble opinion.

[79] *Idem*, . . . *Matthieu*, p. 519.
[80] [See n. 64, above.—Tr.]

*   *   *

But let us give the upper hand to tradition and "harmonistics."
Let us grant the incredible.

Let us grant that this strange Roman procurator—he too transformed with the wave of a magic wand—was inclined to release the
Jew Jesus, accused of messianic pretensions and agitation.

Let us grant that there existed in Judea that singular custom oblig-
ing him to free a prisoner, no matter which, at the will of the crowd
on each Feast of Passover.

Let us grant that there was a notorious Jewish agitator in the
Roman prisons named Barabbas (or Jesus Barabbas), charged with
sedition and murder.

Let us grant that the crowd had massed before the praetorium
around the chief priests, and that Pilate had given them a choice between Barabbas and Jesus (of Nazareth), hoping they would choose
the Nazarene and not the other, the other Jesus.

Let us grant that the excellent Pilate readily consented to free Barabbas, that seditionist, that murderer perhaps.

Let us grant that he then asked the Jewish crowd, he, the Roman
procurator, what he should do with Jesus, accused of having called
himself Messiah and King.

Let us grant that the crowd began to howl at the top of their
voices, "Crucify him! Crucify him!"

Let us grant everything. Let us take from all hands. Let us grant
with Matthew that Pilate "washed his hands in innocence" in keeping
with the Jewish rite and the Psalmist's phrase, and let us also grant,
let us even grant—with Matthew—that in answer "all the people"
carried their savagery, their blindness to the point of daring to cry
out, "His blood be on us and on our children!" Let us grant with John
that the spectacle of Jesus bruised and bleeding after the scourging,
got up (by the Roman soldiers) in the crown of thorns and robe of
purple, that this pitiable, unbearable spectacle only revived, stimulated the rage of the people, drove it to paroxysm. Yes, let us grant
everything, including the ending: Pilate finally ceding to the frenzied
Jews, sending Jesus to his death, to the cross, only because of their
threatening blackmail. . . .

Impossible to go any farther on the road of concessions, in renounc-
ing critical judgment.

Well, then, with all these points granted, with all these contradictions, with the incredible raised to the level of historic truth, I say

that even this, this total acceptance of tradition, does not give anyone the right to conclude that Israel is guilty of the crime, that the Jewish people are fully responsible for it (nor to state it on every occasion to the Christian people, nor to teach it to children in the catechism).[81]

I say it and I prove it.

First, and with a view to our demonstration, let us turn to the commentaries of the most traditional exegetes. All their efforts—to explain—are oriented in the same direction: to find a solution for what seems to them to be the principal problem or difficulty, "the about-face of the crowd," [82] that Jewish crowd who were still enthusiastic over their prophet, who still "hung upon his words," the day before.

One, Father Charue, explains, without offering the slightest proof, that this had been developing for a long time; an evolution had taken place in the minds of the popular masses.[83]

Another, Father Lebreton, carefully leaves aside the testimony of the Synoptics, and submits certain texts of John to support his assertion that the people had long been split, "divided between the influence of the Pharisees and that of the new prophet." [84]

Father Lagrange knows the events and the texts too well not to feel some embarrassment, visible particularly in his first commentary, on Mark: "It is . . . strange that this multitude, which had been sympathetic to Jesus up to this point, shifted opinion so fast. . . . we do not

[81] [This "right" is still invoked today, as Father René Laurentin relates in his remarkable paper, written in 1965 and addressed to the representatives at Vatican II, in which he argues for a strengthening of the Statement on the Jews, then still in draft form. He writes: ". . . the Fathers who asked [for] and obtained . . . the deletion of the clause on deicide based themselves on the following arguments: 'The doctrine [rejecting the accusation] is not certain, it is dangerous, it is contradicted in the Gospel.' . . . 'The Jewish people, as a people, is evidently guilty of material deicide through those who led them.' . . . 'We cannot wholly free the Jewish people from the offense of deicide.'" Father Laurentin goes on to remark: "The Secretariat [responsible for reviewing the Fathers' arguments], to be sure, did not credit these arguments," and did proffer explanations for the deletion which explicitly denied the traditional accusation. But "Unfortunately, these explanations . . . lack the authority of the conciliar text," Father Laurentin comments, "for they do not engage (or at least not directly) the authority of the Council. Those who do not agree with these explanations will have no difficulty dismissing them" ("Vote No. 6 on the Deletion of 'Deicide' from the Schema on Non-Christian Religions," Rome, n.d. [Fall, 1965], monograph [mimeo.], pp. 9–10).—Ed.]

[82] Lebreton, op. cit., II, 405.

[83] Father André Charue, L'Incrédulité des Juifs dans le Nouveau Testament, Louvain, Gembloux, 1929, p. 179.

[84] Lebreton, loc. cit.

know all the motives which were brought into play. . . ." [85] A few years later, commenting on Matthew, Father Lagrange had progressed, and considered quite "natural" the abrupt turnabout which seemed so strange to him a little earlier:

The crowd turned when it was suggested they call for Barabbas. All this is so natural—the right instinct of the masses readily perverted, the unexplained intervention . . .—that we could not think of debating the authenticity of the events. [86]

We know that Father Lagrange expresses himself badly when he is ill at ease. I am prepared to say to the contrary: all this is so little natural that we are indeed forced to the point of debating the authenticity of the events. The hesitations, the contradictions (not to say the stammerings) of an honest man themselves have an eloquence.

I beg pardon of these respectable authors, whom I too respect: in this particular case, of the intervention of the crowd, of "the [Jewish] people," their argument—varied and fluctuating—seems extremely weak. How hard it is to plead a poor case. All these great efforts to explain explain nothing, and go awry.

They explain nothing because it is not enough to recall what everyone knows: that crowds are fickle; or what is in the realm of possibility: that Jesus' arrest destroyed his prestige. The commentators have to go farther, and find some acceptable motive for that unprecedented, unheard-of fury, for that paroxysm of murderous rage, for that sudden extinction of nationalist feeling in a people of "fanatical" nationalism. [87] But they find none, they give none, there is none, other than "the desire to show how the Jewish people . . . fully assumed responsibility for the death of their Christ" (Lagrange *dixit*). [88]

And then, and above all, the explanation goes awry because it is absolutely outside reality. It is this buried reality, submerged below a whole ocean of legends and myths, that we would want to try to grasp, to revive, to bring back from the depths where it resides to the surface of history.

✿   ✿   ✿

Passover at Jerusalem. Palestinian springtime.

For pity's sake, do not expect me to deliver the classic and romantic declamation, the evocation of the city in festival under the burn-

[85] Lagrange, . . . *Marc*, p. 416.
[86] *Idem*, . . . *Matthieu*, p. 529.
[87] Daniel-Rops, *op. cit.*, p. 510.
[88] Lagrange, . . . *Matthieu*, p. 522.

ing Asian sun. The wash of "local color," the Orientalism of the ba-
zaar, the eye-deceiving archaeological setting are for others to
describe. The reality we are involved in seeking here is not a reality
of objects and scenes but of facts, figures, and souls, pragmatic, math-
ematic, psychic.

Passover at Jerusalem. Passover in the year 29 or 30. At the moment when I was writing these lines, then, exactly nineteen hundred
and sixteen or seventeen years ago, close to two millennia. And it
seems almost yesterday to me, "It is so simple," dear Péguy, it is so
clear. Great distances in time, what optical illusions! Your people,
Yahweh, "the people of [Your] first servants," [89] the witness people,
are they not there, still there, dragged from martyrdom to martyrdom
toward the mysterious destiny which has been assigned them? And
the populace screaming for death, is it not there too, still there? And
Caiaphas, born collaborator for the upholding of the "moral
order"? [90] And Pontius Pilate, not the Pontius Pilate of legend "washing his hands in innocence," but the real, the genuine, the eternal
Pontius Pilate, washing his hands in blood, with jubilation—
Schadenfreude?

Passover at Jerusalem. Passover in the year 29 or 30. From the
height of Antonia Fortress' tower, men of the Roman garrison survey
the Temple courtyards. Shame and suffering, defilement and profana-
tion: all of Judea is territory under Roman occupation; the pagan, the
idolater, commands and rules in David's capital. God knows Jerusalem loathed Herod, the Idumean tyrant, of late; but the man who
now occupies Herod's old palace, this procurator Pontius Pilate, who
has come from his residence in Caesarea expressly to oversee the city
in festival and the enormous gathering of people who jam it, is a
thousand times more detested, loathed! Who is not familiar with his
brutality, his insolent contempt for everything Jewish, men, customs,
beliefs, beliefs especially, for that exclusive, aggressive faith in a paradoxical God Who does not even have a statue in His Temple!

Passover at Jerusalem. Passover in the year 29 or 30. On these holy
days, in the Holy City, the ardent fervor of the Jews is exacerbated
—to paroxysm—by the presence, visible or invisible, of the unworthy
conqueror, unworthy before Yahweh. Intolerable memories—of vio-

---

[89] Charles Péguy, *Note conjointe sur M. Descartes et la philosophie cartésienne,* in *Oeuvres complètes de Charles Péguy,* Paris, NRF, 1924, IX, 135.
    [90] [The allusion is to the Vichy government, whose officials commonly spoke
of "defending the moral order."—Ed.]

lence, of blood, of torture—haunt minds, oppress hearts. Young people excepted, who do not remember this atrocious spectacle: two thousand Jews put on the cross by the order of Varus, the governor of Syria,[91] two thousand Jews crucified at the gates of Jerusalem. Two thousand. Can we imagine this, do we dare imagine this? Will the Frenchmen who saw a hundred and twenty of their own die at Tulle on June 9, 1944, hanged from balconies and street lamps along five hundred yards of the Avenue de la Gare, forget in thirty years? And two thousand men on crosses, two thousand bodies hideously tortured, spilling out their agony, their slow death throes, in the Judean sun—given two yards per cross, that makes two and a half miles of a sight only a Goya could evoke, more than would be needed to line both sides of our royal road, the Champs-Élysées, from the Tuileries to the Arch of Triumph—can we believe that thirty years later the Jews, Jewish patriot hearts, would have forgotten? At least Varus and his legions atoned, in a German forest,[92] as it is written:

Now the Lord said to Abram, ". . . him who curses you I will curse. . . ."
Gen. 12:1, 3

Passover at Jerusalem. First day or eve of Passover. It little matters whether it is before or after the Seder, the paschal meal, with its unleavened bread, lamb, bitter herbs, the mashed red fruit mixture *haroset,* four cups of wine, Hallel songs; one day or the other, one and the other, both days of purification, of consecration to God. Days of feast and days of joy. Feast and joy of springtime. Feast and joy of the great liberation, the Exodus after the persecution in Egypt. But joy always shadowed with fear and anguish, as it befits Israel's tormented heart, as it should be with a people marked by God for a mission beyond their strength. The fourteenth of the month of Nisan, the eve of Passover, while the women are busy cooking the supply of unleavened bread needed to last through the feastdays, while the head of the family oversees the detailed preparation of the ritual meal, the eldest son fasts to redeem himself before Yahweh, for the price of the Exodus must be paid to Him Who killed the firstborn of Egypt: how terrible is Thy right hand, O All-Powerful!

Passover at Jerusalem. Passover in the year 29 or 30. What You did

[91] Josephus, *The Jewish Antiquities,* 17:295 (=17:10:10), and *The Jewish War,* 2:75 (=2:5:2). Suppression of an uprising which erupted shortly after the death of Herod the Great.
[92] [Quintilius Varus and his entire army were slain in A.D. 9 by the Cherusci, an ancient tribe of western Germany.—Tr.]

to Pharaoh, what You did to Antiochus, Lord, can't You, won't You do the same to this greedy She-Wolf, insatiable and savage? [93] How many are there this feastday (or day of preparation for the feast), how many pious Israelites, emulators of Zechariah, whose heart burned with hope for "a mighty Savior . . . to save us from our enemies, / And from the power of all those who hate us" (Lk. 1:69, 71 [ABS])? Not, of course, the Annases and the Caiaphases, ready—in all times, in all places—for fruitful collaboration, but the innumerable resisters among a people who do not accept servitude because to accept it means for them to deny God? Some, men of action, quick to draw the knife—whether they are called "Zealots" or "hired assassins," "murderers" or "terrorists," and perhaps we should rank among them Jesus Barabbas, and the one of the Twelve named Simon the Zealot; others, condemning bloody violence and weak submission alike, peaceable but resolute, expecting nothing except from God and His omnipotent power, such as those Pharisees who at a future moment will declare themselves ready to submit to death rather than transgress the Law,[94] those Essenes whose faithfulness to the holy commandments no torture succeeds in breaking.[95] And would it not be appropriate to add the Eleven, the Apostles themselves, whose first question to the risen Jesus (Acts 1:6) will be, "Lord, will you at this time restore the kingdom to Israel?"

Passover in the year 29 or 30. Passover at Jerusalem. A miracle which is renewed each year: the world at Jerusalem. All peoples pass by, all languages are heard. The crowd invades everything, engulfs everything. Flavius Josephus, speaking of the 60s, counts as many as two and a half or even three million pilgrims who have come from all points on the horizon to celebrate Passover in the Holy City. Exaggeration is usual with him. But there is no doubt that the pilgrims number in the tens or hundreds of thousands; Philo assures us of this; the normal population of the city—a hundred thousand souls at most —must be tripled, quadrupled, if not multiplied tenfold. A city of tents in the nearby countryside is coupled to the city of stone. Such is

[93] [Antiochus IV (reigned 175–163 B.C.), one of the thirteen Seleucid kings in the Near East, provoked the successful Machabee rebellion by his strictures against the Jews and Judaism, in particular his attempts to impose the practice of pagan rites on the Jews.—Tr. The She-Wolf, according to Roman legend, suckled Romulus and Remus, the traditional founders of Rome; and by extension, the expression came to stand for Rome itself.—Ed.]

[94] Josephus, *The Jewish Antiquities*, 18:8:3.

[95] *Idem, The Jewish War*, 2:8:10.

the major reality which the historian must take into account: the Passover multitude, a density of multitude which the word of Jesus definitely does not have the time to pass through, to penetrate. "Who is this?" they ask in the city seeing the Master pass on the young ass, followed by the cortege of the disciples (Mt. 21:10).

And it would be "all [these] people," all the people of Jerusalem, augmented by the enormous influx of pilgrims, both groups suddenly mobilized at daybreak one Nisan 14 or 15—the eve or the first day of Passover; snatched from their sleep, turned away from their devotions, even more, from their strongest sentiments, their most steadfast sentiments, and if I may say it, changed in their souls, who are supposedly transformed into that "tiger" thirsting for blood—Jewish blood—spoken of by an eminent member of the Church of Christ,[96] to leap to the praetorium of the Roman magistrate, roar for the death and wrench from Pilate the crucifixion (by Roman soldiers) of this Jew whom the day before some of them were following, admiring, exalting as a prophet, if not as the Messiah!

I say that this is not only incredible but inconceivable; not only inconceivable but impossible, of an absolute impossibility.

Finally, now, open your eyes, take the trouble to look: suppose you had an immense Place de la Concorde before Pilate's praetorium, which even so your four or five hundred thousand Jews would overflow; how could the urgings of the chief priests mentioned in Mark 15:11 and Matthew 27:20 have had the slightest effect on such a human flood, on such a massive herd of people? If some morsels of truth subsist in these catechetical accounts, what could be the real size of the crowd stirred up by the chief priests in front of the praetorium? A few hundred men, a few thousand maximum, an infinitesimal percentage of the human mass at Jerusalem during Passover, more infinitesimal yet in relation to the mass of the Jewish people in the world of antiquity.

And then I ask: what need is there to assume—and explain—a supposed turning, an "about-face of the [Jewish] crowd"? Why insist at all costs that these few hundred, these few thousand Jews be the same as those who the day before "hung upon [Jesus'] words"? And particularly why insist at all costs that they were the voice of Israel?

Yes, why? Unless to carry out the desire, always the same, that Father Lagrange has described so well, "the desire to show how the

[96] Dom Prosper Guéranger; see p. 330, above.

Jewish people . . . fully assumed responsibility for the death of their Christ." This is necessary; therefore, this is. Doctrinal truth, in no way historical, in no way symbolic, in no way real; simply desirable.

It is obviousness itself. Matthew's "all the people" (27:25) can and does mean only one thing: all the people who were there, before the praetorium. And all the people who were there, before the praetorium, were decidedly not all of Israel, not even all the people of Palestine, or all the people on pilgrimage, or even all the people of Jerusalem, not even a qualified delegation from that people.

One of two things:

either this was a random crowd, fairly small for the chief priests to have been able to work them up against Jesus in a matter of minutes;

or else—an infinitely more believable hypothesis—this was a hired mob, of the sort that it is so easy to whip up in big cities, bought cheap by Annas' and Caiaphas' police. We all know how these spontaneous demonstrations work.

Whoever takes the trouble to weigh the realities, to scrutinize the events and the texts, will see clearly—and I think I have demonstrated this—that Jesus did not die as the victim of his people.

To maintain the contrary demands an inveterate, an absolute prejudice, or blind submission to a tradition which we know, however, is not "normative," and thus should not be considered an obligatory rule of thought by even the most docile son of the Church. But a hardy tradition, utterly poisonous, a murderous tradition which I have said and I repeat leads to Auschwitz—Auschwitz and other places. Some six million Jews, murdered uniquely because they were Jews. For without the centuries of Christian catechesis, preaching, and vituperation, Hitlerian catechesis, propaganda, and vituperation would have been impossible.

This is why the historian has the duty, today more than ever, to state categorically:

no, you do not have the right to say, to write, to teach that "the Jewish people . . . fully assumed responsibility for the death of their Christ," that Christ whom most of the Jews did not know, and whose mission, the mission of Christ, of Messiah, even those who knew him were unaware of.

Jesus died sentenced by the Roman procurator Pilate, tortured and crucified by Roman soldiers, for acts of messianic agitation, doubtless at the instigation of a Jewish clan whose active elements were or

seem to have been the high priests Annas and Caiaphas. History does
not know, does not apprehend, and cannot say anything more.[97]

On this specific point—the major, the total responsibility of the
Jewish people—never will tendentious commentaries and calumnious
imputations, piled up from century to century, compensate for the absence of valid testimony in the mind of the honest man.

✿   ✿   ✿

Will we accept as "valid testimony" the texts that will be mounted
against us as a last resort, some drawn from the Epistles of Saint
Paul, others from the Acts of the Apostles?

We have already taken up these texts [98] and set them aside—
provisionally. We ask nothing better than to consider them a second
and last time.

Let us say right away that the same is true of them as of the Gospels: nothing can change the fact that they too are prosecution evidence, and for that precise reason subject to caution and—
particularly on this specific point, Jewish responsibility—marked for
suspicion.

Furthermore, they contradict each other, having been inspired far
less by a concern for historic exactness than by preoccupations with
doctrine, catechesis, polemics.

The oldest—dating back to perhaps the years 50–52—and the one
most readily given in reference is the Pauline text of 1 Thessalonians
2:14–16:

For you, brethren, became imitators of the churches of God in Christ Jesus
which are in Judea; for you suffered the same things from your own countrymen as they did from the Jews, who killed both the Lord Jesus and the
prophets, and drove us out, and displease God and oppose all men by hindering us from speaking to the Gentiles that they may be saved—so as always to fill up the measure of their sins. But God's wrath has come upon
them at last! [Or: for ever! (RSV, n. b)]

[97] [Father Laurentin raises the identical points in his 1965 monograph: "Since
it is declared that the chiefs of the Jews perpetrated the death of Jesus, why not
speak also of *the part taken in his death* by the Romans, on whom depended the
efficacious juridical decision and the execution? Evangelical truth seems to ask
for this complement. This is a significant fact within this framework, for no one
has ever dreamed of attributing a special guilt to the Roman people as such, nor
to the descendants of the Romans" (Laurentin, *op. cit.*, p. 3b).—Ed.]

[98] See pp. 236–238, above.

Evidence or imprecation? Saint Paul was hardly gentle with those he found blocking his way. It leaps to the eye that such a diatribe must not be taken literally. Even were it so taken, it in no wise implies Israel's collective responsibility for the Crucifixion: "the Jews, who killed both the Lord Jesus and the prophets" is a formulation that can just as well mean "that evil species of Jews," always the same, the same as those Jesus had denounced a little earlier, "the chief priests and the scribes and the elders"—"hypocrites" (Mk. 11:27; 7:6, etc.).

Should one reject this restrictive interpretation and apply the Pauline text to the whole of the Jewish people, then one must resolutely disregard other texts of Saint Paul's, the most fundamental, the great Epistles in which the Apostle's inspiration propels him to matchless heights. In 1 Corinthians 2:7–8, speaking of the wisdom he is preaching, "a secret and hidden wisdom of God," Saint Paul writes: "None of the rulers of this age understood this [wisdom]; for if they had, they would not have crucified the Lord of glory." The "rulers of this age"—doubtless those who held the political power, the Roman or Jewish, Roman and Jewish authorities—are thus designated as responsible for the Crucifixion.

Is it not even more significant that the magnificent Epistle to the Romans, in which the Apostle, writing sometime around the years 56–58, broached and treated the problem of Israel in all its ramifications, contains not one phrase, not one word to be heard about the responsibility of the Jewish people? Not the slightest allusion to the sinister exclamation reported in Matthew 27:25, "His blood be on us and on our children!" And the same is true of his most passionate "philippics," such as Philippians 3:2. What an argument, this silence, which lasted into the middle of the second century [99] and possibly longer.[100]

Of the non-Pauline Epistles in the New Testament, only one raises the issue of the responsible authors of the Crucifixion:

---

[99] Justin Martyr, writing in the mid-second century, makes no reference to it in his anti-Jewish polemic, *Dialogue with Trypho*, which is at least strange if he used the first Gospel as is generally agreed.

[100] In his book on anti-Semitism, Lovsky notes that he found Matthew 27:25 cited for the first time, to the best of his knowledge, in Tertullian's treatise *Against the Jews*, written shortly after 200; still, Tertullian deduced nothing from it concerning a curse of the Jewish people. Nor did Origen. The pejorative interpretation did not prevail until the fourth century and after. (See Fadley Lovsky, *Antisémitisme et le Mystère d'Israël* [Anti-Semitism and the Mystery of Israel], Paris, Albin Michel, 1955, p. 435.)

Come now, you rich, weep and howl over your miseries which will come
upon you. . . . You have condemned and put to death the just, and he did
not resist you.

Jas. 5:1, 6 [CCD]

What is the reason for the silence that is generally maintained on
this text? Would it be because it takes the *rich* to task?

The Acts of the Apostles are closely linked to the Gospel of Luke,
to which they form a sequel attributed to the same writer. Concerning the Passion, therefore, they do not introduce new evidence, new
information, distinct from and independent of the Gospels. They ema-
nate from the same witness—if this title can be given to the physician
Luke—as the third Gospel: it is not surprising that they confirm its
principal particulars; it is not surprising either that their reliability is
challenged or dismissed.

If the Apostle Peter, haranguing the people of Jerusalem, expressed
himself thus in Acts 2:22–23, 36 and again in 3:14–15,

. . . Jesus of Nazareth . . . you crucified and killed by the hands of lawless
men. . . . God has made him both Lord and Christ [Messiah], this Jesus
whom you crucified. . . . / But you . . . killed the Author of life, whom
God raised from the dead,

this is because it is well understood from the Lucan account of the
Passion that the people, following their leaders, pressured Pilate to
have Jesus put on the cross. Even so, they are not accused of deicide,
but of homicide and of sinning out of ignorance:

. . . Jesus of Nazareth, a man attested to you by God. . . .
And now, brethren, I know that you acted in ignorance, as did also your
rulers.

Acts 2:22; 3:17

And hardly have these Jewish crucifiers, these "tigers" thirsting for
blood who according to Matthew 27:25 have just shouted in murderous frenzy, "His blood be on us and on our children!", hardly have
they heard Peter's discourse before "they were cut to the heart," have
themselves baptized to the number of three thousand, and form the
admirable first Christian community in Jerusalem, admirable for their
"fellowship," their total acceptance of Christ's teachings (". . . they
sold their possessions and goods and distributed them to all . . ."),
as also for their faithfulness in "attending the temple" (Acts 2:37,
41–46).

But perhaps it is permissible to think that certain expressions of accusation here should not be taken literally, and that when Peter cries, "this Jesus whom you crucified," this means specifically, "this Jesus whom the Romans crucified, at the instigation not of yourselves personally but of your own, our own"; for Peter could just as well and even better have said, "this Jesus whom we crucified."

If in Acts 4:27 the Apostles Peter and John and their first followers, all Jews, "lifted their voices together to God" (4:24), recalling to Him that

. . . there were gathered together against thy holy servant Jesus, whom thou didst anoint, both Herod and Pontius Pilate, with the Gentiles and the peoples of Israel . . . ,

this is because it is well understood from the Lucan account of the Passion that Herod had a certain part in it, took his share of responsibility for it. Again, in this pious effusion, which it would be excessive to regard as historic witness, Herod and Pontius Pilate, Jews and pagans, are placed on a par, on the same plane, without any distinction.

Let us pass over Acts 4:10; 5:30; and 7:52, in which the accusations cast by the Apostles and by Stephen are addressed only to the leaders, the Sanhedrin.

There remain Peter's discourse at Caesarea, before the centurion Cornelius,

And we are witnesses to all that he [Jesus] did both in the country of the Jews and in Jerusalem. They put him to death by hanging him on a tree . . .

                                                                    Acts 10:39

and Paul's discourse in the synagogue at Antioch of Pisidia,

For the people who live in Jerusalem, and their leaders, did not know that he is the Savior, nor did they understand the words of the prophets. . . . Yet they made the prophets' words come true by condemning Jesus. And even though they could find no reason to pass the death sentence on him,[101] they asked Pilate to have him put to death.

                                                        Acts 13:27–28 [ABS]

In the first case, the accusation seems to encompass the Jews of Palestine collectively; in the second case, it encompasses explicitly and uniquely the inhabitants of Jerusalem.

But what are we to gather from these diverse, confused, often con-

---

[101] On this point there seems to be a contradiction between the Gospels and Acts. We could see these words as reminiscent of Pilate's statement: "I have found in him no crime deserving death . . ." (Lk. 23:22).

flicting imputations? The most limited—the last—are again only abusive generalizations, which history cannot really take into consideration. And then who would venture to guarantee the literal exactness of words reproduced some forty years after they were uttered, and reproduced in Greek although they were for the most part spoken in Aramaic?

We do not pretend [writes a Catholic exegete, Eugène Jacquier] that the discourses in Acts were reproduced literally, that is, absolutely as they were uttered. The fact, which all recognize, that we have here only summaries would in itself be proof that they were reproduced only in substance.[102]

Aimé Puech says similarly: "There is almost unanimous agreement today that these discourses were freely composed by Luke." And this author recognizes a manifest desire in the writing of Acts "to deal with the Roman authority tactfully" and "to attribute Christianity's major trials to the Jews." [103] In this regard, there is no distinction between Acts and the Gospels.

✿   ✿   ✿

The universal responsibility of the Jewish people, of the Jewish nation, of Israel in Jesus' condemnation to death is thus a fact of legend-based belief, without solid historic foundation.

In truth, it is an anachronism, and only that: the transposition, considered opportune, of a quite different and later fact—that after a first burst of conversions, and for reasons we will not examine at present, the mass of the Jewish people became resistant to Christian preaching. Now, it was precisely at this time that the accounts of the Passion were being detailed. But historic reality still shows through these accounts, however tendentious they may be. And it does not allow the indictment of the Jewish people, who are not identifiable with Annas or Caiaphas, nor with "the rabble" their police stirred up, nor even with the Sanhedrin.

Péguy said, "It is not the Jews who crucified Jesus Christ, but the sins of all of us; and the Jews, who were but the instrument, participate like others in the font of salvation." [104] Here, it seems to me, is

[102] Eugène Jacquier, Les Actes des Apôtres [The Acts of the Apostles], Paris, Lecoffre, 1905 [repub. Paris, Gabalda, 1926], p. cclxi.

[103] Aimé Puech, Histoire de la littérature grecque chrétienne, 3 vols., Paris, Belles Lettres, 1928–1930, I, 382, 398.

[104] Charles Péguy, Lettres et entretiens, ed. Marcel Péguy, Paris, Artisans du Livre, 1927, p. 135.

Christian language, Christian conviction. It is also sound and orthodox Christian doctrine, too often forgotten. The Catechism of the
Council of Trent teaches: "In this guilt [for Jesus' death] are involved all those who fall frequently into sin; for . . . our sin consigned Christ the Lord to the death of the cross. . . ." [105] We can relate this to the seventh of the Ten Points of Seelisberg, drawn up by
the International Emergency Conference of Christians and Jews in
1947: ". . . the Cross which saves us all reveals that it is for the sins
of us all that Christ died." [106]

This is the conviction, I know, of a Christian elite, Catholic and
Protestant. But it is a tiny minority, with a tiny audience, while the
murderous tradition continues to be planted in defenseless souls by
routine theologians, heedless writers, more concerned with worldly
success than with pure truth.

When will authoritative voices be raised, then, to recall them to
love of truth and love of neighbor, neither of which can be separated
from love of God? [107]

[105] [Quotation taken from *Catechism of the Council of Trent for Parish Priests*,
tr. Fathers John A. McHugh, O.P., and Charles J. Callan, O.P., New York, Wag-
ner, 1923, Pt. I, Chap. 5, para. 11.—Tr.]

[106] The Ten Points of Seelisberg are included in the Appendix on pp. 404–405,
below.

[107] [Since these lines were written, other authoritative Christian voices have
been raised: in a statement titled "The Christian Approach to the Jews" com-
mended to affiliated churches by the First Assembly of the World Council of
Churches, meeting at Amsterdam, the Netherlands, August 22–September 4,
1948, and in a "Resolution on Anti-Semitism" adopted by the Third Assembly of
the same organization, held at New Delhi November 19–December 5, 1961;
in a series of statements formulated by the Consultation on the Church and the
Jewish People, convoked by the Department of World Mission of the Lutheran
World Federation at Logumkloster, Denmark, April 26–May 2, 1964; in a "Resolution on Jewish-Christian Relations" adopted by the General Board of the National Council of the Churches of Christ in the U.S.A., June 5, 1964; in the statement on "Deicide and the Jews" adopted by the House of Bishops of the
Protestant Episcopal Church at its Sixty-First General Convention, St. Louis, Oc-
tober 22, 1964; in the Declaration on Non-Christian Religions promulgated at the
Second Vatican Ecumenical Council, Rome, October 28, 1965 (see n. 16, above);
and in the "Guidelines for Catholic-Jewish Relations" issued by the National
Conference of Catholic Bishops, Washington, D. C., March 15, 1967. Except for
the last-named, these commendable statements are quoted in whole or in part in
Joseph L. Lichten, ed., *The Sin of Anti-Semitism: Statements by Christian
Churches*, New York, Anti-Defamation League of B'nai B'rith, n.d. (1966).—Ed.]

PROPOSITION 20

TO CROWN ITS INJUSTICES, A CERTAIN SO-CALLED CHRISTIAN DEVOTION, ONLY TOO HAPPY TO FALL IN WITH A CENTURIES-OLD PREJUDICE WHICH IS COMPLICATED BY IGNORANCE OR MISUNDERSTANDING OF THE GOSPEL, HAS NEVER WEARIED OF USING THE GRIEVOUS THEME OF THE CRUCIFIXION AGAINST THE JEWISH PEOPLE AS A WHOLE.

In view of the Cross erected on Calvary, it is hard to pursue a discussion we would so fervently prefer to be able to avoid. Yet we must. We must pursue it to the end, just because of that deep fervor. What need does Jesus crucified have, to enlighten hearts, of that halo of legends which Christian piety, especially in the Middle Ages, happily spun around the Cross, out of faith in an uncertain tradition or out of its own inspiration? Legends so beautifully enshrined in art that they have come down to our own day living, moving, and poisonous.

Thus, if the only legend were that of a succoring Veronica bent to wipe the flow of blood and sweat from the Holy Face, how tempting it would be to say with François Mauriac:

Veronica is unknown to the evangelists. . . . (The fact is that she does not appear in pious legends before the fifteenth century. . . .) But she exists; this is not an invented character. It cannot be that a woman could have resisted the desire to wipe that terrible face.[1]

No, it cannot be that a woman, a Jewish woman. . . . For François Mauriac omits that word, that simple word, and all the Christian narrators, all the commentators, all the writers do the same,[2] reserving it

[1] François Mauriac, *Vie de Jésus*, Paris, Flammarion, 1936, p. 266.
[2] Except Charles Péguy, projecting a Veronica of whom he says, "A mere slip of a Jewish woman, a youngster, little Veronica, pulls out her handkerchief, and takes an eternal imprint of Jesus' face" (*Lettres et entretiens*, ed. Marcel Péguy, Paris, Artisans du Livre, 1927, p. 156).

for exclusive application to the savages who raged against Jesus, and who, these, are "the Jews," the qualified representatives of the whole Jewish people.

Such is the major orientation of the innumerable more or less legendary accounts of the Crucifixion: anti-Jewish, basically, profoundly anti-Jewish. And such is their major omission, their major injustice, their major misreading: everything happens as if there were the Jews, evil, cruel, Satanic, on one side, and on the other some charitable souls, these being unidentified. Everything happens as if Jesus himself were not a Jew who lived among the Jews, never wanted to leave the framework of Jewish Palestine; as if—putting the Roman occupation forces aside—Jesus' friends and foes, adherents and adversaries could not be Jews too, naturally, necessarily.

To include all the Jews, "all the [Jewish] people," in the camp of Jesus' enemies at the hour of the Crucifixion is a simplistic position that glares simultaneously with prejudice, ignorance, disdain for reality, and the purest pharisaism, in the pejorative sense of the word.

For we must reiterate an observation made earlier, which is the key to all this:

the Jewish people are here but representatives; they are representatives of the whole of humanity.

✿   ✿   ✿

First example of falsification, deliberate, determined, cavalier, going so far as to give the lie to Scripture:

the crowning with thorns, which is the act of Roman soldiers, is ascribed to the Jews.

What does Scripture say? We have signaled its discrepancies. Mark, Matthew, John at least are agreed in attributing to the Romans, to Pilate's soldiers, the ignominy, the cruelty of these derisive attentions.[3]

Yet from the second to the nineteenth century and beyond, there was no hesitation, there is no hesitation even today, in following the example given by one of the apocryphal gospels, the Gospel of Peter, whose author Father Léon Vaganay characterizes severely as "an accomplished forger." [4]

[3] In Luke 23:16 (see p. 327, above), Pilate proposes to the Jews that he release Jesus after a beating; but nothing in the following account indicates that Jesus was beaten, nor does Luke say anything about the crowning with thorns.

[4] Father Léon Vaganay, ed., Évangile de Pierre, Paris, Gabalda, 1930, p. 124.

We have already quoted Saint Augustine preaching against the Jews to the catechumens.[5] At sixteen hundred years' remove, Léon Bloy echoed him in this passage, splendidly worded but truly filthy:

The universal Church, born of the divine Blood, had the Poor One as its share, and the Jews, entrenched in the impregnable fortress of an obstinate despair, kept Money, the ghastly money clawed from their sacrilegious thorns and dishonored by their spit, as they might have kept unburied the corpse of a God subject to corruption, so that it would poison the universe![6]

Father Journet, conscientious but indulgent, may point out what he calls Léon Bloy's "inexactness," but it cannot prevent him from admiring the fact that it "inspired one of his most magnificent vituperations against the Jews."[7] Magnificent stylistically, I agree, but what is the value of magnificence based on falseness? "The visible traces the footsteps of the invisible,"[8] and I believe it, but not the visible travestied. The spirit of truth comes before everything. And nothing, not the narrow limitations on historic knowledge, nor history's groping, its uncertainties, not the transports of faith either, gives license to the lie.

❁   ❁   ❁

After these indescribable readings, perhaps I may be allowed to introduce a short digression here. At bottom, far from leading me away from the Cross, it brings me closer.

Léon Bloy's book, his favorite book, *Salvation Is from the Jews*, dates from 1892. At that time, Raïssa Maritain assures us, "He did not know the Jews, after all. . . ."[9] Some years later, having made friends with some Jews, having experienced their generosity, the same Léon Bloy wrote:

What people is as poor as the Jewish people? Ah! I know very well, there are the bankers, the speculators. Legend, tradition would have it that all Jews are usurers. People refuse to believe anything else. And

---

[5] See p. 242, above.

[6] Léon Bloy, *Le Salut par les Juifs*, Paris, Mercure de France, 1933, p. 67; "the Poor One" here means Jesus Christ: "It is not necessary to have done intensive work in exegesis to understand that the real Poor One was Jesus Christ . . ." (*ibid.*, p. 61).

[7] Father Charles Journet, *Destinées d'Israël*, Paris, Egloff, 1945, p. 428.

[8] Quoted in Albert Béguin, *Léon Bloy l'impatient* [Léon Bloy, the Impatient], Fribourg, Switz., Egloff, 1944, p. 153. [See, in English, in *idem, Leon Bloy: A Study in Impatience*, London, Sheed & Ward, 1947, p. 137.—Tr.]

[9] Raïssa Maritain, *Les Grandes amitiés* [Great Friendships], New York, Maison Française, 1941, p. 178. [See, in English, as *idem, We Have Been Friends Together*, tr. Julie Kernan, New York, Longmans, Green, 1942.—Tr.]

this legend is a lie. That kind are the scum of the Jewish world. Those who know it and look upon it without prejudice realize that this people has other aspects and, bearing the misery of all centuries, suffers infinitely.[10]

Now I ask Father Journet, what remains of the "magnificent vituperation," of the symbolism of Money, "the ghastly money," Israel's idol, "clawed from [its] sacrilegious thorns and dishonored by [its] spit"?

I do not deny that this hallucinatory symbolism glimmers with rays of light. *Salvation Is from the Jews,* in which the sublime skirts the filthy, is a great book. But this book, little known in times past, has only too many readers today: dreading the ravages of filth in ill-prepared souls, I would hope that they would be put on guard against such hazardous reading.

Then again, is it certain that even alerted minds, interpreters of the quality of Albert Béguin, for example, have not suffered deleterious effects from this writing? In Béguin's analysis of Léon Bloy completed in 1943 and published in 1944, I read:

If Jewish baseness blazes before our eyes, it has at least this in its favor . . . that it is balanced against enormous sufferings. Let us not forget for an instant that while it is glaring because it is the faithlessness of the elder Race, it remains a *figure* of general ignominy.[11]

What! In those years of 1943–1944, it was "Jewish baseness" that blazed before our eyes? It was not German baseness, pagan baseness, Christian baseness, human baseness? And was not "general ignominy" flaunted shamelessly enough to spare us the need to seek a *figure* of it among the Jews, tortured, massacred by the thousands, by the millions?

And why "Jewish baseness"? Albert Béguin's answer: because the persecuted—the wretched persecuted Jews—as much as their persecutors remained "blind to any symbolic understanding of the events, to any penetration of Revelation. . . . A clamor rises from their ranks . . . , but it is the clamor of a herd whose animal life is threatened." [12]

What atrocious injustice toward so many Jewish martyrs who have borne their cross, witnessed to God, and what dreadful assurance in a Christian who, as far as I know, has not borne his cross!

Opposite this page from Albert Béguin I will place only one text, a

[10] Léon Bloy, *Le Vieux de la Montagne,* Paris, Mercure de France, 1907; quoted in Maritain, *op. cit.,* pp. 182–183 [and pp. 128–129.—Tr.].
[11] Béguin, *op. cit.,* p. 137.
[12] *Ibid.,* p. 136.

document read at the Nuremberg trials, the deposition of a German engineer named Graede who was an eyewitness to the massacre of several thousand Jews near Dubno, Russia, in October, 1942.

Men, women, and children of all ages got undressed under the eyes of the S.S., who strolled among them with a riding crop or whip in their hand. Then they went and put their clothes at the place they were shown, pieces of clothing on one side, shoes on the other.

Without crying out or weeping, all these naked people grouped together by families. After embracing and bidding each other farewell, they waited for a sign from the S.S. man standing at the edge of the ditch, a crop in his hand too. I stood near one of them for a quarter of an hour, and I didn't hear anyone complain or ask for mercy. . . .

I saw a whole family [Graede says farther on]: a man and a woman about fifty, with their children eight or nine years old and two grown girls around twenty. A white-haired woman was holding a year-old child in her arms, singing him a song and tickling him . . . ; the child laughed, the father and mother looked at their child with tears in their eyes. The father of a ten-year-old child was holding him by the hand and speaking to him softly; the child was trying not to cry; the father pointed to the sky, caressed his hair; he seemed to be explaining something to him. At that moment an S.S. man standing near the ditch called out something to his comrade, and the latter counted off about twenty people and made them go behind the hillock of earth.

The family I spoke of a while ago were among these twenty people. . . . The twenty people were executed by an S.S. man who machine-gunned them as he sat on the edge of the ditch, smoking a cigarette. The next group had to take their places on the still warm corpses.[13]

It was perhaps the same day, at the same hour, that Albert Béguin, seated at his work table, wrote: "A clamor rises from their ranks . . . , but it is the clamor of a herd whose animal life is threatened. . . . If Jewish baseness blazes before our eyes. . . ."

✿   ✿   ✿

Let us close the digression, and let us pass by way of this detour from the crowning with thorns to "the Way of the Cross."

For the Christian people taken as a whole, and particularly for the Catholic people, who are still generally less accustomed to reading the Gospels than are Protestants, I think it would be truly surprising to learn that the evangelists—except for Luke—say almost nothing of the ascent to Calvary, called "the Way of the Cross."

[13] *Le Monde*, January 3, 1946.

There is no specific detail in whose behalf we can summon agreement from the four Gospels, except that Jesus was led to be crucified
at a place called Golgotha, more exactly *Gogoltha* in Aramaic or *Gul-
goleth* in Hebrew, which is translated as *Kranion* in Greek and *Cal-
varia* (Calvary) in Latin, and means "skull."

Nothing in John on the Way of the Cross except that Jesus carried
his cross (19:17). Nothing in Mark-Matthew except that Jesus did not
carry his cross—indubitably because after the flogging he was not in
a state to do so—and that the Roman troops requisitioned a passerby,
Simon of Cyrene, to carry it (Mk. 15:20–21; Mt. 27:31–32).

Of the four evangelists, Luke is alone in mentioning the crowd following Jesus in procession (23:27). And what does he say about it?
Not a word about sarcasm or insults; on the contrary, he writes of
women who are beating their breast and mourning over him [RK]
and whom Jesus addresses with words of compassion.[14] Such is the
one and only piece of information to be found in the (canonical) Gospels on the attitude of the Jewish crowd along the Way of the Cross.
All the rest is legend and literary embroidery.

Are not this deep silence from the evangelists and this single description from the Greek doctor Luke heavy with meaning? How real,
how obvious must the sympathy of the Jewish crowd have been in the
face of Roman brutality for there to be nothing, absolutely nothing,
not one passage, not one word denying it, except the disordered and
mendacious imaginings of the apocrypha!

That over the course of the following centuries Christian piety applied itself to meditating on the *Via dolorosa* was its right, was its
duty. Far from us the paltriness of looking for chicanery in the number of "Stations of the Cross"—there were fourteen from the sixteenth
century on, but two, three, or four earlier. Similarly, who would think

[14] Catholic interpretation and teaching: "If it goes so hard with the tree that is
still green (that is, with our Lord), what will become of the tree that is already
dried up (that is, of the Jewish nation which is committing an infamous deicide)?" (Father A. Brassac, *Nouveau Testament*, vol. III of Fathers Fulcran G.
Vigouroux and A. Brassac, *Manuel biblique, ou Cours d'Écriture sainte à l'usage
des séminaires*, ed. Fathers A. Brassac and Louis Bacuez, 4 vols., 12th ed., Paris,
Roger et Chernoviz, 1906–1909, p. 698). [See p. 254, n. 55, above.—Tr.] But the
interpretation is arbitrary. The contrast evoked here is between the innocent (the
green tree) and the guilty (the dried-up tree). Nothing justifies an extension of
this guilt to "the Jewish nation." Oscar Cullmann is of the same opinion. He
gives Jesus' saying this meaning: "If the Romans put me to death as a Zealot, I
who have never been one and who have always warned against Zealotism, what
will they do someday to the real Zealots?" (*Dieu et César*, Neuchâtel, Delachaux
et Niestlé, 1956, p. 51).

of taking umbrage at Christian piety for having adopted the mythical but moving episodes of Veronica's wiping Jesus' face or Jesus' meeting with Mary, even though they have no foundation in history? Little matter; the heart has reasons that reason knows not why.[15]

But where devotion errs, where it more than exceeds the limits of its rights, where it fails its Christian duty as well as simple honesty is when it does not hesitate to fill in the silence of the Gospels with a profusion of details inspired by millennial prejudice, when pious meditation ceases to be the most fervent *mea culpa* and tends to become the most venomous diatribe against a scapegoat Israel.

"It is a great misfortune," Father de Lubac quotes someone as saying, "to have learnt the catechism against someone." [16] Never was a word more truly spoken than about the present case.

I find a typical example in that great compendium of Catholic piety, Dom Prosper Guéranger's *Liturgical Year*,[17] which has already been quoted more than once. Nor do others among the most serious modern authors, like Louis-Claude Fillion and Father Jules Lebreton,[18] completely escape that deplorable tradition; nor can they resign themselves to Scripture's silence.

And Father Lagrange? Alas, Father Lagrange comes along too with his little stone. Of course, as a historian concerned with reality, he takes the care to write, "The bulk of the people, pacified by Pilate's capitulation, went about their major business, preparing for Passover," but he adds: "Jews who were enemies of Jesus, and whom we will rediscover at the foot of his cross, formed a procession, and did not abstain from the jeers that the mob pours on those who are going to die." [19] It is possible; strictly speaking, we know nothing about it. How much better grounded is the pertinent recollection of

---

[15] Blaise Pascal, *Opuscules et pensées*, ed. Léon Brunschvicg, Paris, Hachette, 1897, pt. II, sec. 2, chap. VI, para. 477.

[16] Father Henri de Lubac, S.J., *Catholicisme, les aspects sociaux du dogme* [Catholicism: The Social Aspects of Dogma], Paris, Le Cerf, 1938, p. 239. [Quotation taken from *idem, Catholicism: A Study of Dogma in Relation to the Corporate Destiny of Mankind*, tr. Lancelot C. Sheppard, New York, Longmans, Green, 1950, p. 164.—Tr.]

[17] See Dom Prosper Guéranger, O.S.B., *La Passion et la Semaine sainte*, vol. III of *L'Année liturgique* (6 vols.), 24th ed., Tours, Mame, 1921, pp. 25, 185, 509–513.

[18] See Louis-Claude Fillion, *Vie de Notre Seigneur Jésus-Christ*, 22nd ed., Paris, Letouzey, 1929, III, 473n., 476–477; Father Jules Lebreton, S.J., *La Vie et l'enseignement de Jésus-Christ*, 2 vols., Paris, Beauchesne, 1931, II, 419–422.

[19] Father Marie-Joseph Lagrange, O.P., *L'Évangile de Jésus-Christ*, Paris, Gabalda, 1928, p. 563.

Passover, for one ends by forgetting it in this atmosphere of legend: the day of the Passion was the first day of Passover according to the Synoptics, the eve of Passover according to John, a feastday or day of preparation for the feast, a day of worship, a day of recollection, involving for Jews the prohibition of trials and all the more of capital sentencing.

If the most learned doctors stumble in this way, what can we expect of men of letters? Let us pay homage to the exceptional discretion of a François Mauriac, respectful of the texts, of their very silence. It is a happy contrast to the babbling and unbridled fantasying of a Giovanni Papini.[20]

In Daniel-Rops's highly popular *Sacred History: Jesus in His Time*, which has drawn the admiration of the reading public, the French Academy—and even Georges Bernanos—there is no less fantasy; it is simply hidden carefully under a thin but brilliant scholarly veneer. The author assures us that "Most of the fourteen Stations of the Cross illustrate scenes taken from the Gospel." The problem here is that he tends to fail to distinguish between canonical and apocryphal accounts and to make a skillful amalgam of them, flavored with opportune talmudic references—which are incompatible with evangelic tradition, moreover. Thus "The Death Procession" in his Chapter XI takes on the dual character of a Jewish and Roman procession: "There is mention in the Gospel of a centurion and his men, but one also sees Priests and Sanhedrists, only too pleased to follow their victim to the end." One sees them when one wants to see them, for "the Gospel"—look at the texts cited above—says nothing about them. "It does not seem that a single cry was sounded, a single demonstration attempted in his favor." And yet:

Jewish Law provided that, up to the last minute, the intervention of a single member of the community could bring about the suspension of a condemned man's execution. . . . The crowd could hear the Sanhedrin's bailiff repeat the instruction: "If you can prove Jesus' innocence, hurry!" (supposing that this clause of the Law was observed).

The parenthesis is the author's, but what is this reminder of Jewish Law doing in an execution decided by the Roman magistrate? It is there primarily to introduce some banal (or borrowed) considerations

---

[20] Mauriac, *op. cit.*; cf. Giovanni Papini, *Histoire du Christ*, tr., Paris, Payot, 1922, pp. 375–378.

on "the monstrous indifference," "the incomprehensible about-face" of the Jewish people.[21]

I know very well that there is also Péguy, *The Mystery of the Charity of Joan of Arc*.[22] But we must take the measure of all the distance there is between "mystery" and history. And we know for the rest that Péguy's thought at bottom joins our own: that the Jewish people are here but a figure; they are the figure of the whole of humanity.

◊   ◊   ◊

The last hours. The Cross on Golgotha (surveying a world of sin, of derisive pride, of flourishing villainy).

The texts:

And they brought him to the place called Golgotha (which means the place of a skull). And they offered him wine mingled with myrrh; but he did not take it. And they crucified him, and divided his garments among them, casting lots for them, to decide what each should take. And it was the third hour, when they crucified him. And the inscription of the charge against him read, "The King of the Jews." And with him they crucified two robbers, one on his right and one on his left. (And the scripture was fulfilled which says, "He was reckoned with the transgressors.") [23] And those who passed by derided him, wagging their heads, and saying, "Aha! You who would destroy the temple and build it in three days, save yourself, and come down from the cross!" So also the chief priests mocked him to one another with the scribes, saying, "He saved others; he cannot save himself. Let the Christ, the King of Israel, come down now from the cross, that we may see and believe." Those who were crucified with him also reviled him.

And when the sixth hour had come, there was darkness over the whole land [or: earth] until the ninth hour. And at the ninth hour Jesus cried with a loud voice, "Elo-i, Elo-i, lama sabach-thani?" which means, "My God, my God, why hast thou forsaken me?" And some of the bystanders hearing it said, "Behold, he is calling Elijah." And one ran and, filling a sponge full of vinegar, put it on a reed and gave it to him to drink, saying, "Wait, let us see whether Elijah will come to take him down." And Jesus uttered a loud cry, and breathed his last. And the curtain of the temple was torn in two, from top to bottom. And when the centurion, who stood facing

[21] Henry Daniel-Rops, *Histoire sainte: Jésus en son temps*, Paris, Fayard, 1945, pp. 530–536.

[22] See Charles Péguy, *Le Mystère de la charité de Jeanne d'Arc*, in *Cahiers de la Quinzaine*, 11th ser., no. 6, December, 1909, pp. 150, 170–171.

[23] This verse, 28, is omitted by the oldest manuscripts, and its authenticity seems dubious.

him, saw that he thus breathed his last, he said, "Truly this man was the Son of God!"

There were also women looking on from afar, among whom were Mary Magdalene, and Mary the mother of James the younger and of Joses, and Salome, who, when he was in Galilee, followed him, and ministered to him; and also many other women who came up with him to Jerusalem.

Mk. 15:22–41 [incorporating nn. g and h]

And when they came to a place called Golgotha (which means the place of a skull), they offered him wine to drink, mingled with gall; but when he tasted it, he would not drink it. And when they had crucified him, they divided his garments among them by casting lots; then they sat down and kept watch over him there. And over his head they put the charge against him, which read, "This is Jesus the King of the Jews." Then two robbers were crucified with him, one on the right and one on the left. And those who passed by derided him, wagging their heads and saying, "You who would destroy the temple and build it in three days, save yourself! If you are the Son of God, come down from the cross." So also the chief priests, with the scribes and elders, mocked him, saying, "He saved others; he cannot save himself. He is the King of Israel; let him come down now from the cross, and we will believe in him. He trusts in God; let God deliver him now, if he desires him; for he said, 'I am the Son of God.'" And the robbers who were crucified with him also reviled him in the same way.

Now from the sixth hour there was darkness over all the land [or: earth] until the ninth hour. And about the ninth hour Jesus cried with a loud voice, "Eli, Eli, lama sabach-thani?" that is, "My God, my God, why hast thou forsaken me?" And some of the bystanders hearing it said, "This man is calling Elijah." And one of them at once ran and took a sponge, filled it with vinegar, and put it on a reed, and gave it to him to drink. But the others said, "Wait, let us see whether Elijah will come to save him." And Jesus cried again with a loud voice and yielded up his spirit.

And behold, the curtain of the temple was torn in two, from top to bottom; and the earth shook, and the rocks were split; the tombs also were opened, and many bodies of the saints who had fallen asleep were raised, and coming out of the tombs after his resurrection they went into the holy city and appeared to many. When the centurion and those who were with him, keeping watch over Jesus, saw the earthquake and what took place, they were filled with awe, and said, "Truly this was the Son of God!"

There were also many women there, looking on from afar, who had followed Jesus from Galilee, ministering to him; among whom were Mary Magdalene, and Mary the mother of James and Joseph, and the mother of the sons of Zebedee.

Mt. 27:33–56 [incorporating n. m]

And when they came to the place which is called The Skull, there they crucified him, and the criminals, one on the right and one on the left. And Jesus said, "Father, forgive them; for they know not what they do." And they cast lots to divide his garments. And the people stood by, watching;

but the rulers scoffed at him, saying, "He saved others; let him save himself, if he is the Christ of God, his Chosen One!" The soldiers also mocked him, coming up and offering him vinegar, and saying, "If you are the King of the Jews, save yourself!" There was also an inscription over him, "This is the King of the Jews."

One of the criminals who were hanged railed at him, saying, "Are you not the Christ? Save yourself and us!" But the other rebuked him, saying, "Do you not fear God, since you are under the same sentence of condemnation? And we indeed justly; for we are receiving the due reward of our deeds; but this man has done nothing wrong." And he said, "Jesus, remember me when you come in your kingly power." And he said to him, "Truly, I say to you, today you will be with me in Paradise."

It was now about the sixth hour, and there was darkness over the whole land [or: earth] until the ninth hour, while the sun's light failed [or: the sun was eclipsed]; and the curtain of the temple was torn in two. Then Jesus, crying with a loud voice, said, "Father, into thy hands I commit my spirit!" And having said this he breathed his last. Now when the centurion saw what had taken place, he praised God, and said, "Certainly this man was innocent!" And all the multitudes who assembled to see the sight, when they saw what had taken place, returned home beating their breasts. And all his acquaintances and the women who had followed him from Galilee stood at a distance and saw these things.

Lk. 23:33–49 [incorporating nn. *q* and *r*]

[They arrived at] the place called the place of a skull, which is called in Hebrew Golgotha. There they crucified him, and with him two others, one on either side, and Jesus between them. Pilate also wrote a title and put it on the cross; it read, "Jesus of Nazareth, the King of the Jews." Many of the Jews read this title, for the place where Jesus was crucified was near the city; and it was written in Hebrew, in Latin, and in Greek. The chief priests of the Jews then said to Pilate, "Do not write, 'The King of the Jews,' but, 'This man said, I am King of the Jews.'" Pilate answered, "What I have written I have written."

When the soldiers had crucified Jesus they took his garments and made four parts, one for each soldier; also his tunic. But the tunic was without seam, woven from top to bottom; so they said to one another, "Let us not tear it, but cast lots for it to see whose it shall be." This was to fulfil the scripture,

> "They parted my garments among them,
> and for my clothing they cast lots."

So the soldiers did this. But standing by the cross of Jesus were his mother, and his mother's sister, Mary the wife of Clopas, and Mary Magdalene. When Jesus saw his mother, and the disciple whom he loved standing near, he said to his mother, "Woman, behold, your son!" Then he said to the disciple, "Behold, your mother!" And from that hour the disciple took her to his own home.

After this Jesus, knowing that all was now finished, said (to fulfil the scripture), "I thirst." A bowl full of vinegar stood there; so they put a sponge full of the vinegar on hyssop and held it to his mouth. When Jesus had received the vinegar, he said, "It is finished"; and he bowed his head and gave up his spirit.

Since it was the day of Preparation, in order to prevent the bodies from remaining on the cross on the sabbath (for that sabbath was a high day), the Jews asked Pilate that their legs might be broken, and that they might be taken away. So the soldiers came and broke the legs of the first, and of the other who had been crucified with him; but when they came to Jesus and saw that he was already dead, they did not break his legs. But one of the soldiers pierced his side with a spear, and at once there came out blood and water. He who saw it has borne witness—his testimony is ture, and he knows that he tells the truth—that you also may believe. For these things took place that the scripture might be fulfilled, "Not a bone of him shall be broken." And again another scripture says, "They shall look on him whom they have pierced."

Jn. 19:17–37

It is unfortunately not possible either to accept these texts in their totality or to "harmonize" at least some of their discrepancies.

Discrepancies little noticeable in Mark and Matthew, for the good reason that Matthew's account seems to have been traced almost line by line from Mark's; we will see where the few modifications or amplifications to be found in them lie. Discrepancies more conspicuous —to the point of contradiction—between Mark and Luke and John, the last two of whom relied on other traditions and accounts, though they knew and used Mark's account.

What are the most important of these divergences?

The ignominy of the jeering at the Crucified: in Mark-Matthew this is attributed to passersby, chief priests, and scribes (Matthew adds: "and elders," so that all the members of the Sanhedrin would have a share in it), in Luke only to "the rulers" and to Roman soldiers; John makes no mention of it.

The attitude of the two thieves: in Mark-Matthew they are at one in deriding Jesus, they too, both of them, while Luke distinguishes the "good" thief, touched by grace, from the criminal who insults Jesus. John is mute on this point too.

The presence of the holy women: the four evangelists have noted the presence of women loyal to Jesus at Calvary; according to the Synoptics, they remain at a distance "looking on from afar"; according to John, they are at the foot of the cross, where Jesus can speak to them. Mark supplies three names: "Mary Magdalene, and Mary the mother of James the younger and of Joses, and Salome." Matthew writes "the mother of the sons of Zebedee" in place of Salome. Luke gives no names. John furnishes two, Mary Magdalene and "Mary the wife of Clopas"—who is perhaps "the mother of James the younger and of Joses"; and he is the only evangelist, moreover, to note the presence of Jesus' mother, her sister (Clopas' wife), and "the disciple whom [Jesus] loved."

The centurion's witness: John says nothing about it; in Mark it is the loud cry of Jesus expiring that makes the Roman officer say, "Truly this man was the Son of God!"; in Matthew it is the "awe" inspired in the centurion and his men by the earthquake; Luke is less specific with respect to motivation ("Now when the centurion saw what had taken place . . ."), more prudent with respect to expression ("Certainly this man was innocent!").

These several discrepancies and contradictions are secondary. More serious is this observation: if we look closely, we see with blinding clarity that the account of the Crucifixion in the four Gospels is more or less influenced by what I will call a "preoccupation with references," the determination—half-admitted—to show that Scripture has been fulfilled in every detail. The result is that no matter what we do, we will not be able to distinguish the elements of reality from the elements of myth or legend—a deliberate legend.

For example: Mark 15:23 relates that at the moment Jesus is being put on the cross, they want to give him "wine mingled with myrrh"; giving a man about to be executed a cup of flavored wine was not a Roman but a Jewish custom whose purpose was to attenuate the sufferings of the condemned, and it is specified in the Talmud (Sanhedrin 43a); in Jerusalem a society of pious women performed this service; nothing prevents us from presuming that they did this charitable deed for Jesus. But Matthew 27:34 substitutes "wine . . . mingled with gall"—several manuscripts of Matthew even say "vinegar . . . mingled with gall"—for Mark's "wine mingled with myrrh"; this is quite the contrary of a charitable act. Why this change or difference? Because Matthew is preoccupied with applying Psalm 68:22 [CCD] to Jesus: "Rather they put gall in my food, and in my thirst they gave me vinegar to drink."

Isn't it likewise this verse 22 of Psalm 68 which stands behind the detail of the vinegar (Lk. 23:36) or the sponge filled with vinegar (Mk. 15:36; Mt. 27:48; Jn. 19:29) offered to Jesus by the soldiers? It is certainly not impossible that the prophecy was fulfilled on this point:

Roman soldiers always had with them their *posca*, a mixture of water and vinegar; they could very well have filled a sponge with some to assuage the thirst of the dying Crucified. In Mark, Matthew, and John, the act of one or more Roman soldiers seems in fact a compassionate act, but it is a derisive act in Luke, surely under the influence of Psalm 68:22. How far does that influence go? Who can say?

Another example: in the four Gospels, the soldiers divide the garments of the Crucified among themselves; they cast lots for their shares, according to Mark, Matthew, and Luke; according to John, they make four parts of them which they distribute among the four of them, and cast lots only for the tunic "without seam." Such an allotment was in keeping with Roman custom, and in itself it is nothing if not plausible. But we cannot ignore that it is also in keeping with Psalm 22:18 [RSV]: ". . . they divide my garments among them, / and for my raiment they cast lots." How can we not believe that this verse 18, explicitly recalled by John, influenced or even dictated the version he gives us of the division of the garments, which is at once more literal and more symbolic? In reality, the distinction drawn by the fourth Gospel for purposes of symbolism forces the meaning of Psalm 22:18, in which the two elements of the sentence indeed seem to apply to but one operation (and the Synoptics understand it this way): dividing up the garments by casting lots.

There is almost not a line, not a detail of the Gospel accounts of the Crucifixion which does not betray the influence of Hebrew Scripture. It is visible in all four Gospels, striking in Matthew and John.

Mark and Matthew recount that passersby derided Jesus, "wagging their heads"; how can we fail to perceive here, with Father Lagrange, "recollections of the Old Testament"? [24] It is written in the Lamentations of Jeremiah 2:15: "All who pass along the way . . . hiss and wag their heads. . . ." It is written in Psalm 22:7–8: "All who see me mock at me, . . . they wag their heads; 'He committed his cause to the Lord; let him deliver him, . . . for he delights in him!'" It is written in the Book of Wisdom 2:13, 16, 18 [JB]:

> [The virtuous man] claims to have knowledge of God,
> and calls himself a son of the Lord. . . .
> and boasts of having God for his father. . . .
> If the virtuous man is God's son, God will take his part
> and rescue him from the clutches of his enemies.

[24] Father Marie-Joseph Lagrange, O.P., ed. and tr., *Évangile selon saint Marc*, Paris, Gabalda, 1910, p. 430.

Matthew, inspired by these texts, will thus judge it opportune to add
to the gibes that Mark puts in the mouths of the chief priests, "He
trusts in God; let God deliver him now, if he desires him; for he said,
'I am the Son of God'" (Mt. 27:43). In this connection, D. F. Strauss
observes that the words drawn from Psalm 22 are "attributed in the
Old Testament to the enemies of the virtuous man; consequently, the
Sanhedrin members could not have adopted them without thereby
declaring themselves impious, and they would certainly have avoided
this."[25]

Yet these waggings of head, these sneers, these gibes, more ritual
than real, are used to vilify the Jewish people once again, to give
them a veritably Satanic face. Not that I find it surprising—however
odious it might be—that some passersby mocked Jesus: vileness is the
commonest thing in the world; no people has a monopoly on it; I
need take only a dozen steps to find it in my path. More improbable
is the lengthy presence of chief priests, of Sanhedrists, on such a day,
in such a place. And what do we do with the contradiction between
the accounts? In Luke, where do we see that the attitude of the people is hostile? They are there, they look on, say not a word, and when
it is finished, go away "beating their breasts."[26]

❁   ❁   ❁

On this question, having come to the end of my demonstration, I
would like to yield the word one last time to Christian authors, cleric
and lay.

The illustrious liturgist Dom Guéranger:

[Mass for Tuesday of Holy Week, commentary on the Epistle (Jer. 11)]:
. . . the Jews nail him to the tree. . . .

[Good Friday afternoon:] . . . but these people have only insults for
him. Their insolent and pitiless voices rise to him. . . . never has insult to
divine majesty risen to [God] with such presumption. Let us Christians,
who adore him whom the Jews blaspheme, offer him at this moment the
reparation to which he is so entitled.[27]

[25] D. F. Strauss, Vie de Jésus [Life of Jesus], tr. Émile Littré, 2 vols., 3rd
ed., Paris, Ladrange, 1839, II, 568.

[26] "The attitude of the people who, struck with wonder, turn away beating
their breasts belongs to that group of features and episodes rooted in a primitive
tradition in which the people had no part in Christ's condemnation" (Alfred
Wautier d'Aygalliers, Les Sources du récit de la Passion chez Luc [The Sources
of the Passion Account in Luke], Alençon, Coueslant, 1920, p. 236).

[27] Guéranger, op. cit., pp. 287, 556–557. [The liturgy of the Oriental Church
speaks likewise: "The children of the Hebrews are not content with treason, O

The professor of Sacred Scripture A. Brassac:

Jesus crucified knew every humiliation. Instead of being surrounded with the respect and pity which are due even to criminals at the point of death, he saw an insulting crowd turn against him: the people drawn by curiosity, passersby, Sanhedrists, soldiers.[28]

The consultant to the Pontifical Biblical Commission Louis-Claude Fillion:

Insults will pursue him all the way to the cross. . . .
   [After Jesus' death:] At Jerusalem, the earth began to shake, as if it were seized with convulsive movements and wanted to follow the example of the firmament in showing the horror that the deicide of the Jews caused it.[29]

The learned theologian Jules Lebreton, S.J.:

Jesus spoke thus ["Father, forgive them; for they know not what they do" (Lk. 23:34)], while they nailed him on the gibbet. Those for whom he interceded were neither only nor primarily the soldiers: "Those poor devils, it is only too obvious they did not know what they were doing . . ."; it was the chief offenders, those against whom Jesus' death armed divine justice, those who called down on themselves the curse of spilled blood: the Jews.[30]

That great novelist François Mauriac, in his chapter on "The Placing in the Tomb" as in other passages, using Saint John's editorial procedure of writing the word *Jews* in a pejorative sense:

A secret disciple of Jesus, of the kind who had been afraid of the Jews as long as he lived, Joseph of Arimathea, obtained the Procurator's permission to take the body. Nicodemus, a timorous man himself, a politician, stepped forward at this point. . . . It was a time for timorous people. . . . What should they be afraid of? The Jews can no longer do them any harm. . . .[31]

Up to the reader to make his way here and figure out that Nicodemus, that Joseph of Arimathea are themselves Jews too, like the Apostles, like the holy women.

Christ, but they raise their heads to spit at you their mockeries and their venom. But you, O Lord, repay them according to their works, because they did not understand your humility. . . . Reward them as they deserve, Lord, because they contrive plans against you" (Eleventh Antiphon of Matins, Good Friday, in the Byzantine liturgy; quoted in Sister Marie Despina, "Jews in Oriental Christian Liturgy," *Sidic* [Rome], October–November, 1967, p. 15).—Ed.]
   [28] Brassac, *op. cit.*, p. 707.
   [29] Fillion, *op. cit.*, III, 488, 500.
   [30] Lebreton, *op. cit.*, II, 422.
   [31] Mauriac, *op. cit.*, p. 271.

The bombastic rhetorician Giovanni Papini:

A clamor of demoniac laughter, of exultant exclamations, of ferocious jests rose from the crowd about Golgotha. . . .

There they are, clustered on the slopes of Golgotha, dehumanized by hate! Look at them well, look them in the face, one by one; you will recognize them all, for they are immortal. See how they thrust out their twitching muzzles, their scrawny necks, their noses humped and hooked, their rapacious eyes, gleaming under their bristling eyebrows. See how hideous they are, branded with the mark of Cain. Count them over well, for they are all there, just like the men whom we now know, brothers of the men whom we meet every day in our streets. . . .

The death-struggle was over and the Jews were satisfied.[32]

The devout provincial relaxing from his usual labors by writing a *Way of the Cross*, in which he huffs and puffs to create what he thinks is pious literature but which is neither pious nor literature; the cross has been erected, and here before it are Jews and Christians who speak in turn:

[The (Jewish) crowd:] We do not make blood run: our hands are clean. We have respect for the Law: our hearts are clean. But the hangman works for us. How our eyes feast on the blood of the blasphemer!

In contrast to the "cunning" of these Jews is the nobility of soul of the Christians (who apparently have nothing to do with this Drama, nothing in common with the Jews, with the Gentiles, and who have doubtless dropped from heaven):

We were not around you, Lord . . . , like those Romans who saw you, who touched you, and who nailed you; like those Jews who saw you and who did not want to touch you and who delivered you up and who nailed you. . . . We too want to contemplate that Passion which a delirious crowd gorged itself on. . . . [But] we are afraid that a glance cast at the Cross would wound you more frightfully than the brutal cruelty of those Pagans or the hypocritical cruelty of those Jews.[33]

[32] Papini, *op. cit.*, pp. 387–403. [Quotations taken from *idem, Life of Christ*, tr. Dorothy Canfield Fisher, New York, Harcourt, 1923, pp. 361, 369, 374.—Tr. The Oberammergau Passion Play speaks in the same tone:

Captain: Let him be. We will halt a little while, so that he may recover before ascending the hill.
Caiphas: Still another halt! When shall we come to Calvary? . . .
People: Oh! on to Golgotha! To the cross with him! To the cross! He dies on the cross! Hail Israel! The enemy is overthrown! His death is our safety! We are freed!

(*The Passion Play of Oberammergau*, English version of the official text of the 1970 performances, "revised and newly published," Oberammergau, Community of Oberammergau, 1970, pp. 111, 112.)—Ed.]
[33] Anon., *Chemin de Croix* [Way of the Cross], 1944, pp. 58–63.

On the last page of this work, we read: printing completed July 19, 1944; and the signature is that of a distinguished university professor. Let us grant him the benefit of anonymity.

*   *   *

And now, good reader, for the last time, make the comparisons that are necessary. Reread the Gospel texts: Mark-Matthew, where the people are represented only by a few passersby; Luke, where they appear silent at first, mute, then grieved; John, where they are mentioned nowhere. And then reread the commentaries of the theologians, the elaborations of the men of letters, renowned or obscure.

What emerges from these comparisons?

The savagery of the Jewish people in their inexplicable, unjustifiable cruelty? Or, in the guise of Christian piety, the savagery against the Jewish people of a pharisaic devotion which nothing can stop, not even deference to the most frightful martyrdom? And which, in its fashion (that has no resemblance to Jewish "cunning," Jewish "hypocrisy," does it?), pushes them, very gently, toward new martyrdoms.

In the name of Christ.

"FATHER, FORGIVE THEM; FOR THEY KNOW NOT
WHAT THEY DO."

◇◇

Conclusion

Christians stand between Christ and the Jews, concealing the Savior's true image from them.

NIKOLAI BERDYAEV [*]

[*] Nicolas Berdiaeff, "Le Christianisme et le danger du communisme matérialiste," *Le Christianisme social*, no. 2–3, April, 1939.

PROPOSITION 21 AND LAST

WHATEVER THE SINS OF THE PEOPLE OF ISRAEL MAY BE, THEY ARE INNOCENT, TOTALLY INNOCENT OF THE CRIMES OF WHICH CHRISTIAN TRADITION ACCUSES THEM: THEY DID NOT REJECT JESUS, THEY DID NOT CRUCIFY HIM. AND JESUS DID NOT REJECT ISRAEL, DID NOT CURSE IT: JUST AS "THE GIFTS . . . OF GOD ARE IRREVOCABLE" (ROM. 11:29), THE EVANGELICAL LAW OF LOVE ALLOWS NO EXCEPTION. MAY CHRISTIANS COME TO REALIZE THIS AT LAST—MAY THEY REALIZE AND REDRESS THEIR CRYING INJUSTICES. AT THIS MOMENT, WHEN A CURSE SEEMS TO WEIGH UPON THE WHOLE HUMAN RACE, IT IS THE URGENT DUTY TO WHICH THEY ARE CALLED BY THE MEMORY OF AUSCHWITZ.

It remains for us to measure the road we have traveled. Where we started from. Where we have come to. What lands, under what skies.

We started from a first certainty, hard as a rock: the indissoluble bond that unites the New Testament to the Old, the Christian faith to the Jewish faith.

It is certain that Christianity was born out of Judaism. "It is certain," states the good Catholic historian Louis Duchesne, "that Christianity has its roots in Jewish tradition, that the first crises in its history are comparable to the one which separates a child from its mother . . . , that the sacred books of Israel are also its sacred books, and even that there was a time when it knew no others." [1] It is certain that the first Christians, at their head Peter, James, and John, the Apostles, were pious Israelites and that, in company with the other Jews, they worshiped Yahweh in His Temple.

Father Journet speaks of "eternal gratitude to those first Jews [the

[1] Msgr. Louis Duchesne, *Histoire ancienne de l'Église*, 3 vols., 5th ed., Paris, Fontemoing, 1911, I, 37.

first Christians] to whom the mission was confided . . . of transferring from the Mosaic religion to the evangelic religion . . . the sacred patrimony of the Jewish people, notably its most revered treasure, the Law and the prophets." [2] There would be much to say about this transfer, this mission. And there is better to say; Father Journet omits the essential, the essential claim of the Jews to Christians' "eternal gratitude." For what Christians received above all from Jews is faith in God, in God One and Eternal, the God of Abraham, Isaac, and Jacob (Mk. 12:29). What more miraculous gift could there be! They received God. Simply. They received Him from the Jews.

Should not the recollection, the proclamation of this first truth suffice to impose mutual respect, to instill a burning desire for love and union, for joined prostration before "the thrice-holy Face"? [3] The anti-Semitism of Christians, the anti-Christianism of Jews are equal insults to God. "Whatever difference there may appear to be to us, Moses and Jesus Christ meet closely, the Synagogue and the Church extend hands to each other." Who said this? A prince of the Church, Bossuet.[4]

The Synagogue and the Church extend hands to each other. But between them are the Cross and the Crucified: Jesus the Messiah means the Christ, God incarnate for the ones, neither Messiah nor God for the others; Jesus the cornerstone (Eph. 2:20), but also the stumbling block. And there is also the Christian accusation: "The people who were to find fulfillment in the coming of the Messiah they were awaiting refused that Messiah; and so, since then, they have been fragmented, dispersed, rejected by men, and, in the eyes of the faith, rejected by God." [5] And the more relentless Christians are in their accusation, the more stubborn the stubborn Jews remain in their denial.

*   *   *

We started from another certainty, no less solid, no less rocklike: the Jewish stock whence Jesus issued, the Jewish national and reli-

[2] Father Charles Journet, *Destinées d'Israël,* Paris, Egloff, 1945, p. 114.

[3] Father Henri de Lubac, in Father Henri de Lubac, S.J., *et al., Israël et la foi chrétienne,* "Manifeste contre le Nazisme" series, Fribourg, Switz., Éd. de la Librairie de l'Université, 1942, p. 38.

[4] Jacques-Bénigne Bossuet, sermon for the Feast of the Visitation, 1656; quoted in Journet, *op. cit.,* p. 105, n. 1.

[5] Franz-J. Leenhardt, *L'Antisémitisme et le mystère d'Israël,* Geneva, Labor et Fides, 1939, p. 26.

gious framework in which he exercised his ministry, preached his Gospel, recruited his disciples.

It is certain that Jesus was a Jew, a Jew "according to the flesh" (Rom. 1:3); it is certain that his mother, Mary, all his family were Jews; Jewish was the Precursor, John the Baptist; Jewish were all of Jesus' companions who became the Apostles of Christ, Peter, James, and John, the Twelve, the seventy; Jewish were Mary Magdalene, Martha and Mary of Bethany; Jewish was Saul of Tarsus who became the Apostle Paul; Jewish were all those who formed the first Christian community, the admirable initial Church of Jerusalem, of which Father Journet has found it possible to say: "Never will the Church here below be so fervent, so loving, so pure as it was in the time when it was entirely Jewish." [6]

Truly, this Jew—Jesus, Yeshua—was necessary, all these Jews before Jesus, around Jesus, after the Passion were necessary, these thousands, these myriad Jews counted in the Acts of the Apostles were necessary to build the primitive Church. Should not this next recollection, a simple observation of facts taken from history, suffice to stop certain insulting words short on Christian lips, tear certain inadmissible sentiments out of Christian hearts forever?

Jesus was a Jew, a humble Jewish artisan. A fact of history and also a truth of faith, since such was the will of God. Why then do commentators apply themselves to "de-Judaizing" him? Jesus, "born under the law" (Gal. 4:4), was circumcised, and Jesus wanted to be only "a servant to the circumcised" (Rom. 15:8). Jesus spoke a Semitic language, Aramaic; the Word, which Christian peoples receive refracted by translations of translations, was a Semitic Word. Jesus was raised, grew up, and as we have demonstrated, contrary to certain groundless assertions, Jesus lived in respect of the Mosaic Law and the Jewish cult. Jesus preached in synagogues and the Jewish Temple. And the first article of faith for Christians has been to recognize in Jesus the Christ, that is, the Messiah announced by the Jewish Prophets.

To which Christians, millions of Christians reply (and in what a positive tone!): here exactly, Jews, is where the shoe pinches, because the Jew Jesus was the Christ announced by the Scriptures, indeed more, because he was "the Son of the living God" (Mt. 16:16), "the Word" miraculously incarnate,

[6] Journet, op. cit., p. 42.

and as the Jewish people not only failed to recognize him, rejected him, but insulted, tortured, crucified him,

it is for this Crime, this deliberate acceptance of the Crime ("His blood be on us and on our children!") which the "deicide people" are expiating, that they are cast out, dispersed, hunted, abhorred, that they are subjected to "the wrath of God," crucifiers themselves crucified, felled by the blow of "providential"—some add: eternal— punishment.

Hence their wretched destiny, their torments beyond remedy (because these come not from men but from God), the almost uninterrupted succession of their bloody trials up to the most recent, the bloodiest being Auschwitz:

> It doubtless did not rest with Israel not to kill its God after having failed to recognize him, and, as blood calls mysteriously to blood, it perhaps no more rests with Christian charity to prevent the horror of the pogrom from compensating for the unbearable horror of the Crucifixion in the secret balance sheet of the divine intentions.[7]

But we do not accept, we will never accept this inhuman tradition, this barbaric conception of God's justice, even though—as we have noticed, alas!—the vast majority of Christian doctors and peoples accept it, implicitly or explicitly.[8] (Praised be the infinitesimal and noble minority!)

And how valid is the crushing accusation on which that tradition is based? How valid are all those Christian accusations, taken up again unendingly from century to century?

To decipher the murky and monstrous enigma, we have lengthily,

[7] Anon. (a German Catholic), "Le Sang retombe," in Paul Claudel et al., Les Juifs, "Présences" series, Paris, Plon, 1937, p. 19; Henry Daniel-Rops, Histoire sainte: Jésus en son temps, Paris, Fayard, 1945, p. 527, but changed in more recent editions (see p. 260, n. 70, above).

[8] [The tragic aptness of Professor Isaac's comment, twenty years after he wrote it, can be seen in the weakening process which the Vatican Council's Statement on the Jews underwent between its 1964 draft and the 1965 version which the Council adopted (see the Foreword; p. 319, n. 16, and p. 352, n. 81, above). It is true that the Statement can be interpreted as rejecting the deicide charge, and that prominent Church spokesmen were quick to confirm this interpretation. The unfortunate fact remains, as Father René Laurentin observes, that the final document "seemed to make no formal refutation or exclusion of collective culpability, but only of individual guilt" (Father René Laurentin and Joseph Neuner, S.J., The Declaration on the Relation of the Church to Non-Christian Religions of Vatican II, "Vatican II Documents" series, Glen Rock, N. J., Paulist Press, 1966, pp. 39–40).—Ed.]

minutely, honestly interrogated the events and the texts, without excluding a single one.

What have they said in answer to the fundamental questions?

✿   ✿   ✿

First this, which every historian knows, which a good number of theologians disregard—or want to disregard—and which commands the attention of every man of good faith:

in the time of Jesus, in that beginning of the first century of the Christian era, which corresponds with the beginnings of the Roman imperial regime, at the apogee of Roman power and civilization, in that time, understand,

the Dispersion of the Jewish people had been an accomplished fact for centuries.

Although history cannot reach any numerical certainty on this point, it is overwhelmingly probable that, of the whole of the Jewish nation, the Jews of Palestine were the minority, the Jews of the Dispersion, or Diaspora, the majority.

Two consequences.

First: in all likelihood, the majority of the Jewish people did not know Jesus, did not benefit from his ministry. And since it appears in the Gospels that this ministry was exercised principally in the limited area of the Sea of Galilee, it is overwhelmingly probable that in Palestine itself a great number of Jews did not know Jesus, did not benefit from his ministry. In all likelihood, Jesus reached only a minority of Jews; one could almost say: a minority of a minority.

Then what is the meaning of the common statement: "The Jewish people rejected Jesus"?

The Jewish people? As a whole, they did not even know him.

And second, what is the meaning of that other common and traditional statement, that the Dispersion of the Jewish people was a "providential punishment" [9] consequent on the Crime, the Crucifixion: "The [Jewish] people . . . refused that Messiah; and so, *since then,* they have been fragmented, dispersed, rejected by men . . . ," as says Franz-J. Leenhardt?

---

[9] Louis-Claude Fillion, *Vie de Notre Seigneur Jésus-Christ,* 22nd ed., Paris, Letouzey, 1929, III, 197, among many other users of this phrase.

Dispersed since then? They had already been dispersed for centuries.

The Palestinian Jews themselves were not "dispersed" "since then." They were decimated, it is true, after two fierce wars of national independence (66–70 and 132–135), like the Gauls after theirs, and a hundred times more than the Gauls were, because they were a hundred times more fanatical and more heated, more dogged, and tougher fighters. The Temple was destroyed in 70; Jerusalem became a forbidden city (to Jews) in 135; but not the rest of the country. And in the whole of the Empire, "since then" until Constantine—or for three centuries—it was the Christians who were persecuted, "rejected by men," while the Jews—except for a short period—retained their privileged status.

First flat contradiction of theology by history.

✿   ✿   ✿

After this recall to truth, a recall to "critical honesty."

We cannot broach and resolve the problem of Jesus and Israel in their reciprocal relations except through a critical examination of the only texts at our disposal, the Gospels.

In the Christian's eyes, the Gospels are inspired texts. They are nonetheless texts set down by the hand of man, and for that reason necessarily subject to the laws of criticism, textual, literary, historical, which no exegesis, even the most orthodox, may evade. One must decipher the manuscripts, collate them, choose between variants, eliminate copyists' errors and suspect interpolations: textual criticism. One must discern the peculiarities of the evangelical Greek, of the Greek of each evangelist, the Semitisms that have more or less penetrated into it: literary criticism. For each Gospel, one must establish (if possible) by whom and when (at least approximately) it was written, in what surroundings, under what conditions: historical criticism. And these three kinds of criticism envisage the same aim: to reach evangelical truth, to extricate it from all the dross, from all human impurities, as the archaeologist, discovering a marvelous buried statue that is stained, battered, broken, sets to work enthusiastically, reverently, to extricate it from the earth that holds it, stand it up in the light, restore its integral and divine beauty. What nobler task, provided that love of God and of truth—the one inseparable from the other—is the deep impulse that inspires it!

Now, from the standpoint of historical criticism, we know, and it is necessary to know, that the Gospels were written in a time when a breach was tending to form between Jews faithful to the Law of Moses and adherents to the new faith, in a time when the latter, reacting to the intense hostility of official Judaism, were seeking support from the Gentile world, when the recruiting of Christian communities among the Jews seemed to be flagging. Inevitably these trends, these events would have to leave traces in the writing of the Gospels, and they did leave some, all the stronger and more visible as the deplorable quarrels waxed bitterer. Historical criticism is obliged to seek out these traces carefully, just as is literary criticism to seek out traces of Semitisms. It is obliged to seek out scrupulously, to define as closely as possible, the position of each evangelist toward the Jews—toward the priests, the doctors, the people; to discern the greater or lesser influence attributable to polemics, greater in the Gospel of John because it is the latest in date, greater in all the Gospels when it comes to the account of the Passion because, with regard to Roman public opinion and the Roman authorities, the "scandal of the cross" (Gal. 5:11 [JB]), the Roman punishment, was the most burning question. If historical criticism does not do this, it fails in its duty, it exposes itself to the most serious errors in interpretation—even on the religious plane—and it confesses itself incapable of extricating the deposit of historic reality which is to be found in these texts but which is often found hidden, or veiled.

Unhappily, and for centuries, preconception prevailed over critical wisdom. A tradition formed, if not doctrinal, at least in fact, in word, in teaching. A habit. Far from rejecting certain elements of dross, theologians have treated them as pure Gospel substance. Far from putting the faithful on guard against certain tendentious, fallacious formulations (such as John's *oi Ioudaioi*—"the Jews"—for the chief priests and scribes), they have made an even more tendentious use of them, a murderous abuse. I have shown through many quotations— they could have been a thousand times more numerous—what aberrations of language, sometimes even of thought, Christian authors have willingly let themselves be led to express in this direction. This said, and this initial false step (which falsifies everything) duly noted, I can now define the principal theses which I contrast with what may rightly be called the traditional Christian theses, even if the tradition is not "normative" in the eyes of the Roman Church.[10]

✿ ✿ ✿

To say that the Jewish people did not acknowledge Jesus, that they rejected him, that they categorically refused to recognize him as the Messiah, the Son of God, is not an opinion peculiar to one or another theologian, Catholic or Protestant; it has been an almost unanimous opinion, professed by all Christians somewhat instructed in their religion and sacred history, the opinion preached, the opinion taught: it has had currency in Christendom ever since there has been a Christendom.

But counterfeit currency.

Merely examining the events would be enough, as we have just seen, to shake if not overthrow the traditional assertion. Since the Dispersion was already an accomplished fact in the time of Jesus, the majority of the Jewish people did not know Jesus, did not benefit from his ministry, thus did not refuse to acknowledge him, did not reject him.

More convincing still in this regard is an examination of the texts, a simple and wholesome reading of the Gospels.

They show us clearly, beyond any possible debate, that if Jesus.

[10] [Just how normative these "traditional Christian theses" do remain for some Catholics may be judged from Father Laurentin's report on an expert at the Second Vatican Ecumenical Council, who, though ". . . he is very prominent in efforts to foster Jewish-Christian friendship, thought he should argue in the following terms to justify the suppression of the clause on deicide [from the conciliar Statement on the Jews]: 'We must be clear. . . . the expression [deicide] is altogether traditional. . . . it is theologically correct'" (Father René Laurentin, "Vote No. 6 on the Deletion of 'Deicide' from the Schema on Non-Christian Religions," Rome, n.d. [Fall, 1965], monograph [mimeo.], p. 9). In the same train of thought, Bishop Luigi Carli, of Segni, Italy, made the following assertions in February of 1965: "Can the Jews be said to be 'cursed' by God? This is not a formal curse. . . . With this being stated, [however,] I hold that Judaism (still taken in the religious and not in the ethnic-political sense) can legitimately be called accursed. . . . The thesis according to which Judaism must be held responsible for deicide, reprobated and accursed by God in the sense and within the limits stated above, is always legitimately tenable, or at least the legitimate object of opinion" (in Palestro del clero, February, 1965, pp. 200–201; quoted in Laurentin and Neuner, op. cit., pp. 99–100). If "Judaism . . . can legitimately be called accursed" (and this of course is a controversial theological issue), how could Bishop Carli expect Christians unfamiliar with the subtleties of clerical thinking not to regard its adherents—that is, the Jews—as accursed too? That is precisely what they have done, for centuries. It should be noted, moreover, that Bishop Carli saw fit to expound these notions in the influential Italian clerical review three months after the Council had formally adopted the 1964 draft of the Statement on the Jews, with its explicit rejection of such "theses," on November 20.—Ed.]

preaching his Gospel to the Palestinian Jews, and to the Jews alone, ran up against the open hostility of the doctors—certain doctors— and the priestly oligarchy, he received an enthusiastic welcome from the popular masses. The three Synoptic Gospels give us multiple and striking testimony of this. The fourth Gospel is more difficult to interpret because it is a coded message: decoded, its testimony joins with that of the Synoptics. The divisions it notes among "the Jews" on the subject of Jesus are divisions among doctors, among Pharisees, for the doctors, the Pharisees themselves were not unanimously opposed to Jesus; far from it. And how could we know from the Gospels—whose authors unquestionably had a bias against the Jewish doctors—what was the attitude toward Jesus of the most respected masters, the authentic spiritual leaders of Judaism, who were quite obviously neither Annas nor Caiaphas?

What we do know gives us the right to say:

Jesus' enemies in Palestine were the same that the Prophets had encountered, the same he would have encountered in any other country, in any other time, the same he still encounters among all peoples: the clan of the "proper," the clan of the "notables," and less the clan of the Pharisees than what is commonly called today the "pharisaic spirit."

But a unique company issued from Israel, the chosen company of the disciples, whom we do not know could have possibly been found elsewhere than in Israel.

With regard to the Jewish people as a whole, or more precisely that fraction of the Jewish people to whom it was given to know Jesus and receive his Gospel, this restricted group, far from repulsing Jesus, welcomed him almost everywhere with admiration, fervor, wonderment.

They welcomed him as a prophet sent by God, it is true, not as the Messiah, not as God's own Son, the incarnate Word. But could they do otherwise? To maintain that they could is to pass the limits of justice and understanding.

To the day of his entry into Jerusalem, and thus to the last days of his ministry—on the eve of the Passion—Jesus forbade himself and his disciples to make any revelation of his messianic office. The "small ovation of the palm branches" [11] could not have profoundly changed the opinion of the Jewish people in this respect.

[11] Father Marie-Joseph Lagrange, O.P., ed. and tr., *Évangile selon saint Luc*, Paris, Gabalda, 1921, p. cxxxviii.

To these last hours, no more than he declared himself Messiah-King did Jesus publicly, explicitly declare himself God's own Son. On this point, the testimony of the fourth Gospel, dominated by doctrinal concerns, does not prevail against the testimony of the other three Gospels.

Jewish tradition, moreover, had established no link between these two terms, *Messiah* and *Son of God*. To the latter it had never given anything but a figurative meaning. Based on Scripture, the most widespread messianic hopes were for the coming of a King-Messiah, a new and glorious David, a liberator in the spiritual and the temporal order, destined to bring the world peace and justice, the triumph of faith in Yahweh, the reign of God. As we have seen,[12] the Master of Righteousness in the Dead Sea Scrolls was recognized as Prophet and Messiah, suffering Messiah in the image of the suffering Servant evoked in Isaiah 53. But this interpretation was restricted to a tiny minority.

I ask, then, what can the Jewish people be reproached for? How could Jesus' final declarations before his judges (Jewish judges), whose exact nature it is impossible to know, which the Synoptics give us in varying versions, which the fourth Gospel says nothing about, reach the Jewish people in a few minutes and shake their faith to its depths?

✿　　✿　　✿

This first Christian accusation, whose lack of substance leaps to the eye, has an equivalent counterpart.

It is not true that Israel rejected Jesus. No more is it true that Jesus rejected Israel.

Saying that God, in the person of Jesus, through His Word, pronounced the downfall, the reprobation, the rejection of Israel, or even that He hurled a terrifying curse against "the whole Israelite race,"[13] also has currency in Christendom, in Christian teaching, in Christian preaching, and is no less counterfeit currency.

With regard to Israel and its sins, the harshness of the Gospels does not exceed the customary harshness of the Prophets.

As for Israel's "reprobation," most Christian commentators see this

[12] See p. 139, above.
[13] Hébert Roux, *L'Évangile du Royaume*, Geneva, Labor et Fides, 1934, p. 272.

everywhere in the Gospels: it exists nowhere. They see it through an abusive and tendentious interpretation of the evangelical texts or in some cases through the hasty exploitation of a few verses which cannot be accepted without reservations, either because they are in contradiction with others and with the very principles of the Gospel or because in themselves, as it happens, they reveal obvious prejudice in the writer (whether the original or later).

Thus does the bright light of the Gospel illuminating textual criticism expose in all its falseness the inhuman and odious thesis of the anticipatory and "providential" hardening of the Jewish people, linked with the teaching of parables, popular teaching if ever there was.

There is not one allegedly reprobative parable, not even the parable of the homicidal (and deicidal) vineyard tenants, there is not one allegedly reprobative sentence which cannot clearly be shown to envisage, not the Jewish people, "the whole Israelite race," but very much rather the leaders of Israel as expressly distinguished from the people,[14] and the most often a race of men who can in no wise be identified with Israel, who are of all times and all countries, of all religions and all churches, the race of pious hypocrites, proud doctors, rich men enslaved by money, timeless "pharisees."

Such is "the race" to which are addressed the harshest condemnations, the explicit maledictions of the Gospels. Beyond the Jewish people, they envisage the whole of humanity.

         ❉   ❉   ❉

The next Christian accusation brought against Israel, the accusation of deicide, an accusation of murder which is itself murderous, is the most serious, the most poisonous: it is also the most iniquitous.

Jesus was sentenced to the punishment of the cross, a Roman punishment, by Pontius Pilate, the Roman procurator. He was sentenced on charges of public agitation, of messianic pretensions, to say it another way for a crime of rebellion, a specifically Roman crime. He was flogged—on the orders of the Roman Pilate—by Roman soldiers. He was crucified—on the orders of the Roman Pilate—by Roman soldiers.

Those are the facts.

[14] [A distinction which is clearly made by Joachim Jeremias in his book *Die Gleichnisse Jesu.* See p. 212, n. 84, above.—Ed.]

But the four evangelists, in agreement for once, assert: it was the Jews who delivered Jesus to the Romans; it was irresistible pressure from the Jews that impelled Pilate, who wanted to find Jesus innocent, to have him punished nonetheless. Hence it is the Jews on whom the responsibility for the Crime devolves, on them that it weighs, with a supernatural weight, which crushes them.

All right. The Jews. But history asks for clarifications: which Jews, according to the evangelists' statements?

On this the agreement of the four disappears.

Shall we take the word of the Synoptics—Mark, Matthew, and Luke? In those few hours (of the feastday or eve of the feastday) or few days,[15] there would have been two trials of Jesus, a Jewish trial prior to the Roman trial; Jesus arraigned first before the Sanhedrin and condemned first by the Sanhedrin for the crime of blasphemy, then delivered to the Roman and condemned a second time by him, for a quite different crime (of messianism), under pressure from the Sanhedrists but with the support of the excited mob of people.

Shall we take the word of the fourth Gospel, John's? Only the high priests, Annas and Caiaphas, and their confederates are on the scene; Jesus is summoned first before Annas, then before Caiaphas, who delivers him to Pilate; no mention of the Sanhedrin, of a Jewish trial, of a Jewish condemnation; no mention of an excited mob of people. "The Jews" who put pressure on Pilate, those Jews whom Pilate does not dare resist, are the high priests and their men, the Temple police.

Let us accept the authenticity, the historicity, and even the "harmony" of these divergent accounts. Do they justify the verdict of the global responsibility of the Jewish people, of "the whole Israelite race"?

Of course not.

Not Annas or Caiaphas, nor the Temple police, nor the Sanhedrin dominated by an oligarchic caste, nor the crowd—whoever they were —gathered in a mob before the praetorium, none of these was remotely qualified to represent "the Jewish nation," all of Israel. They represented only themselves, their own baseness, the savagery of influential people, common vileness.

You pose the axiom of Israel's joint responsibility with its leaders. But what do you call "leaders"? The ringleaders—if I may call them this—the Annases, the Caiaphases, were official leaders, religious

[15] See p. 288, n. 2, above.

leaders; they were not spiritual leaders. And what do you call "joint
responsibility"? How do you mean this? No joint responsibility of the
French people, the Christian people, the Church itself with Joan of
Arc's judges, French judges, Church judges. No joint responsibility of
the Roman Church with Alexander Borgia and other unworthy popes,
though these were elected leaders. No joint responsibility of the
whole of the Christian masses drawn from paganism with Jesus'
Roman judge, Jesus' Roman executioners. But joint responsibility forever of the whole of the Jewish people, "the whole Israelite race,"
with Caiaphas, the high priest designated by Rome, or with "the rabble" stirred up by his men. Truly, what an excess of injustice; and to
claim that God is mixed up in this!

Yet I have treated the accusation too leniently. I have not pointed
out the reservations that "critical honesty" must exercise—unless
it abdicates its responsibilities—when it considers accounts swarm-
ing with contradictions, with improbabilities, bursting with the
predetermination to exonerate Pilate, to lay on "the Jews" all the
odium of the most odious of crimes. We have taken care not to run to
the opposite extreme: we do not intend for an instant to acquit the
Jewish authorities of their share of responsibility. But who could
strictly demarcate that share from Pilate's? The Pilate of evangelic
tradition, so oddly different from the Pilate of history, is a legendary
person, doubtless as legendary as the cry of "all the [Jewish] people":
"His blood be on us and on our children!"

✿   ✿   ✿

One wonders, I myself have wondered: given the groundlessness of
the Christian accusation, how can we explain that it was accepted in
this way, transmitted from generation to generation, from antiquity to
our own day, almost without any contradiction?

How can we explain it? Let us say rather: how can we be surprised
at it? It is a common observation that error, legend, untruth, myth
fit man's measure far better than truth, and hence are more readily
propagated in time and space. First of all, truth is discouraging;
it is discoverable only at the price of long effort, and when it appears
—that nuisance—in the clear light of day, it is customarily not greeted
happily. Look around you: it is because it was basically dishonest,
grounded in the grossest scientific errors (but in a psychological
understanding of the masses), that Hitlerian racism was propagated,

continues to be propagated at the speed of lightning: *Blitzlüge,* the lightning lie. And in the past, how much time did men need to accept the double notion, the double fact of the earth's roundness and rotation? *Eppur si muove!* [16] This is all the truer when it is question of a critical truth, I mean a truth based on textual criticism; first, its very nature prevents it from having a large audience, and then in the present case, progress in critical study—in exegesis—is closely tied to progress, recent and slow, in the philological and historical sciences.

But it is possible to be more specific.

Intentionally or not, the accusers have started from a point of confusion. Fundamental confusion. Which has been sustained from century to century. Which is still sustained and reigns over minds.

Confusion of two historical problems, two historical facts, which are entirely distinct.

The first of these problems is one we have examined: Jesus and Israel, Jesus and his people. In the apparently rather narrow Jewish sphere in which he lived, preached, spread the Gospel, Jesus found adversaries, enemies, disciples, the sympathies of the masses. These are the facts. There was neither a rejection of the Jewish people by Jesus nor a rejection of Jesus by the Jewish people.

The second problem is quite other: Judaism and Christianity. We have not broached it but have only alluded to it. It is also a fact, but later and quite other, that at a given moment, after a strong surge of conversions, the Jewish people, regrouped behind their doctors, became resistant to Christian preaching. What the Jewish people rejected at that moment was not Jesus, not even the Christ; it was the Christian faith and rule, as they were defined by the new Church. Moreover, there was a parallel and mutual rebuff, of Christianity by Judaism and of Judaism by Christianity, the two rebuffs closely related to one another. Which was cause, which effect? Let us not forget, primitive Christianity was Judeo-Christianity. From the day when it ceased to be so, when Judeo-Christianity saw itself relegated to the rank of an inferior sect, then a heresy, a breach opened between the two confessions: to ask the Jewish people to cast off a Law they venerated as dictated by God Himself, to ask them that, which Jesus had never asked, was truly to ask the impossible. The growing

---

[16] ["And yet it moves!"—Italian phrase supposedly uttered by Galileo after he had been forced in effect to recant his theories of the earth's motion, which were considered contrary to Scripture, during an Inquisition trial in 1632.—Tr.]

mutual hostility of the doctors (Christian and Jewish) and the development of Christian dogmatics did the rest: the breach became an
abyss.

It was easy and it was tempting to Christian doctors to let themselves confuse these two series of facts, distant and distinct though
they were from each other. And they have done so. Since the era
when it can be established that the canonical Gospels were written.
More so thereafter. From this arose certain stylistic practices in the
Gospels, certain equivocal, tendentious formulations which we have
discussed. From this, and in connection with the incessant Judeo-
Christian disputes, was born an even more tendentious tradition,
which emptied the Gospels as it were of their historic substance and
substituted the myth of rejection, of reprobation, of deicide for an entirely different reality. Could people have stopped themselves on this
slope? They were the less inclined to follow it, on the Christian side,
the more the adversary remained aggressive and not without influence
among half-Christianized populations. If there was an abyss between
the theologians, this was not the case between the bodies of faithful
in many areas for centuries: Jewish proselytism—the attraction of Judaism and the synagogue for the Christian people—lasted infinitely
longer than it is thought, well into the Middle Ages.[17] Thus defensive
weapons were sought in the arsenal of reprobation quite as often as
offensive. Then when Judaism, outcast, reviled, hunted, seemed definitively out of the battle, the habit had taken hold, the tradition was
set. The myth of Crime had engendered the myth of Punishment: together they explained, covered, if not justified Israel's martyrdom.
Enough to reassure and lull Christian consciences.

✿   ✿   ✿

But in present times there is enough to awaken and trouble them.
Cursed times, when the mounting tide of inhumanity threatens to
wash over everything, times fertile in crimes of unprecedented mon-
strosity.

The German responsibility for these crimes, as overwhelming as it
has been, is only a derivative responsibility, grafted like a most hide-

----

[17] On this point, see the highly interesting details furnished in Robert Anchel,
Les Juifs de France [The Jews of France], Paris, Janin, 1884, pp. 23–30; and see
Jules Isaac, *Genèse de l'antisémitisme*, Paris, Calmann-Lévy, 1956, pp. 142, 157,
161, 175, 221, 224, 275, 282, n. 1, 286, 325.

ous parasite on a centuries-old tradition which is a Christian tradition. How can we forget that Christianity, especially from the eleventh century on, practiced a policy of degradation and pogroms against the Jews which has extended—among certain Christian peoples—into the contemporary era, and whose survival is observable still in Poland, with its highly Catholic history, whose Hitlerian system was merely an atrociously perfected copy?

Anti-Judaism will retain its virulence as long as the Christian Churches and peoples do not recognize their initial responsibility, as long as they do not have the heart to wipe it out. Latent anti-Semitism exists everywhere, and the contrary would be surprising: for the perennial source of this latent anti-Semitism is none other than Christian religious teaching in all its forms, the traditional and tendentious interpretation of Scripture, the interpretation which I am absolutely convinced is contrary to the truth and love of him who was the Jew Jesus. The Jewish problem is not only a temporal problem; it is first and fundamentally a spiritual problem, whose resolution can be found only in a profound spiritual and religious renewal.

I urge true Christians, and also true Israelites, to undertake this effort of renewal, of purification, this strenuous examination of conscience. Such is the aim I have envisaged. Such is the major lesson that emerges from meditation on Auschwitz, which I cannot release myself from, which no man of heart could abstain from. The glow of the Auschwitz crematorium is the beacon that lights, that guides all my thoughts. Oh, my Jewish brothers, and you as well, my Christian brothers, do you not think that it mingles with another glow, that of the Cross?

APPENDIX AND PRACTICAL
CONCLUSION

For purposes of greater clarity, may I be allowed to submit for the examination of Christians of good will—who are agreed in principle on the need for rectification—the following Eighteen Points, meant to serve at least as a basis for discussion.

Christian teaching worthy of the name should

1. give all Christians at least an elementary knowledge of the Old Testament; stress the fact that the Old Testament, essentially Semitic—in form and substance—was the Holy Scripture of Jews before becoming the Holy Scripture of Christians;

2. recall that a large part of Christian liturgy is borrowed from it, and that the Old Testament, the work of Jewish genius (enlightened by God), has been to our own day a perennial source of inspiration to Christian thought, literature, and art;

3. take care not to pass over the singularly important fact that it was to the Jewish people, chosen by Him, that God first revealed Himself in His omnipotence; that it was the Jewish people who safeguarded the fundamental belief in God, then transmitted it to the Christian world;

4. acknowledge and state openly, taking inspiration from the most reliable historical research, that Christianity was born of a living, not a degenerate Judaism, as is proved by the richness of Jewish literature, Judaism's indomitable resistance to paganism, the spiritualization of worship in the synagogues, the spread of proselytism, the multiplicity of religious sects and trends, the

broadening of beliefs; take care not to draw a simple caricature of historic Phariseeism;

5. take into account the fact that history flatly contradicts the theological myth of the Dispersion as providential punishment for the Crucifixion, since the Dispersion of the Jewish people was an accomplished fact in Jesus' time and since in that era, according to all the evidence, the majority of the Jewish people were no longer living in Palestine; even after the two great Judean wars (first and second centuries), there was no dispersion of the Jews of Palestine;

6. warn the faithful against certain stylistic tendencies in the Gospels, notably the frequent use in the fourth Gospel of the collective term "the Jews" in a restricted and pejorative sense—to mean Jesus' enemies: chief priests, scribes, and Pharisees—a procedure that results not only in distorting historic perspectives but in inspiring horror and contempt of the Jewish people as a whole, whereas in reality this people is in no way involved;

7. state very explicitly, so that no Christian is ignorant of it, that Jesus was Jewish, of an old Jewish family, that he was circumcised (according to Jewish Law) eight days after his birth; that the name *Jesus* is a Jewish name, Yeshua, Hellenized, and *Christ* the Greek equivalent of the Jewish term *Messiah;* that Jesus spoke a Semitic language, Aramaic, like all the Jews of Palestine; and that unless one reads the Gospels in their earliest text, which is in the Greek language, one knows the Word only through a translation of a translation;

8. acknowledge—with Scripture—that Jesus, "born under the [Jewish] law" (Gal. 4:4), lived "under the law"; that he did not stop practicing Judaism's basic rites to the last day; that he did not stop preaching his Gospel in the synagogues and the Temple to the last day;

9. not fail to observe that during his human life, Jesus was uniquely "a servant to the circumcised" (Rom. 15:8); it was in Israel alone that he recruited his disciples; all the Apostles were Jews like their master;

10. show clearly from the Gospel texts that to the last day, except on rare occasions, Jesus did not stop obtaining the enthusiastic sympathies of the Jewish masses, in Jerusalem as well as in Galilee;

11. take care not to assert that Jesus was personally rejected by the Jewish people, that they refused to recognize him as Messiah and

God, for the two reasons that the majority of the Jewish people did not even know him and that Jesus never presented himself as such explicitly and publicly to the segment of the people who did know him; acknowledge that in all likelihood the messianic character of the entry into Jerusalem on the eve of the Passion could have been perceived by only a small number;

12. take care not to assert that Jesus was at the very least rejected by the qualified leaders and representatives of the Jewish people; those who had him arrested and sentenced, the chief priests, were representatives of a narrow oligarchic caste, subjugated to Rome and detested by the people; as for the doctors and Pharisees, it emerges from the evangelical texts themselves that they were not unanimously against Jesus; nothing proves that the spiritual elite of Judaism was involved in the plot;

13. take care not to strain the texts to find in them a universal reprobation of Israel or a curse which is nowhere explicitly expressed in the Gospels; take into account the fact that Jesus always showed feelings of compassion and love for the masses;

14. take care above all not to make the current and traditional assertion that the Jewish people committed the inexpiable crime of deicide, and that they took total responsibility on themselves as a whole; take care to avoid such an assertion not only because it is poisonous, generating hatred and crime, but also because it is radically false;

15. highlight the fact, emphasized in the four Gospels, that the chief priests and their accomplices acted against Jesus unbeknownst to the people and even in fear of the people;

16. concerning the Jewish trial of Jesus, acknowledge that the Jewish people were in no way involved in it, played no role in it, probably knew nothing about it; that the insults and brutalities attributed to them were the acts of the police or of some members of the oligarchy; that there is no mention of a Jewish trial, of a meeting of the Sanhedrin in the fourth Gospel;

17. concerning the Roman trial, acknowledge that the procurator Pontius Pilate had entire command over Jesus' life and death; that Jesus was condemned for messianic pretensions, which was a crime in the eyes of the Romans, not the Jews; that hanging on the cross was a specifically Roman punishment; take care not to impute to the Jewish people the crowning with thorns, which in the Gospel accounts was a cruel jest of the Roman soldiery; take

care not to identify the mob whipped up by the chief priests
with the whole of the Jewish people or even the Jewish people
of Palestine, whose anti-Roman sentiments are beyond doubt;
note that the fourth Gospel implicates exclusively the chief
priests and their men;

18. last, not forget that the monstrous cry, "His blood be on us and
on our children!" (Mt. 27:25), could not prevail over the Word,
"Father, forgive them; for they know not what they do" (Lk.
23:34).[1]

*　　*　　*

These Eighteen Points have in fact served as a basis of discussion
for a (Christian) commission, the Third Commission of the International Emergency Conference of Christians and Jews at Seelisberg,
Switzerland, in August, 1947.[2] From these deliberations emanated the
important document known under the title of the Ten Points of Seelisberg, whose text is as follows:

1. Remember that it is the same living God Who speaks to us all through
the Old and the New Testaments.
2. Remember that Jesus was born of a Jewish mother of the seed of
David and the people of Israel, and that his everlasting love and forgiveness embrace his own people and the whole world.
3. Remember that the first disciples, the Apostles, and the first martyrs
were Jews.

[1] [See the Eighteen Points, in English, in Jules Isaac, *The Christian Roots of
Antisemitism*, tr. Dorothy and James Parkes, London, pub. for the Council of
Christians and Jews and the Parkes Library, 1960, pp. 17–20; and in *idem, Has
Anti-Semitism Roots in Christianity?*, tr. Dorothy and James Parkes, New York,
National Conference of Christians and Jews, 1961, pp. 77–85.—Tr.]

[2] ["Faced by the appalling effects of antisemitism, [the Conference] sought
to study the causes and means to combat it 'through educational, political, religious and social channels'. The sixty-four participants . . . came from nineteen
countries, and worked in five Commissions. The Third Commission was charged
with examining the task of the Churches in the fight against antisemitism." This
quotation is from the opening paragraph of the Ten Points of Seelisberg, printed
in Jules Isaac's *Christian Roots of Antisemitism* (p. 21). It is also to be noted that
the participants, Professor Isaac included among them, represented Catholic,
Protestant, and Jewish confessions, though after the Eighteen Points had been
presented to the Third Commission, the Jews withdrew. The Christians then
"drew up together a project which Protestants and Catholics later examined separately" and which were thereafter "redrafted by a Christian sub-committee, but
the results of the discussions were all the time submitted to the Jewish delegation" (*ibid.*, p. 22). The document finally adopted by the Conference, in full session, contains the Ten Points of Seelisberg. These are quoted below, along with a
concluding paragraph of "practical suggestions," largely from the Parkes translation (*ibid.*, pp. 23–25), with minor alterations for conformity with the French text
in *Jésus et Israël.*—Ed.]

4. Remember that the fundamental commandment of Christianity, to love God and one's neighbor, proclaimed already in the Old Testament and confirmed by Jesus, is binding upon both Christians and Jews in all human relationships, without any exception.

5. Avoid disparaging biblical or postbiblical Judaism with the object of extolling Christianity.

6. Avoid using the word "Jews" in the exclusive sense of "the enemies of Jesus," and the words "the enemies of Jesus" to designate the whole Jewish people.

7. Avoid presenting the Passion in such a way as to bring the odium of the killing of Jesus upon all the Jews or upon the Jews alone. In fact, it was not all the Jews who demanded the death of Jesus. It is not the Jews alone who are responsible, for the Cross which saves us all reveals that it is for the sins of us all that Christ died.

   Remind all Christian parents and teachers of the grave responsibility which they assume when they present the Gospels and particularly the Passion story in a simplistic manner. By so doing, they run the risk of implanting an aversion in the conscious or subconscious minds of their children or hearers, intentionally or unintentionally. Psychologically speaking, in the case of simple minds, moved by a passionate love and compassion for the crucified Savior, the horror which they feel quite naturally toward the persecutors of Jesus will easily be turned into an undiscriminating hatred of the Jews of all times, including those of our own day.

8. Avoid referring to the scriptural curses, or the cry of a raging mob, "His blood be on us and on our children!", without remembering that this cry could not prevail against the infinitely more weighty prayer of Jesus: "Father, forgive them; for they know not what they do."

9. Avoid promoting the superstitious notion that the Jewish people is reprobate, accursed, reserved for a destiny of suffering.

10. Avoid speaking of the Jews as if the first members of the Church had not been Jews.

We make the following practical suggestions:

to introduce or develop in school instruction and elsewhere, at each stage, a more objective and deeper study of the biblical and postbiblical history of the Jewish people, as well as of the Jewish problem;

in particular, to promote the spread of this knowledge by publications adapted to different Christian groups;

to ensure the correction of anything in Christian publications and above all in educational handbooks which would be in conflict with the above principles.

We place our common effort under the sign of the words of Saint Paul in Romans 11:28–29: ". . . they are beloved for the sake of the forefathers. For the gifts and the call of God are irrevocable."

FINIS